The Re
COMP
LIBF

E. A. J. HONIGMANN former editor
J. R. MULRYNE R. L. SMALLWOOD and PETER CORBIN general editors

For over thirty years *The Revels Plays* have offered the most
authoritative editions of Elizabethan and Jacobean plays by
authors other than Shakespeare. The *Companion Library*
provides a fuller background to the main series by publishing
worthwhile dramatic and non-dramatic material that will be
essential for the serious student of the period.

Three Jacobean witchcraft plays

MANCHESTER
UNIVERSITY PRESS

THE REVELS PLAYS COMPANION LIBRARY

Three Jacobean witchcraft plays

The Tragedy of Sophonisba
The Witch
The Witch of Edmonton

edited by PETER CORBIN
and DOUGLAS SEDGE

Manchester University Press

Manchester and New York

distributed exclusively in the USA by Palgrave

Published by
Manchester University Press
Oxford Road, Manchester M13 9NR, UK
and Room 400, 175 Fifth Avenue, New York, NY 10010, USA
http://www.manchesteruniversitypress.co.uk

Distributed exclusively in the USA by
Palgrave, 175 Fifth Avenue, New York,
NY 10010, USA

Distributed exclusively in Canada by
UBC Press, University of British Columbia, 2029 West Mall,
Vancouver, BC, Canada V6T 1Z2

British Library Cataloguing-in-Publication Data
A catalogue record for this book is available from the British Library

Library of Congress Cataloging-in-Publication Data applied for

ISBN 0 7190 1953 2 *paperback*

First published 1986

08 07 06 05   10 9 8 7 6 5

Printed in Great Britain
by Bell & Bain Ltd, Glasgow

CONTENTS

LIST OF ILLUSTRATIONS

GENERAL EDITORS' PREFACE

Since the late 1950s the series known as the Revels Plays has provided for students of the English Renaissance drama carefully edited texts of the major Elizabethan and Jacobean plays. The series now includes some of the best known drama of the period and has continued to expand, both within its original field and, to a lesser extent, beyond it, to include some important plays from the earlier Tudor and from the Restoration periods. The Revels Plays Companion Library is intended to further this expansion and to allow for new developments.

The aim of the Companion Library is to provide students of the Elizabethan and Jacobean drama with a fuller sense of its background and context. The series includes volumes of a variety of kinds. Small collections of plays, by a single author or concerned with a single theme and edited in accordance with the principles of textual modernisation of the Revels Plays, offer a wider range of drama than the main series can include. Together with editions of masques, pageants, and the non-dramatic work of Elizabethan and Jacobean playwrights, these volumes make it possible, within the overall Revels enterprise, to examine the achievement of the major dramatists from a broader perspective. Other volumes provide a fuller context for the plays of the period by offering new collections of documentary evidence on Elizabethan theatrical conditions and on the performance of plays during that period and later. A third aim of the series is to offer modern critical interpretation, in the form of collections of essays or of monographs, of the dramatic achievement of the English Renaissance.

So wide a range of material necessarily precludes the standard format and uniform general editorial control which is possible in the original series of Revels Plays. To a considerable extent, therefore, treatment and approach is determined by the needs and intentions of individual volume editors. Within this rather ampler area, however, we hope that the Companion Library maintains the standards of scholarship which have for so long characterised the Revels Plays, and that it offers a useful enlargement of the work of the series in preserving, illuminating, and celebrating the drama of Elizabethan and Jacobean England.

E. A. J. HONIGMANN
J. R. MULRYNE
R. L. SMALLWOOD

PREFACE AND ACKNOWLEDGEMENTS

As editors of the first volume of play texts to appear in the Revels Plays Companion Library we have been conscious of the pioneering nature of the project. Whilst we have adhered to the basic principles and editorial practices of previous Revels editions, it has not proved practicable, in a volume containing three complete plays, to provide the elaborate textual apparatus, with its exhaustive collation and compositorial analysis, that characterises the single editions in the Revels Plays series. However, within the space available, we have attempted to provide introductory material, notes and collation sufficient to allow the reader to place the plays within their historical and theatrical context, to understand the complexity of the phenomenon of witchcraft in the period and to have access to bibliographical information reflecting the nature of the texts and their treatment by previous editors.

As always in editing Renaissance drama one stands on giants' shoulders and our debt to previous editors and scholars is immense. In addition, we are grateful for the help and advice of Miss Susan Hankey, Professor Gãmini Salgãdo, Professor Paul Doe and particularly to Dr Gareth Roberts, whose learning in the field of witchcraft has saved us from many errors. We are also indebted to the staff of the University of Exeter Library, the British Library, the Bodleian Library and particularly to Susan Brock of the Shakespeare Institute. Conventional typing thanks must go to the inventors of that 'modern witchcraft', the word-processor, and in particular to the University of Exeter Pallas Computing Project for the loan of a machine at a crucial time. A special debt is owed to our General Editor, Robert Smallwood, for his support and encouragement. Above all we thank our families for patience and forbearance.

P.C.
D.S.

ABBREVIATIONS AND REFERENCES

All references to Shakespeare's plays are to Alexander's *Complete Works*, London, 1951. Abbreviation of the titles of Shakespeare's plays follows that of Onions's *A Shakespeare Glossary*. *OED* and Onions are the basis of most glossarial notes; Partridge and Colman have been consulted for bawdy word-play; Sugden for topographical references; Linthicum for costume; Tilley's reference number only is given in the case of most of the proverbial expressions in the plays.

EDITIONS

In the commentary and textual collation the following abbreviations have been used for the various editions and textual commentators:

Sophonisba (Soph.)

Q   *The Wonder of Woman, or The Tragedy of Sophonisba*, 1606.
O   *The Works of John Marston*, 1633.
Bu.   *The Plays of John Marston*, ed. A. H. Bullen, 3 vols., 1887.
Deighton   Kenneth Deighton, *Marston's Works: Conjectural Readings*, 1893.
H   *The Works of John Marston*, ed. J. O. Halliwell, 3 vols., 1856.
K   *John Marston's The Wonder of Women or The Tragedy of Sophon-isba*, ed. William Kemp, 1979.
Thorssen   Michael West and Marilyn Thorssen, 'Observations on the Text of Marston's *Sophonisba*', *Anglia*, 98 (1980), 348–56.
Wo.   *The Plays of John Marston*, ed. H. Harvey Wood, 3 vols., 1934–9.

The Witch (Wi.)

MS   Bodleian MS Malone 12.
1673   *Macbeth* (Cademon's Quarto), 1673.
1810   *Ancient British Drama* (vol. 3 contains *The Witch*), ed. William Miller, 1810.
1813 Var.   *The Plays of William Shakespeare*, ed. George Stevens and Samuel Johnson, 6th ed., 21 vols., 1813.
Bod.   Bodleian MS Mus b. 1. fol. 21.
Bu.   *The Works of Thomas Middleton*, ed. A. H. Bullen, 8 vols., 1885–6.
D   *The Works of Thomas Middleton*, ed. A. Dyce, 5 vols., 1840.

Dav.   *Macbeth, A Tragedy. With all the Alterations, Amendments and New Songs* [Adapted by William Davenant], 1674.

Dr.   Drexel MS 4175.

Drees   *Thomas Middleton: The Witch*, eds. I. Drees and Henry de Vocht, 1945.

Ellis   *Thomas Middleton*, ed. Havelock Ellis, 2 vols., Mermaid, 1890.

G   *The Witch*, eds. W. W. Greg and F. P. Wilson, Malone Society, 1948 (1950).

R   *The Witch*, ed. Isaac Reed, 1778.

The Witch of Edmonton (W.Ed.)

Q   *The Witch of Edmonton*, 1658.

Ba.   *Elizabethan and Stuart Plays*, ed. C. R. Baskerville, V. B. Heltzel and A. H. Nethercot, 1935.

Bo.   *The Dramatic Works of Thomas Dekker*, ed. Fredson Bowers, 4 vols., 1953–61.

D   *The Dramatic Works of John Ford*, ed. William Gifford, revised by Alexander Dyce, 3 vols., 1869.

Gi.   *The Works of John Ford*, ed. William Gifford, 2 vols., 1827.

La.   *Jacobean and Caroline Comedies*, ed. R. G. Lawrence, 1973.

On.   *The Witch of Edmonton, A Critical Edition*, ed. E. S. Onat, 1980.

Rh.   *Thomas Dekker*, ed. Ernest Rhys, Mermaid, 1887.

We.   *The Dramatic Works of John Ford*, ed. Henry Weber, 2 vols., 1811.

GENERAL

Appian   *Appian, The Roman History*, trans. Horace White, 2 vols., 1899.

AR   John Marston, *Antonio's Revenge*, ed. W. Reavley Gair, Revels, 1978.

Bentley   G. E. Bentley, *The Jacobean and Caroline Stage*, 7 vols., 1941–68.

Bentley, *Profession*   G. E. Bentley, *The Profession of Dramatist in Shakespeare's Time, 1560–1642*, 1971.

Briggs, *Anatomy*   K. M. Briggs, *The Anatomy of Puck*, 1959.

Briggs, *PHT*   K. M. Briggs, *Pale Hecate's Team*, 1962.

Bromham   A. A. Bromham, 'The Date of *The Witch* and the Essex Divorce Case', *Notes and Queries*, 225 (1980), 149–52.

Chambers, *MS*   E. K. Chambers, *The Medieval Stage*, 2 vols., 1903.

Chambers, *ES*   E. K. Chambers, *The Elizabethan Stage*, 4 vols., 1923.

Colman   E. A. M. Colman, *The Dramatic Use of Bawdy in Shakespeare*, 1974.

Faustus   Christopher Marlowe, *Dr Faustus*, ed. John D. Jump, Revels, 1962.

Goodcole   Henry Goodcole, *The wonderful discoverie of Elizabeth Sawyer a Witch*, 1621.

Greg   W. W. Greg, 'Some Notes on Crane's Manuscript of *The Witch*', *The Library*, n.s.22 (1942), 208–22.

Harris   A. Harris, *Night's Black Agents: Witchcraft and Magic in Seventeenth Century English Drama*, 1980.

Harrison   *The Trial of the Lancaster Witches, A.D. MDCXII*, ed. G. B. Harrison, 1929.

Hartnoll   Phyllis Hartnoll, *The Oxford Companion to the Theatre*, 1951.

Hoy   Cyrus Hoy, *Introductions, Notes and Commentaries to texts in 'The Dramatic Works of Thomas Dekker'* [ed. Fredson Bowers], 4 vols., 1980.

Ingram   R. W. Ingram, 'The Use of Music in the Plays of Marston', *Music and Letters*, 37 (1956), 154–64.

Kittredge   George Lyman Kittredge, *Witchcraft in Old and New England*, 1929, repr. 1956.

Linthicum   M. C. Linthicum, *Costume in the Drama of Shakespeare and his Contemporaries*, 1936.

Livy   Livy, *The War with Hannibal, Books XXI–XXX of The History of Rome from its Foundation*, trans. Aubrey de Selincourt, 1965.

Long   John H. Long, *Shakespeare's Use of Music: The Histories and Tragedies*, 1971.

Lucan   Lucan, *Pharsalia*, trans. Robert Graves, 1956.

Machiavelli, *Discourses*   Nicolo Machiavelli, *Discourses*, trans. Leslie J. Walker, SJ, ed. with an Introduction by Bernard Crick, 1983.

Machiavelli, *The Prince*   Nicolo Machiavelli, *The Prince*, trans. Luigi Ricci, revised by E. R. P. Vincent, 1935.

Montaigne   *Montaigne's Essays*, trans. John Florio, 3 vols., Everyman's Library, 1910.

MQ   Ben Jonson, *The Masque of Queenes*, vol. 7 of *Ben Jonson*, ed. C. H. Herford and P. and E. Simpson, 1941.

Nosworthy   J. M. Nosworthy, *Shakespeare's Occasional Plays: Their Origin and Transmission*, 1965.

Onions   C. T. Onions, *A Shakespeare Glossary*, 1911.

Partridge   Eric Partridge, *Shakespeare's Bawdy: A Literary and Psychological Essay and a Comprehensive Glossary*, 1947 (rev. & enlarged, 1969).

Roberts   Gareth Roberts, 'A Re-examination of the Sources of the Magical Material in Middleton's *The Witch*', *Notes and Queries* (1976), 216–19.

Rosen   *Witchcraft*, ed. Barbara Rosen, 1969.

Russell   *The Witch of Edmonton*, with a commentary by Simon Trussler and notes by Jacqui Russell, 1983.

Schanzer   Ernest Schanzer, 'Marriage Contracts in *Measure for Measure*', *ShS*, 13 (1960), 81–9.

Scot   Reginald Scot, *The Discoverie of Witchcraft*, 1584.

ShS   Shakespeare Survey.

Sugden   E. H. Sugden, *A Topographical Dictionary to the Works of Shakespeare and his Fellow Dramatists*, 1925.

Thomas   Keith Thomas, *Religion and the Decline of Magic*, 1971 (repr. 1978).

Tilley   M. P. Tilley, *A Dictionary of the Proverbs in England in the Sixteenth and Seventeenth Centuries*, 1950.

Wickham   Glynne Wickham, *Early English Stages*, 4 vols., 1966–81.

Ure   Peter Ure, *Elizabethan and Jacobean Drama, Critical Essays*, 1974.

Wentersdorf   Karl P. Wentersdorf, 'The Marriage Contracts in *Measure for Measure*', *ShS*, 32 (1979), 129–44.

INTRODUCTION

GENERAL

The three plays in this volume reflect the variety of witch belief and practice in the Jacobean period. Marston's *Sophonisba* dramatises classical practices within a world of Romano-Carthaginian conflict; Middleton's *The Witch*, set in 'Jacobean' Italy, draws heavily upon literary and academic witchcraft knowledge; *The Witch of Edmonton* by Dekker, Ford and Rowley attempts to place on stage topical events drawn from a contemporary witch pamphlet presenting common superstitions within a sharply delineated English rural community.

For Jacobean society witchcraft presented a real and frightening danger which posed a threat to everyone from the highest to the lowest in the land. A pamphlet of 1591, *Newes from Scotland, Declaring the Damnable life and death of Doctor Fian*,[1] relates how witchcraft placed King James in mortal danger on his voyage from Denmark with his new Queen in 1590. The children of the scholar and gentleman, Edward Fairfax, the translator of Tasso, were alleged to have been bewitched in 1621 by six women who lived in Knaresborough Forest;[2] and at numerous trials countless ordinary citizens testified to their belief that they had suffered from witchcraft practices. If witchcraft provoked great anxiety it also stimulated considerable academic and religious debate. The modern scholar might interpret witchcraft practice and belief in terms of the customs of vestigial paganism transmitted via folk-lore, simple superstition or a deep-rooted desire to retain the half-understood practices and rituals of Roman Catholicism in the face of the insecure Protestant reformation, but many of those who attended the first performances of the plays in this volume would have accepted the notion of the devil's direct intervention in the affairs of men and the attempt by individuals to invoke his personal assistance. An incident relating to the performance of Marlowe's *Dr Faustus* at Exeter illustrates this point memorably, for in the course of the presentation certain of the actors were incapacitated by the conviction that 'there was one devell too many amongst them; and so after a little pause desired the people to pardon them, they could go no further with this matter; the people also understanding the thing as it was, every man hastened to be first out of dores'.[3]

English judicial attitudes and practice towards witchcraft were com-
paratively tolerant compared to those common on the continent and in
Scotland. It was not until 1563 that the first comprehensive act was passed
specifically directed towards witchcraft and, significantly, although
bewitching to death attracted the death penalty, injuring persons or goods
or cattle and seeking treasure, warranted only prison and pillory for the
first offences; the second conviction, however, rendered the criminal liable
to execution. That political considerations were of major importance is
evidenced by a subsequent clarification to the act which nominates astrological calculation and divination of the length of the Queen's life as indic-
table offences. The law was strengthened under James I. The act of 1604
makes the keeping of familiars an offence together with the exhumation of
bodies for conjuration or evocation. In contrast to continental practice,
English witches were almost always examined by Justices rather than by
officials of the church and the accused were usually examined on factual
evidence rather than hearsay. Horrendous tortures, practised on the continent, to elicit confession and to determine guilt, which have coloured
modern perceptions of such trials,[4] were not common experience in
England. The penalty, should a trial lead to conviction of a capital offence,
was death by hanging, not by burning. However, whilst we may accept
that English justice was less savage than that of its neighbours, it must be
admitted that a society, often desperate and on the edge of unaccountable
natural disaster, was inclined to seek out its scapegoats amongst the
weakest and most vulnerable. Women, and especially the elderly, eccentric
and deprived, frequently became the objects of gossip and fear, and thus
the subjects of persecution. It is significant, perhaps, that all the 'witches'
of these plays are females.

Undoubtedly the work which most influenced views on witchcraft and
demonology was *Malleus Maleficarum*. Published in 1486, it was designed
by its authors, Jacob Sprenger and Heinrich Kramer (Institor), to provide
a *summa* of witchcraft and its practices, and a set of procedures for the
discovery, examination, torture and trial of witches. To what extent the
work was a response to or a provocation of the witch hysteria which swept
the continent, and especially Germany, in the late fifteenth and sixteenth
centuries is open to argument; but by means of its many reprintings it
initiated a lengthy, complex and sharp debate between the absolute be-
lievers in witchcraft and those more sceptically inclined. Although
England largely escaped witch mania until the late sixteenth century, the
controversy was eventually taken up by many English writers. Reginald
Scot, sceptical of the claims made against witches, published *The
Discoverie of Witchcraft* (1584) soon after the witch trials at St Osyth in
1582, and argued against the unwarranted persecution of the old and
simple-minded who were frequently branded as witches. Subsequently the
non-conforming preacher, George Gifford, published his *A Discourse of*

the subtill Practices of Devilles in 1587 and *A Dialogue concerning Witches and Witchcraftes* in 1593, which also demonstrate considerable scepticism, arguing that the devil has no need for old women to do his work and that much innocent blood may be shed because of unreliable confessions. Such views were vigorously opposed. King James VI of Scotland's *Demonology* (1597) was expressly written against Scot whose *Discoverie* was banned immediately on James's accession to the English throne in 1603. King James's absolutist stance, although qualified in later years, owed much to continental theory, and was paradoxically supported, if not surpassed in vehemence, by the puritan William Perkins, whose *Discourse of the Damned Art of Witchcraft* was published in 1608.

The dramatists drew heavily from such intellectual discourse but they also borrowed from more popular and transient writing. Pamphleteers and ballad-makers reported the trials and executions of witches in a journalistic fashion and thus recorded the more commonplace witch-lore.[5] Such literature provides a very different viewpoint on our subject from the academic controversialists; here we are in contact with everyday life, small and isolated communities at war with themselves, in which petty rivalries and old scores are worked out with accusations of witchcraft. It is not surprising that dramatists should exploit the dramatic potential of contemporary sensation or the esoteric mysteries of the learned investigator. Harris notes a significant surge in theatrical use of the more spectacular aspects of witchcraft belief in the early years of James I's reign.[6] Although dating is not precise it seems likely that *Sophonisba* set the trend at the Blackfriars, followed soon after by *Macbeth*, in its initial state as performed at the Globe.[7] Both plays are notable for their emphasis on the less comic, more disturbing aspects of the subject.

This trend received stimulus from two important developments in 1608–9: the performance at court of Jonson's *The Masque of Queenes* and the acquisition by the King's Men of the Blackfriars Theatre. The first event, by exploiting the full resources of music, dance and spectacle of the court masque, with the elaborate stage-machinery of Whitehall and extravagant costuming, under the design of Inigo Jones, gave Jonson an opportunity to demonstrate in the anti-masque the potential of witchcraft material to embody the concept of chaos and disorder. The second event gave the foremost acting company of the period access to sophisticated stage-machinery allowing the enactment of the more spectacular facets of witchcraft lore. This they were able to exploit in an impressively organised scene in Act III of *The Witch*, exploring the rituals whereby witches achieved transvection by means of anointing and the summoning of spirits 'in the air'. So successful was this spectacle that *Macbeth* was revived in a version which includes two songs and a dance from *The Witch* and introduces Hecate, who, like Middleton's witch of the same name, takes advantage of the Blackfriars flying machinery. Although the extent of the revisions of the original *Macbeth* script remains the subject of controversy,[8] it seems likely that the cauldron scene was also a later addition, possibly under the influence of Middleton's treatment in *The Witch*, though in this respect Jonson's extensive and learned ingredients and charms from *The Masque of Queenes* may have been the example which they both followed. Whatever the exact relations between the three works, each exploited the cauldron motif to present 'grotesque rituals, with their gruesome ingredients [which] add immensely to the aura of superhuman wickedness that surrounds the witches'.[9]

By contrast with such sophisticated staging effects, *The Witch of Edmonton* relies upon a strong sense of locality and the texture of domestic life to convey its vision of the perils of witchcraft. Unlike Heywood's *The Late Lancashire Witches* (1634) which is also based on contemporary witch-trial material, the dramatists do not trivialise their material in the stage-presentation. One striking stage effect indicates the gravity of the approach as well as the originality of the conception. Animals as familiars to witches had been presented previously on stage—Malkin, the great Cat, is employed to spectacular effect in *The Witch*—but the Dog in this play is presented with a resourcefulness and variety that encompass both an engaging intimacy in the Cuddy Banks scenes and a savage cynicism of Marlovian dimensions in his entrapment and destruction of his victims.

THE TRAGEDY OF SOPHONISBA

The writing of *Sophonisba* (1604–6), Marston's last complete play before his retirement from theatre activity,[10] seems to have involved a very special ambition on the part of the author. In his Preface to *The Fawne* (1604) he refers to his work in progress, a 'Tragedy . . . which shall boldly abide the most curious perusal' and in the Epilogus to *Sophonisba* itself he shows a marked anxiety about the reader's judgement of the play, together with a confidence that he has achieved 'words well sensed, best suiting subject grave'. Further evidence of Marston's solicitude concerning the reputation of his tragedy is provided by the curious note appended to the quarto edition of the play in which he shows concern that the conditions of the original performance, 'the fashion of the entrances and music of this tragedy . . . as it was presented by youths', may have adversely affected the final product. It is difficult to see the precise grounds of Marston's anxiety. Bentley points out that the custom of musical interludes between the acts was so well established as a tradition at the Blackfriars Theatre that it was continued when the King's Men took over from the Boys' Company in 1608.[11] If the musical expertise of the boy-actors constrained Marston to provide opportunities for a display of their talents, the effects, as suggested in the quarto stage directions, do not seem ill-adapted to Marston's artistic purposes. Indeed, the subtle orchestration of music and ritual is one of the most striking features of the play and Marston's earlier work shows that the exploiting of musical effects, both as regards musical theory and its practice, was a particular concern of the dramatist.[12] Possibly conscious that he was attempting something new, he seems to be at pains to make clear in this 'Author's Note' that the talents of the boy actors for parody and mock-heroic,[13] which he himself had encouraged in previous plays, were not appropriate in this tragic piece.

Marston's choice of subject matter and setting also reflects his concern to achieve a serious and elevated tone for his tragedy. In choosing to focus upon and dramatise an episode in the second Punic or Hannibalic War, taken from Appian's *Roman History*, Book VIII, he was seeking to acquire the gravity and authority of a classical subject and, perhaps, enter into competition with Jonson whose *Sejanus* had been published in 1605. The savage, satirical tone of his earlier plays of court and citizen life is abandoned for a severely classical play-world within which we are invited to admire the protagonists' ability to withstand the vagaries of fortune and malice. Marston makes no discrimination between the historical cultures of Carthage and Rome. Massinissa, historically a prince of the Massyllian tribe, initially allied to Carthage, was probably a black, yet is presented as an entirely Roman figure in attitude and manner. In addition, the ethos of the setting is Roman in its ceremonies and values.[14] The characters invoke Roman deities and perform Roman sacrifices; the marriage ceremony between Sophonisba and Massinissa is classical in tone if not authority; Scipio enters with the compliments of a Roman general; and, in the final movement, Sophonisba's corpse is adorned with Roman triumphal regalia.

Appian's *History* provides the dramatist with almost all the main events of the action: the sexual rivalry between Massinissa and Syphax for Sophonisba, the Carthaginians' betrayal of Massinissa by handing over Sophonisba to his rival, the campaign which leads to the defeat of Syphax and the Carthaginians, and Sophonisba's heroic suicide. Marston's handling of the material is, however, in marked contrast to the documentary practice of Jonson which he rejects in his Address to the General Reader. Where Jonson 'followed his sources so closely that he provided something of a verse translation of them',[15] Marston shapes and alters Appian, develops and enriches his source's sketchy characterisation of the protagonists and incorporates material from Montaigne, Machiavelli and Lucan in order to sharpen and deepen the dramatic argument. Appian, unlike Livy (who also relates Sophonisba's history),[16] offers only unembellished and straightforward narrative and thus there is a necessary expansion of source material. The dramatist considerably develops and explores the intrigue within the Carthaginian power structure which leads to

Massinissa's betrayal, frequently drawing on Machiavelli and Montaigne to provide supportive argument and comment.[17] From Appian's statements on Syphax's duplicity is developed a character of extreme and cynical appetite; whilst Sophonisba and Massinissa, no more than ciphers in the source, are transformed into epic figures.

However, Marston's most radical departure in dramatising his source material is the incorporation into his plot of the Erictho episode from Lucan's *Pharsalia*, Book VI. Lucan's Erictho is an arch-witch of terrifying power of whom even the Olympian gods are fearful, but it is with the underworld and the newly dead that she is most engaged. Lucan narrates how Sextus Pompey sought her out so that she might reveal the outcome of the battle of Pharsalia and the civil war. This she accomplished by reanimating the body of a dead soldier who prophesied the defeat of Pompey's faction and the destruction of his family. Although he changes her function from prophetess to demonic procuress—Syphax seeks her help in forcing Sophonisba's love—Marston draws on Lucan for Syphax's description of her fearsome appearance and loathsome practices,[18] adding some embellishments of his own.[19] The witch's ghastly pallor, matted hair and necrophilic rites are taken directly from Lucan and even the dramatist's additions have their genesis in the source. Erictho's description of her cell and its surroundings (IV.i.161–7) recalls the scene in Lucan where she reanimates the corpse: 'Soon she reached the dell selected as the scene for her ghastly miracle; this lay sheltered by a beetling precipice at the bottom of a steep slope, almost as far down as the Underworld itself, and vaguely seen yew plantations, too thick for the sun's rays to penetrate, leaned forward to screen it' (p. 144). The dramatist's handling of Lucan has occasioned sharp criticism. Reed comments that Erictho is 'a monster shaped and exaggerated by the distorted brain of the author' and adds that her language and some of her actions 'are so unnatural as to lack all verisimilitude'.[20] It has been argued that the episode is no more than 'a well articulated string of ghoulish detail',[21] that it 'out-Lucans Lucan'[22] and that it is 'a scene of gratuitous horror, introduced merely to make our flesh creep'.[23] Such charges of excessive ornamentation and mere sensationalism are invalid[24] for Marston resists the opportunity of dramatising some of Lucan's most sensational detail such as the procedure for reanimating the dead: 'Then she made several cuts in the corpse's breast, and after washing out the contents of his veins, poured in warm menstrual blood mixed with every kind of unnatural poison . . . To these commoner ingredients she added the bewitched leaves of plants that she had spat upon when they first appeared, thereby steeping them in the venom of her own body' (p. 155). Thus Marston's presentation of Erictho accords closely in tone and manner with Lucan who has been called 'the father of yellow journalism', for his love of sensational detail.[25]

Erictho, in contrast to Hecate and Elizabeth Sawyer, is essentially a witch of the classical tradition to which Marston has added a number of seventeenth-century beliefs and practices. In common with her Thessalian forbears she has power over the weather, the sea and the earth and can control wild beasts and natural phenomena. She is the mistress of potent charms which influence even the Gods of the Underworld and, as we have seen, her practices are drawn directly from Lucan. She is thus a witch 'of the severely classical kind' and 'the only fully fledged example of her kind in Elizabethan drama'.[26] Marston's alteration of her function to procuress, however, allies her more closely to Renaissance witch belief. In her deception of Syphax by a bed-trick she adopts the role of a succubus, a devil in female form, who seduces and betrays men. Her dramatic escape from Syphax's wrath, by slipping into the ground, would suggest her demonic status and although there was controversy on the subject of sexual intercourse with spirits—Scot, IV.10, denying the possibility—it may be assumed that a contemporary audience would have judged that Syphax had placed himself in the devil's power. Although Thessalian witches were noted for their love philters which were effective on even the strongest heart, the dramatist denies Erictho such powers:

> Why, fool of kings, could thy weak soul imagine
> That 'tis within the grasp of heaven or hell
> To enforce love? Why know, love dotes the Fates;
> Jove groans beneath his weight.   (V.i.4–7)

Here, too, there may be a reflection of popular witch belief which parallels the devil-dog's confession in *The Witch of Edmonton* (II.i.156–60) that he cannot touch the life of Old Banks because of his virtue and charity. Erictho's necrophilic practices also place her within contemporary witch belief, since the Act of 1604 specifically cites such activity as incurring the death penalty. One section of the Act is precisely directed to witches who 'take up any dead man, woman or child out of his, her or their grave, or any other place where the dead body resteth, or the skin, bone, or any other part of any dead person, to be employed or used in any manner of witchcraft, sorcery, charm, or enchantment'.[27]

Marston's Erictho is therefore an amalgam, a successful mixture of classical and exotic authority which contributes to the overall gravity of the play together with an adjustment to contemporary attitudes which would make her immediate and recognisable to the Blackfriars audience.

Both Marston's treatment of his military sources and his use of classical witchcraft indicate the elevated tone aimed at in this tragedy. These effects are echoed very noticeably by the style of the blank verse and the nature of the rhetoric employed throughout, praised by T. S. Eliot for their consistency.[28] In this respect the play has affinities with such closet dramas as Fulke Greville's *Mustapha* and *Alaham* where the expectation of readership rather than theatre-performance allows a compression in the speeches demanding and repaying close study. But whilst it is true that Marston's style becomes at times perplexingly elliptical[29] and occasionally in danger of falling into rhodomontade or bathos,[30] it is an exaggeration to suggest, as Finklepearl does, that the style is 'always more or less obscure'.[31] On the contrary, Marston's handling of narrative, argument and emotion is often arrestingly varied and pithy. For example, Carthalo's disclosure, in the role of nuntius, of the imminent arrival of the Roman forces is conveyed in a startlingly vivid association of images which Shakespeare seems to have remembered when writing a similar nuntius speech in *Macbeth*:[32]

> . . . Descried from off the watch three hundred sail,
> Upon whose tops the Roman eagles stretched .
> Their large spread wings, which fanned the evening air,
> To us cold breath; for well we might discern
> Rome swam to Carthage. (I.ii.71–5)

Although the frequent debates in the play are weighted with *sententiae* and aphorism, often signalled by italics in the quarto text, Marston is as much concerned with dialectical interplay and force of rejoinder as he is with generality and compression of thought. Such effects, whilst demanding careful delivery from the actors, can offer sharp discriminations to the auditors, as in Sophonisba's riposte to Carthalo:

> *Carthalo.* The gods foresaw, 'tis fate we thus are forced.
> *Sophonisba. Gods naught foresee, but see, for to their eyes*
> *Naught is to come or past;* nor are you vile
> Because the gods foresee. *For gods, not we,*
> *See as things are; things are not as we see.* (II.i.131–5)

Moreover, Wood's claim that Marston's style is 'almost grotesquely strained and inflated in its attempt to match the dignity of the subject and the importance of the occasion'[33] fails to acknowledge Marston's variations of rhetorical style. Particularly significant is Marston's ability to undermine rhetorical tropes as when Sophonisba eschews 'stage-like passion':

> I should now curse the gods,
> Call on the Furies, stamp the patient earth,
> Cleave my stretched cheeks with sound, speak from all sense,
> But loud and full of player's eloquence.
> No, no.—What shall we eat? (IV.i.23–27)

At such moments Marston bracingly reminds the audience of the 'mingled reality and unreality of the stage world'.[34]

Although Marston shows considerable resourcefulness in his handling of rhetoric, what distinguishes *Sophonisba* from the closet dramas of Greville and the Roman plays of Jonson is the dramatic integration of dialogue and stage action. Ritual, dumb show, processional entries and exits are all exploited with Marston's characteristic originality and resourcefulness. In the Prologus Marston takes over the primitive technique from the popular history play tradition of using a dumb show to replace or assist the exposition.[35] Not only does the elaborate double entry reinforce the stature of the opposed 'princes of proud sceptres' but the audience becomes immediately engaged with the principal characters in the conflict, and the 'ill-boding' atmosphere of the 'nuptial pomp' is established, producing a dynamic, urgent quality to Syphax's expression of outrage in the play's opening scene. A similar power is gained at the opening of Act II with a more sophisticated use of dumb show. Here, Gelosso's protest against the dishonourable proceedings of the Carthaginian council is magnified when silent action erupts into speech, 'My hand? My hand? Rot first. Wither in aged shame!'[36] Marston's boldness in the use of stage spectacle goes well beyond the creation of striking local effects, making full use of, and sometimes straining to the utmost, the resources of the Blackfriars stage. Trap-doors not only act as a means of escape from Syphax's bedchamber but also as a cave's mouth or vault opening into Belos' Forest, as a means by which Asdrubal's ghost arises out of the altar, and as Erictho's sudden exit when she *slips into the ground*. Some critics have felt that Marston makes unwarrantable demands upon his audience in IV.i by transposing the action from Belos' Forest to Syphax's bed-chamber without Syphax leaving the stage.[37] It is not the case, however, that Marston is crudely invoking the primitive convention of continuous staging here. On the contrary, by dwelling on specific aspects of the initial location, he draws attention to the transposition which occurs and thus makes it a positive feature of Erictho's impressive powers. The change of venue becomes expressive of the witch's psychological power over Syphax, her use of 'brain-sleights' (V.i.18).

A particularly interesting feature of the staging of this play which suggests how deeply Marston sought to integrate staging and theme is the extensive use of the curtained bed, which is an essential focus of several scenes and is used by Marston emblematically. This effect is prepared for by the ritualised laying of Sophonisba *in a fair bed* for consummation of her wedding to Massinissa where their sexual union is given an emblematic significance by a series of ceremonies. Sophonisba is discovered to Massinissa who performs the ceremony of drawing *a white ribbon forth of the bed as from the waist of* SOPHONISBA and initiating the formal dedication *Io to Hymen*. The emblematic effect is further heightened when Carthalo enters *his shield stuck full of darts*, at the moment when Massinissa is *ready for bed*, encouraging the audience to observe the polarity between the honour of marriage and that of warfare, a central concern of the play. A marked contrast to this use of the marriage-bed occurs in III.i when the drugged Vangue is laid in Syphax's bed ('There lie Syphax bride') and the curtains drawn for a very different discovery, when Syphax, *ready for bed*, invokes a very different order of music to celebrate his supposed union with Sophonisba: 'Cupid, thy flame; 'bove all, O Hercules, / Let not thy back be wanting' (III.i.183–4) before leaping into bed with the befuddled Vangue. Marston shows the degree to which this presentation is consciously shaped when Syphax exclaims, 'Ha! Can any woman turn to such a devil?', for these words ironically prefigure his final devastating use of the curtained bed. This occurs at the end of Act IV and the beginning of Act V when, in a further attempt to ravish Sophonisba, Syphax unwittingly, but appropriately to the lustful passion that he consistently displays, commits the heinous sin of intercourse and propagation with a demon. Once again the occasion is accompanied by ceremonial invocations and the use of music, the degree of inversion of decorum being indicated by Syphax's assertion that 'hell and heaven rings / With music spite of Phoebus'.

In his use of stage spectacle and especially in the provision of music, Marston seems intent on integrating theatrical means with thematic purpose. Although speculation in this area must be kept within bounds in the absence of the original music,[38] it would appear that the choice of instruments is designed to underpin and support the developing action in a carefully designed fashion.[39] Evidence of this may be found in Marston's use of the convention of music between the acts, where the audience seem to be prepared for changes of setting and mood. The nature of the music between Acts IV and V is exceptionally effective in that the instruments used, '*a bass viol and a treble lute*', have already been associated with lovemaking by Syphax, so that the music may be thought to relate to Syphax's intercourse with Erictho which occurs in the interval.[40] That Marston attaches a particular significance to the role of music in the bewitching of Syphax is made quite clear in Erictho's declared aim to employ music in the accomplishment of Syphax's desires.[41] The association between Erictho and a certain kind of music is in fact so strong that her entry and silent presence whilst Syphax invokes her throughout twenty-four lines, is accompanied by '*infernal music*' which plays softly. This music is later identified by Syphax as:

> The deep fetched groans
> Of labouring spirits that attend
> Erictho.   (IV.I.192–4)

The source of this music seems to show Marston at his most demanding in terms of theatrical resources. It may be assumed that the infernal music called for at lines 101 and 191 in this scene was provided from beneath the stage as in the direction from Shakespeare's *Antony and Cleopatra*, '*Music of Hautboys as under the stage*'.[42] The music appears then to shift ground at line 198, '*A treble viol and a bass lute, play softly within the canopy*', associating the source of the music with the bed where Syphax's demonic intercourse is to take place; whilst at line 208 a further shift appears to

occur, 'A short song to soft music above', reminding us of Erictho's promise to 'force / The air to music'.[43] The series of surprises implied by this
staging is wholly in keeping with Marston's restlessly innovative drama-
turgy throughout the scene. Whatever the actual music used here, the
association of music and female lust provides a total contrast with the
music formerly associated with Sophonisba. As O'Neil remarks, 'Syphax's
gloating about defeating Phoebus brings to mind that his god of music is
Sophonisba's "patron"... It is not, ironically, the love of Sophonisba
which is won by Syphax, but the love of Syphax which is won by
Erictho'.[44]

The poetic justice of Syphax's fate indicates Marston's concern to articulate a moral debate in his play. Although Syphax does not perish, his
association with demonic powers is appropriate to his distorted appetite,
and, in the eyes of the contemporary audience, he would be damned. The
play presents a didactic patterning of morally opposed characters and
attitudes, a structure which is intimated by the emblematic dumb-show of
the prologue. As the play develops, characters are quickly delineated as
inhabiting opposed moral worlds. Massinissa, Sophonisba and Gelosso
represent honour, propriety and stoical integrity in the face of malice and
misfortune, whilst the Carthaginian establishment, Syphax and, most
dramatically, Erictho embody unprincipled passion for power and sexual
gratification.

Through the course of the play the protagonists' stoical integrity is
tested by the play-world's dominant chaotic passion and Machiavellian
self-interest. The frustration of their marital consummation draws from
them honourable commitment to Carthage (I.ii.135–205), whilst
Massinissa's betrayal and the gift of Sophonisba to Syphax, from cynical
motives, provokes a response which establishes her stoical values as lying
beyond the play-world's sublunary limitations:

> What power can make me wretched? What evil
> Is there in life to him that knows life's loss
> To be no evil? (II.i.145–7)

Confronted with the politic trading of his wife to Syphax and his betrayal
by Carthage, Massinissa attempts to maintain a stoic detachment
(III.ii.50–61) despite intense emotional pressure. The audience is invited to
admire such strength of character and the more so in Sophonisba's response to Syphax's intention of winning his pleasure by force:

> Show but one strain of force,
> Bow but to seize this arm, and by myself,
> Or more, by Massinissa, this good steel
> Shall set my soul on wing. Thus formed gods see,
> And men with gods' worth envy nought but me. (IV.i.53–7)

Her release from Syphax's power, not to Massinissa but to her potential humiliation at the hands of Scipio and the dishonour of her husband, provokes her suicide and a rejection of earthly expectations:

> How near was I unto the curse of man, joy!
> How like was I yet once to have been glad!
> He that ne'er laughed may with constant face
> Contemn Jove's frown. Happiness makes us base.   (V.iii.89–92)

Her coronation, in the final scene, with the Roman triumphal regalia, intended for Massinissa, establishes Sophonisba as the focal dramatic image of the final tableau and thus provokes the audience's admiration.

Marston handles the forces opposed to such stoical virtue in a carefully controlled and ascending structure. We are first introduced to the cynical politicking of the Carthaginians whose criteria for action are purely Machiavellian: 'Prosperous success gives blackest actions glory; / The means are unremembered in most story' (II.i.33–4). Only Gelosso stands against the politic statesman in the council to argue for absolute values of honour and integrity, and his commitment forces him to betray his loyalty to his country. Similarly, Massinissa and Sophonisba are forced to choose between their personal integrity and their public loyalties. Massinissa allies himself with Scipio, the Roman invader, and Sophonisba deceives both the Carthaginian council and Syphax to maintain her vows to her husband. The fallible and fallen world seems not to allow virtue to flourish untainted.

Sophonisba's essential opponent in the play is Erictho. Although the Erictho episode has been dismissed as 'totally unrelated to anything else in the play'[45] and has been described as no more than a late addition to compete with *Macbeth*,[46] the Erictho scenes are central to Marston's moral scheme. The witch represents the extreme of distorted appetite. Where Asdrubal and his advisers pragmatically seek cynical security, she, single-mindedly, strives for her own carnal pleasures:

> Know we, Erictho, with a thirsty womb,
> Have coveted full threescore suns for blood of kings...
> We, in the pride and height of covetous lust,
> Have wished with woman's greediness to fill
> Our longing arms with Syphax' well-strung limbs.   (V.i.8–15)

Her grave-robbing, her control of base creatures and her manipulation of the air to produce erotic and sensual music mark her as a figure of unconstrained appetite over against Sophonisba who can forgo the pleasures of the bridal-bed and maintain her virtue in the face of physical and moral pressures; whilst her human opponent, Syphax, on the other hand, is linked with Erictho in her necrophilic practices by his threat to satisfy his lust on Sophonisba's corpse should she commit suicide (IV.i.58–62). The Erictho scenes, although they constitute a brief period of the play's action, are an essential part of Marston's argument, for the witch is the play's most potent emblem of lust and appetite in action and an agent of Syphax's moral, if not physical, destruction. In contrast, Sophonisba maintains her integrity in death, denies the claims and compromise values of the human world to receive a coronation which suggests that she belongs to the element of fire beyond the base earth.

Thus Marston opposes Sophonisba, 'the wonder of women', who rises above the baseness of human passions, against Erictho, a witch, whose appetital nature is bound to the underworld, the flesh and, for Marston's audience, the devil. The classical witchcraft of Marston's play draws a distinction between the human and demonic more sharply and in a more horrifying way than both Middleton's *The Witch*, where an easy and even casual interaction occurs between the two worlds, and *The Witch of Edmonton*, where the devil is given domestic and familiar form.

THE WITCH

Since its emergence from obscurity with Reed's limited printing from the manuscript in 1778, critical interest in Middleton's *The Witch* has centred on the fact that two of its songs (in abbreviated form) and a dance known as 'The Witches' Dance' also occur in the Folio text of Shakespeare's *Macbeth*.[47] The songs are given in their full form in Middleton's play and are integral to the staging of their respective scenes, whereas they seem to be unwarranted intrusions, if not positive violations of tone and mood, in the Shakespeare text. Thus it is now generally accepted that they were inserted into a pre-Folio revival of *Macbeth* to catch the prevailing fashion for theatrical spectacle.[48] That Middleton's play was a failure on the stage, and thus fair game for such cannibalism, has been widely assumed from the admission in the Dedication that the play was 'ignorantly ill-fated'.[49] Further speculation on the circumstances of the original composition has added to this assumption of the play's failure. It has been suggested that the play was hastily composed to capitalise on the recent witchcraft vogue created by Ben Jonson's *The Masque of Queenes* and even that properties, costumes, dances and stage effects were imported from the court production of that masque.[50]

Associated with these speculations concerning the play's relationship to other works dealing with witchcraft has been the attempt to assign a precise date to the original composition. Since the manuscript, a transcript by Ralph Crane, scrivener to the King's Men, almost certainly belongs to the period 1619–27,[51] and contains a reference in the Dedication to its long 'imprisoned obscurity', it is likely that the play belongs to a period prior to Middleton's major tragic work; whilst the statement on the first page of the manuscript, 'long since acted by his Majesty's servants at the Blackfriars' places it later than Middleton's city comedies written for the Boys' Companies since the King's Men did not play there before the autumn of 1609. Stylistic grounds lend some support to this impression—in particular the character of Francisca seems a forerunner of Beatrice-Joanna in *The Changeling*—and would suggest a most likely dating of *c.* 1613–16, close to *More Dissemblers Besides Women* (1615) with which it has affinities,[52] and the tragicomedy *A Fair Quarrel* (1616) whose central theme of honour *The Witch* presents in a starkly reductive form. Such a dating is also implied by the striking parallel with the divorce case of the Earl of Essex in the main Isabella/Sebastian/Antonio plot.[53]

Sebastian procures from the witch Hecate a charm to 'starve up generation' (I.ii.152) in the newly celebrated marriage between Antonio and Isabella. It acts selectively on Antonio, enabling him to continue to satisfy Florida, his whore, but not to consummate his marriage with Isabella. This *maleficium*, whilst readily current in Jacobean folk-lore, bears close resemblance to the real-life court case in which divorce was granted to the Earl of Essex on the grounds of non-consummation due to impotence induced by bewitchment. The case was perhaps the most notorious social and political scandal of the decade, beginning as early as 1610 and flaring into great prominence with the actual divorce proceedings of 1613 and the subsequent revelations of love philters and poisons in the trial of 1615–16 which culminated in the execution of the accomplices to the Overbury murder.[54] Annulment of the marriage between the Earl and Countess of Essex was only granted after the active support and politicking of James I in packing the commission trying the case with commissioners prepared to support his own belief that selective impotence could be caused by witchcraft. James I, himself a believer in the dangers of witchcraft,[55] argued that by the devil's 'filthy witchcraft' a man may be made 'unable *versus hanc*' (i.e. sexually incapable towards a specific woman) and that 'if the power of witchcraft may reach to our life, [so] much more to a member (i.e. sexual organ) . . . wherein the Devil hath his principal operation'.[56] It seems likely that Middleton's play, whatever its precise dating, would have been interpreted by theatre audiences during the protracted period of this scandal as an allusion to the Essex affair and for this reason there exists a serious possibility that the play's original neglect was due to censorship rather than its failure to entertain.[57]

The possible mirroring of events from Jacobean court life might seem at odds with the play's Italian setting, but in fact there is little attempt to present a consistent sense of place or society in the four rather tenuously linked plots of the play. The opening scene introduces us, against a background of heady marriage celebrations, to the main plot in which the returned soldier, Sebastian, determines to uphold the integrity of his betrothal vow to Isabella despite her match with Antonio. The ritual drinking during the wedding breakfast also sets up the slighter affair, based on an episode from Montaigne's *The Florentine History*, of the Duchess's revenge on her husband for his cruel trick of making her drink healths out of the skull-cup of her conquered father. These sketchily Italian motifs are sharply contrasted with the closely observed domestic detail of a third, largely discrete strand, the strategems employed by Aberzanes to keep secret and dispose of Francisca's unwanted pregnancy. This story, reminiscent of Middleton's city comedies, furnishes such realistic details as caudels for lying-in, aphrodisiacs and muddy journeys into the country. Interacting with the first and second plots, but not the third, are the witches, whose unspecified domain is conveniently adjacent to the environs of Ravenna. Thus we are offered an indeterminate world in which there are frequent references to London settings—the Cat and Fiddle tavern, Rutneys brothel, Thames watermen, law-term dissolutes, tobacco-smoking knights, etc.—and so little does the decorum of place concern the dramatist that a Scottish accent is used for inhabitants of northern Italy.

Some scholars have felt that such a melange of material indicates hasty composition[58] and such an impression might at first seem to be confirmed by Middleton's wholesale borrowings of witchcraft lore from Scot's *The Discoverie of Witchcraft* (1584). In some cases whole lists of demons and cauldron ingredients, and an Ovidian invocation, are taken over *verbatim* by the dramatist and there is no discernible attempt, as there is so notably in *The Witch of Edmonton*, to create a coherent social background within which witchcraft operates. Continental and English witchcraft practices are mingled indiscriminately. The meeting of groups of witches in a sabbath in which the Devil was worshipped, the sexual assaults on the community by incubus and succubus, the transvection of witches into the air by means of anointing—all vigorously presented in Middleton's play—belong essentially to continental conceptions of witchcraft[59] and reflect the literary nature of Middleton's source material. They co-exist in the play alongside more characteristically English ingredients of witch-lore such as the familiar, the use of waxen effigies and the laming of cattle in reprisal for neglect to lend 'barm and milk / Goose-grease and tar'.[60] At times Middleton's presentation of material moves in a shockingly casual way from the trivial to the painful, as when, in a moment of black humour, the 'red-haired girl' joins the ingredients in the cauldron:

> *Firestone.*   Here's bear-breech and lizard's brain, forsooth.
> *Hecate.*   Into the vessel;
> And fetch three ounces of the red-haired girl
> I killed last midnight.
> *Firestone.*   Whereabouts, sweet mother?
> *Hecate.* Hip; hip or flank. Where is the *acopus*?   (V.ii.53–7)

The dramatist seems less concerned to establish a credible social context for witchcraft than to display an impressive variety of charms under the command of the chief witch, Hecate, who, although associated with the moon-goddess and with rituals of moon-worship, is, nevertheless, of mortal status with a finite, if protracted, life expectancy (I.ii.69–77). Opportunities are blatantly engineered in order to allow for recitals of her capabilities; for example, the deep grief and reluctance of Sebastian to consult her gives a cue for the listing of a menu of available *maleficia* at I.ii.133ff. and likewise, at V.ii.18ff., the scepticism of the Duchess prompts a haughty recital in Latin to demonstrate her professional credentials. In this way Hecate is established with an impressive authority, enjoying shrewd telepathic powers and particularly notable for her joyful and appreciative response to moonlit flight and the pleasures of music and dance:

> *Hecate.*   I'm so light
> At any mischief! There's no villainy
> But is a tune methinks.   (V.ii.78–80)

None the less, Hecate is not viewed as all-powerful. Her charms require careful tending and can only work within their own capacities. Thus her method of murder by use of waxen pictures requires a full month for its successful operation and, in the case of matrimony, she frankly admits her powerlessness:

> *Hecate.*   We cannot disjoin wedlock.
> 'Tis of heaven's fastening. Well may we raise jars,
> Jealousies, strifes and heart-burning disagreements,
> Like a thick scurf o'er life, as did our master
> Upon that patient miracle, but the work itself
> Our power cannot disjoint.   (I.ii.172–7)

That Middleton achieves more in the witch scenes than mere 'dramatic illustrations of the books on demonology'[61] is indicated not merely by the vitality of his presentation of Hecate. The dramatist, suppressing Scot's sceptical attitude towards his material, creates a positively celebratory air by resourceful use of stage spectacle, music, dance and ritual. A comparison with the conditions under which the potent herbs are gathered by the witches in this play and in *Macbeth* suggests the lesser degree of malignity involved in Middleton's play.[62] Here they are gathered by moonlight, appropriate to Hecate's close association with the moon (III.iii.30); in Shakespeare, in total darkness, 'Slivered in the moon's eclipse' (IV.i.28).

Middleton carefully arranges his presentation of these witch scenes in such a way as to arouse curiosity and to avoid repetition of effects. Thus, in the first of them, attention is centred on Hecate and her dealings with the mortals who seek her, rather than on the preparations of the magical herbs; these are kept largely offstage, though Middleton does bring the scene to a spectacular climax in the entry of Hecate's great cat, her familiar, leading in the banquet, one which is, one may assume, suitably more fantastic than that of the mortals in I.i. In the second witch scene the fruits of Hecate's skills are demonstrated in terms of the witches' moonlit flight in an effect combining music and spectacle.[63] The stage-business here clearly calls for elaborate and spectacular stage-effects complemented by the divided song with its skilful use of voices 'in the air',[64] an effect which was to inspire Davenant's Restoration revival of *Macbeth*. The deadly potency of Hecate's cauldron brew is reserved for the final witch scene. It is important to remember here that Shakespeare's famous cauldron scene in *Macbeth* probably derives from Middleton's original *tour de force*, though both may be in part inspired by Jonson's *The Masque of Queenes*.[65] In this scene, ritual and song culminate in the presentation of a special dance, which in its manner and performance was doubtless designed to complement the grotesque and noxious nature of the witches' cauldron brew.[66]

The tone of the witch scenes is partly established by the manner in which the court of Ravenna interacts with the world of witchcraft. An easy commerce seems to exist in which the human world is viewed by the witches largely as a means by which to satisfy their lechery. When no mortals are available, Hecate is forced to be content with incest with her loutish son Firestone.[67] For the mortals, consulting witches seems to be far from an unusual activity; even Sebastian, who has perhaps the strongest sense of moral scruple in the play, announces his intended visit to the witches in a surprisingly perfunctory manner. In terms of the relative corruption revealed in the play it seems that it is the human world which is the more vicious. By contrast Hecate and her followers appear, in their uncomplicated delight in their activities, almost innocent; though guilty of coarse and brutal crimes, they seem not much more culpable than neutral executors of the hypocritical and wicked intents of the court figures. Middleton partly achieves this impression by the zest with which he presents the witches' activities and the comic role which is played by Firestone, who typically goes joy-riding on that malignant spirit, the Nightmare (I.ii.94–104); but also by the extent to which the mortal world is given to the pursuit of appetite and greed. In this respect the witch scenes may be said to act as a foil to, or parody of, the unrestrained desires of the inhabitants of Ravenna. Significantly the emphasis in the presentation of the witches' evil is sexual, as it is in the human world, and in this sense Hecate symbolises the unwholesome sexual desire which is a major concern of the play as a whole.[68]

Most commentators on the play have seen the inconsistencies of plotting and startling juxtapositions of mood as evidence of incompetent or careless construction. Swinburne's reaction in this respect, otherwise admiring the play's language and manner, is typically dismissive: 'so ridiculous a reconciliation between intending murderers and intended victims as here exceeds in absurdity the chaotic combination of accident and error which disposes of inconvenient or superfluous underlings'.[69] It is true that the details of Sebastian's intrigues to gain Isabella are so elaborate in IV.ii as to be impenetrable. In particular it is impossible to make clear sense of his use of Florida. If his intention is to use her to confirm Isabella's belief that Ferdinand's house is used by Antonio for assignations, why does he give her the key to Isabella's chamber? If the plan is that Isabella will discover her on her return, it remains an unnecessary and confusing duplication. The cause of this muddle is doubtless in part hasty composition; but an ancillary cause seems to be Middleton's desire to pile on the confusions and misunderstandings thick and fast in the final act. Thus, anticipating the much more skilful plotting of Women Beware Women, Florida's presence in Isabella's chamber is necessary for Middleton's plan to show the spiralling accidents associated with Francisca's counterplot.

It has recently been argued that The Witch is a concerted parody or burlesque of Fletcherian romantic tragicomedy.[70] Whilst close identification with specific plays by Fletcher is rather speculative, Middleton's handling of the final resolution of the intrigue lends some support to this approach. In particular, Antonio's reported death at V.iii.25–33ff., like the death of Raggozine in Shakespeare's Measure for Measure, is so palpably contrived as to draw attention to the dramatic artifice.[71] This effect is further heightened in the subsequent incredible revelation that the Duchess's 'honour' remains intact after all, and further capped by the amazing decision by the Duke that the woman who has ruthlessly plotted murders, including his own, demonstrates 'virtue's noblest ends' (V.iii.130). Whilst it seems likely that Middleton aimed at a parodic effect here, however, the result is not entirely successful because it seems at odds with the ironies aimed at in the self-destructive counterplots of Francisca. The latter's deadly intents merit Antonio's punishment of marriage to the worthless Aberzanes, followed by poisoning in the wedding-toast, but the tragicomic framework, aided by the very active intervention of the good servant Hermio, moves the resolution of this plot to a more equivocal conclusion.

That Middleton is experimenting with tragicomic conventions in this play is clearly evident in his use of surprise and withheld information. Stage-whispering is frequent; the audience is not informed of events which are presumed to have taken place offstage and, more significantly, striking deceptions occur, as when the audience suddenly learns at V.iii.100ff. that the Duchess did not lose her honour to Almachildes in III.i as it had been led to believe. Perhaps the device that suggests Middleton's approach to his material most revealingly is the withholding until V.i of the information that Antonio, in collaboration with Gaspero, has misled Isabella, with a story of Sebastian's death in battle, in order to gain her consent to the marriage that takes place at the opening of the play. Our only clue that Isabella is under such a misapprehension occurs in a soliloquy at IV.ii.92–4. The effect of delaying this information until so late in the play is to inhibit our sympathy for Sebastian and Isabella's plight which would otherwise accrue had Antonio's villainy been revealed to the audience at the outset. Unless we interpret this as an incompetent use of tragicomic convention, it would seem to suggest that Middleton intends to prevent the audience's emotional engagement with the couples' formal role as thwarted lovers.

Although Sebastian's opening appeal to heavenly sanction of his prior marriage contract might arouse audience sympathy, it is immediately clear from Fernando's comment that his friend's state of mind is desperate, an impression confirmed by Sebastian's prompt consultation with Hecate and his obsession with the physical aspects of the situation:

> *Sebastian.* I fear they're now a-kissing. What's o'clock?
> 'Tis now but supper-time, but night will come
> And all new-married couples make short suppers. (I.ii.119–21)

When the charm of impotency has evidently worked on Antonio, Sebastian exults that Antonio has 'no content' but the emphasis seems to fall on his own sexual frustration, casting doubt on the integrity of his claim, 'Holy vows witness that our souls were married!' (II.i.222). Further doubt of the correspondence between his rhetoric and his barely control-led emotions is created by a singularly insensitive interpretation of Isa-bella's 'waspishness' (III.ii.48). His elaborate plan to achieve consumma-tion of his 'marriage' to Isabella by deception and rape, which he justifies to his friend Fernando in a sanctimonious speech (IV.ii.6ff.), sorts ill with his scornful remarks on the morals of Florida, currently being employed by him to aid his deception. It is true that Sebastian stops short of violating Isabella and that he appears to undergo an important change of heart, but even here his rationale for so doing casts some doubt on the credibility of the language of his conclusion: 'No, he that would soul's sacred comfort win / Must burn in pure love, like a seraphin' (IV.ii.110–11). In a parallel way, Isabella is far from being the perfect creation that her role of abused integrity might suggest. Initially she seems only to show sexual disappoint-ment at her husband's failure to consummate their marriage. She sings the first verse of a song whose remaining verses are bawdy[72] in order to gain a kiss from Antonio and plays the smug housewife to the world. Her willing-ness to believe the disguised Sebastian's criticisms of her husband are surprisingly prompt as is her wish that these criticisms should prove true and rid her of her husband.

By inhibiting audience sympathy for the 'virtuous' characters in this way, Middleton seems to be aiming for an all-pervasive irony such as one finds in the later *Women Beware Women* and *The Changeling*. The figures at the court of Ravenna offer a largely reductive view of moral awareness. The Duke's habit of taunting his wife with her father's skull, which is tolerated in public even by the Governor, seems whimsical and arbitrary. The Duchess's resort to revenge seems mechanical and casual rather than deeply felt and her proud insistence that she is only a murderess, not an adulteress, appears as moral delinquency. Even the Governor displays a strikingly neutral attitude towards his neice together with an alarmingly complacent reliance on providence to protect Isabella:

> I'll not speak
> To have her spared if she be base and guilty.
> If otherwise, heaven will not see her wronged;
> I need take no care for her.   (V.i.106–9)

The widespread emptiness of moral perception, which Middleton suggests in his portrayal of this court, is thrown into sharp relief by the openly shameless depravity of the sixteen-year-old sister of Antonio, Francisca. Her sharp, insolent *doubles entendres* in her dialogue with Isabella and Antonio lend to her character a vitality which is matched by the frankness of her soliloquies:

> These bastards come upon poor venturing gentlewomen
> Ten to one faster than your legitimate children.
> If I had been married, I'll be hanged if I had been with child so soon now. When
> they are once husbands they'll be whipped ere they take such pains as a friend
> will do: to come by water to the back-door at midnight; there stay perhaps an
> hour in all weathers with a pair of reeking watermen laden with bottles of wine,
> chewets and currant-custards.   (II.i.42–49)

Such colloquial admission of callous depravity is likely to affect an audience more directly than the more conventionally sensational scenes of the play and allows for moments of shocking energy in the struggle to survive, as when Francisca prays for the success of her plan to discredit Isabella: 'I trust he's spoiled 'em both—too dear a happiness! / O, how I tremble between doubts and joys!' (IV.iii.43–4). At such moments one perceives how the title of the play might apply more widely than merely to Hecate, and one gains a hint of the potential of the witchcraft material to underline a tragic view, such as one finds in *The Changeling*, of man's enslavement to appetite and passion.

THE WITCH OF EDMONTON

The title-page of the first and only early edition of *The Witch of Edmonton*, published in 1658, gives the authors as '*William Rowley, Thomas Dekker, John Ford, &c.*' The play dates, however, from 1621 for there is a record of a performance at Court on 29 December of that year.[73] No doubt it received its first performance at the Cockpit earlier in the year since it dramatises the events which led to the execution of Elizabeth Sawyer for witchcraft on 19 April 1621 and Prince Charles's Company would have wished to capitalise on the current sensation. The 1658 quarto would appear to derive not from the original production but from a revival of the play in the mid 1630s as is evidenced by the Prologue and references to the actors, Bird, Hamluc and Fenn.[74] The Prologue makes much of Edmonton as the setting for the earlier anonymous play, *The Merry Devil of Edmonton*, which appears to have been extremely popular, being performed at Court three times, twice in the 1630s, and reprinted six times between 1608 and 1655. The author of the Prologue perhaps judged that reference to the earlier and still popular play would drum up custom. In fact the association of the two plays is misleading since *The Merry Devil* offers no substantial presentation of witchcraft or magic, Peter Fabell, the central protagonist, being a pale Faustian figure within an environment of romantic comedy.

The collaborative nature of *The Witch of Edmonton* has given rise to extended debate on the dramatists' individual responsibilities. The general consensus suggests that Dekker was the leader of the overall project, having the main responsibility for the Elizabeth Sawyer area of the play, whilst Ford's hand is most apparent in the Frank Thorney plot and Rowley's main contribution lies in the Cuddy Banks scenes. The argument, however, is in no way conclusive[75] and the title page's '&c.' has led at least one critic to suggest that there may be other participants in the collaboration.[76] Collaborative play-writing was a commonplace during the period and the question of precise attribution is probably vain and certainly largely irrelevant to the dramatic quality of the text except in so far as it has affected its reputation, as, for example, in the case of the misplaced view that the play is loosely constructed.[77]

In contrast to Middleton's quasi-Italian setting for *The Witch*, *The Witch of Edmonton* is precisely located in the rural environment of Jacobean Edmonton and its surroundings, the contemporary audience's familiarity and association with the play-world being supported by frequent references to neighbouring villages such as Enfield and Waltham, and to districts and locations in nearby London. One of the play's most striking characteristics is its detailed evocation of the life of such a community, its social structure, concerns, and activities. We are presented with a world in which a local knight, Sir Arthur Clarington, occupies the apex of the social hierarchy whilst beneath him are ranged in due order, minor gentry, yeoman and tenant farmers, country-men and peasants. At the bottom of the social order is Elizabeth Sawyer, the Witch of Edmonton, destitute, isolated and both feared and abused by her neighbours.

It is a coherent and comprehensive community in which the social divisions are clearly drawn. The Thorneys, minor gentry, are bankrupt and needs must mend their fortune by dowry-hunting. Thus Frank Thorney is tempted into a bigamous marriage with the daughter of the wealthy yeoman, Old Carter, who though socially inferior is none the less proud of his

yeoman status and way of life (I.ii.4–6). His constant recourse to proverbial expression creates an impression of sound if limited intelligence and
understanding. Farmers such as Old Banks and his neighbours show less
perception and his concern for the sickness of his horse and their fears for
the health of their cattle (IV.i.1–14) suggest not only a society acutely
aware of the small margin between prosperity and disaster, but also a cast
of mind which is credulous in seeking for immediate and simple explan-
ations for natural misfortune. The coherence of the community is further
enhanced by the dramatists' presentation of its shared activities. The
elaborate preparations by Cuddy Banks and his companions for the morris
dance, with detailed discussion of the quality of the bells to be employed,
the refurbishing of the Hobby Horse and the parts to be played by individuals, together with the references to the marriage celebration with its
feasting and tilting at the barrels, combine to create a concrete sense of the
community's social texture. It is this community which is the background
for and the victim of the witch-mania and hysteria which is instrumental in
pursuing Elizabeth Sawyer to execution.

The 'convincing tone of realism'[78] which contributes so much to the
dramatic action derives in large measure from the dramatists' main source,
Goodcole's pamphlet, *The wonderful discoverie of Elizabeth Sawyer, a
Witch* (1621), and the manner in which they adapt it. In modern parlance
the play might be termed a 'docudrama' for almost all the events of the
Elizabeth Sawyer action are drawn from Goodcole's report although such
incidents as the thatch burning and Anne Radcliffe's suicide, dismissed by
Goodcole as 'ridiculous fictions' (sig. A3v), are more likely to have been
drawn from ballad literature. The dramatists did not slavishly follow
Goodcole. Two examples suggest their concern to heighten the dramatic
quality of the material. Goodcole's references to the witch's husband and
children are suppressed so that she is presented as a woman entirely isolated from human support and comfort. Secondly, Elizabeth Sawyer's
statement that the devil appeared to her in the form of both a black and a
white dog (Goodcole, sig. C2v) is developed symbolically to presage her
condemnation and execution. No source has been discovered for the
Cuddy Banks plot but K. M. Briggs has suggested the trace of a possible
source for Frank Thorney's murder of Susan in a ballad published between
1640 and 1655.[79]

The realistic social observation supports and adds authenticity to the
dramatists' presentation of popular witch beliefs and practices. The play,
which has been described as 'a comprehensive study of Elizabethan ideas
of witchcraft'[80] and 'the soberest and most factual of all the witch plays',[81]
dramatises an almost complete range of witchcraft practice. Elizabeth
Sawyer's social position and appearance precisely conform to the common
image of a witch. She is old, isolated from the community, 'poor, deformed
and ignorant / And like a bow buckled and bent together' (II.i.2–3) and she

has only one eye (II.i.89–90). Scot writes that those who are said to be witches 'are women who are commonly old, lame, bleare-eied, pale, fowle, and full of wrinkles; poore, sullen, superstitious... They are leane and deformed, shewing melancholie in their faces... They are doting, scolds, mad, divelish' (I.3). Elizabeth Sawyer certainly has a sharp tongue which she uses with effect in her confrontation with Old Banks and in her arguments with Sir Arthur and the Justice, whilst the motivation for her *malificia*, revenge for the denial of small requests and for injuries and insults, also accords with common belief.[82] Cursing her persecutors, Elizabeth Sawyer falls into witchcraft through ignorance and temptation. Since she is treated as a witch, though ignorant of witchcraft practices, she expresses the desire to become one in order to revenge herself on Old Banks. At once the devil appears to her in the shape of a black dog and she is cajoled and pressured into a compact with him. The pact is sealed, to the accompaniment of thunder and lightning, when she allows the devil-dog to suck blood from her arm (II.i.147), the common means by which such contracts were believed to be concluded. From this point the play dramatises a sequence of common witch beliefs and practices as Elizabeth Sawyer's career develops towards its pathetic conclusion on the scaffold.

The devil-dog, a strikingly effective theatrical creation, whom she calls Tom or Tommy, performs the role of her familiar, the instrument of her malice and revenge. He it is who is sent to spoil Old Banks's corn and injure his cattle, to lame his horse, nip the suckling child and prevent the butter from coming. The concept of the familiar, a belief unique to English witchcraft lore, occurs again and again in English witch trials, accused witches being said to be served by toads, ferrets, cats, frogs, moles etc.[83] Tom is, however, much more than a conventional familiar since the dramatists, elaborating on their source material, present him as an agent of evil, independent of Elizabeth Sawyer, in crystalising Frank Thorney's murderous thoughts and disrupting the morris. The Dog's leading rôle is emphasised by his instruction of the novice witch in the formula which invokes his presence: *'If thou to death or shame pursue 'em / Sanctibicetur nomen tuum'* (II.i.175–6). The quarto's various spellings of the prayer suggest that Elizabeth Sawyer, in her ignorance, achieves an imperfect grasp of the Latin, a perversion of 'Hallowed be Thy Name' from the Lord's Prayer.[84] Nonetheless, Tommy consistently appears when she chants the formula, until V.i.27.1 when, having deserted her, he returns in the shape of a white dog in order to put her in mind of her winding sheet. It is characteristic of witch lore that the relationship between Tom and his mistress includes the sucking of her blood, so forming a teat or witch's mark (IV.i.153–6). The witch's mark, supposedly insensitive to pain, was frequently regarded as the most telling evidence of witchcraft[85] and much significance is attached to it in Goodcole's pamphlet.

One of the methods by which a witch might harm her enemies was by means of the devil's touch.[86] The familiar 'touches' the victim and thus transmits the *maleficium*. Elizabeth Sawyer seeks the death of Old Banks (II.i.153) and Anne Radcliffe (IV.i.173–90) by this means. Since Banks is 'loving to the world' and charitable, the devil-dog has no power to injure him. With Anne Radcliffe, however, he is more successful. She loses her mind and finally dashes out her brains, a dramatic exaggeration of Goodcole's report. Fears of such *maleficia* could provoke communal hysteria and recourse to superstitious procedures, both to identify the witch and nullify her power. In IV.i Hamluc enters with thatch and link in an attempt to prove Elizabeth Sawyer a witch: 'A handful of thatch plucked off a hovel of hers; and they say, when 'tis burning, if she be a witch she'll come running in' (17–18). Mother Sawyer duly appears, though whether by accident or compulsion is not clear. This superstition seems to have been widely accepted by country people,[87] but is dismissed by Goodcole as 'an old ridiculous custome' (sig. A4). Similarly, Anne Radcliffe appears to attempt to remove the witch's *maleficium* by trying to scratch Mother Sawyer's face,[88] for it was a common belief into the last century that to wound a witch or to draw blood 'above the breath' annulled the spell.

The devil-dog's activities in other areas of the play illustrate further popular beliefs. The manner in which he is able to encourage Frank Thorney's unspoken, and perhaps unconscious, impulse to murder suggests that the devil can read minds or quickly take advantage of our darker thoughts, a view confirmed by Tom's subsequent discussion with Cuddy Banks, whilst Cuddy's frustrated courting of Katherine dramatises the belief that the devil or his agents might take on any shape they pleased. It would be a mistake, however, to see *The Witch of Edmonton* as no more than a catalogue of accepted witch beliefs and practices designed to provoke fear and moral condemnation. Elizabeth Sawyer is presented in such a way that the audience is invited to respond to her with sympathy as a victim both of the devil's wiles and the social prejudices of the community in which she lives. Her opening soliloquy establishes a pattern for compassionate response:

> Some call me witch,
> And, being ignorant of myself, they go
> About to teach me how to be one, urging
> That my bad tongue, by their bad usage made so,
> Forspeaks their cattle, doth bewitch their corn,
> Themselves, their servants and their babes at nurse.
> This they enforce upon me, and in part
> Make me to credit it. (II.i.8–15)

Her complaint is immediately substantiated with the entrance of Old Banks who abuses and beats her for gathering sticks on his land. The half fearful, half mocking behaviour of the morris dancers towards her (II.i.87–98) serves to emphasise her point. If society does not exactly make witches it predisposes them to feel and behave in ways which expose them to the devil's temptations. Mother Sawyer's understandable anger and desire for revenge provokes the devil-dog to appear: 'Ho! Have I found thee cursing? Now thou art mine own' (II.i.121). Her response is ambiguous; whilst she desires revenge she is also fearful of giving up her soul. It is significant that she agrees to the pact only after the devil threatens to tear her into a thousand pieces. Thus it is a persecuted and isolated old woman who is entrapped into witchcraft rather than an evil and malicious criminal who purposely seeks to acquire devilish power.

Whilst the witch employs the devil-dog to pursue her revenge, it is noteworthy that the relationship which she develops with her 'Tom' is close and affectionate. She looks on the Dog as her confidant, her companion and comfort, and it is therefore the more poignant when Tom, in the guise of a white dog, abandons her to conviction and execution. Furthermore the dramatists present her actions within a wider social context which suggests that her crimes are paralleled elsewhere in society. Examined by Sir Arthur and the Justice (IV.i), she is given the opportunity to deliver a penetrating critique of the sexual and financial corruption of legitimate society (IV.i.103–146). We are therefore encouraged to see Elizabeth Sawyer as much as a victim as a criminal, a view which is reinforced by the note of scepticism within the play with regard to popular witch beliefs. The thatch-burning is described by the Justice, a figure of authority, as ridiculous. Banks's report of his embarrassing behavioural compulsion with his cow (IV.i.53–68) is dismissed as sport by Sir Arthur whilst the Justice admonishes the countrymen's treatment of the witch, reminding them that she is a subject and entitled to the law's protection.

The audience is also placed in a complex judgemental position in the case of Frank Thorney. He too is a victim, caught between affection for and marriage to Winnifride and his responsibility to restore the family fortune by acquiring Susan's dowry. Again we are not allowed to see him as a complete villain. Not only is he placed under a family obligation but, early in the play, we are made aware that he is ignorant of Winnifride's previous sexual liaison with her master, Sir Arthur. Faced with contrary demands, Frank seeks an easy way through. He marries bigamously and plans to flee the country with Winnifride. Susan's unwillingness to see him leave provokes his unspoken desire to be rid of her and at once the devil-dog appears to crystalise his murderous impulses (III.iii.14–16). Unaware of the Dog's influence, Frank casts suspicion for the murder on Warbeck and Somerton who are arrested and charged. Subsequently, in a scene in which the Dog appears to celebrate his success in claiming Frank for his own, the truth is discovered and Young Thorney is carried off to prison and eventual execution. Frank is presented with dramatic subtlety as a character of weak moral resolve yet also possessed by a painful and disruptive consciousness of his sins. As with Elizabeth Sawyer, social pressures acting upon human inadequacies allow the devil to do his work.

The Frank/Winnifride/Susan plot strongly reflects the genre of domestic and homiletic tragedy.[89] The textures of family interests and tensions are sharply drawn and scenes such as the discovery of Susan's murder by Old Carter and Old Thorney and that in which the injured Frank is attended by Katherine provide both an acute dramatic irony and a moving articulation of familial grief and distress. Frank's speech before execution draws the community together in grief at his untimely death and in the charity of mutual forgiveness. Repenting his sins, he makes his peace with those whom he has injured, presents himself as an exemplum of wrongdoing, but puts his trust in a higher mercy:

> A court hath been kept where I am found
> Guilty; the difference is, my impartial judge
> Is much more gracious than my faults
> Are monstrous to be named, yet they are monstrous.   (V.iii.87–90)

Similarly, Elizabeth Sawyer delivers her homily to both the on-stage and off-stage audience: 'Bear witness. I repent all former evil; / There is no damnèd conjuror like the devil' (V.iii.50–1). Only Sir Arthur is excluded from this communion of forgiveness. Reflecting Mother Sawyer's penetrating critique of court and citizen morality, his sexual exploitation of Winnifride and selfish manipulation of Frank are punished by a considerable fine and, more significantly, since it points the audience's response towards a deeper social corrosion, by Old Carter's potent dismissal: 'If luck had served, Sir Arthur, and every man had his due, somebody might have tottered ere this without paying fines, like it as you list' (V.iii.161–3).

The tragic intervention of the devil in the life of the community is burlesqued in the play's third narrative strand, the Cuddy Banks plot. The Dog's frustration of Cuddy's romantic aspirations, the disruption of the morris dance and the nature of the relationship established between Cuddy and Tom comically parallel the tragic structures elsewhere in the play. Where Elizabeth Sawyer recognises the Dog as the devil and employs him as a familiar and Frank's dissembling ends in tragedy, Cuddy treats the Dog 'doggedly' as a dog and is punished with no more than a ducking for his unsuccessful pursuit of Katherine, whilst the communal witch mania of the countrymen (IV.i) is replicated in comic terms by Tom's intervention in the morris (III.iv). Such potent counterpointing of tragic and comic tones demonstrates a conception of tragi-comedy less sophisticated than the quasi-Fletcherian mode of The Witch where the tragic impetus is denied by an entirely unexpected catastrophe.

The Witch of Edmonton has been criticised for a lack of overall coherence of thematic development and tone,[90] a view to which the collaborative process of composition has leant support. Such responses, however, underestimate the skill of the dramatists, for the play explores the consequences of allowing the devil to penetrate, work in and corrupt a small but representative community. The devil-dog operates in the three areas of the play and thus draws them together. Here an analogy may be drawn with a play such as *The Spanish Tragedy* where Kyd reveals the unforeseen consequences of invoking revenge for Andrea's personal satisfaction, an act which results in general destruction. Elizabeth Sawyer's unexpected and untutored invocation of the devil leads not only to her own corruption and execution but to the exploitation of Frank's moral weakness and the tragedy which befalls his family. Ironically the innocent, the clown Cuddy Banks, survives the confrontation with the devil and it is he who defuses the devil's terror and influence by demonstrating the pettiness of his stratagems and suggests that his success depends on human fallibility.[91] Thus the play has a strong and focused moral impulse, not only in revealing how susceptible humankind is to temptation but also in arguing for the potential for human kindness and understanding.[92] The sympathetic light in which Elizabeth Sawyer is often presented, her affection for 'Tom', Young Banks's treatment of the devil-dog and his partial sympathy for the witch reveal a human warmth which finds its most dramatic expression at the conclusion of the Frank Thorney plot. Frank is presented not as a villain meeting his just end but rather as a penitent young man led astray and thus the focus of communal distress and forgiveness. He is forgiven in turn by all those whom he has injured and Old Carter engages to comfort his unfortunate father and support his 'distressed widow'. The play's final movement celebrates an ideal of charity achieved in the face of personal tragedy and human fallibility.

The Witch of Edmonton has received five professional British productions in this century; the Phoenix Society at the Lyric, Hammersmith, April 1921; the Old Vic, December 1936; the Mermaid Theatre, November 1962; the Royal Shakespeare Company at The Other Place, September 1981; and the Bristol Old Vic, June 1984. These have included a number of notable actors and performances. In the Phoenix Society production Sybil Thorndike played Mother Sawyer and Russell Thorndike played the Dog, whilst at the Old Vic the witch's role was taken by Edith Evans. However, judging from reviews of these earlier productions, the revival which was most successful in revealing the text's potential was Barry Kyle's at The Other Place. Great care was taken to establish a sense of the everyday life of the community. The set 'with its stiles, barrels, straw, pails, dirty linen and dead birds reminds us that Edmonton was once a rural community'.[93] The cast was frequently engaged in hauling sacks, inspecting their contents, fetching water, churning butter and other such activities so that, as Michael Billington observed, 'we get ... a strong sense of a tight-knit hypocritical community on which Mother Sawyer seeks reasonable revenge'. Miles Anderson's Dog was 'blacked all over, with a curly spaniel wig and a black harness incorporating a tail'[94] and was at times terrifying but also engaging, whilst Miriam Karlin's witch conveyed 'a poignant sense of defiant vulnerability'.[95] For James Fenton the production showed how 'in a society where the failure of a crop may come as an irremediable disaster, a society where the question of survival is most pressing, phenomena such as witch-hunts are a way of responding to a fearful common danger'.[96]

That *The Witch of Edmonton* can find both an audience and a production which gains critical praise encourages the hope that *Sophonisba* and *The Witch* may also be revived.

A NOTE ON THE TEXTS

Two early editions of John Marston's *Sophonisba* survive, a quarto edition of 1606 and a collected octavo edition of 1633. Since Marston was still alive in 1633 there must remain a possibility that some of the variants of the octavo text are authorial. However, all the evidence suggests otherwise. The fact that the collected edition was re-issued in the same year expunging Marston's name from the general title-page and also from prefatory matter and individual title-pages,[97] would seem to suggest active hostility to the publication, making it unlikely that Marston co-operated in revising his texts. Examination of the octavo variants makes it even less likely that the corrector's hand was Marston's. Kemp, in his recent edition, argues convincingly that with the exception of a few obviously superior readings and a brilliant emendation at II.iii.108, 'many of its new readings are simply literary sophistications, and some even convert the quarto's sense into nonsense'.[98]

The quarto edition of 1606 must then provide the copy-text for any modern edition of the play,[99] though the present edition is less conservative than Kemp's old-spelling text in adhering to quarto readings. The quarto text gives the impression, consistent with Marston's concern expressed in the note after the Epilogus, of being printed from a carefully prepared author's copy which is particularly notable for the elaborate and carefully visualised stage-directions. Less easy to interpret is the extraordinarily elaborate and persistent proof-reading that occurred in John Windet's printing shop, made the more tantalising by the possibility of Marston's contribution.[100] The present edition, based on the Bodleian copy (Malone 186) and collated with the two copies in the British Library (Ashley 1102 and C. 34.d.33) also draws upon the more comprehensive collations of Kemp's edition. Some readings in the Textual Collation are listed as 'variants' rather than 'corrected' or 'uncorrected' readings because of the bewildering nature of the proof-reading of certain forms of the quarto.[101] The quarto copy text has also been collated with the Huntington Library copy of the 1633 octavo and the three copies in the British Library have been consulted.

Middleton's *The Witch* survives only in manuscript form (Bodleian Library MS Malone 12) in a copy which has been identified as by Ralph Crane,[102] a scrivener used from time to time by the King's Men and from the evidence of the Epistle employed here by Middleton to furnish a copy at the request of Thomas Holmes, Esq. This copy forms the basis of the present edition. In line with the principles of this series the persistent habit in the manuscript of indicating elision by an apostrophe accompanied by the uncontracted phrase (e.g. "I' have byn", "thou' hast", etc.) has been brought into line with standard modern practice.[103] From the evidence of the anticipatory directions for entrance (often not precisely aligned in the margins with the dialogue) it would seem likely that Crane's original was probably a playhouse manuscript. The manuscript has been collated against the subsequent printed editions listed in the Abbreviations. The Malone Society edition by W. W. Greg and F. P. Wilson has proved invaluable in confirming a number of manuscript readings.

On 21 May 1658 Edward Blackmore 'Entred for his Copie (under ye hand of Mr Thomason Warden) a booke called The Witch of Edmonton a TragiComedy by Will: Rowley &c', some thirty-seven years after the publication of Goodcole's pamphlet and the play's first production. The 1658 quarto, the only early text, shows signs of careless printing and a lack of proof-reading. Four pages in Act V are misnumbered, act and scene divisions are inconsistently presented and there are a number of major variations in the forms of speech-prefixes.[104] Such textual deficiencies, together with the inclusion of references to the actors W. Hamluc, W. Mago, Theophilus Bird and Ezekiel Fenn[105] have given rise to speculation about the manuscript which lies behind the quarto. Bentley (I.251–2; II.378; III.271–2) conjectures that it was a prompt copy of the revived production of 1635/6. Bowers (III.483–6) on the other hand, whilst accepting that the manuscript had some connection with the theatre and that it may have been in the possession of an actor, argues that it was more likely to have been autograph papers or 'a rather literal scribal copy preliminary to the prompt book'.

The Bodleian copy (Malone 238) has provided the copy-text for this edition and in addition the two other Bodleian copies were consulted together with two copies in the British Library and the copy in the Henry E. Huntington Library. No press variants were observed.

NOTES

1 Reprinted by Rosen, pp. 190–203.
2 *Fairfax's Daemonologia*, with a Biographical Introduction by William Grainge (1882).
3 Chambers, *ES*, III, 424.
4 For example, Caryl Churchill's play, *Vinegar Tom, TQ* Publications, 1978.
5 For an excellent collection of witch pamphlets see Rosen.
6 p. 157.
7 See Nosworthy, pp. 32–45.
8 See Nosworthy, pp. 8–45, *Macbeth*, ed. Muir, pp. xxiv–vi and Harris, pp. 158–60.
9 Harris, p. 88.
10 Chambers, *ES*, III, 433, suggests that the omission of the acting company on the title-page indicates performance late in 1605 or early in 1606, after Queen Anne's patronage had been withdrawn from the Revels Boys' Company playing at the Blackfriars; however, the title-page may simply indicate the printer's acknowledgement of the loss of patronage at the time of printing; see R. A. Foakes, 'Tragedy at the Children's Theatres after 1600: A Challenge to the Adult Stage', *Elizabethan Theatre*, II, ed. D. Galloway (Toronto, 1970), p. 52, who argues for the slightly earlier dating, 1604–5.
11 Bentley, VI, 9–11.
12 See David G. O'Neil, 'The Influence of Music in the Works of John Marston, I, II & III', *Music and Letters*, 53 (1972), pp. 122–33, 293–308 and 400–10. See also R. W. Ingram, *John Marston* (Boston, 1978), pp. 144–5, who suggests that 'Marston may have felt that the rich directions for music printed in *Sophonisba* read awkwardly'.
13 See R. A. Foakes, pp. 37–59, who links this play closely with Chapman's *Bussy D'Ambois*.
14 See Peter Ure, 'John Marston's *Sophonisba*: a Reconsideration', *Elizabethan and Jacobean Drama* (1974), p. 78.
15 W. F. Bolton, ed. *Sejanus*, New Mermaid (1966), p. xiii.
16 See Livy, pp. 633–7. Marston only draws on Livy in V.ii.68–86 and V.iii.13–28.
17 See, for example, II.i.33–4 and 68 for Machiavelli, and II.i.118–19 and III.i.178 for Montaigne.
18 See IV.i.102–125 and notes.
19 See IV.i.143–60 and notes. Lines 157–160 have drawn sharp criticism from commentators.
20 Robert R. Reed, Jnr, *The Occult on the Tudor and Stuart Stage* (1965), p. 163.
21 Una Ellis Fermor, *The Jacobean Drama* (1965. ed.), p. 87n.
22 George Lyman Kittredge, *Witchcraft in Old and New England* (1929), p. 312.
23 T. S. Eliot, *Selected Essays*, 3rd enlarged ed. (1951), p. 230, commenting on Bullen's discussion of the play in Bullen's *Marston*, I.xliv–v.
24 T. S. Eliot grasps the point though he expresses it somewhat obscurely, '[the episode] is integral to the plot of the play; and is one of those moments of a double reality, in which Marston is saying something else, which evidence his poetic genius' (*Selected Essays*, p. 230).
25 Lucan, Introduction, p. 13.
26 Ure, pp. 78–9.
27 Rosen, p. 57.
28 *Selected Essays*, p. 232.
29 For example, see commentary, I.ii.163, II.i.166, III.ii.77 and IV.i.187–8.
30 See Philip J. Finklepearl, *John Marston of the Middle Temple*, (Cambridge, Mass., 1969), p. 250 and W. Bridges-Adams, *The Irresistible Theatre* (1957), p. 278.
31 Finklepearl, p. 249.

32 For a list of parallels between the two plays, see A. C. Bradley, *Shakespearean Tragedy* (1904), p. 471 and K. Muir in his Arden edition of *Macbeth*, pp. xx–xxii, who suggests that Shakespeare was probably the borrower.

33 *The Plays of John Marston*, ed. H. Harvey Wood, 3 vols (1938), II, xii.

34 R. W. Ingram, *John Marston*, p. 143, in referring to the debate between Carthalo and Gelosso at II.i.49ff.

35 Dieter Mehl, *The Elizabethan Dumb Show* (1964), p. 134.

36 Mehl, p. 137, notes Marston's fondness for beginning the dialogue 'at full speed'.

37 See commentary note to IV.i.182.

38 Mary Chan, *Music in the Theatre of Ben Jonson* (1980), p. 15.

39 See commentary notes to III.i.o.1, IV.i.o.1 and V.i.o.1, and Ingram, 'The Use of Music', pp. 154–64.

40 Cf. *The Insatiate Countess*, III, where a short song accompanies the offstage love-making between Isabella and Gniaca; see also Ingram, *John Marston*, p. 146.

41 O'Neil, pp. 306–7.

42 *Antony and Cleopatra*, IV.iii. and O'Neil, p. 307.

43 IV.i.177–8.

44 O'Neil, p. 308.

45 Finklepearl, p. 244.

46 See Harris, p. 65.

47 For a comprehensive discussion of this issue see Nosworthy, pp. 24–45.

48 See Nosworthy, p. 39.

49 For a rebuttal of this general assumption, see Ann Lancashire, '*The Witch*: Stage Flop or Political Mistake?', in '*Accompaninge the players*', *Essays in Celebration of Thomas Middleton, 1580–1980*, ed. Kenneth Friedereich (New York, 1983), pp. 161–81.

50 See W. J. Lawrence, 'The Mystery of *Macbeth*' in *Shakespeare's Workshop* (1928), pp. 28–33.

51 See *The Witch*, ed. W. W. Greg and F. P. Wilson, Malone Society, 1948 (1950), pp. vii–viii.

52 See John F. McElroy, *Parody and Burlesque in the Tragicomedies of Thomas Middleton* (Salzburg, 1972), p. 155.

53 First noted by R. C. Bald, 'The Chronology of Middleton's Plays', *MLR*, 32 (1937), p. 41.

54 See Lancashire, pp. 163–7.

55 See above, pp. 1–3.

56 Quoted by Lancashire, p. 177.

57 See Lancashire, pp. 161–72; see also Heinemann, *Puritanism and Theatre* (1980), pp. 107–14.

58 See commentary, I.i.38, I.ii.108 and V.iii.54.

59 See Thomas, p. 529.

60 I.ii.53–4. See Thomas, pp. 530 and 663.

61 R. H. Barker, *Thomas Middleton* (1958), p. 94.

62 See Briggs, *PHT*, p. 80.

63 See Glynne Wickham, 'To Fly or Not to Fly? The Problem of Hecate in Shakespeare's *Macbeth*' in *Essays on Drama and Theatre: Liber Amicorum Benjamin Hunningher* (Amsterdam, Baarn, 1973), pp. 175–9.

64 See Appendix for the music to this song.

65 See Nosworthy, p. 43 and notes 8 and 9 above.

66 See Commentary, V.ii.84.1 and Appendix.

67 I.ii.96ff.

68 See B. J. Baines, *The Lust Motif in the Plays of Thomas Middleton* (Salzburg, 1973), p. 58.

69 [*The Plays of*] *Thomas Middleton*, ed. H. Ellis, vol. 1, p. xxvi.

70 See McElroy, pp. 155–215.

71 For a contrary view that Antonio's death presents an 'allegorical descent into hell pit', see Lancashire, p. 172–3.

72 See Appendix.
73 Bentley, I, 213.
74 See note to Prologue.
75 For a summary of the debate see Onat, pp. 98ff.
76 See Bentley, *Profession*, pp. 216–17.
77 See L. L. Brodwin, 'The Domestic Tragedy of Frank Thorney in *The Witch of Edmonton*', *Studies in English Literature*, 7 (1967), p. 319n and Victoria Radin, 'The Witch and the Cobblers', *The Observer*, 3 October 1982.
78 Reed, p. 184.
79 Briggs, *PHT*, p. 96.
80 Reed, p. 181.
81 Briggs, *PHT*, p. 94.
82 See Rosen, p. 29 and Kittredge, p. 19.
83 See Rosen, pp. 182–9, 'More Executions at Chelmsford'.
84 See Goodcole, sig. C4v. For misuse of prayers and sacraments see Kittredge, pp. 145ff.
85 See Rosen, pp. 17–18 and Thomas, pp. 530–1.
86 See IV.i.189n.
87 See Kittredge, p. 102.
88 See IV.i. 184n., Kittredge, p. 47 and Thomas, p. 634.
89 See L. L. Brodwin, note 77 above.
90 See note 73 above.
91 V.i.128–37 and II.i.121n.
92 Harris, p. 95 and Reed, pp. 182–3.
93 Michael Billington, *The Guardian*, 17 September 1981.
94 B. A. Young, *The Financial Times*, 17 September 1981.
95 R. V. Holdsworth, *TLS*, 25 September 1981.
96 James Fenton, *The Sunday Times*, 3 October 1982.
97 See Robert E. Brettle, 'Bibliographical Notes on Some Marston Quartos and Early Collected Editions', *The Library*, n.s. 8 (1927), p. 347 and *The Wonder of Women or The Tragedy of Sophonisba*, ed. Kemp, 1979, pp. 36–7. See also W. W. Greg, *Bibliography of the English Printed Drama to the Restoration*, III, 1089–91, for description of copies which seem to represent intermediate stages in the removal of Marstonian traces from the original 1633 issue.
98 Kemp, pp. 39–40.
99 Some copies of this edition have a variant title-page, possibly, but by no means certainly, to clarify the play's title as 'Sophonisba' rather than 'The Wonder of Women'; see Kemp, pp. 38–9.
100 Kemp, pp. 44–5.
101 See Kemp, pp. 60–7, for an extensive demonstration and discussion of this phenomenon.
102 F. P. Wilson, *The Library*, n.s. 7 (1926), pp. 194–215.
103 See W. W. Greg, 'Some Notes on Crane's Manuscript of *The Witch*', *The Library*, n.s. 22 (1942), pp. 208–22.
104 For example, pp. 55, 57, 60 and 61 are misnumbered as 35, 41, 43 and 44; Acts I, II and IV are divided into scenes at points where the stage is cleared, whereas Acts III and V have no scene divisions despite the fact that the stage is cleared on a number of occasions; Elizabeth Sawyer is variously nominated 'Sawy.', 'The Witch', 'Elizabeth Sawyer', 'Mother Sawyer' and 'Sawyer'; Young Banks is nominated 'Clow.', 'Clown', 'Young Banks' and 'Cuddy Banks'.
105 See notes to Actors' Names and Prologue.

JOHN MARSTON

THE WONDER OF WOMEN *or*
THE TRAGEDY OF SOPHONISBA

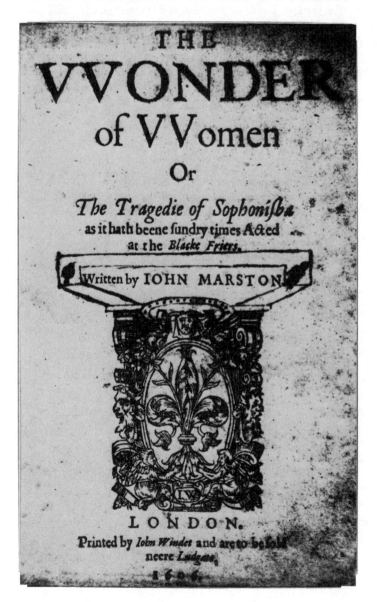

THE
VVONDER
of VVomen
Or

The Tragedie of Sophonisba
as it hath beene sundry times Acted
at the *Blacke Friers.*

Written by IOHN MARSTON

LONDON.
Printed by *Iohn Windet* and are to be sold
neere *Ludgate.*
1606.

TO THE GENERAL READER

Know that I have not laboured in this poem to tie myself to relate anything as an historian, but to enlarge everything as a poet. To transcribe authors, quote authorities, and translate Latin prose orations into English blank verse, hath, in this subject, been the least aim of my studies. Then, equal reader, peruse me with no prepared dislike; and if ought shall displease thee, thank thyself; if ought please thee, thank not me: for I confess in this it was not my only end.

JO[HN] MARSTON.

ARGUMENT

A grateful heart's just height; ingratitude,
And vow's base breach with worthy shame pursued;
A woman's constant love, as firm as fate;
A blameless counsellor well born for state;
The folly to enforce free love. These, know,
This subject with full light doth amply show.

INTERLOCUTORS

[PROLOGUE]

MASSINISSA, } kings in Libya, rivals for Sophonisba.
SYPHAX,

ASDRUBAL, father to Sophonisba.

GELOSSO, ⎫
BYTHEAS, ⎬ senators of Carthage.   5
CARTHALO, ⎭

HANNO MAGNUS, captain for Carthage.

JUGURTH, Massinissa's nephew.

SCIPIO, } generals of Rome.   10
LAELIUS,

VANGUE, an Ethiopian slave.

GISCO, a surgeon of Carthage.

NUNTIUS.

SOPHONISBA, daughter to Asdrubal of Carthage.   15

34

ZANTHIA, *her maid.*
ERICTHO, *an enchantress.*
ARCATHIA, ⎫
                 ⎬ *waiting-women to Sophonisba.*
NYCEA,   ⎭
[Soldier.]   20
[Pages. Troops. Boys. Ushers. Chorus.]

PROLOGUS

Cornets sound a march.
Enter at one door the PROLOGUE, *two* Pages *with torches,*
ASDRUBAL *and* JUGURTH, *two* Pages *with lights,* MASSINISSA
leading SOPHONISBA, ZANTHIA *bearing* SOPHONISBA'S *train,*
ARCATHIA *and* NYCEA, HANNO *and* BYTHEAS. *At the other door*
two Pages *with targets and javelins, two* Pages *with lights,*
SYPHAX *armed from top to toe;* VANGUE *follows. These, thus*
entered, stand still, whilst the PROLOGUE, *resting between both*
troops, speaks.

[*Prologue.*] The scene is Libya, and the subject thus:
    Whilst Carthage stood the only awe of Rome,
    As most imperial seat of Libya,
    Governed by statesmen each as great as kings—
    For seventeen kings were Carthage feodars—   5
    Whilst thus she flourished, whilst her Hannibal
    Made Rome to tremble, and the walls yet pale,
    Then in this Carthage Sophonisba lived,
    The far-famed daughter of great Asdrubal;
    For whom, 'mongst others, potent Syphax sues,   10
    And well-graced Massinissa rivals him,
    Both princes of proud sceptres. But the lot
    Of doubtful favour Massinissa graced,
    At which Syphax grows black. For now the night
    Yields loud resoundings of the nuptial pomp;   15
    Apollo strikes his harp, Hymen his torch,
    Whilst louring Juno, with ill-boding eye,
    Sits envious at too forward Venus. Lo,
    The instant night! And now, ye worthier minds,
    To whom we shall present a female glory,   20
    The wonder of a constancy so fixed
    That fate itself might well grow envious,
    Be pleased to sit, such as may merit oil

And holy dew 'stilled from diviner heat.
For rest thus knowing, what of this you hear,   25
The author lowly hopes, but must not fear:
  For just worth never rests on popular frown,
  To have done well is fair deeds' only crown.
                              Nec se quaesiverit extra.

Cornets sound a march. The PROLOGUE *leads* MASSINISSA'S
troops over the stage, and departs. SYPHAX'S *troops only stay.*

ACT I

Scene i

[SYPHAX'S *troops remaining, enter*] SYPHAX *and* VANGUE.

Syphax. Syphax, Syphax! Why wast thou cursed a king?
    What angry god made thee so great, so vile?
    Contemned, disgracèd! Think, wert thou a slave,
    Though Sophonisba did reject thy love,
    Thy low neglected head unpointed at,   5
    Thy shame unrumoured, and thy suit unscoffed,
    Might yet rest quiet. Reputation,
    Thou awe of fools and great men, thou that chok'st
    Freest addictions, and mak'st mortals sweat
    Blood and cold drops in fear to lose, or hope   10
    To gain, thy never-certain seldom-worthy gracings.
    Reputation!
    Wert not for thee, Syphax could bear this scorn,
    Not spouting up his gall among his blood
    In black vexations. Massinissa might   15
    Enjoy the sweets of his preferrèd graces
    Without my dangerous envy or revenge;
    Wert not for thy affliction, all might sleep
    In sweet oblivion. But—O greatness' scourge!—
    We cannot without envy keep high name,   20
    Nor yet disgraced can have a quiet shame.
Vangue. Scipio—
Syphax. Some light in depth of hell. Vangue, what hope?
Vangue. I have received assured intelligence
    That Scipio, Rome's sole hope, hath raised up men,   25
    Drawn troops together for invasion—
Syphax. Of this same Carthage?
Vangue.   With this policy,
    To force wild Hannibal from Italy—
Syphax. And draw the war to Afric?
Vangue.   Right.
Syphax.   And strike
    This secure country with unthought of arms?   30
Vangue. My letters bear he is departed Rome,
    Directly setting course and sailing up—

Syphax. To Carthage, Carthage! O thou eternal youth,
          Man of large fame, great and abounding glory,
          Renownful Scipio, spread thy two-necked eagles,   35
          Fill full thy sails with a revenging wind,
          Strike through obedient Neptune till thy prows
          Dash up our Libyan ooze and thy just arms
          Shine with amazeful terror on these walls!
          O now record thy father's honoured blood   40
          Which Carthage drunk; thy uncle Publius' blood
          Which Carthage drunk; three hundred hundred souls
          Of choice Italians Carthage set on wing.
          Remember Hannibal, yet Hannibal,
          The consul-queller. O then enlarge thy heart,   45
          Be thousand souls in one! Let all the breath,
          The spirit of thy name and nation, be mixed strong
          In thy great heart! O fall like thunder-shaft,
          The winged vengeance of incensèd Jove
          Upon this Carthage! For Syphax here flies off   50
          From all allegiance, from all love or service,
          His now freed sceptre once did yield this city.
          Ye universal gods, light, heat, and air
          Prove all unblessing Syphax if his hands
          Once rear themselves for Carthage but to curse it!   55
          It had been better they had changed their faith,
          Denied their gods, than slighted Syphax' love,
          So fearfully will I take vengeance.
          I'll interleague with Scipio.—Vangue,
          Dear Ethiopian negro, go wing a vessel,   60
          And fly to Scipio. Say his confederate,
          Vowed and confirmed, is Syphax. Bid him haste
          To mix our palms and arms. Will him make up,
          Whilst we are in the strength of discontent,
          Our unsuspected forces well in arms.   65
          For Sophonisba, Carthage, Asdrubal,
          Shall feel their weakness in preferring weakness
          And one less great than we. To our dear wishes
          Haste, gentle negro, that this heap may know
          Me and their wrong.
Vangue.   Wrong?   70
Syphax. Ay, though 'twere not, yet know while kings are strong,
          What they'll but think, and not what is, is wrong.
          I am disgraced in and by that which hath
          No reason—love, and woman. My revenge
          Shall therefore bear no argument of right: 75

Passion is reason when it speaks from might.
I tell thee, man, nor kings nor gods exempt,
But they grow pale if once they find contempt.
Haste!   [*Exeunt.*]

[ACT I] SCENE ii

Enter ARCATHIA; NYCEA, *with tapers;* SOPHONISBA, *in her night*
attire, followed by ZANTHIA.

Sophonisba. Watch at the doors. And till we be reposed
   Let no one enter. Zanthia, undo me.
Zanthia. With this motto under your girdle:
   You had been undone if you had not been undone.
   Humblest service.   5
Sophonisba. I wonder, Zanthia, why the custom is
   To use such ceremony, such strict shape,
   About us women. Forsooth, the bride must steal
   Before her lord to bed; and then delays
   Long expectations, all against known wishes.   10
   I hate these figures in locution,
   These about-phrases forced by ceremony.
   We must still seem to fly what we most seek
   And hide ourselves from that we fain would find.
   Let those that think and speak and do just acts   15
   Know form can give no virtue to their acts
   Nor detract vice.
Zanthia. 'Las, fair princess, those that are strongly formed
   And truly shaped may naked walk, but we,
   We things called women, only made for show   20
   And pleasure, created to bear children
   And play at shuttlecock, we imperfect mixtures,
   Without respective ceremony used,
   And ever complement, alas, what are we?
   Take from us formal custom and the courtesies   25
   Which civil fashion hath still used to us,
   We fall to all contempt. O women, how much,
   How much, are you beholding to ceremony!
Sophonisba. You are familiar. Zanthia, my shoe.

    [ZANTHIA *removes and examines* SOPHONISBA'S *shoes.*]

Zanthia. 'Tis wonder, madam, you tread not awry.   30
Sophonisba. Your reason, Zanthia.

Zanthia.   You go very high.
Sophonisba. Hark! Music, music!

> *The* Ladies *lay the Princess in a fair bed, and close the curtains,*
> *whilst* MASSINISSA *enters.*

Nycea. The bridegroom!

Arcathia.   The bridegroom!
Sophonisba. Haste, good Zanthia! Help, keep yet the doors!
Zanthia. Fair fall you, lady; so, admit, admit.   35

> *Enter four* Boys, *antiquely attired, with bows and quivers,*
> *dancing to the cornets a fantastic measure;* MASSINISSA *in his*
> *night-gown, led by* ASDRUBAL *and* HANNO, *followed by* BYTHEAS
> *and* JUGURTH. *The* Boys *draw the curtains, discovering*
> SOPHONISBA, *to whom* MASSINISSA *speaks.*

Massinissa. You powers of joy, gods of a happy bed,
    Show you are pleased! Sister and wife of Jove,
    High-fronted Juno, and thou Carthage patron,
    Smooth-chinned Apollo, both give modest heat
    And temperate graces!

> MASSINISSA *draws a white ribbon forth of the bed as from the*
> *waist of* SOPHO[NISBA].

                    Lo, I unloose thy waist!   40
She that is just in love is godlike chaste.
    Io to Hymen!
Chorus. (with cornets, organ and voices.) Io to Hymen!
Sophonisba. A modest silence, though't be thought
        A virgin's beauty and her highest honour;
        Though bashful feignings nicely wrought   45
        Grace her that virtue takes not in, but on her;
    What I dare think I boldly speak.
        After my word my well-bold action rusheth;
    In open flame then passion break!
        Where virtue prompts, thought, word, act never blusheth.   50
    Revenging gods, whose marble hands
        Crush faithless men with a confounding terror,
    Give me no mercy if these bands
        I covet not with an unfeigned fervour;
    Which zealous vow when ought can force me t'lame,   55
    Load with that plague Atlas would groan at, shame.
        Io to Hymen!

Chorus.   *Io to Hymen!*
Asdrubal. Live both high parents of so happy birth,
        Your stems may touch the skies and shadow earth;
        Most great in fame, more great in virtue shining,   60
        Prosper, O powers, a just, a strong divining.
        Io to Hymen!
Chorus.   *Io to Hymen!*

        Enter CARTHALO, *his sword drawn, his body wounded, his*
        shield struck full of darts; MASSINISSA *being ready for bed.*

Carthalo. To bold hearts fortune! Be not you amazed,
        Carthage, O Carthage! Be not you amazed.
Massinissa. Jove made us not to fear. Resolve, speak out: 65
        The highest misery of man is doubt. Speak Carthalo.
Carthalo. The stooping sun, like to some weaker prince,
        Let his shades spread to an unnatural hugeness,
        When we, the camp that lay at Utica,
        From Carthage distant but five easy leagues,   70
        Descried from off the watch three hundred sail,
        Upon whose tops the Roman eagles stretched
        Their large spread wings, which fanned the evening air,
        To us cold breath; for well we might discern
        Rome swam to Carthage.   75
Asdrubal. Hannibal, our anchor is come back; thy slight,
        Thy stratagem, to lead war unto Rome,
        To quit ourselves, hath now taught desperate Rome
        T'assail our Carthage. Now the war is here.
Massinissa. He is nor blest, nor honest, that can fear.   80
Hanno Magnus. Ay, but to cast the worst of our distress—
Massinissa. To doubt of what shall be is wretchedness.
        Desire, fear, and hope, receive no bond,
        By whom we in ourselves are never, but beyond. On!
Carthalo. Th'alarum beats necessity of fight;   85
        Th'unsober evening draws out reeling forces,
        Soldiers, half men, who to their colours troop
        With fury, not with valour; whilst our ships
        Unrigged, unused, fitter for fire than water,
        We save in our barred haven from surprise.   90
        By this our army marcheth toward the shore,
        Undisciplined young men, most bold to do,
        If they knew how or what; when we descry
        A mighty dust beat up with horses' hooves;
        Straight Roman ensigns glitter. Scipio—
Asdrubal.   Scipio!   95

Carthalo. Scipio, advancèd like the god of blood,
 Leads up grim war, that father of foul wounds,
 Whose sinewy feet are steeped in gore, whose hideous voice
 Makes turrets tremble and whole cities shake;
 Before whose brows flight and disorder hurry;   100
 With whom march burnings, murder, wrong, waste, rapes;
 Behind whom a sad train is seen; woe, fears,
 Tortures, lean need, famine, and helpless tears.
 Now make we equal stand in mutual view.
 We judged the Romans eighteen thousand foot,   105
 Five thousand horse. We almost doubled them
 In number, not in virtue; yet in heat
 Of youth and wine, jolly and full of blood,
 We gave the sign of battle. Shouts are raised
 That shook the heavens. Pell-mell our armies join— 110
 Horse, targets, pikes—all against each opposed,
 They give fierce shock, arms thundered as they closed.
 Men cover earth, which straight are coverèd
 With men and earth; yet doubtful stood the fight,
 More fair to Carthage, when lo, as oft you see   115
 In mines of gold, when labouring slaves delve out
 The richest ore, being in sudden hope
 With some unlooked-for vein to fill their buckets
 And send huge treasure up, a sudden damp
 Stifles them all, their hands yet stuffed with gold,— 120
 So fell our fortunes; for look, as we stood proud
 As hopeful victors, thinking to return
 With spoils worth triumph, wrathful Syphax lands
 With full ten thousand strong Numidian horse
 And joins to Scipio. Then lo, we all were damped; 125
 We fall in clusters, and our wearied troops
 Quit all. Slaughter ran through us straight. We fly,
 Romans pursue, but Scipio sounds retreat
 As fearing trains and night. We make amain
 For Carthage most and some for Utica,   130
 All for our lives.—New force, fresh arms with speed!
 You have sad truth of all.—No more, I bleed.
Bytheas. [*Tearing his hair.*] O wretched fortune!
Massinissa.   Old lord, spare thy hairs:
 What, dost thou think baldness will cure thy grief?
 What decree the Senate?   135

   Enter GELOSSO *with commissions in his hand, sealed.*

Gelosso. Ask old Gelosso, who returns from them

Informed with fullest charge. Strong Asdrubal,
Great Massinissa, Carthage general,
So speaks the Senate: counsel for this war
In Hanno Magnus, Bytheas, Carthalon,   140
And us, Gelosso, rests. Embrace this charge
You never yet dishonoured. Asdrubal,
High Massinissa, by your vows to Carthage,
By th' god of great men, glory, fight for Carthage!
Ten thousand strong Massulians, ready trooped,   145
Expect their king; double that number waits
The leading of loved Asdrubal. Beat loud
Our Afric drums! And whilst our o'ertoiled foe
Snores on his unlaced cask all faint, though proud
Through his successful fight, strike fresh alarms.   150
Gods are not if they grace not bold, just arms.
Massinissa. Carthage thou straight shalt know
Thy favours have been done unto a king.
                Exit [MASSINISSA] *with* ASDRUBAL *and the* Page.
Sophonisba. My lords, 'tis most unusual such sad haps
Of sudden horror should intrude 'mong beds   155
Of soft and private loves; but strange events
Excuse strange forms. O you that know our blood,
Revenge if I do feign. I here protest,
Though my lord leave his wife a very maid,
Even this night, instead of my soft arms   160
Clasping his well-strung limbs with glossful steel,
What's safe to Carthage shall be sweet to me.
I must not, nor am I once ignorant
My choice of love hath given this sudden danger
To yet strong Carthage. 'Twas I lost the fight;   165
My choice vexed Syphax; enraged Syphax struck
Arms' fate; yet Sophonisba not repents:
O *we were gods if that we knew events.*
But let my lord leave Carthage, quit his virtue,
I will not love him; yet must honour him,   170
As still good subjects must bad princes. Lords,
From the most ill-graced hymeneal bed
That ever Juno frowned at, I entreat
That you'll collect from our loose-formed speech
This firm resolve: that no low appetite   175
Of my sex' weakness can or shall o'ercome
Due grateful service unto you or virtue.
Witness, ye gods, I never until now
Repined at my creation. Now I wish

I were no woman, that my arms might speak   180
My heart to Carthage. But in vain: my tongue
Swears I am woman still. I talk too long.

Cornets [sound] a march. Enter two Pages *with targets and
javelins; two* Pages *with torches.* MASSINISSA *armed cap-a-pie;*
ASDRUBAL *armed.*

Massinissa. Ye Carthage lords, know Massinissa knows
Not only terms of honour, but his actions;
Nor must I now enlarge how much my cause   185
Hath dangered Carthage, but how I may show
Myself most pressed to satisfaction.
The loathsome stain of kings—ingratitude—
From me O much be far! And since this torrent,
War's rage, admits no anchor—since the billow   190
Is risen so high we may not hull, but yield
This ample state to stroke of speedy swords—
What you with sober haste have well decreed,
We'll put to sudden arms. No, not this night,
These dainties, this first fruits of nuptials,   195
That well might give excuse for feeble ling'rings,
Shall hinder Massinissa. Appetite,
Kisses, loves, dalliance, and what softer joys
The Venus of the pleasing'st ease can minister,
I quit you all. Virtue perforce is vice;   200
But he that may, yet holds, is manly wise.
Lo then, ye lords of Carthage, to your trust
I leave all Massinissa's treasure. By the oath
Of right good men stand to my fortune just:
Most hard it is for great hearts to mistrust.   205
Carthalo. We vow by all high powers.
Massinissa.   No, do not swear;
I was not born so small to doubt or fear.
Sophonisba. Worthy, my lord—
Massinissa.   Peace, my ears are steel.
I must not hear thy much-enticing voice.
Sophonisba. By Massinissa Sophonisba speaks,   210
Worthy his wife. Go with as high a hand
As worth can rear. I will not stay my lord.
Fight for our country. Vent thy youthful heat
In fields, not beds. The fruit of honour, fame,
Be rather gotten than the oft disgrace   215
Of hapless parents, children. Go, best man,
And make me proud to be a soldier's wife

That values his renown above faint pleasures.
Think every honour that doth grace thy sword
Trebles my love. By thee I have no lust   220
But of thy glory. Best lights of heaven with thee!
Like wonder, stand or fall; so, though thou die,
My fortunes may be wretched, but not I.
Massinissa. Wondrous creature! Even fit for gods, not men.
Nature made all the rest of thy fair sex   225
As weak essays to make thee a pattern
Of what can be in woman. Long farewell!
He's sure unconquered in whom thou dost dwell,
Carthage Palladium. See that glorious lamp,
Whose lifeful presence giveth sudden flight   230
To fancies, fogs, fears, sleep and slothful night,
Spreads day upon the world. March swift amain.
Fame got with loss of breath is god-like gain!

The Ladies *draw the curtains about* SOPHONISBA; *the rest accompany* MASSINISSA *forth: the cornets and organs playing loud
full music for the Act.*

ACT II

SCENE i

Whilst the music for the first Act sounds, HANNO, CARTHALO,
BYTHEAS, GELOSSO, *enter. They place themselves to counsel,*
GISCO, *the impoisoner, waiting on them;* HANNO, CARTHALO
and BYTHEAS *setting their hands to a writing, which being offered to* GELOSSO, *he denies his hand, and, as much offended,
impatiently starts up and speaks.*

Gelosso. My hand? My hand? Rot first. Wither in agèd shame!
Hanno Magnus. Will you be so unseasonably wood?
Bytheas. Hold such preposterous zeal as stand against
The full decree of Senate? All think fit.
Carthalo. Nay, most inevitable necessary   5
For Carthage safety, and the now sole good
Of present state, that we must break all faith
With Massinissa. Whilst he fights abroad
Let's gain back Syphax, making him our own
By giving Sophonisba to his bed.   10
Hanno Magnus. Syphax is Massinissa's greater, and his force

Shall give more side to Carthage; as for's queen,
And her wise father, they love Carthage fate:
Profit and honesty are one in state.
Gelosso. And what decrees our very virtuous Senate   15
Of worthy Massinissa that now fights
And, leaving wife and bed, bleeds in good arms
For right old Carthage?
Carthalo.   Thus 'tis thought fit:
Her father, Asdrubal, on sudden shall take in
Revolted Syphax; so with doubled strength,   20
Before that Massinissa shall suspect,
Slaughter both Massinissa and his troops,
And likewise strike with his deep stratagem
A sudden weakness into Scipio's arms,
By drawing such a limb from the main body   25
Of his yet powerful army. Which being done,
Dead Massinissa's kingdom we decree
To Sophonisba and great Asdrubal
For their consent; so this swift plot shall bring
Two crowns to her, make Asdrubal a king.   30
Gelosso. So, first faith's breach, adultery, murder, theft!
Carthalo. What else!
Gelosso.   Nay, all is done, no mischief left.
Carthalo.   Pish!
Prosperous success gives blackest actions glory;
The means are unremembered in most story.
Gelosso. Let me not say gods are not.
Carthalo.   This is fit: 35
Conquest by blood is not so sweet as wit,
For, howsoe'er nice virtue censures of it,
He hath the grace of war that hath war's profit.
But Carthage, well advised that states come on
With slow advice, quick execution,   40
Have here [*indicating* GISCO] an engineer long bred for plots,
Called an impoisoner, who knows this sound excuse:
The only dew that makes men sprout in courts is use.
Be't well or ill, his thrift is to be mute;
Such slaves must act commands, and not dispute,   45
Knowing foul deeds with danger do begin,
But with rewards do end. Sin is no sin,
But in respects—
Gelosso. Politic lord, speak low. Though heaven bears
A face far from us, gods have most long ears;   50
Jove has a hundred hundred marble hands.

Carthalo. O ay, in poetry or tragic scene!
Gelosso. I fear gods only know what poets mean.
Carthalo. Yet hear me, I will speak close truth and cease:
    Nothing in Nature is unserviceable, 55
    No, not even inutility itself.
    Is then for nought dishonesty in being?
    And if it be sometimes of forcèd use,
    Wherein more urgent than in saving nations?
    State shapes are soldered up with base, nay faulty, 60
    Yet necessary functions. Some must lie,
    Some must betray, some murder, and some all.
    Each hath strong use, as poison in all purges;
    Yet when some violent chance shall force a state
    To break given faith, or plot some stratagems, 65
    Princes ascribe that vile necessity
    Unto heaven's wrath. And sure, though't be no vice,
    Yet 'tis bad chance. States must not stick too nice;
    For Massinissa's death sense bids forgive.
    Beware to offend great men, and let them live; 70
    For 'tis of empire's body the main arm:
    He that will do no good shall do no harm.
    You have my mind.
Gelosso. Although a state-like passion and weak heat
    Full of an empty wording might suit age, 75
    Know I'll speak strongly truth. Lords, ne'er mistrust
    That he who'll not betray a private man
    For his country, will ne'er betray his country
    For private men; then give Gelosso faith.
    If treachery in state be serviceable, 80
    Let hangmen do it. I am bound to lose
    My life, but not my honour, for my country.
    Our vow, our faith, our oath, why they're ourselves,
    And he that's faithless to his proper self
    May be excused if he break faith with princes. 85
    The gods assist just hearts, and states that trust
    Plots before Providence are tossed like dust.
    For Massinissa—O, let me slake a little
    Austere discourse and feel humanity!—
    Methinks I hear him cry, 'O fight for Carthage! 90
    Charge home! Wounds smart not for that so just, so great,
    So good a city.' Methinks I see him yet
    Leave his fair bride even on his nuptial night
    To buckle on his arms for Carthage. Hark!
    Yet, yet, I hear him cry, 'Ingratitude, 95

Vile stain of man, O ever be most far
From Massinissa's breast! Up, march amain:
Fame got with loss of breath is god-like gain.'
And see, by this he bleeds in doubtful fight,
And cries for Carthage, whilst Carthage—memory,   100
Forsake Gelosso!—would I could not think,
Nor hear, nor be, when Carthage is
So infinitely vile! See, see! Look here!

Cornets. Enter two Ushers, SOPHONISBA, ZANTHIA, ARCATHIA.
HANNO, BYTHEAS *and* CARTHALO *present* SOPHONISBA *with a
paper which she having perused, after a short silence, speaks.*

[*Sophonisba.*] Who speaks? What, mute? Fair plot! What, blush
                                               to break it?
    How lewd to act when so shamed but to speak it.   105
    Is this the Senate's firm decree?
Carthalo.   It is.
Sophonisba. Hath Syphax entertained the stratagem?
Carthalo. No doubt he hath or will.
Sophonisba.   My answer's thus,
    What's safe to Carthage shall be sweet to me.
Carthalo. Right worthy.
Hanno Magnus.   Royalest.
Gelosso.   O very woman!   110
Sophonisba. But 'tis not safe for Carthage to destroy,
    Be most unjust, cunningly politic;
    Your head's still under heaven. O trust to Fate:
    Gods prosper more a just than crafty state.
    'Tis less disgrace to have a pitied loss,   115
    Than shameful victory.
Gelosso.   O very angel!
Sophonisba. We all have sworn good Massinissa faith.
    Speech makes us men, and there's no other bond
    'Twixt man and man but words. O equal gods,
    Make us once know the consequence of vows—   120
Gelosso. And we shall hate faith-breakers worse than man-eaters.
Sophonisba. Ha! Good Gelosso, is thy breath not here?
Gelosso. You do me wrong. As long as I can die,
    Doubt you that old Gelosso can be vile?
    States may afflict, tax, torture, but our minds   125
    Are only sworn to Jove. I grieve, and yet am proud
    That I alone am honest. High powers, you know
    Virtue is seldom seen with troops to go.

Sophonisba. Excellent man! Carthage and Rome shall fall
    Before thy fame. [*To the rest*] Our lords, know I the worst?   130
Carthalo. The gods foresaw, 'tis fate we thus are forced.
Sophonisba. *Gods naught foresee, but see, for to their eyes*
    Naught is to come or past; nor are you vile
    Because the gods foresee. *For gods, not we,*
    See as things are; things are not as we see.   135
    But since affected wisdom in us women
    Is our sex' highest folly, I am silent.
    I cannot speak less well, unless I were
    More void of goodness. Lords of Carthage, thus:
    The air and earth of Carthage owes my body.   140
    It is their servant. What decree they of it?
Carthalo. That you remove to Cirta, to the palace
    Of well-formed Syphax, who with longing eyes
    Meets you. He that gives way to Fate is wise.
Sophonisba. I go. What power can make me wretched? What evil   145
    Is there in life to him that knows life's loss
    To be no evil? Show, show thy ugliest brow,
    O most black chance! Make me a wretched story:
    Without misfortune virtue hath no glory.
    Opposèd trees make tempests show their power,   150
    And waves forced back by rocks make Neptune tower,—
      Tearless, O see a miracle of life,
      A maid, a widow, yet a hapless wife!

Cornets. SOPHO[NISBA], *accompanied with the* Senators,
depart[*s*]; [GISCO *goes out separately*]; *only* GELOSSO *stays.*

Gelosso. A prodigy! Let Nature run cross-legged,
    Ops go upon her head, let Neptune burn,   155
    Cold Saturn crack with heat, for now the world
    Hath seen a woman!
    Leap nimble lightning from Jove's ample shield
    And make at length an end! The proud hot breath
    Of thee, contemning greatness, the huge drought   160
    Of sole self-loving vast ambition,
    Th'unnatural scorching heat of all those lamps
    Thou rear'dst to yield a temperate fruitful heat,
    Relentless rage, whose heart hath not one drop
    Of human pity,—all, all loudly cry,   165
    'Thy brand, O Jove!' For know the world is dry.
    O let a general end save Carthage fame!
    When worlds do burn, unseen's a city's flame.

Phoebus in me is great. Carthage must fall.
Jove hates all vice, but vows' breach worst of all.   *Exit.*   170

[ACT II] SCENE ii

Cornets sound a charge. Enter MASSINISSA *in his gorget and
shirt, shield, sword; his arm transfixed with a dart.* JUGURTH
follows, with his cuirass and cask.

Massinissa. Mount us again. Give us another horse!
Jugurth. Uncle, your blood flows fast. Pray ye withdraw.
Massinissa. O Jugurth, I cannot bleed too fast, too much,
    For that so great, so just, so royal Carthage!
    My wound smarts not, blood's loss makes me not faint   5
    For that loved city. O nephew, let me tell thee
    How good that Carthage is. It nourished me,
    And when full time gave me fit strength for love,
    The most adorèd creature of the city,
    To us, before great Syphax, did they yield,   10
    Fair, noble, modest, and 'bove all, my,
    My Sophonisba! O Jugurth, my strength doubles.
    I know not how to turn a coward, drop
    In feeble baseness I cannot. Give me horse.
    Know I am Carthage' very creature, and I am graced   15
    That I may bleed for them. Give me fresh horse.
Jugurth. He that doth public good for multitude,
    Finds few are truly grateful.
Massinissa. O Jugurth, fie! You must not say so, Jugurth.
    Some commonweals may let a noble heart   20
    Too forward bleed abroad, and bleed bemoaned,
    But not revenged, at home. But Carthage, fie!
    It cannot be ungrate, faithless through fear.
    It cannot, Jugurth; Sophonisba's there.
    Beat a fresh charge!   25

Enter ASDRUBAL, *his sword drawn, reading a letter;* GISCO
follows him.

Asdrubal. Sound the retreat! Respect your health, brave prince.
    The waste of blood throws paleness on your face.
Massinissa. By light, my heart's not pale. O my loved father,

We bleed for Carthage, balsam to my wounds,
We bleed for Carthage. Shall's restore the fight?   30
My squadron of Massulians yet stands firm.
Asdrubal. The day looks off from Carthage. Cease alarms!
   A modest temperance is the life of arms.
   Take our best surgeon, Gisco. He is sent
   From Carthage to attend your chance of war.   35
Gisco. We promise sudden ease.
Massinissa.   Thy comfort's good.
Asdrubal. [*Aside*] That nothing can secure us but thy blood!
   [*To Gisco, handing him poison*] Infuse it in his wound,
                                        'twill work amain.
Gisco. [*To Asdrubal*] O Jove!
Asdrubal.   [*To Gisco*] What Jove? Thy god must be thy gain,
   And as for me, Apollo Pythian;   40
   Thou know'st a statist must not be a man.   *Exit.*

   Enter GELOSSO *disguised like an old soldier, delivering to*
   MASSINISSA *(as he* [*is*] *preparing to be dressed by* GISCO*)* [*a*]
   letter, which MASSINISSA *reading, starts, and speaks to* GISCO.

Massinissa. Forbear! How art thou called?
Gisco.   Gisco, my lord.
Massinissa. Um, Gisco, ha, touch not mine arm! (*To Gelosso*)
                                        Most only man!
   [*To Gisco*] Sirrah, sirrah, art poor?
Gisco.   Not poor.
Massinissa.   Nephew,
                                           command

              MASSINISSA *begins to draw.*

Our troops of horse make undisgraced retreat,   45
Trot easy off.—Not poor!—Jugurth, give charge
My soldiers stand in square battalia,
Entirely of themselves.   *Exit* JUGURTH.
              Gisco, thou'rt old.
'Tis time to leave off murder. Thy faint breath
Scarce heaves thy ribs, thy gummy blood-shot eyes   50
Are sunk a great way in thee, thy lank skin
Slides from thy fleshless veins. Be good to men.
Judge him, ye gods! I had not life to kill
So base a creature. [GISCO *attempts to drink his own poison.*]
              Hold, Gisco, live:
The god-like part of kings is to forgive.   55

Gisco. Command astonished Gisco.
Massinissa.   No, return.
    Haste unto Carthage. Quit thy abject fears,
    Massinissa knows no use of murderers.   [*Exit* GISCO.]

                Enter JUGURTH, *amazed, his sword drawn.*

    Speak, speak! Let terror strike slaves mute,
    Much danger makes great hearts most resolute.   60
Jugurth. Uncle, I fear foul arms. Myself beheld
    Syphax, on high speed, run his well-breathed horse
    Direct to Cirta, that most beauteous city
    Of all his kingdom; whilst his troops of horse
    With careless trot pace gently toward our camp   65
    As friends to Carthage. Stand on guard, dear uncle,
    For Asdrubal, with yet his well-ranked army,
    Bends a deep threat'ning brow to us as if
    He waited but to join with Syphax' horse
    And hew us all to pieces. O my king,   70
    My uncle, father, captain over all!
    Stand like thyself, or like thyself now fall!
    Thy troops yet hold good ground. Unworthy wounds
    Betray not Massinissa!
Massinissa.   Jugurth, pluck,
    Pluck. [JUGURTH *removes the dart from* MASSINISSA'S *arm.*]
        So, good coz.
Jugurth.   O God! Do you not feel?   75
Massinissa. Not, Jugurth, no. Now all my flesh is steel.
Gelosso. Off, base disguise! [*Discovers himself.*] High lights
                                        scorn not to view
    A true old man. Up, Massinissa! Throw
    The lot of battle upon Syphax' troops
    Before he join with Carthage. Then amain   80
    Make through to Scipio; he yields safe abode.
    Spare treachery and strike the very gods.
Massinissa. Why wast thou born at Carthage, O my fate,
    Divinest Sophonisba? I am full
    Of much complaint, and many passions,   85
    The least of which expressed would sad the gods
    And strike compassion in most ruthless hell.
    Up, unmaimed heart, spend all thy grief and rage
    Upon thy foe! The field's a soldier's stage
    On which his action shows. If you are just,   90
    And hate those that contemn you, O you gods,
    Revenge worthy your anger, your anger! O,

Down man, up heart! Stoop, Jove, and bend thy chin
To thy large breast. Give sign thou'rt pleased and just.
Swear good men's foreheads must not print the dust. *Exeunt.*   95

[ACT II] SCENE iii

Enter ASDRUBAL, HANNO, BYTHEAS.

Asdrubal. What Carthage hath decreed, Hanno, is done.
    Advanced and born was Asdrubal for state.
    Only with it his faith, his love, his hate,
    Are of one piece. Were it my daughter's life
    That fate hath sung, to Carthage safety brings,   5
    What deed so red but hath been done by kings?
    Iphigenia! He that's a man for men,
    Ambitious as a god, must, like a god,
    Live clear from passions; his full aimed-at end,
    Immense to others, sole self to comprehend,   10
    Round in's own globe; not to be clasped but holds
    Within him all, his heart being of more folds
    Than shield of Telamon, not to be pierced, though struck:
    The god of wise men is themselves, not luck.

Enter GISCO.

See him by whom now Massinissa is not.   15
    Gisco, is't done?
Gisco.   Your pardon, worthy lord,
    It is not done; my heart sunk in my breast,
    His virtue mazed me, faintness seized me all:
    Some god's in kings, that will not let them fall.
Asdrubal. His virtue mazed thee! Um. Why now I see   20
    Thou'rt that just man that hath true touch of blood,
    Of pity and soft piety. Forgive?
    Yes, honour thee. We did it but to try
    What sense thou hadst of blood. Go, Bytheas,
    Take him into our private treasury –   25
    [*Aside to Bytheas*] And cut his throat; the slave hath all
                                        betrayed.
Bytheas. [*To Asdrubal*] Are you assured?
Asdrubal.   [*To Bytheas*] Assured; for this I know,
    Who thinketh to buy villainy with gold,
    Shall ever find such faith so bought, so sold.
    Reward him thoroughly.

A shout; the cornets giving a flourish.

Hanno Magnus.   What means this shout?   30
Asdrubal. Hanno, 'tis done. Syphax' revolt by this
    Hath secured Carthage; and now his force come in
    And joined with us, give Massinissa charge,
    And assured slaughter. O ye powers, forgive!
    Through rotten'st dung best plants both sprout and live;   35
    By blood vines grow.
Hanno Magnus.   But yet think, Asdrubal,
    'Tis fit at least you bear grief's outward show;
    It is your kinsman bleeds. What need men know
    Your hand is in his wounds? 'Tis well in state
    To do close ill, but 'void a public hate.   40
Asdrubal. Tush, Hanno, let me prosper; let routs prate,
    My power shall force their silence or my hate
    Shall scorn their idle malice. Men of weight
    Know, he that fears envy let him cease to reign;
    The people's hate to some hath been their gain.   45
    For howsoe'er a monarch feigns his parts,
    Steal anything from kings but subjects' hearts.

Enter CARTHALO *leading in bound* GELOSSO.

Carthalo. Guard, guard the camp! Make to the trench! Stand firm!
Asdrubal. The gods of boldness with us! How runs chance!
Carthalo. Think, think how wretched thou canst be, thou art.   50
    Short words shall speak long woes.
Gelosso.   Mark, Asdrubal.
Carthalo. Our bloody plot to Massinissa's ear
    Untimely by this lord was all betrayed.
Gelosso. By me it was, by me, vile Asdrubal,
    I joy to speak't.
Asdrubal.   Down, slave!
Gelosso.   I cannot fall.   55
Carthalo. Our train's disclosed, straight to his well-used arms
    He took himself, rose up with all his force
    On Syphax' careless troops—Syphax being hurried
    Before to Cirta fearless of success,
    Impatient Sophonisba to enjoy—   60
    Gelosso rides to head of all our squadrons,
    Commands make stand in thy name, Asdrubal,
    In mine, in his, in all. Dull rest our men,
    Whilst Massinissa now with more than fury,
    Chargeth the loose and much-amazèd ranks   65

Of absent Syphax, who with broken shout
—In vain expecting Carthage secondings—
Give faint repulse. A second charge is given;
Then look as when a falcon towers aloft,
Whole shoals of fowl and flocks of lesser birds   70
Crouch fearfully and dive, some among sedge,
Some creep in brakes; so Massinissa's sword
Brandished aloft, tossed 'bout his shining cask,
Made stoop whole squadrons. Quick as thought he strikes.
Here hurls he darts and there his rage-strong arm   75
Fights foot to foot. Here cries he 'Strike!' They sink
And then grim slaughter follows; for by this,
As men betrayed, they curse us, die, or fly, or both.
Of ten, six thousand fell. Now was I come,
And straight perceived all bled by his vile plot.   80
Gelosso. Vile? Good plot! My good plot, Asdrubal.
Carthalo. I forced our army beat a running march,
But Massinissa struck his spurs apace
Unto his speedy horse, leaves slaughtering.
All fly to Scipio, who with open ranks   85
In view receives them. All I could effect
Was but to gain him.
Asdrubal.   Die!
Gelosso.   Do what thou can,
Thou canst but kill a weak old honest man.

                              GELOSSO *departs, guarded.*

Carthalo. Scipio and Massinissa by this strike
Their claspèd palms, then vow an endless love;   90
Straight a joint shout they raise, then turn they breasts
Direct on us, march strongly toward our camp,
As if they dared us fight. O Asdrubal,
I fear they'll force our camp.
Asdrubal.   Break up and fly!
—This was your plot.
Hanno Magnus.   But 'twas thy shame to choose it.   95
Carthalo. He that forbids not offence, he does it.
Asdrubal. The curse of women's words go with you. Fly!
You are no villains! Gods and men, which way?
Advise, vile things!
Hanno Magnus.   Vile?
Asdrubal.   Ay!
Carthalo.   Not.
Bytheas.   You did all.

Asdrubal. Did you not plot?
Carthalo.   Yielded not Asdrubal?   100
Asdrubal. But you enticed me.
Hanno Magnus.   How?
Asdrubal.   With hope of place.
Carthalo. He that for wealth leaves faith, is abject.
Hanno Magnus.   Base.
Asdrubal. Do not provoke my sword; I live.
Carthalo.   More shame,
    T'outlive thy virtue and thy once great name.
Asdrubal. Upbraid ye me?
Hanno Magnus.   Hold!
Carthalo.   Know that only thou   105
    Art treacherous. Thou shouldst have had a crown.
Hanno Magnus. Thou didst all, all; he for whom mischief's done,
    He does it.
Asdrubal.   Brook open scorn, faint powers!
    Make good the camp!—No, fly!—Yes, what? Wild rage!
    To be a prosperous villain! Yet some heat, some hold;   110
    But to burn temples and yet freeze, O cold!
    Give me some health, now your blood sinks: thus deeds
    Ill nourished rot; without Jove nought succeeds.   *Exeunt.*

ACT III

SCENE i

Organ mixed with recorders for this act. SYPHAX, *his dagger*
twined about her hair, drags in SOPHONISBA *in her nightgown-*
petticoat; and ZANTHIA *and* VANGUE *following.*

Syphax. Must we entreat? Sue to such squeamish ears?
    Know, Syphax has no knees, his eyes no tears;
    Enragèd love is senseless of remorse.
    Thou shalt, thou must. Kings' glory is their force.
    Thou art in Cirta, in my palace, fool.   5
    Dost think he pitieth tears that knows to rule?
    For all thy scornful eyes, thy proud disdain,
    And late contempt of us, now we'll revenge;
    Break stubborn silence. Look, I'll tack thy head
    To the low earth, whilst strength of two black knaves   10
    Thy limbs all wide shall strain. Prayer fitteth slaves,
    Our courtship be our force. Rest calm as sleep,

Else at this quake. Hark, hark, we cannot weep.
Sophonisba. Can Sophonisba be enforced?
Syphax.   Can? See.
Sophonisba. Thou mayest enforce my body, but not me.   15
Syphax. Not?
Sophonisba.   No.
Syphax.   No?
Sophonisba.   No; off with thy loathèd arms,
   That lie more heavy on me than the chains
   That wear deep wrinkles in the captive's limbs!
   I do beseech thee.
Syphax.   What?
Sophonisba.   Be but a beast,
   Be but a beast.
Syphax.   Do not offend a power   20
   Can make thee more than wretched. Yield to him
   To whom fate yields. Know, Massinissa's dead.
Sophonisba. Dead?
Syphax.   Dead.
Sophonisba.   To gods of good men, shame!
Syphax. Help, Vangue, my strong blood boils.
Sophonisba. O yet save thine own fame.   25
Syphax. All appetite is deaf; I will, I must.
   Achilles' armour could not bear out lust.
Sophonisba. Hold thy strong arm, and hear me, Syphax. Know
   I am thy servant now. I needs must love thee,
   For—O my sex forgive!—I must confess   30
   We not affect protesting feebleness,
   Entreats, faint blushings, timorous modesty;
   We think our lover is but little man,
   Who is so full of woman. Know, fair prince,
   Love's strongest arm's not rude; for we still prove,   35
   Without some fury there's no ardent love.
   We love our love's impatience of delay;
   Our noble sex was only born t'obey
   To him that dares command.
Syphax.   Why this is well;
   Th'excuse is good. Wipe thy fair eyes, our queen,   40
   Make proud thy head; now feel more friendly strength
   Of thy lord's arm. Come, touch my rougher skin
   With thy soft lip. Zanthia, dress our bed.
   Forget old loves and clip him that through blood
   And hell acquires his wish. Think not, but kiss,   45
   The flourish 'fore love's fight is Venus' bliss.

Sophonisba. Great dreadful lord, by thy affection,
    Grant me one boon. Know I have made a vow.
Syphax. Vow? What vow? Speak.
Sophonisba.   Nay, if you take offence
    Let my soul suffer first, and yet—
Syphax.   Offence?   50
    No, Sophonisba, hold; thy vow is free
    As—Come, thy lips!
Sophonisba.   Alas, cross misery!
    As I do wish to live I long to enjoy
    Your warm embrace, but, O my vow, 'tis thus:
    If ever my lord died, I vowed to him   55
    A most, most private sacrifice, before
    I touched a second spouse. All I implore
    Is but this liberty.
Syphax.   This? Go, obtain.
    What time?
Sophonisba.   One hour.
Syphax.   Sweet, good speed, speed, adieu!
    [*Aside*] Yet, Syphax, trust no more than thou mayst view.   60
    Vangue shall stay.
Sophonisba.   He stays.

    Enter a *Page, delivering a letter to* SOPHO[NISBA], *which she*
                 privately reads.

Syphax.   Zanthia, Zanthia,
    Thou art not foul, go to; some lords are oft
    So much in love with their known ladies' bodies,
    That they oft love their maids. Hold, hold, thou'st find
    To faithful care kings' bounty hath no shore.   65

             [*Gives* ZANTHIA *money.*]

Zanthia. You may do much.
Syphax.   But let my gold do more.
Zanthia. I am your creature.
Syphax.   Be, get, 'tis no stain;
    The god of service is however gain.   *Exit* [SYPHAX.]
Sophonisba. Zanthia, where are we now? Speak worth my
                            service;
    Ha' we done well?
Zanthia.   Nay, in height of best.   70
    I feared a superstitious virtue would spoil all,
    But now I find you above women rare.
    She that can time her goodness hath true care

Of her best good. Nature at home begins;
She whose integrity herself hurts, sins.   75
For Massinissa, he was good, and so—
But he is dead, or worse distressed, or more
Than dead, or much distressed. O sad, poor—
Who ever held such friends? No, let him go.
Such faith is praised, then laughed at, for still know   80
Those are the living women that reduce
All that they touch unto their ease and use,
Knowing that wedlock, virtue, or good names,
Are courses and varieties of reason,
To use or leave as they advantage them,   85
And absolute within themselves reposed,
Only to greatness ope, to all else closed.
Weak sanguine fools are to their own good nice;
Before I held you virtuous but now wise.
Sophonisba. Zanthia, victorious Massinissa lives,   90
    My Massinissa lives. O steady powers,
    Keep him as safe as heaven keeps the earth,
    Which looks upon it with a thousand eyes,
    That honest valiant man! And, Zanthia,
    Do but record the justice of his love,   95
    And my forever vows, forever vows!
Zanthia. Ay, true madam; nay, think of his great mind,
    His most just heart, his all of excellence,
    And such a virtue as the gods might envy.
    Against this, Syphax is but—and you know,   100
    Fame lost, what can be got that's good. For—
Sophonisba.   Hence!
    Take; nay, with one hand.
Zanthia.   My service.
Sophonisba.   Prepare
    Our sacrifice.
Zanthia.   But yield you, ay or no?
Sophonisba. When thou dost know—
Zanthia.   What then?
Sophonisba.   Then thou wilt
                                                      know.
                                        Exit ZANTHIA.

    Let him that would have counsel 'void th' advice   105
    Of friends, made his with weighty benefits,
    Whose much dependence only strives to fit
    Humour, not reason, and so still devise
    In any thought to make their friend seem wise.

But above all, O fear a servant's tongue,   110
Like such as only for their gain do serve.
Within the vast capacity of place
I know no vileness so most truly base.
Their lord's their gain; and he that most will give,
With him they will not die, but they will live.   115
Traitors and these are one. Such slaves once trust,
Whet swords to make thine own blood lick the dust.

Cornets and organs playing full music. Enters the solemnity of a
sacrifice [supervised by ZANTHIA, *and observed by* VANGUE];
which being entered, whilst the attendants furnish the altar,
     SOPHO[NISBA *sings a] song; which done, she speaks.*

[*Sophonisba.*] Withdraw, withdraw.
                   All but ZANTHIA *and* VANGUE *depart.*
I not invoke thy arm, thou god of sound,
Nor thine, nor thine, although in all abound   120
High powers immense. But jovial Mercury,
And thou, O brightest female of the sky,
Thrice-modest Phoebe, you that jointly fit
A worthy chastity and a most chaste wit,
To you corruptless honey and pure dew   125
Upbreathes our holy fire. Words just and few,
O deign to hear if in poor wretches' cries
You glory not! If drops of withered eyes
Be not your sport, be just. All that I crave
Is but chaste life or an untainted grave.   130
I can no more. Yet hath my constant tongue
Let fall no weakness, though my heart were wrung
With pangs worth hell. Whilst great thoughts stop our tears,
Sorrow unseen, unpitied, inward wears.
You see now where I rest, come is my end.   135
Cannot heaven virtue against weak chance defend?
When weakness hath outborne what weakness can,—
What should I say?—'tis Jove's, not sin of man.
Some stratagem now! Let wit's god be shown;
Celestial powers by miracles are known.   140
I have't; 'tis done.—Zanthia, prepare our bed.
Vangue!
Vangue.   Your servant.
Sophonisba.   Vangue, we have performed
Due rites unto the dead.

     SOPHONISBA *presents a carouse to* VANGUE, *[and urges him to*
             drink].

Now to thy lord, great Syphax, healthful cups;
Which done, the king is right much welcome.   145
Vangue. Were it as deep as thought, off it should thus. *He drinks.*
Sophonisba. [*Aside*] My safety with that draught.
Vangue. Close the vault's mouth lest we do slip in drink.
Sophonisba. To what use, gentle negro, serves this cave
Whose mouth thus opens so familiarly   150
Even in the king's bedchamber?
Vangue.   O, my queen,
This vault with hideous darkness and much length
Stretcheth beneath the earth into a grove
One league from Cirta—I am very sleepy—
Through this, when Cirta hath been strong begirt   155
With hostile siege the king hath safely 'scaped
To, to –
Sophonisba. The wine is strong.
Vangue.   Strong!   [VANGUE *falls.*]
Sophonisba.   Zanthia!
Zanthia. What means my princess?
Sophonisba.   Zanthia, rest firm
And silent. Help us. Nay, do not dare refuse.
Zanthia. The negro's dead!
Sophonisba.   No, drunk.
Zanthia.   Alas!
Sophonisba.   Too late!   160
Her hand is fearful whose mind's desperate.
It is but sleepy opium he hath drunk.
Help, Zanthia!

They lay VANGUE *in* SYPHAX' *bed and draw the curtains.*

There lie Syphax' bride.
A naked man is soon undressed;
There bide dishonoured passion.   165
They knock within! Forthwith Syphax comes.
Syphax. [*Within*] Way for the king!
Sophonisba.   Straight for the king. I fly
Where misery shall see nought but itself.
Dear Zanthia, close the vault when I am sunk
And whilst he slips to bed, escape. Be true.   170
I can no more. Come to me. [*Embraces her.*] Hark, gods, my
                                                                     breath
Scorns to crave life, grant but a well-famed death.
                                        She descends.

Enter SYPHAX, *ready for bed* [*with* Attendants.]

Syphax. Each man withdraw, let not a creature stay
    Within large distance.
Zanthia.   Sir!
Syphax.   Hence, Zanthia!
    Not thou shalt hear; all stand without ear-reach   175
    Of the soft cries nice shrinking brides do yield,
    When—
Zanthia.   But, sir—
Syphax.   Hence!   [ZANTHIA *retires.*]
    Stay, take thy delight by steps,
    Think of thy joys, and make long thy pleasures.
    O silence, thou dost swallow pleasure right;   180
    Words take away some sense from our delight.
    Music! [*Music plays.*] Be proud, my Venus; Mercury, thy
                                      tongue;
    Cupid, thy flame; 'bove all, O Hercules,
    Let not thy back be wanting; for now I leap
    To catch the fruit none but the gods should reap.   185

Offering to leap into [*the*] *bed, he discovers* VANGUE.

    Ha! Can any woman turn to such a devil?
    Or—or—Vangue, Vangue—
Vangue.   Yes, yes.
Syphax.   Speak, slave!
    How cam'st thou here?
Vangue.   Here?
Syphax.   Zanthia, Zanthia!

           [ZANTHIA *comes forward.*]

    Where's Sophonisba? Speak at full, at full.
    Give me particular faith, or know thou art not—   190
Zanthia. Your pardon, just-moved prince, and private ear.
                                   [*Whispers.*]
Syphax. Ill actions have some grace, that they can fear.
Vangue. How came I laid? Which way was I made drunk?
    Where am I? Think, or is my state advanced?
    O Jove, how pleasant is it but to sleep   195
    In a king's bed!
Syphax.   Sleep there thy lasting sleep,
    Improvident, base, o'er-thirsty slave.

         SY[PHAX] *kills* VA[NGUE].

    Die pleased, a king's couch is thy too-proud grave.

Through this vault, sayst thou?
Zanthia.   As you give me grace
To live, 'tis true.
Syphax.   We will be good to Zanthia;   200
Go, cheer thy lady, and be private to us.
Zanthia. As to my life.   *She descends after* SOPHONISBA.
Syphax.   I'll use this Zanthia,
And trust her as our dogs drink dangerous Nile,
Only for thirst, then fly the crocodile.
Wise Sophonisba knows love's tricks of art,   205
Without much hindrance pleasure hath no heart.
Despite all virtue or weak plots I must:
Seven-wallèd Babel cannot bear out lust.
                              Descends through the vault.

[ACT III] SCENE ii

Cornets sound marches. Enter SCIPIO *and* LAELIUS, *with the
compliments of a Roman General before them. At the other
door,* MASSINISSA *and* JUGURTH.

Massinissa. Let not the virtue of the world suspect
Sad Massinissa's faith; nor once condemn
Our just revolt. Carthage first gave me life,
Her ground gave food, her air first lent me breath:
The earth was made for men, not men for earth.   5
Scipio, I do not thank the gods for life,
Much less vile men, or earth. Know, best of lords,
It is a happy being breathes well-famed,
For which Jove fees thee thus. Men, be not fooled
With piety to place, tradition's fear: 10
A just man's country Jove makes everywhere.
Scipio. Well urgeth Massinissa. But to leave
A city so ingrate, so faithless, so more vile
Than civil speech may name, fear not. Such vice
To scourge is heaven's most grateful sacrifice.   15
Thus all confess, first they have broke a faith
To thee most due, so just to be observed
That barbarousness itself may well blush at them.
Where is thy passion? They have shared thy crown,
Thy proper right of birth, contrived thy death.   20
Where is thy passion? Given thy beauteous spouse
To thy most hated rival. Statue, not man!

And last, thy friend Gelosso—man worth gods—
With tortures they have rent to death.
Massinissa.   O Gelosso!
    For thee full eyes—
Scipio.   No passion for the rest?   25
Massinissa. O Scipio, my grief for him may be expressed by tears,
    But for the rest, silence and secret anguish
    Shall waste – shall waste! – Scipio, he that can weep,
    Grieves not, like me, private deep inward drops
    Of blood. My heart – for god's rights give me leave   30
    To be a short time man.
Scipio.   Stay prince.
Massinissa.   I cease.
    Forgive if I forget thy presence. Scipio,
    Thy face makes Massinissa more than man,
    And here before your steady power a vow
    As firm as fate I make: when I desist   35
    To be commanded by thy virtue, Scipio,
    Or fall from friend of Rome's, revenging gods
    Afflict me with your torture. I have given
    Of passion and of faith, my heart.
Scipio.   To counsel then:
    Grief fits weak hearts, revenging virtue men.   40
    Thus I think fit, before that Syphax know
    How deeply Carthage sinks, let's beat swift march
    Up even to Cirta, and whilst Syphax snores
    With his, late thine—
Massinissa.   With mine! No, Scipio,
    Libya hath poison, asps, knives, and too much earth   45
    To make one grave. With mine! No, she can die,
    Scipio. With mine? Jove, say it, thou dost lie.
Scipio. Temperance be Scipio's honour.
Laelius.   Cease your strife,
    She is a woman.
Massinissa.   But she is my wife.
Laelius. And yet she is no god.
Massinissa.   And yet she's more.   50
    I do not praise god's goodness, but adore.
    Gods cannot fall, and for their constant goodness,
    Which is necessitated, they have a crown
    Of never-ending pleasures. But faint man,
    Framed to have his weakness made the heavens' glory,   55
    If he with steady virtue holds all siege
    That power, that speech, that pleasure, that full sweets,

A world of greatness can assail him with—
Having no pay but self-wept misery—
And beggars treasure heaped; that man I'll praise   60
Above the gods.
Scipio.   The Libyan speaks bold sense.
Massinissa. By that by which all is, proportion,
    I speak with thought.
Scipio.   No more.
Massinissa.   Forgive my admiration.
    You touched a string to which my sense was quick.
    Can you but think? Do, do. My grief! My grief   65
    Would make a saint blaspheme. Give some relief.
    As thou art Scipio, forgive that I forget
    I am a soldier. Such woes Jove's ribs would burst:
    Few speak less ill that feel so much of worst.
    My ear attends.
Scipio.   Before then Syphax join   70
    With new-strengthened Carthage, or can once unwind
    His tangled sense from out so wild amaze,
    Fall we like sudden lightning 'fore his eyes.
    Boldness and speed are all of victories.
Massinissa. Scipio, let Massinissa clip thy knees!   75
    May once these eyes view Syphax! Shall this arm
    Once make him feel his sinew? O ye gods!
    My cause, my cause! Justice is so huge odds
    That he who with it fears, heaven must renounce
    In his creation.
Scipio.   Beat then a close quick march.   80
    Before the morn shall shake cold dews through skies,
    Syphax shall tremble at Rome's thick alarms.
Massinissa. Ye powers, I challenge conquest to just arms.
                With a full flourish of cornets, they depart.

ACT IV

SCENE i

Organs, viols and voices play for this act.

Enter SOPHONISBA *and* ZANTHIA, *as out of a cave's mouth.*

Sophonisba. Where are we, Zanthia?
Zanthia.   Vangue said the cave
    Opened in Belos' forest.
Sophonisba.   Lord, how sweet
    I scent the air! The huge long vault's close vein,

What damps it breathed! In Belos' forest, sayst?
Be valiant, Zanthia. How far's Utica   5
From these most heavy shades?
Zanthia.   Ten easy leagues.
Sophonisba. There's Massinissa. My true Zanthia,
 Shall's venture nobly to escape, and touch
 My lord's just arms? Love's wings so nimbly heave
 The body up, that, as our toes shall trip   10
 Over the tender and obedient grass,
 Scarce any drop of dew is dashed to ground.
 And see the willing shade of friendly night
 Makes safe our instant haste! Boldness and speed
 Make actions most impossible succeed.   15
Zanthia. But, madam, know the forest hath no way
 But one to pass, the which holds strictest guard.
Sophonisba. Do not betray me, Zanthia.
Zanthia.   I, madam?
Sophonisba.   No,
 I not mistrust thee, yet—but—
Zanthia.   Here you may
 Delay your time.
Sophonisba.   Ay, Zanthia, delay,   20
 By which we may yet hope—yet hope. Alas,
 How all benumbed's my sense! Chance hath so often struck
 I scarce can feel. I should now curse the gods,
 Call on the furies, stamp the patient earth,
 Cleave my stretched cheeks with sound, speak from all sense,   25
 But loud and full of players' eloquence.
 No, no.—What shall we eat?
Zanthia.   Madam, I'll search
 For some ripe nuts which autumn hath shook down
 From the unleaved hazel; then some cooler air
 Shall lead me to a spring; or I will try   30
 The courteous pale of some poor foresters
 For milk.   *Exit* ZANTHIA.
Sophonisba. Do, Zanthia. O happiness
 Of those that know not pride or lust of city!
 There's no man blessed but those that most men pity.
 O fortunate poor maids, that are not forced   35
 To wed for state, nor are for state divorced;
 Whom policy of kingdoms doth not marry,
 But pure affection makes to love or vary;
 You feel no love which you dare not to show,
 Nor show a love which doth not truly grow.   40

O, you are surely blessèd of the sky!
You live, that know not death before you die.

Through the vault's mouth, in his night-gown, torch in his
*   hand,* SYPHAX *enters just behind* SOPHON[ISBA].

You are—
Syphax.   In Syphax' arms. Thing of false lip,
    What god shall now release thee?
Sophonisba.   Art a man?
Syphax. Thy limbs shall feel. Despite thy virtue, know   45
    I'll thread thy richest pearl. This forest's deaf
    As is my lust. Night and the god of silence
    Swells my full pleasures, no more shalt thou delude
    My easy credence. Virgin of fair brow,
    Well-featured creature, and our utmost wonder,   50
    Queen of our youthful bed, be proud.

        SYPHAX *setteth away his light, and prepareth to embrace*
                    SOPHO[NISBA].

I'll use thee—

            SOPHONISBA *snatcheth out her knife.*

Sophonisba. Look thee, view this! Show but one strain of force,
    Bow but to seize this arm, and by myself,
    Or more, by Massinissa, this good steel   55
    Shall set my soul on wing. Thus formed gods see,
    And men with gods' worth envy nought but me.
Syphax. Do, strike thy breast. Know, being dead, I'll use
    With highest lust of sense thy senseless flesh,
    And even then thy vexèd soul shall see,   60
    Without resistance, thy trunk prostitute
    Unto our appetite.
Sophonisba.   I shame to make thee know
    How vile thou speakest. Corruption then as much
    As thou shalt do, but frame unto thy lusts
    Imagination's utmost sin. Syphax,   65
    I speak all frightless. Know I live or die
    To Massinissa; nor the force of fate
    Shall make me leave his love or slake thy hate.
    I will speak no more.
Syphax. Thou hast amazed us. [*Aside*] Woman's forcèd use,   70
    Like unripe fruits, no sooner got but waste;
    They have proportion, colour, but no taste.

Think, Syphax—[*To her*] Sophonisba, rest thine own.
Our guard!

Enter a Guard.

    Creature of most astonishing virtue,
If with fair usage, love, and passionate courtings,   75
We may obtain the heaven of thy bed,
We cease no suit; from other force be free.
We dote not on thy body, but love thee.
Sophonisba. Wilt thou keep faith?
Syphax.   By thee, and by that power
By which thou art thus glorious, trust my vow.   80
Our guard, convey the royal'st excellence
That ever was called woman to our palace.
Observe her with strict care.

    [*Re-enter* ZANTHIA.]

Sophonisba.   Dread Syphax, speak!
As thou art worthy, is not Zanthia false?
Syphax. To thee she is.
Sophonisba.   As thou art then thyself,   85
Let her not be.
Syphax.   She is not!

   The Guard *seizeth* ZANTHIA.

Zanthia.   Thus most speed:
When two foes are grown friends, partakers bleed.
Syphax. When plants must flourish, their manure must rot.
Sophonisba. Syphax, be recompensed, I hate thee not.
     Ex[eun]t SOPH[ONISBA, ZANTHIA, *and* Guard].
Syphax. A wasting flame feeds on my amorous blood   90
Which we must cool or die. What way all power,
All speech, full opportunity, can make,
We have made fruitless trial. Infernal Jove,
You resolute angels that delight in flames,
To you, all-wonder-working spirits, I fly.   95
Since heaven helps not, deepest hell we'll try!
Here, in this desert, the great soul of charms,
Dreadful Erictho lives, whose dismal brow
Contemns all roofs or civil coverture.
Forsaken graves and tombs, the ghosts forced out,   100
She joys to inhabit.

Infernal music plays softly whilst ERICTHO *enters and when she
speaks ceaseth.*

A loathsome yellow leanness spreads her face,
A heavy hell-like paleness loads her cheeks,
Unknown to a clear heaven. But if dark winds
Or thick black clouds drive back the blinded stars   105
When her deep magic makes forced heaven quake
And thunder spite of Jove, Erictho then
From naked graves stalks out, heaves proud her head
With long unkempt hair loaden, and strives to snatch
The night's quick sulphur. Then she bursts up tombs,   110
From half-rot cerecloths then she scrapes dry gums
For her black rites. But when she finds a corse
New graved whose entrails yet not turn
To slimy filth, with greedy havoc then
She makes fierce spoil and swells with wicked triumph   115
To bury her lean knuckles in his eyes.
Then doth she gnaw the pale and o'ergrown nails
From his dry hand. But if she find some life
Yet lurking close, she bites his gelid lips,
And sticking her black tongue in his dry throat,   120
She breathes dire murmurs which enforce him bear
Her baneful secrets to the spirits of horror.
To her first sound the gods yield any harm,
As trembling once to hear a second charm.
She is—
Erictho.   Here, Syphax, here. Quake not, for know   125
I know thy thoughts. Thou wouldst entreat our power
Nice Sophonisba's passion to enforce
To thy affection. Be all full of Jove,
'Tis done, 'tis done. To us heaven, earth, sea, air,
And Fate itself obeys. The beasts of death   130
And all the terrors angry gods invented,
T'afflict th'ignorance of patient man,
Tremble at us. The rolled-up snake uncurls
His twisted knots at our affrighting voice.
Are we incensed? The king of flames grows pale,   135
Lest he be choked with black and earthy fumes,
Which our charms raise. Be joyed, make proud thy lust.
I do not pray, you gods: my breath's 'You must'.
Syphax. Deep-knowing spirit, mother of all high
Mysterious science, what may Syphax yield   140
Worthy thy art, by which my soul's thus eased?
The gods first made me live, but thou live pleased.
Erictho. Know then, our love, hard by the reverend ruins
Of a once glorious temple reared to Jove,

Whose very rubbish, like the pitied fall 145
Of virtue most unfortunate, yet bears
A deathless majesty, though now quite razed,
Hurled down by wrath and lust of impious kings,
So that, where holy Flamens wont to sing
Sweet hymns to heaven, there the daw and crow, 150
The ill-voiced raven and still-chattering pie
Send out ungrateful sound and loathsome filth;
Where statues and Jove's acts were vively limned,
Boys with black coals draw the veiled parts of nature
And lecherous actions of imagined lust; 155
Where tombs and beauteous urns of well-dead men
Stood in assurèd rest, the shepherd now
Unloads his belly; corruption most abhorred
Mingling itself with their renownèd ashes.
Ourself quakes at it. 160
There once a charnel-house, now a vast cave,
Over whose brow a pale and untrod grove
Throws out her heavy shade; the mouth, thick arms
Of darksome yew, sun-proof, for ever choke.
Within rests barren darkness; fruitless drought 165
Pines in eternal night. The steam of hell
Yields not so lazy air. There, that's my cell;
From thence a charm, which Jove dare not hear twice,
Shall force her to thy bed. But, Syphax, know,
Love is the highest rebel to our art. 170
Therefore I charge thee, by the fear of all
Which thou knowest dreadful, or more, by ourself,
As with swift haste she passeth to thy bed,
And easy to thy wishes yields, speak not one word,
Nor dare, as thou dost fear thy loss of joys, 175
T'admit one light, one light.
Syphax. 　　　　　　　　　As to my fate
I yield my guidance.
Erictho. 　　　　　　　Then, when I shall force
The air to music, and the shades of night
To form sweet sounds, make proud thy raised delight.
Meantime, behold, I go a charm to rear, 180
Whose potent sound will force ourself to fear.

　　　　　　　　　　　　　　　　　[*Exit* ERICTHO.]
Syphax. Whither is Syphax heaved? At length shall's joy
Hopes more desired than heaven? Sweet labouring earth,
Let heaven be unformed with mighty charms;
Let Sophonisba only fill these arms, 185

Jove we'll not envy thee. Blood's appetite
Is Syphax' god. My wisdom is my sense,
Without a man I hold no excellence.
Give me long breath, young beds, and sickless ease.
For we hold firm, that's lawful which doth please.   190

Infernal music, softly.

Hark, hark! Now rise infernal tones,
    The deep-fetched groans
Of labouring spirits that attend
Erictho.

Erictho. (Within.)   Erictho!
Syphax.   Now crack the trembling earth, and send   195
    Shrieks that portend
Affrightment to the gods which hear
Erictho.

Erictho. (Within.)   Erictho!

*A treble viol, and a bass lute, play softly within the
canopy.*

Syphax. Hark, hark! Now softer melody strikes mute
Disquiet Nature. O thou power of sound,   200
How thou dost melt me! Hark, now even heaven
Gives up his soul amongst us. Now's the time
When greedy expectation strains mine eyes
For their loved object; now, Erictho willed,
Prepare my appetite for love's strict gripes.   205
O you dear founts of pleasure—blood and beauty—
Raise active Venus, worth fruition
Of such provoking sweetness. Hark, she comes!

A short song to soft music above.

Now nuptial hymns enforcèd spirits sing.
Hark, Syphax, hark!

Cantant.

    Now hell and heaven rings   210
With music spite of Phoebus. Peace!

Enter ERICTHO *in the shape of* SOPHONISBA, *her face veiled, and
hasteth in the bed of* SYPHAX.

    She comes!
Fury of blood's impatient! Erictho,
'Bove thunder sit. To thee, egregious soul,

Let all flesh bend. Sophonisba, thy flame
But equal mine, and we'll joy such delight,   215
That gods shall not admire, but even spite!

SYPHAX *hasteneth within the canopy, as to* SOPHONISBA'S *bed.*

ACT V

SCENE i

A bass lute and a treble viol play for the act.

SYPHAX *draws the curtains and discovers* ERICTHO *lying with
him.*

Erictho. Ha! Ha! Ha!
Syphax.   Light! Light!
Erictho.   Ha! Ha!
Syphax. Thou rotten scum of hell—
         O my abhorrèd heat! O loathed delusion!

   They leap out of the bed; SYPHAX *takes him to his sword.*

Erictho. Why, fool of kings, could thy weak soul imagine
      That 'tis within the grasp of heaven or hell   5
      To enforce love? Why know, love dotes the Fates;
      Jove groans beneath his weight. More ignorant thing,
      Know we, Erictho, with a thirsty womb,
      Have coveted full threescore suns for blood of kings.
      We that can make enragèd Neptune toss   10
      His huge curled locks without one breath of wind;
      We that can make heaven slide from Atlas' shoulder;
      We, in the pride and height of covetous lust,
      Have wished with woman's greediness to fill
      Our longing arms with Syphax' well-strung limbs.   15
      And dost thou think, if philters or hell's charms
      Could have enforced thy use, we would have damned
      Brain-sleights? No, no. Now are we full
      Of our dear wishes. Thy proud heat well wasted
      Hath made our limbs grow young. Our love, farewell,   20
      Know he that would force love, thus seeks his hell.

   ERICTHO *slips into the ground as* SYPHAX *offers his sword to her.*

Syphax. Can we yet breathe? Is any plagued like me?
      Are we—Let's think. O now contempt, my hate

To thee, thy thunder, sulphur, and scorned name!
He whose life's loathed, and he who breathes to curse   25
His very being, let him thus with me

       SYPHAX *kneels at the altar.*

Fall 'fore an altar sacred to black powers
And thus dare heavens! O thou whose blasting flames
Hurl barren droughts upon the patient earth,
And thou, gay god of riddles and strange tales,   30
Hot-brainèd Phoebus, all add if you can
Something unto my misery! If aught
Of plagues lurk in your deep-trenched brows,
Which yet I know not, let them fall like bolts
Which wrathful Jove drives strong into my bosom!   35
If any chance of war, or news ill-voiced,
Mischief unthought-of lurk, come, give't us all,
Heap curse on curse, we can no lower fall!

   Out of the altar the ghost of ASDRUBAL *ariseth.*

Asdrubal. Lower, lower!
Syphax.   What damned air is formed
Into that shape? Speak, speak, we cannot quake!   40
Our flesh knows not ignoble tremblings. Speak!
We dare thy terror. Methinks hell and fate
Should dread a soul with woes made desperate.
Asdrubal. Know me the spirit of great Asdrubal,
Father to Sophonisba, whose bad heart   45
Made justly most unfortunate. For know,
I turned unfaithful, after which the field
Chanced to our loss, when of thy men there fell
Six thousand souls, next fight, of Libyans ten.
After which loss we unto Carthage flying,   50
Th'enragèd people cried their army fell
Through my base treason. Straight my revengeful fury
Makes them pursue me. I with resolute haste
Made to the grave of all our ancestors,
Where poisoned, hoped my bones should have long rest.   55
But see, the violent multitude arrives,
Tear down our monument, and me now dead
Deny a grave; hurl us among the rocks
To stanch beasts' hunger. Therefore, thus ungraved,
I seek slow rest. Now dost thou know more woes   60
And more must feel. Mortals, O fear to slight
Your gods and vows. Jove's arm is of dread might.

Syphax. Yet speak. Shall I o'ercome approaching foes?
Asdrubal. Spirits of wrath know nothing but their woes.   *Exit.*

Enter NUNTIUS.

Nuntius. My liege, my liege, the scouts of Cirta bring intelligence   65
    Of sudden danger. Full ten thousand horse,
    Fresh and well-rid, strong Massinissa leads,
    As wings to Roman legions that march swift,
    Led by that man of conquest, Scipio.
Syphax.   Scipio?
Nuntius. Direct to Cirta.

A march far off is heard.

Hark, their march is heard   70
  Even to the city.
Syphax.   Help, our guard! My arms!

[*Enter* Servants *with armour.*]

  Bid all our leaders march! Beat thick alarms!
[*Exit* NUNTIUS.]
  I have seen things which thou wouldst quake to hear.
  Boldness and strength, the shame of slaves be fear.
  Up, heart! Hold, sword! Though waves roll thee on shelf,   75
  Though fortune leave thee, leave not thou thyself!
Exit [SYPHAX,] *arming* [*attended by* Servants].

[ACT V] SCENE ii

Enter two Pages *with targets and javelins,* LAELIUS *and*
JUGURTH, *with halberds,* SCIPIO *and* MASSINISSA *armed, cornets
sounding a march.*

Scipio. Stand!
Massinissa.   Give the word—Stand!
Scipio.   Part the file!
Massinissa.   Give way!
  Scipio, by thy great name, but greater virtue,
  By our eternal love, give me the chance
  Of this day's battle! Let not thy envied fame
  Vouchsafe t'oppose the Roman legions   5
  Against one weakened Prince of Libya.
  This quarrel's mine. Mine be the stroke of fight!
  Let us and Syphax hurl our well-forced darts

Each unto other's breast. O—what should I say?—
Thou beyond epithet, thou whom proud lords of fortune   10
May even envy,—alas, my joy's so vast
Makes me seem lost,—let us thunder and lightning
Strike from our brave arms! Look, look, seize that hill!
Hark! He comes near. From thence discern us strike
Fire worth Jove; mount up, and not repute   15
Me very proud though wondrous resolute.
My cause, my cause is my bold-heart'ning odds,
That sevenfold shield: just arms should fright the gods.
Scipio. Thy words are full of honour. Take thy fate.
Massinissa. Which we do scorn to fear. To Scipio state   20
    Worthy his heart. Now let the forcèd brass
    Sound on!

Cornets sound a march. SCIPIO *leads his train up to the mount.*

    Jugurth, clasp sure our cask,
Arm us with care; and Jugurth, if I fall
Through this day's malice or our fathers' sins,
If it in thy sword lie, break up my breast   25
And save my heart that never fell nor sued
To aught but Jove and Sophonisba. Sound,
Stern heart'ners unto wounds and blood. Sound loud,
For we have namèd Sophonisba!

Cornets, a flourish.

So!

Cornets, a march far off.

Hark, hark, he comes! Stand blood, now multiply   30
Force more than fury. Sound high, sound high, we strike
For Sophonisba!

Enter SYPHAX, *armed, his* Pages *with shields and darts before,
cornets sounding marches.*

Syphax.   For Sophonisba!
Massinissa. Syphax!
Syphax.   Massinissa!
Massinissa.   Betwixt us two,
    Let single fight try all.
Syphax.   Well urged.
Massinissa.   Well granted.
    Of you, my stars, as I am worthy you,   35
    I implore aid, and O, if angels wait

Upon good hearts, my genius be as strong
As I am just.

Syphax.   Kings' glory is their wrong.
He that may only do just acts' a slave.
My god's my arm, my life my heaven, my grave   40
To me all end.

Massinissa.   Give day, gods, life not death
To him that only fears blaspheming breath.
For Sophonisba!

Syphax.   For Sophonisba!

Cornets sound a charge. MASSINISSA *and* SYPHAX *combat.*
SYPHAX *falls.* MASSINISSA *unclasps* SYPHAX' *cask, and as ready*
to kill him, [then] *speaks* SYPHAX.

Syphax. Unto thy fortune, not to thee, we yield.

Massinissa. Lives Sophonisba yet unstained—speak just—   45
Yet ours, unforced?

Syphax.   Let my heart fall more low
Than is my body if, only to thy glory,
She lives not yet all thine.

Massinissa.   Rise, rise! Cease strife.
Hear a most deep revenge: from us take life!

Cornets sound a march. SCIPIO *and* LAELIUS *enter.* SCIPIO *pas-*
seth to his throne. MASSINISSA *presents* SYPHAX *to* SCIPIO'S *feet,*
cornets sounding a flourish.

To you all power of strength; and next to thee,   50
Thou spirit of triumph, born for victory,
I heave these hands. March we to Cirta straight,
My Sophonisba with swift haste to win,
In honour and in love all mean is sin.
                    Ex[*eunt*] MA[SSINISSA] *and* JUG[URTH].

Scipio. As we are Rome's great general, thus we press   55
Thy captive neck. But as still Scipio,
And sensible of just humanity,
We weep thy bondage. Speak, thou ill-chanced man.
What spirit took thee when thou wert our friend,
Thy right hand given both to gods and us   60
With such most passionate vows and solemn faith,
Thou fledst with such most foul disloyalty
To now weak Carthage, strengthening their bad arms,
Who lately scorned thee with all loathed abuse,
Who never entertain for love but use?   65

Syphax. Scipio, my fortune is captivèd, not I.

Therefore I'll speak bold truth; nor once mistrust
What I shall say, for now, being wholly yours,
I must not feign. Sophonisba, 'twas she,
'Twas Sophonisba that solicited   70
My forced revolt. 'Twas her resistless suit,
Her love to her dear Carthage, 'ticed me break
All faith with men. 'Twas she made Syphax false;
She that loves Carthage with such violence,
And hath such moving graces to allure,   75
That she will turn a man that once hath sworn
Himself on's father's bones her Carthage foe,
To be that city's champion and high friend.
Her hymeneal torch burnt down my house,
Then was I captived when her wanton arms   80
Threw moving clasps about my neck. O charms,
Able to turn even fate! But this, in my true grief,
Is some just joy, that my love-sotted foe
Shall seize that plague; that Massinissa's breast
Her hands shall arm, and that, ere long you'll try,   85
She can force him your foe as well as I.
Scipio. Laelius, Laelius, take a choice troop of horse
And spur to Cirta. To Massinissa thus:
Syphax' palace, crown, spoil, city's sack,
Be free to him. But if our new-laughed friend   90
Possess that woman of so moving art,
Charge him with no less weight than his dear vow,
Our love, all faith, that he resign her thee.
As he shall answer Rome, will him give up
A Roman prisoner to the Senate's doom;   95
She is a Carthaginian, now our law's.
Wise men prevent not actions, but ever cause.
Syphax. [*Aside*] Good malice, so, as liberty so dear,
Prove my revenge. What I cannot possess
Another shall not: that's some happiness.   100
                              Exeunt, the cornets flourishing.

                          [ACT V] SCENE iii

*The cornets afar off sounding a charge. A Soldier wounded at
one door. Enters at the other* SOPHONISBA, *two* Pages *before her
        with lights, two women bearing up her train.*

Soldier. Princess, O fly! Syphax hath lost the day,
And captived lies. The Roman legions

Have seized the town, and with inveterate hate
Make slaves or murder all. Fire and steel,
Fury and night, hold all. Fair Queen, O fly!   5
We bleed for Carthage, all of Carthage die!   *Exit.*

The cornets sounding a march. Enter Pages *with javelins and
    targets,* MASSINISSA *and* JUGURTH, MASSINISSA'S *beaver shut.*

Massinissa. March to the palace.
Sophonisba.   Whate'er man thou art,
    Of Libya thy fair arms speak. Give heart
    To amazed weakness; hear her, that for long time
    Hath seen no wishèd light. Sophonisba,   10
    A name for misery much known, 'tis she
    Entreats of thy graced sword this only boon:
    Let me not kneel to Rome, for though no cause
    Of mine deserves their hate, though Massinissa
    Be ours to heart, yet Roman generals   15
    Make proud their triumphs with whatever captives.
    O 'tis a nation which from soul I fear,
    As one well knowing the much-grounded hate
    They bear to Asdrubal and Carthage blood.
    Therefore with tears that wash thy feet, with hands   20
    Unused to beg, I clasp thy manly knees.
    O save me from their fetters and contempt,
    Their proud insults and more than insolence!
    Or, if it rest not in thy grace of breath
    To grant such freedom, give me long-wished death;   25
    For 'tis not much loathed life that now we crave,
    Only an unshamed death and silent grave
    We will now deign to bend for.
Massinissa.   Rarity!

MAS[SINISSA] *disarms his head.*

    By thee and this right hand, thou shalt live free!
Sophonisba. We cannot now be wretched.
Massinissa.   Stay the sword!   30
    Let slaughter cease! Sounds soft as Leda's breast
    Slide through all ears!

Soft music.

                    This night be love's high feast.
Sophonisba. O'erwhelm me not with sweets. Let me not drink
    Till my breast burst, O Jove, thy nectar. Think—

She sinks into MASSI[NISSA'S] *arms.*

Massinissa. She is o'ercome with joy.
Sophonisba.   Help, help to bear   35
    Some happiness, ye powers! I have joy to spare,
    Enough to make a god. O Massinissa!
Massinissa.   Peace.
    A silent thinking makes full joys increase.

Enter LAELIUS.

Laelius. Massinissa!
Massinissa.   Laelius!
Laelius.   Thine ear.
Massinissa.   Stand off.
                                [*Takes* LAELIUS *aside.*]
Laelius. From Scipio thus: by thy late vow of faith,   40
    And mutual league of endless amity,
    As thou respect'st his virtue, or Rome's force,
    Deliver Sophonisba to our hand.
Massinissa. Sophonisba?
Laelius.   Sophonisba.
Sophonisba.   My lord
    Looks pale, and from his half-burst eyes a flame   45
    Of deep disquiet breaks. The gods turn false
    My sad presage.
Massinissa.   Sophonisba?
Laelius.   Even she.
Massinissa. She killed not Scipio's father, nor his uncle,
    Great Cneius.
Laelius.   Carthage did.
Massinissa.   To her what's Carthage?
Laelius. Know 'twas her father Asdrubal struck off   50
    His father's head. Give place to faith and fate.
Massinissa. 'Tis cross to honour.
Laelius.   But 'tis just to state.
    So speaketh Scipio. Do not thou detain
    A Roman prisoner due to this great triumph,
    As thou shalt answer Rome and him.
Massinissa.   Laelius,   55
    We now are in Rome's power. Laelius,
    View Massinissa do a loathèd act,
    Most sinking from that state his heart did keep.
    Look, Laelius, look, see Massinissa weep!
    Know I have made a vow, more dear to me   60

Than my soul's endless being; she shall rest
Free from Rome's bondage.

Laelius.   But dost thou forget
Thy vow, yet fresh, thus breathed: 'When I desist
To be commanded by thy virtue, Scipio,
Or fall from friend of Rome, revenging gods,   65
Afflict me with your torture.'

Massinissa.   Laelius, enough.
Salute the Roman, tell him we will act
What shall amaze him.

Laelius.   Wilt thou yield her then?

Massinissa. She shall arrive there straight.

Laelius.   Best fate of men
To thee.

Massinissa.   And Scipio.   [*Exit* LAELIUS *with* Pages.]
                        Have I lived, O heavens,   70
To be enforcedly perfidious?

Sophonisba. What unjust grief afflicts my worthy lord?

Massinissa. Thank me, ye gods, with much beholdingness;
For mark, I do not curse you.

Sophonisba.   Tell me, sweet,
The cause of thy much anguish.

Massinissa.   Ha, the cause?   75
Let's see. Wreathe back thine arms, bend down thy neck,
Practise base prayers, make fit thyself for bondage.

Sophonisba. Bondage!

Massinissa.   Bondage, Roman bondage.

Sophonisba.   No, no!

Massinissa. How then have I vowed well to Scipio?

Sophonisba. How then to Sophonisba?

Massinissa.   Right, which way?   80
Run mad! Impossible distraction!

Sophonisba. Dear lord, thy patience, let it maze all power;
And list to her in whose sole heart it rests
To keep thy faith upright.

Massinissa.   Wilt thou be slaved?

Sophonisba. No, free.

Massinissa.   How then keep I my faith?

Sophonisba.   My death   85
Gives help to all. From Rome so rest we free;
So brought to Scipio, faith is kept in thee.

Enter a Page *with a bowl of wine.*

Massinissa. Thou dar'st not die—some wine. Thou dar'st not die.

Sophonisba. How near was I unto the curse of man, joy!
          How like was I yet once to have been glad!   90
          He that ne'er laughed may with a constant face
          Contemn Jove's frown. Happiness makes us base.

          She takes a bowl into which MAS[SINISSA] *puts poison.*

          Behold me, Massinissa, like thyself,
          A king and soldier; and I prithee keep
          My last command.
Massinissa.   Speak, sweet.
Sophonisba.   Dear, do not weep.   95
          And now with undismayed resolve behold,
          To save you, you—for honour and just faith
          Are most true gods, which we should much adore—
          With even disdainful vigour I give up
          An abhorred life.

                    She drinks.

                              You have been good to me,   100
          And I do thank thee, heaven. O my stars,
          I bless your goodness, that with breast unstained,
          Faith pure, a virgin wife, tried to my glory,
          I die, of female faith the long-lived story;
          Secure from bondage and all servile harms,   105
          But more, most happy in my husband's arms.

                    She sinks.

Jugurth. Massinissa, Massinissa!
Massinissa.   Covetous,
          Fame-greedy lady, could no scope of glory,
          No reasonable proportion of goodness,
          Fill thy great breast, but thou must prove immense,   110
          Incomprehence in virtue? What, wouldst thou
          Not only be admired, but even adored?
          O glory ripe for heaven! Sirs, help, help, help!
          Let us to Scipio with what speed you can;
          For piety make haste, whilst yet we are man.   115
                    Exeunt, bearing SOPH[ONISBA] *in a chair.*

                    [ACT V, SCENE iv]

          Cornets, a march. Enter SCIPIO *in full state, triumphal orna-*
          ments carried before him, and SY[PHAX] *bound; at the other*
                              door, LAELIUS.

Scipio. What answers Massinissa? Will he send
 That Sophonisba of so moving tongue?
Laelius. Full of dismayed unsteadiness he stood,
 His right hand locked in hers, which hand he gave
 As pledge from Rome she ever should live free.   5
 But when I entered and well urged this vow
 And thy command, his great heart sunk with shame,
 His eyes lost spirit, and his heat of life
 Sank from his face, as one that stood benumbed,
 All mazed, t'affect impossibilities;   10
 For either unto her or Scipio
 He must break vow. Long time he tossed his thoughts;
 And as you see a snow-ball being rolled,
 At first a handful, yet, long bowled about,
 Insensibly acquires a mighty globe,   15
 So his cold grief through agitation grows,
 And more he thinks, the more of grief he knows.
 At last he seemed to yield her.
Syphax.   Mark, Scipio.
 Trust him that breaks a vow?
Scipio.   How then trust thee?
Syphax. O, misdoubt him not, when he's thy slave like me. 20

    Enter MASSINISSA, *all in black.*

Massinissa. Scipio!
Scipio.   Massinissa!
Massinissa.   General!
Scipio.   King!
Massinissa. Lives there no mercy for one soul of Carthage,
 But must see baseness?
Scipio.   Wouldst thou joy thy peace,
 Deliver Sophonisba straight and cease.
 Do not grasp that which is too hot to hold.   25
 We grace thy grief, and hold it with soft sense.
 Enjoy good courage, but 'void insolence.
 I tell thee Rome and Scipio deign to bear
 So low a breast. As for her, say we fear.
Massinissa. Do not, do not. Let not the fright of nations 30
 Know so vile terms. She rests at thy dispose.
Syphax. To our soul, joy. Shall Sophonisba then
 With me go bound, and wait on Scipio's wheel?
 When th' whole world's giddy, one man cannot reel.
Massinissa. Starve thy lean hopes; and, Romans, now behold 35
 A sight would sad the gods, make Phoebus cold.

Organ and recorders play to a single voice. Enter in the mean-
time the mournful solemnity of MASSINISSA'S *presenting*
SOPHON[ISBA'S] *body.*

Look, Scipio, see what hard shift we make
To keep our vows. Here, take, I yield her thee;
And Sophonisba, I keep vow, thou art still free.
Syphax. Burst, my vexed heart! The torture that most racks   40
    An enemy is his foe's royal acts.
Scipio. The glory of thy virtue live for ever.
    Brave hearts may be obscured, but extinct never.

SCIPIO *adorns* MASSINISSA.

Take from the general of Rome this crown,
This robe of triumph, and this conquest's wreath,   45
This sceptre and this hand. For ever breathe
Rome's very minion. Live worth thy fame,
As far from faintings as from now base name.
Massinissa. Thou whom, like sparkling steel, the strokes of
                               chance
    Made hard and firm, and, like wild-fire turned,   50
    The more cold fate, more bright thy virtue burned,
    And in whole seas of miseries didst flame;
    On thee, loved creature of a deathless fame,

MASSINISSA *adorns* SOPHONISBA.

Rest all my honour. O, thou for whom I drink
So deep of grief, that he must only think,   55
Not dare to speak, that would express my woe;
Small rivers murmur, deep gulfs silent flow.
My grief is here, [*Pointing to his heart.*] not here.
        [*Pointing to* SOPHONISBA'S *body.*]
                        Heave gently then,
Women's right wonder, and just shame of men.

Cornets a short flourish.

Exeunt, MA[SSINISSA] *remains.*

EPILOGUS

[*Massinissa.*] And now with lighter passion, though with most
                             just fear,

I change my person, and do hither bear
Another's voice, who with a phrase as weak
As his deserts, now willed me, thus formed, speak:
 If words well sensed, best suiting subject grave,   5
Noble true story may once boldly crave
Acceptance gracious; if he whose fires
Envy not others nor himself admires;
If scenes exempt from ribaldry or rage,
Of taxings indiscreet, may please the stage,   10
If such may hope applause, he not commands,
Yet craves as due, the justice of your hands.
But freely he protests, howe'er it is,
Or well or ill, or much, not much amiss,
 With constant modesty he doth submit   15
 To all, save those that have more tongue than wit.

(AUTHOR'S NOTE.)

After all, let me entreat my reader not to tax me for the fashion
of the entrances and music of this tragedy, for know it is printed
only as it was presented by youths, and after the fashion of the
private stage. Nor let some easily amended errors in the printing afflict thee, since thy own discourse will easily set upright
any such unevenness.

THOMAS MIDDLETON

A TRAGICOMEDY CALLED
THE WITCH

Hee. giue mē soome Lizard-Brains: quickly Firstsone
    where's Grannam Stadlin, and all y᷂ rest oͭ yͤ Sisters.
Fir. all at hand forsooth.
Hee. giue mē Marmaritin: soome Beare-britch: when.
Fir. here's Beare-Britch, and Lizard braines forsooth
Hee. Into yͤ vessell;
    and fetch three ounces of y᷂ red-haird-Girle
    I̅ killd last midnight.
Fir. whereabouts, sweet Mother!
Hee. Hip: Hip, or Flanck: where is yͤ Acopus.
Fir. you shall haue Acopus. forsooth;
Hee. Stir: Stir about: whilst I̅ begin the Charme.

    A Charme Song: about a Vessell.

  Black Spiritts, and white: Red Spiritts, and Gray
  Mingle, Mingle, Mingle, you that mingle may.
     Titty, Tiffin: keepe it stiff in
     Firr-Drake, Puckey, make it Luckey.
     Liard, Robin, you must bob in
  Round, a-round, a-round, about, about
  All ill come runnig in all good keepe-out.

    1 witch. Here's the Blood of a Bat.
    Hee. Put in that: oh put in that.
    2 Here's Libbards Bane

                    pul

THE PERSONS

DUKE.
L[ORD] GOVERNOR [OF RAVENNA].
SEBASTIAN, *contracted to Isabella.*
FERNANDO, *his friend.*
ANTONIO, *husband to Isabella.*   5
ABERZANES, *a gent[leman] neither honest, wise, nor valiant.*
ALMACHILDES, *a fantastical gentleman.*
GASPERO,⎫|*servants to Antonio.*
HERMIO, ⎭
FIRESTONE, *the clown and Hecate's son.*   10
DUCHESS.
ISABELLA, *niece to the Governor.*
FRANCISCA, *Antonio's sister.*
AMORETTA, *the Duchess's woman.*
FLORIDA, *a courtesan.*   15
HECATE, *the chief witch.*
STADLIN,⎫ *witches.*
HOPPO, ⎭
[MALKIN, a Spirit like a Cat]
[Three] other Witches [*including* HELLWAIN *and* PUCKLE],⎫   20
Servants,   ⎭ *mutes.*
[Boy.]
[Old Woman.]
[Spirits, Gentlemen, Attendants.]

                        THE SCENE: *Ravenna, Italy*   25

                    [EPISTLE]

To the truly worthy and generously affected *Thomas Holmes*
Esquire.

Noble Sir,
            As a true testimony of my ready inclination to your
service, I have, merely upon a taste of your desire, recovered into my   5
hands—though not without much difficulty—this ignorantly ill-
fated labour of mine. Witches are, *ipso facto*, by the law condemned
and that only, I think, hath made her lie so long in an imprisoned
obscurity. For your sake alone, she hath thus far conjured herself
abroad; and bears no other charms about her but what may tend to   10
your recreation, nor no other spell but to possess you with a belief
that as she, so he that first taught her to enchant, will always be,
                                        Your devoted
                                        Tho[mas]
                                        Middleton.   15

ACT I

SCENE i

Enter SEBASTIAN *and* FERNANDO.

Sebastian. My three years spent in war has now undone
    My peace for ever.
Fernando.   Good, be patient, sir.
Sebastian. She is my wife by contract before heaven
    And all the angels, sir.
Fernando.   I do believe you;
    But where's the remedy now? You see she's gone: 5
    Another has possession.
Sebastian.   There's the torment!
Fernando. This day being the first of your return
    Unluckily proves the first too of her fastening.
    Her uncle, sir, the governor of Ravenna,
    Holding a good opinion of the bridegroom,   10
    As he's fair-spoken, sir, and wond'rous mild—
Sebastian. There goes the devil in a sheep-skin!
Fernando.   – with all speed
    Clapped it up suddenly. I cannot think, sure,
    That the maid over-loves him; though being married,
    Perhaps for her own credit, now she intends   15
    Performance of an honest duteous wife.
Sebastian. Sir, I've a world of business. Question nothing,
    You will but lose your labour; 'tis not fit
    For any, hardly mine own secrecy,
    To know what I intend. I take my leave, sir.   20
    I find such strange employments in myself
    That unless death pity me and lay me down
    I shall not sleep these seven years; that's the least, sir.   *Exit.*
Fernando. That sorrow's dangerous can abide no counsel.
    'Tis like a wound past cure. Wrongs done to love   25
    Strike the heart deeply. None can truly judge on't
    But the poor sensible sufferer, whom it racks
    With unbelievèd pains, which men in health,
    That enjoy love, not possibly can act,
    Nay, not so much as think. In troth, I pity him.   30
    His sighs drink life-blood in this time of feasting.

[*Noise of preparations for a banquet.*]

—A banquet towards too! Not yet hath riot
    Played out her last scene? At such entertainments still
    Forgetfulness obeys and surfeit governs;
    Here's marriage sweetly honoured in gorged stomachs   35
    And overflowing cups!

Enter GASPERO *and* Servant.

Gaspero.   Where is she, sirrah?
Servant. Not far off.
Gaspero.   Prithee where? Go fetch her hither.
                              [*Exit* Servant.]
    [*Aside*] I'll rid him away straight. [*To Fernando*] The duke's
                                now risen, sir.
Fernando. I am a joyful man to hear it, sir,
    It seems he's drunk the less; though I think he   40
    That has the least has certainly enough.   *Exit.*
Gaspero. I have observed this fellow; all the feast-time
    He hath not pledged one cup, but looked most wickedly
    Upon good malego, flies to the black-jack still
    And sticks to small drink like a water-rat.   45

Enter FLORIDA.

O, here she comes! Alas, the poor whore weeps!
    'Tis not for grace now, all the world must judge,
    It is for spleen and madness 'gainst this marriage.
    I do but think how she could beat the vicar now,
    Scratch the man horribly that gave the woman,   50
    The woman worst of all, if she durst do it.
    [*To her*] Why how now, mistress? This weeping needs not;
    For though my master marry for his reputation
    He means to keep you too.
Florida.   How, sir?
Gaspero.   He doth, indeed;
    He swore't to me last night. Are you so simple,   55
    And have been five years traded, as to think
    One woman would serve him? Fie, not an empress!
    Why, he'll be sick o'th' wife within ten nights
    Or never trust my judgement.
Florida.   Will he, thinkst thou?
Gaspero. Will he!
Florida.   I find thee still so comfortable,   60
    Beshrew my heart, if I know how to miss thee.

They talk of gentlemen, perfumers and such things;
Give me the kindness of the master's man
In my distress, say I.
Gaspero.   'Tis your great love, forsooth.
   Please you withdraw yourself to yond private parlour.   65
   I'll send you ven'son, custard, parsnip-pie;
   For banqueting-stuff—as suckets, jellies, syrups—
   I will bring in myself.
Florida.   I'll take 'em kindly, sir.   Exit.
Gaspero. She's your grand strumpet's complement to a tittle.
   'Tis a fair building. It had need, it has   70
   Just at this time some one-and-twenty inmates;
   But half of 'em are young merchants, they'll depart shortly.
   They take but rooms for summer and away they
   When't grows foul weather. Marry then come the termers
   And commonly they're well-booted for all seasons.   75
   But peace, no more: the guests are coming in.   [Retires.]

Enter ALMACHILDES *and* AMORETTA.

Almachildes. The fates have blessed me; have I met you privately?
Amoretta. Why, sir! Why, Almachildes!
Almachildes.   Not a kiss?
Amoretta. I'll call aloud, i'faith.
Almachildes.   I'll stop your mouth.
Amoretta. Upon my love to reputation   80
   I'll tell the duchess once more.
Almachildes.   'Tis the way
   To make her laugh a little.
Amoretta.   She'll not think
   That you dare use a maid of honour thus.
Almachildes. Amsterdam swallow thee for a puritan
   And Geneva cast thee up again, like she that sunk   85
   At Charing-Cross and rose again at Queenhithe!
Amoretta. Ay, these are the holy fruits of the sweet vine, sir—
                       [Retires.]
Almachildes. Sweet venery be with thee and I at the tail
   Of my wish! I am a little headstrong, and so
   Are most of the company. I will to the witches.   90
   They say they have charms and tricks to make
   A wench fall backwards and lead a man herself
   To a country-house some mile out of the town
   Like a fire-drake. There be such whoreson kind girls
   And such bawdy witches, and I'll try conclusions.   95

Enter DUKE, DUCHESS, L[ORD] GOVERNOR, ANTONIO, *and*
ISABELLA, FRANCISCA [*and* Attendants *with a banquet.*]

Duke. A banquet yet? Why surely, my lord governor,
  Bacchus could never boast of a day till now
  To spread his power and make his glory known.
Duchess. [*To Governor*] Sir, you've done nobly; though in
                                                 modesty
  You keep it from us, know we understand so much.   100
  All this day's cost 'tis your great love bestows
  In honour of the bride, your virtuous niece.
Governor. In love to goodness and your presence, madam,
  So understood, 'tis rightly.
Duke.   Now will I
  Have a strange health after all these.
Governor.   What's that, my lord?   105
Duke. A health in a strange cup; and't shall go round.
Governor. Your grace need not doubt that, sir, having seen
  So many pledged already. This fair company
  Cannot shrink now for one, so it end there.
Duke. It shall; for all ends here. Here's a full period.   110
                         [*Produces a skull set as a cup.*]
Governor. A skull, my lord?
Duke.   Call it a soldier's cup, man.
  [*To the skull*] Fie, how you fright the women!—I have sworn
  It shall go round, excepting only you, sir,
  For your late sickness, and the bride herself,
  Whose health it is.
Isabella.   [*Aside*] Marry, I thank heaven for that.   115
Duke. Our duchess I know will pledge us, though the cup
  Was once her father's head; which as a trophy
  We'll keep till death in memory of that conquest.
  He was the greatest foe our steel e'er struck at,
  And he was bravely slain. Then took we thee   120
  Into our bosom's love. Thou mad'st the peace
  For all thy country, thou; that beauty did.
  We're dearer than a father are we not?
Duchess. Yes, sir, by much.
Duke.   And we shall find that straight.
                                                [*Drinks.*]
Antonio. [*Aside*] That's an ill bride-cup for a marriage-day;   125
  I do not like the fate on't.
Governor.   Good my lord,
  The duchess looks pale. Let her not pledge you there.
Duke. Pale?

Duchess.   Sir, not I.
Duke.   See how your lordship fails now;
     The rose's not fresher, nor the sun at rising
     More comfortably pleasing.
Duchess.   Sir, to you,   130
     The lord of this day's honour.   [*Drinks.*]
Antonio.   All first moving
     From your grace, madam, and the duke's great favour.
                                                  [*Drinks.*]
     [*To Francisca*] Sister, it must.
Francisca.   [*Aside*] This's the worst fright that could
                                                  come
     To a concealed great belly. I'm with child
     And this will bring it out, or make me come   135
     Some seven weeks sooner than we maidens reckon. [*Drinks.*]
Duchess. [*Aside*] Did ever cruel, barbarous act match this?
     Twice hath his surfeits brought my father's memory
     Thus spitefully and scornfully to mine eyes,
     And I'll endure't no more. 'Tis in my heart since.   140
     I'll be revenged as far as death can lead me.
Almachildes. Am I the last man then? I may deserve
     To be first one day.   [*Drinks.*]
Governor.   Sir, it has gone round now.
Duke. The round? An excellent way to train up soldiers.
     Where's bride and bridegroom?
Antonio.   At your happy service.   145
Duke. A boy tonight at least! I charge you look to't
     Or I'll renounce you for industrious subjects.
Antonio. Your grace speaks like a worthy and tried soldier.
                         Exeunt [*all but* GASPERO.]
Gaspero. And you'll do well for one that ne'er tossed pike, sir.
                                             Exit.

                    [ACT I] SCENE ii

                    Enter HECATE.

Hecate.   Titty and Tiffin,
             Suckin and Pidgen,
             Liard and Robin,
             White spirits, black spirits;
             Grey spirits, red spirits;   5
             Devil-toad, devil-ram;
             Devil-cat, and devil-dam.

Why Hoppo and Stadlin, Hellwain and Puckle!
Stadlin. [*Within*] Here, sweating at the vessel.
Hecate.   Boil it well.
Hoppo. [*Within*] It gallops now.
Hecate.   Are the flames blue enough?   10
    Or shall I use a little seeton more?
Stadlin. [*Within*] The nips of fairies upon maids' white hips
    Are not more perfect azure.
Hecate.   Tend it carefully.
    Send Stadlin to me with a brazen dish
    That I may fall to work upon these serpents,   15
    And squeeze 'em ready for the second hour.
    Why, when!

        [*Enter* STADLIN *with a brazen dish.*]

Stadlin.   Here's Stadlin and the dish.
Hecate. There, take this unbaptisèd brat;
      [*Giving the dead body of a baby.*]
    Boil it well; preserve the fat.
    You know 'tis precious to transfer   20
    Our 'nointed flesh into the air,
    In moonlight nights o'er steeple-tops,
    Mountains and pine-trees, that like pricks or stops
    Seem to our height; high towers and roofs of princes
    Like wrinkles in the earth. Whole provinces   25
    Appear to our sight then even leek
    A russet mole upon some lady's cheek,
    When hundred leagues in air we feast and sing,
    Dance, kiss and coll, use everything.
    What young man can we wish to pleasure us   30
    But we enjoy him in an incubus?
    Thou knowst it, Stadlin?
Stadlin.   Usually that's done.
Hecate. Last night thou got'st the Mayor of Whelplie's son.
    I knew him by his black cloak lined with yellow;
    I think thou'st spoiled the youth—he's but seventeen.   35
    I'll have him the next mounting. Away, in!
    Go feed the vessel for the second hour.
Stadlin. Where be the magical herbs?
Hecate.   They're down his throat;
    His mouth crammed full; his ears and nostrils stuffed.
    I thrust in *eleoselinum* lately,   40
    Aconitum, frondes populeus, and soot—
    You may see that, he looks so black i'th'mouth—

Then *sium, acarum vulgaro* too,
Pentaphyllon, the blood of a flitter-mouse,
Solanum somnificum et oleum.   45
Stadlin. Then there's all, Hecate?
Hecate.   Is the heart of wax
    Stuck full of magic needles?
Stadlin.   'Tis done, Hecate.
Hecate. And is the farmer's picture and his wife's
    Laid down to th' fire yet?
Stadlin. They're a-roasting both, too.
Hecate.   Good.   [*Exit* STADLIN.]   50
    Then their marrows are a-melting subtly
    And three months' sickness sucks up life in 'em.
    They denied me often flour, barm and milk,
    Goose-grease and tar, when I ne'er hurt their charmings,
    Their brew-locks, nor their batches, nor forspoke   55
    Any of their breedings. Now I'll be meet with 'em.
    Seven of their young pigs I have bewitched already
    Of the last litter, nine ducklings, thirteen goslings,
    And a hog fell lame last Sunday, after evensong too;
    And mark how their sheep prosper, or what sop   60
    Each milch-kine gives to th' pail. I'll send
    Those snakes shall milk 'em all beforehand.
    The dewed-skirted dairy wenches shall stroke
    Dry dugs for this and go home cursing.
    I'll mar their syllabubs and frothy feastings   65
    Under cows' bellies with the parish youths.
    Where's Firestone? Our son, Firestone!

Enter FIRESTONE.

Firestone.   Here am I, mother.
Hecate. Take in this brazen dish full of dear ware.   [*Gives dish.*]
    Thou shalt have all when I die; and that will be
    Even just at twelve o'clock at night come three year.   70
Firestone. And may you not have one o'clock in to th' dozen,
    mother?
Hecate. No.
Firestone. Your spirits are then more unconscionable than bakers;
    you'll have lived then, mother, six-score year to the hundred,   75
    and methinks after six-score years the devil might give you a
    cast, for he's a fruiterer too, and has been from the beginning.
    The first apple that e'er was eaten came through his fingers. The
    costermonger's, then, I hold to be the ancientest trade, though
    some would have the tailor pricked down before him.   80

Hecate. Go, and take heed you shed not by the way.
    The hour must have her portion, 'tis dear syrup;
    Each charmèd drop is able to confound
    A family consisting of nineteen
    Or one-and-twenty feeders.
Firestone.   [*Aside*] Marry, here's stuff indeed!   85
    Dear syrup call you it? A little thing
    Would make me give you a dram on't in a posset
    And cut you three years shorter.
Hecate.   Thou'rt now
    About some villainy.
Firestone.   Not I, forsooth.
    [*Aside*] Truly the devil's in her, I think.   90
    How one villain smells out another straight! There's no
    knavery but is nosed like a dog and can smell out a dog's
    meaning. [*To Hecate*] Mother, I pray give me leave to ramble
    abroad tonight with the Nightmare, for I have a great mind
    to overlay a fat parson's daughter.   95
Hecate. And who shall lie with me then?
Firestone.   The great cat
    For one night, mother. 'Tis but a night—
    Make shift with him for once.
Hecate.   You're a kind son!
    But 'tis the nature of you all, I see that.
    You had rather hunt after strange women still   100
    Than lie with your own mothers. Get thee gone;
    Sweat thy six ounces out about the vessel
    And thou shalt play at midnight. The Nightmare
    Shall call thee when it walks.
Firestone.   Thanks, most sweet mother.
                                            Exit.

Hecate. [*Kneels.*] Urchins, Elves, Hags, Satyrs, Pans, Fawns,   105
    Silens, Kit-with-the-candlestick, Tritons, Centaurs,
    Dwarfs, Imps, the Spoorn, the Mare, the Man-i'-th'oak,
    The Hellwain, the Fire-drake, the Puckle. *A ab hur hus*!

Enter SEBASTIAN.

Sebastian. [*Aside*] Heaven knows with what unwillingness and
                                           hate
    I enter this damned place; but such extremes   110
    Of wrongs in love fight 'gainst religious knowledge,
    That were I led by this disease to deaths
    As numberless as creatures that must die,
    I could not shun the way. I know what 'tis

To pity madmen now; they're wretched things   115
That ever were created, if they be
Of woman's making and her faithless vows.
I fear they're now a-kissing. What's o'clock?
'Tis now but supper-time, but night will come
And all new-married couples make short suppers.   120
[*To Hecate*] Whate'er thou art, I have no spare time to fear
                                                          thee,
My horrors are so strong and great already
That thou seemst nothing. Up and laze not.
Hadst thou my business thou couldst ne'er sit so;
'Twould firk thee into air a thousand mile   125
Beyond thy ointments. I would I were read
So much in thy black power as mine own griefs!
I'm in great need of help; wilt give me any?
Hecate. Thy boldness takes me bravely. We're all sworn
To sweat for such a spirit. See, I regard thee;   130
I rise and bid thee welcome. What's thy wish now?
Sebastian. O my heart swells with't! I must take breath first.
Hecate. Is't to confound some enemy on the seas?
It may be done tonight. Stadlin's within;
She raises all your sudden ruinous storms   135
That shipwreck barks and tears up growing oaks,
Flies over houses and takes *Anno Domini*
Out of a rich man's chimney—a sweet place for't!
He would be hanged ere he would set his own years there;
They must be chambered in a five-pound picture,   140
A green silk curtain drawn before the eyes on't—
His rotten diseased years! Or dost thou envy
The fat prosperity of any neighbour?
I'll call forth Hoppo, and her incantation
Can straight destroy the young of all his cattle,   145
Blast vineyards, orchards, meadows, or in one night
Transport his dung, hay, corn, by ricks, whole stacks
Into thine own ground.
Sebastian.   This would come most richly now
To many a country grazier; but my envy
Lies not so low as cattle, corn or vines.   150
'Twill trouble your best powers to give me ease.
Hecate. Is it to starve up generation?
To strike a barrenness in man or woman?
Sebastian.   Ha!
Hecate. Ha? Did you feel me there? I knew your grief.
Sebastian. Can there be such things done?

Hecate.   Are these the skins   155
  Of serpents? These of snakes?
Sebastian.   I see they are.
Hecate. So sure into what house these are conveyed,

               [*Giving skins to* SEBASTIAN.]

  Knit with these charmèd and retentive knots,
  Neither the man begets nor woman breeds;
  No, nor performs the least desires of wedlock,   160
  Being then a mutual duty. I could give thee
  Chiroconita, adincantida,
  Archimadon, marmaritin, calicia,
  Which I could sort to villainous barren ends;
  But this leads the same way. More I could instance: 165
  As the same needles thrust into their pillows
  That sews and socks up dead men in their sheets;
  A privy gristle of a man that hangs
  After sunset—good, excellent! Yet all's there, sir.
Sebastian. You could not do a man that special kindness   170
  To part 'em utterly now? Could you do that?
Hecate. No, time must do't. We cannot disjoin wedlock.
  'Tis of heaven's fastening. Well may we raise jars,
  Jealousies, strifes and heart-burning disagreements,
  Like a thick scurf o'er life, as did our master   175
  Upon that patient miracle, but the work itself
  Our power cannot disjoint.
Sebastian.   I depart happy
  In what I have then, being constrained to this.
  [*Aside*] And grant, you greater powers that dispose men,
  That I may never need this hag again.   *Exit.*   180
Hecate. I know he loves me not, nor there's no hope on't;
  'Tis for the love of mischief I do this,
  And that we're sworn to—the first oath we take.

               [*Enter* FIRESTONE.]

Firestone. O mother, mother!
Hecate.   What's the news with thee now?
Firestone. There's the bravest young gentleman within and the fine-   185
  liest drunk; I thought he would have fallen into the vessel. He
  stumbled at a pipkin of child's grease, reeled against Stadlin,
  overthrew her, and in the tumbling-cast struck up old Puckle's
  heels with her clothes over her ears.
Hecate. Hoyday!   190
Firestone. I was fain to throw the cat upon her to save her honesty,

and all little enough. I cried out still 'I pray be covered!' See
where he comes now, mother.

Enter ALMACHILDES.

Almachildes. Call you these witches?
    They be tumblers, methinks, very flat tumblers.   195
Hecate. [*Aside*] 'Tis Almachildes—fresh blood stirs in me!—
    The man that I have lusted to enjoy.
    I have had him thrice in incubus already.
Almachildes. Is your name Goody Hag?
Hecate.   'Tis anything.
    Call me the horrid'st and unhallowed'st things   200
    That life and nature trembles at; for thee
    I'll be the same. Thou com'st for a love-charm now?
Almachildes. Why, thou'rt a witch I think.
Hecate.   Thou shalt have
                                        choice
    Of twenty, wet or dry.
Almachildes.   Nay, let's have dry ones!
Hecate. If thou wilt use't by way of cup and potion,   205
    I'll give thee a remora shall bewitch her straight.
Almachildes. A remora? What's that?
Hecate.   A little suck-stone;
    Some call it a sea-lamprey, a small fish.
Almachildes.   And must't
                               be buttered?
Hecate. The bones of a green frog too, wondrous precious,
    The flesh consumed by pismires.
Almachildes.   Pismires? Give me a
                             chamber-pot!   210
Firestone. [*Aside*] You shall see him go nigh to be so unmannerly
    he'll make water before my mother anon.
Almachildes. And now you talk of frogs, I have somewhat here;
    I come not empty-pocketed from a banquet—
    I learned that of my haberdasher's wife.   215
    Look, goody witch, there's a toad in marchpane for you.
                                      [*Gives.*]
Hecate. O, sir, you've fitted me.
Almachildes.   And here's a spawn or two
    Of the same paddock-brood too, for your son.   [*Gives.*]
Firestone. I thank your worship, sir. How comes your handkercher
    so sweetly thus berayed? Sure, 'tis wet sucket, sir.   220
Almachildes. 'Tis nothing but the syrup the toad spit.
    Take all I prithee.

Hecate.   This was kindly done, sir.
    And you shall sup with me tonight for this.
Almachildes. How? With thee? Dost think I'll eat fried rats
    And pickled spiders?
Hecate.   No; I can command, sir,   225
    The best meat i'th' whole province for my friends,
    And reverently served in too.
Almachildes.   How?
Hecate.   In good fashion.
Almachildes. Let me but see that, and I'll sup with you.

>   *She conjures and enter* [MALKIN, *a* Spirit *like*] *a Cat, playing on*
>   *a fiddle, and* Spirits *with meat.*

    The Cat and Fiddle? An excellent ordinary!
    You had a devil once in a fox-skin?   230
Hecate. O, I have him still. Come walk with me, sir.
>   *Exeunt* [*all but* FIRESTONE.]
Firestone. How apt and ready is a drunkard now to reel to the
    devil! Well, I'll even in and see how he eats; and I'll be hanged if
    I be not the fatter of the twain with laughing at him.   *Exit.*

ACT II

SCENE i

Enter ANTONIO *and* GASPERO.

Gaspero. Good sir, whence springs this sadness? Trust me, sir,
    You look not like a man was married yesterday.
    There could come no ill tidings since last night
    To cause that discontent. I was wont to know all
    Before you had a wife, sir. You ne'er found me   5
    Without those parts of manhood—trust and secrecy.
Antonio. I will not tell thee this.
Gaspero.   Not your true servant, sir?
Antonio. True? You'll all flout according to your talent,
    The best a man can keep of you; and a hell 'tis
    For masters to pay wages to be laughed at.   10
    Give order that two cocks be boiled to jelly.
Gaspero. How! Two cocks boiled to jelly?
Antonio. Fetch half an ounce of pearl.   *Exit.*
Gaspero.   This is a cullis
    For a consumption; and I hope one night

Has not brought you to need the cook already,   15
And some part of the goldsmith. What, two trades
In four and twenty hours and less time?
Pray heaven the surgeon and the pothecary
Keep out, and then 'tis well. You'd better fortune,
As far as I see, with your strumpet sojourner,   20
Your little four nobles a week. I ne'er knew you
Eat one ponado all the time you've kept her;
And is't in one night now come up to two-cock broth?
I wonder at the alteration strangely.

Enter FRANCISCA.

Francisca. Good morrow, Gasper.
Gaspero.   Your hearty wishes, mistress,   25
And your sweet dreams come upon you!
Francisca.   What's that, sir?
Gaspero. In a good husband; that's my real meaning.
Francisca. Saw you my brother lately?
Gaspero.   Yes.
Francisca.   I met him now
As sad methought as grief could make a man.
Know you the cause?
Gaspero.   Not I. I know nothing,   30
But half an ounce of pearl and kitchen business,
Which I will see performed with all fidelity;
I'll break my trust in nothing, not in porridge, I.   *Exit.*
Francisca. I have the hardest fortune, I think, of a hundred
gentlewomen.   35
Some can make merry with a friend seven year
And nothing seen; as perfect a maid still,
To the world's knowledge, as she came from rocking.
But 'twas my luck, at the first hour, forsooth,
To prove too fruitful. Sure, I'm near my time.   40
I'm yet but a young scholar, I may fail
In my account; but certainly I do not.
These bastards come upon poor venturing gentlewomen ten to
one faster than your legitimate children. If I had been married, I'll be hanged if I had been with child so soon now. When 45
they are once husbands they'll be whipped ere they take such
pains as a friend will do: to come by water to the back-door at
midnight; there stay perhaps an hour in all weathers with a pair
of reeking watermen laden with bottles of wine, chewets and
currant-custards. I may curse those egg-pies; they are meat that 50
help forward too fast.

This hath been usual with me night by night,
Honesty forgive me, when my brother has been
Dreaming of no such junkets; yet he hath fared
The better for my sake, though he little think   55
For what, nor must he ever. My friend promised me
To provide safely for me, and devise
A means to save my credit here i'th'house.
My brother sure would kill me if he knew't,
And powder-up my friend and all his kindred   60
For an East Indian voyage.

Enter ISABELLA.

Isabella.   Alone, sister?
Francisca. [*Aside*] No, there's another with me, though you see't
                                                                not.
[*To her*] 'Morrow, sweet sister; how have you slept tonight?
Isabella. More than I thought I should. I've had good rest.
Francisca. I'm glad to hear't.
Isabella.   Sister, methinks you are too long
                                                      alone,   65
And lose much good time, sociable and honest.
I'm for the married life. I must praise that now.
Francisca. I cannot blame you, sister, to commend it.
You have happened well, no doubt, on a kind husband,
And that's not every woman's fortune, sister.   70
You know if he were any but my brother
My praises should not leave him yet so soon.
Isabella. I must acknowledge, sister, that my life
Is happily blest with him. He is no gamester
That ever I could find or hear of yet,   75
Nor midnight surfeiter. He does intend
To leave tobacco too.
Francisca.   Why here's a husband!
Isabella. He saw it did offend me and swore freely
He'd ne'er take pleasure in a toy again
That should displease me. Some knights' wives in town   80
Will have great hope, upon his reformation,
To bring their husbands' breaths into th'old fashion
And make 'em kiss like christians, not like pagans.
Francisca. I promise you, sister, 'twill be a worthy work
To put down all these pipers. 'Tis great pity   85
There should not be a statute against them,
As against fiddlers.
Isabella.   These good offices,

If you'd a husband, you might exercise
To th' good o'th' commonwealth, and do much profit.
Beside it is a comfort to a woman   90
T'have children, sister, a great blessing certainly.
Francisca. They will come fast enough.
Isabella.   Not so fast neither
As they're still welcome to an honest woman.
Francisca. [*Aside*] How near she comes to me! I protest she grates
My very skin.
Isabella.   Were I conceived with child,   95
Beshrew my heart, I should be so proud on't.
Francisca. That's natural. Pride is a kind of swelling.
[*Aside*] And yet I've small cause to be proud of mine.
Isabella. You are no good companion for a wife;
Get you a husband; prithee, sister, do,   100
That I may ask your counsel now and then.
'Twill mend your discourse much. You maids know nothing.
Francisca. No, we are fools; but commonly we prove
Quicker mothers than you that have husbands.
[*Aside*] I'm sure I shall else. I may speak for one.   105

Enter ANTONIO.

Antonio. [*Aside*] I will not look upon her. I'll pass by
And make as though I see her not.
Isabella.   Why, sir,
'Pray your opinion, by the way, with leave, sir;
I'm counselling your sister here to marry.
Antonio. To marry? Soft, the priest is not at leisure yet;   110
Some five year hence. Would you fain marry, sister?
Francisca. I have no such hunger to't, sir; [*Aside*] for I think
I've a good bit that well may stay my stomach,
As well as any that broke fast a sinner.
Antonio. Though she seem tall of growth, she's short in years   115
Of some that seem much lower. How old, sister?
Not seventeen, for a yard of lawn!
Francisca.   Not yet, sir.
Antonio. I told you so.
Francisca. [*Aside*] I would he'd laid a wager of old shirts rather,
I shall have more need of them shortly; and yet   120
A yard of lawn will serve for a christ'ning-cloth;
I have use for everything as my case stands.
Isabella. I care not if I try my voice this morning
But I have got a cold, sir, by your means.
Antonio. I'll strive to mend that fault.

Isabella.   I thank you, sir.   125
                                Song.
                    In a maiden-time professed,
                    Then we say that life is best;
                    Tasting once the married life,
                    Then we only praise the wife.
                    There's but one state more to try   130
                    Which makes women laugh or cry—
                    Widow, widow! Of these three,
                    The middle's best, and that give me.

Antonio. There's thy reward. [*Kisses her.*]
Isabella.   I will not grumble, sir,
        Like some musician; if more come, 'tis welcome.   135
Francisca. [*Aside*] Such tricks has made me do all that I have
                                                        done.
        Your kissing married folks spoils all the maids
        That ever live i'th' house with 'em. O here

        Enter ABERZANES [*and* Servants *carrying baked meats and*
                        bottles.]

        He comes with his bags and bottles. He was born
        To lead poor watermen and I.   140
Aberzanes. Go, fellows, into th' larder; let the bake-meats
        Be sorted by themselves.
Antonio.   Why, sir—
Aberzanes. Look the canary bottles be well stopped;
        The three of claret shall be drunk at dinner.
                                        [*Exeunt* Servants.]
Antonio. My good sir, you're too plenteous of these courtesies,   145
        Indeed you are. Forbear 'em, I beseech ye.
        I know no merit in me but poor love
        And a true friend's well-wishing, that can cause
        This kindness in excess. [*Aside*] I'th' state that I am,
        I shall go near to kick this fellow shortly   150
        And send him downstairs with his bag and baggage.
        Why comes he now I'm married? There's the point.
        [*To Aberzanes*] I pray forbear these things.
Aberzanes.   Alas, you know, sir,
        These idle toys, which you call courtesies,
        They cost me nothing but my servants' travail.   155
        One office must be kind, sir, to another—
        You know the fashion. What, the gentlewoman
        Your sister's sad methinks.
Antonio.   I know no cause she has.

Francisca. [*Aside*] Nor shall you, by my good will.
                    [*To Aberzanes*] What do you mean, sir?
    Shall I stay here to shame myself and you?   160
    The time may be tonight for aught you know.
Aberzanes. [*To her*] Peace! There's means wrought I tell thee.
Francisca.   [*To him*] Ay, sir, when?

            Enter SEBASTIAN [*disguised as* CELIO] *and* Gentleman.

Antonio. How now! What's he?
Isabella.   O, this is the man, sir,
    I entertained this morning for my service;
    Please you to give your liking.
Antonio.   Yes, he's welcome;   165
    I like him not amiss. [*To Sebastian*] Thou wouldst speak
                                                    business,
    Wouldst thou not?
Sebastian.   Yes; may it please you, sir,
    There is a gentleman from the northern parts
    Hath brought a letter, as it seems, in haste.
Antonio. From whom?
Gentleman.   Your bonny lady mother, sir.   170
                                        [*Gives letter.*]
Antonio. You're kindly welcome, sir. How doth she?
Gentleman. I left her heal verray well, sir.
[*Antonio.*] ([*Reads*] letter.) *I pray send your sister down with all*
    speed to me. I hope it will prove much for her good, in the way
    of her preferment. Fail me not, I desire you, son, nor let any   175
    excuse of her's withhold her. I have sent, ready furnished, horse
    and man for her.
Aberzanes. [*To Francisca*] Now, have I thought upon you?
Francisca.   [*To him*] Peace, good sir.
    You're worthy of a kindness another time.
Antonio. Her will shall be obeyed. Sister, prepare yourself,   180
    You must down with all speed.
Francisca.   [*Aside*] I know down I must;
    And good speed send me!
Antonio.   'Tis our mother's pleasure.
Francisca. Good sir, write back again, and certify her
    I'm at my heart's wish here. I'm with my friends
    And can be but well, say.
Antonio.   You shall pardon me, sister;   185
    I hold it no wise part to contradict her,
    Nor would I counsel you to't.
Francisca.   'Tis so uncouth

Living i'th' country now I'm used to th' city,
That I shall ne'er endure't.
Aberzanes.   Perhaps, forsooth,
   'Tis not her meaning you shall live there long;   190
   I do not think but after a month or so
   You'll be sent up again: that's my conceit.
   However, let her have her will.
Antonio.   Ay, good sir,
   Great reason 'tis she should.
Isabella.   I am sorry, sister,
   'Tis our hard fortune thus to part so soon.   195
Francisca. The sorrow will be mine.
Antonio.   Please you walk in, sir;
   We'll have one health into those northern parts
   Though I be sick at heart.
            Exeunt [ANTONIO, ISABELLA *and* Gentleman.]
Aberzanes.   Ay, sir, a deep one—
   [*To her*] Which you shall pledge too.
Francisca.   You shall pardon me:
   I have pledged one too deep already, sir.   200
Aberzanes. Peace; all's provided for. Thy wine's laid in,
   Sugar and spice. The place not ten mile hence.
   What cause have maids now to complain of men,
   When a farmhouse can make all whole again?
            Exeunt [ABERZANES *and* FRANCISCA.]
Sebastian. It takes; he's no content. How well she bears it yet!   205
   Hardly myself can find so much from her
   That am acquainted with the cold disease.
   O honesty's a rare wealth in a woman!
   It knows no want, at least will express none,
   Not in a look. Yet I'm not throughly happy.   210
   His ill does me no good. Well may it keep me
   From open rage and madness for a time,
   But I feel heart's grief in the same place still.
   What makes the greatest torment 'mongst lost souls?
   'Tis not so much the horror of their pains,   215
   Though they be infinite, as the loss of joys.
   It is that deprivation is the mother
   Of all the groans in hell and here on earth
   Of all the red sighs in the hearts of lovers.
   Still she's not mine, that can be no man's else   220
   Till I be nothing, if religion
   Have the same strength for me as't has for others.
   Holy vows witness that our souls were married!

Enter GASPERO *and* L[ORD] GOVERNOR, [*with* Attendants.
SEBASTIAN *retires.*]

Gaspero. Where are you, sir? Come, 'pray give your attendance.
    Here's my lord governor come.
Governor.   Where's our new kindred?   225
    Not stirring yet, I think?
Gaspero.   Yes, my good lord.
    Please you walk near?
Governor.   Come gentlemen, we'll enter.
                                [*Exeunt all but* SEBASTIAN.]
Sebastian. I've done't upon a breach; this's a less venture.   [*Exit.*]

[ACT II] SCENE ii

Enter ALMACHILDES.

Almachildes. What a mad toy took me to sup with witches?
    Fie of all drunken humours! By this hand
    I could beat myself when I think on't; and the rascals
    Made me good cheer too; and to my understanding then
    Ate some of every dish, and spoiled the rest.   5
    But coming to my lodging, I remember
    I was as hungry as a tired foot-post.
    What's this? [*Takes from his pocket a ribbon.*]
                    O, 'tis the charm her hagship gave me
    For my duchess' obstinate woman; wound about
    A threepenny silk ribbon of three colours,   10
    Necte tribus nodis ternos Amoretta colores.
    Amoretta!—why, there's her name indeed.
    Necte—Amoretta—again, two boughts;
    Nodo et Veneris dic vincula necte.
    Nay, if *Veneris* be one, I'm sure there's no dead flesh in't.   15
    If I should undertake to construe this now,
    I should make a fine piece of work of it,
    For few young gallants are given to good construction
    Of anything, hardly of their best friends' wives,
    Sisters or nieces. Let me see what I can do now.   20
    Necte tribus nodis—Nick of the tribe of noddies;
    Ternos colores—that makes turned colours;
    Nodo et Veneris—goes to his venery like a noddy;
    Dic vincula—with Dick the vintner's boy.
    Here were a sweet charm now, if this were the meaning on't;   25
    and very likely to overcome an honourable gentlewoman. The

whoreson old hellcat would have given me the brain of a cat
once, in my handkercher—I bad her make sauce with't with a
vengeance!—and a little bone in the nethermost part of a wolf's
tail—I bad her pick her teeth with't, with a pestilence! Nay this   30
is somewhat cleanly yet and handsome—a coloured ribbon? A
fine, gentle charm; a man may give't his sister, his brother's
wife, ordinarily. See, here she comes luckily.

Enter AMORETTA.

Amoretta. Blest powers, what secret sin have I committed
  That still you send this punishment upon me?   35
Almachildes. 'Tis but a gentle punishment; so take it.
Amoretta. Why, sir, what mean you? Will you ravish me?
Almachildes. What, in the gallery? and the sun peep in?
  There's fitter time and place.

    [*As he embraces her, he thrusts the ribbon into her bosom.*]

        [*Aside*] 'Tis in her bosom now.
Amoretta. Go, you're the rudest thing e'er came at court.   40
Almachildes. Well, well. I hope you'll tell me another tale
  Ere you be two hours older—a rude thing!
  I'll make you eat your word; I'll make all split else.   *Exit.*
Amoretta. Nay, now I think on't better, I'm to blame too.
  There's not a sweeter gentleman in court;   45
  Nobly descended too, and dances well.
  Beshrew my heart, I'll take him when there's time;
  He will be catched up quickly. The duchess says
  She's some employment for him and has sworn me
  To use my best art in't. Life of my joys,   50
  There were good stuff! I will not trust her with him.
  I'll call him back again. He must not keep
  Out of my sight so long; I shall go mad then.

Enter DUCHESS.

Duchess. [*Aside*] He lives not now to see tomorrow spent
  If this means take effect, as there's no hardness in't.   55
  Last night he played his horrid game again,
  Came to my bedside at the full of midnight,
  And in his hand that fatal, fearful cup;
  Waked me and forced me pledge him, to my trembling,
  And my dead father's scorn. That wounds my sight   60
  That his remembrance should be raised in spite.
  But either his confusion or mine ends it.
  [*To Amoretta*] O, Amoretta! Hast thou met him yet?
  Speak, wench, hast done that for me?

Amoretta.   What, good madam?

Duchess. Destruction of my hopes! Dost ask that now?   65
    Didst thou not swear to me, out of thy hate
    To Almachildes, thou'dst dissemble him
    A loving entertainment, and a meeting
    Where I should work my will?

Amoretta.   Good, madam, pardon me.
    A loving entertainment I do protest   70
    Myself to give him—with all speed I can too!—
    But as I'm yet a maid, a perfect one
    As the old time was wont to afford, when
    There was few tricks and little cunning stirring,
    I can dissemble none that will serve your turn.   75
    He must have e'en a right one, and a plain one.

Duchess. Thou mak'st me doubt thy health. Speak, art thou well?

Amoretta. O, never better, if he would make haste
    And come back quickly. He stays now too long.
              [*The ribbon falls out of her bosom.*]

Duchess. [*Aside*] I'm quite lost in this woman. What's that fell   80
    Out of her bosom now? Some love-token?   [*Picks up ribbon.*]

Amoretta. Nay, I'll say that for him: he's the uncivilest gentleman
    And every way desertless.

Duchess.   [*Aside*] Who's that now
    She discommends so fast?

Amoretta.   I could not love him, madam,
    Of any man in court.

Duchess.   What's he now, prithee?   85

Amoretta. Who should it be but Almachildes, madam?
    I never hated man so deeply yet.

Duchess. As Almachildes?

Amoretta.   I am sick, good madam,
    When I but hear him named.

Duchess.   How is this possible?
    But now thou saidst thou lovedst him, and didst raise him   90
    'Bove all the court in praises.

Amoretta.   How great people
    May speak their pleasure, madam! But surely I
    Should think the worse of my tongue while I lived then.

Duchess. No longer have I patience to forbear thee,
    Thou that retaint'st an envious soul to goodness!   95
    He is a gentleman deserves as much
    As ever fortune yet bestowed on man:
    The glory and prime lustre of our court.
    Nor can there any but ourself be worthy of him;

And take you notice of that now from me,   100
Say you have warning on't. If you did love him,
You must not now.
Amoretta.   Let your grace never fear it.
Duchess. Thy name is Amoretta as ours is;
It's made me love and trust thee.
Amoretta.   And my faithfulness
Has appeared well i'th' proof still. Has't not, madam?   105
Duchess. But if't fail now, 'tis nothing.
Amoretta.   Then it shall not.
I know he will not be long from fluttering
About this place, now he's had a sight of me,
And I'll perform
In all that I vowed, madam, faithfully.   110
Duchess. Then am I blest both in revenge and love
And thou shalt taste the sweetness.   *Exit.*
Amoretta.   What your aims be
I list not to enquire. All I desire
Is to preserve a competent honesty
Both for mine own and his use that shall have me,   115
Whose luck soe'er it be.

Enter ALMACHILDES.

                        O, he's returned already;
I knew he would not fail.
Almachildes.   [*Aside*] It works by this time
Or the devil's in't, I think. I'll ne'er trust witch else,
Nor sup with 'em this twelvemonth.
Amoretta.   [*Aside*] I must soothe
                                            him now;
And 'tis great pain to do't against one's stomach.   120
Almachildes. Now, Amoretta!
Amoretta.   Now you're welcome, sir,
If you'd come always thus.
Almachildes.   O, am I so?
Is the case altered since?
Amoretta.   If you'd be ruled,
And know your times, 'twere somewhat; a great comfort.
'Las, I could be as loving and as venturous   125
As any woman—we're all flesh and blood, man—
If you could play the game out modestly
And not betray your hand. I must have care, sir;
You know I have a marriage-time to come,
And that's for life. Your best folks will be merry,   130
But look to the main chance—that's reputation—

And then do what they list.
Almachildes.   Wilt hear my oath?
　By the sweet health of youth, I will be careful
　And never prate on't; nor like a cunning snarer
　Make thy clipped name the bird to call in others.   135
Amoretta. Well, yielding then to such conditions
　As my poor bashfulness shall require from you,
　I shall yield shortly after.
Almachildes.   I'll consent to 'em
　And may thy sweet humility be a pattern
　For all proud women living.
Amoretta.   They're beholding to you.   140

                    Exeunt.

[ACT II] SCENE iii

Enter ABERZANES *and an* Old Woman [*carrying a baby.*]

Aberzanes. So, so, away with him! I love to get 'em,
　But not to keep 'em. Dost thou know the house?
[*Old*] *Woman.* No matter for the house, I know the porch.
Aberzanes. There's sixpence more for that. Away, keep close.
                    [*Exit* Old Woman.]
　My tailor told me he sent away a maid-servant   5
　Well ballast of all sides, within these nine days—
　His wife ne'er dreamed on't!—gave the drab ten pound,
　And she ne'er troubles him. A common fashion
　He told me 'twas to rid away a scape,
　And I have sent him this for't. I remember   10
　A friend of mine once served a prating tradesman
　Just on this fashion, to a hair in troth.
　'Tis a good ease to a man: you can swell a maid up
　And rid her for ten pound. There's the purse back again
　Whate'er becomes of your money or your maid.   15
　This comes of bragging now. It's well for the boy too;
　He'll get an excellent trade by't, and on Sundays
　Go like a gentleman that has pawned his rapier.
　He need not care what countryman his father was,
　Nor what his mother was when he was gotten.   20
　The boy will do well, certain, give him grace
　To have a quick hand and convey things cleanly,
　'Twill be his own another day.

                    Enter FRANCISCA.

                    O, well said!

Art almost furnished? There's such a toil always
To set a woman to horse, a mighty trouble.   25
The letter came to your brother's hands I know
On Thursday last by noon; you were expected there
Yesterday night.

Francisca.   It makes the better, sir.

Aberzanes. We must take heed we ride through all the puddles
Twixt this and that now, that your safe-guard there   30
May be most probably dabbled.

Francisca.   [*Looks in mirror.*] Alas, sir,
I never marked till now—I hate myself—
How monstrous thin I look!

Aberzanes.   Not monstrous neither:
A little sharp i'th'nose, like a country woodcock.

Francisca. Fie, fie! How pale I am! I shall betray myself.   35
I would you'd box me well and handsomely
To get me into colour.

Aberzanes.   Not I, pardon me.
That let a husband do when he has married you.
A friend at court will never offer that.
Come, how much spice and sugar have you left now   40
At this poor one-month's voyage?

Francisca.   Sure not much, sir.
I think some quarter of a pound of sugar
And half an ounce of spice.

Aberzanes.   Here's no sweet charge!
And there was thirty pound, good weight and true,
Beside what my man stole when't was a-weighing,   45
And that was three pound more, I'll speak with least.
The Rhenish wine, is't all run out in caudles too?

Francisca. Do you ask that, sir? 'Tis of a week's departure.
You see what 'tis now to get children, sir.
                    [*Enter* Boy.]

Boy. Your mares are ready both, sir.

Aberzanes.   Come we'll up then.   50
Youth, give my sister a straight wand. There's twopence.

Boy. I'll give her a fine whip, sir.

Aberzanes.   No, no, no!
Though we have both deserved it.

Boy.   Here's a new one.

Aberzanes. Prithee talk to us of no whips, good boy;
My heart aches when I see 'em. Let's away.   *Exeunt.* 55

ACT III

SCENE i

Enter DUCHESS *leading* ALMACHILDES *(blindfold).*

Almachildes. This's you that was a maid? How are you born
    To deceive men! I'd thought to have married you;
    I had been finely handled, had I not?
    I'll say that man is wise ever hereafter
    That tries his wife beforehand. 'Tis no marvel   5
    You should profess such bashfulness to blind one,
    As if you durst not look a man i'th' face,
    Your modesty would blush so. Why do you not run
    And tell the duchess now? Go, you should tell all.
    Let her know this too.

            [*Attempts to free himself.*]

                Why here's the plague now!   10
    'Tis hard at first to win 'em; when they're gotten
    There's no way to be rid on 'em. They stick
    To a man like bird-lime. My oath's out—
    Will you release me? I'll release myself else.
Duchess. Nay, sure I'll bring you to your sight again.   15

        [*Removing the blindfold from his eyes.*]

    Say thou must either die or kill the duke,
    For one of them thou must do.
Almachildes.   How, good madam?
Duchess. Thou hast thy choice, and to that purpose, sir,
    I've given thee knowledge now of what thou hast,
    And what thou must do to be worthy on't.   20
    You must not think to come by such a fortune
    Without desert; that were unreasonable.
    He that's not born to honour must not look
    To have it come with ease to him. He must win't.
    Take but into thine actions wit and courage,   25
    That's all we ask of thee. But if through weakness
    Of a poor spirit thou deniest me this,
    Think but how thou shalt die, as I'll work means for't,
    No murderer ever like thee; for I purpose
    To call this subtle, sinful snare of mine   30
    An act of force from thee. Thou'rt proud and youthful;
    I shall be believed. Besides thy wantonness

Is at this hour in question 'mongst our women,
Which will make ill for thee.
Almachildes.   I had hard chance
To light upon this pleasure that's so costly.   35
'Tis not content with what a man can do
And give him breath, but seeks to have that too.
Duchess. Well, take thy choice.
Almachildes.   I see no choice in't, madam,
For 'tis all death methinks.
Duchess.   Thou'st an ill sight then
Of a young man. 'Tis death if thou refuse it;   40
And say my zeal has warned thee. But consenting,
'Twill be new life, great honour, and my love,
Which in perpetual bands I'll fasten to thee.
Almachildes. How, madam?
Duchess.   I'll do't religiously,
Make thee my husband. May I lose all sense   45
Of pleasure in life else and be more miserable
Than ever creature was! For nothing lives
But has a joy in somewhat.
Almachildes.   Then by all
The hopeful fortunes of a young man's rising
I will perform it, madam.
Duchess.   There's a pledge then   50
Of a duchess' love for thee. [*Kisses him.*] And now trust me
For thy most happy safety. I will choose
That time shall never hurt thee. When a man
Shows resolution and there's worth in him
I'll have a care of him. Part now for this time   55
But still be near about us, till thou canst
Be nearer, that's ourself.
Almachildes.   And that I'll venture hard for.
Duchess. Good speed to thee!   *Exeunt.*

[ACT III] SCENE ii

Enter GASPERO *and* FLORIDA.

Florida. Prithee be careful of me, very careful now.
Gaspero. I warrant you. He that cannot be careful of a quean, can
be careful of nobody. 'Tis every man's humour that. I should
ne'er look to a wife half so handsomely.
Florida. O softly, sweet sir! Should your mistress meet me now in   5
her own house, I were undone for ever.

Gaspero. Never fear her. She's at her prick-song close;
 There's all the joy she has or takes delight in.
 Look, here's the garden key, my master gave't me,
 And willed me to be careful. Doubt not you on't. 10
Florida. Your master is a noble complete gentleman
 And does a woman all the right that may be.

    Enter SEBASTIAN [*as* CELIO.]

Sebastian. How now? What's she?
Gaspero.   A kind of doubtful creature;
 I'll tell thee more anon. [*Exeunt* GASPERO *with* FLORIDA.]
Sebastian.   I know that face
 To be a strumpet's, or mine eye is envious 15
 And would fain wish it so where I would have it.
 I fail if the condition of this fellow
 Wears not about it a strong scent of baseness.
 I saw her once before here, five days since 'tis,
 And the same wary, panderous diligence 20
 Was then bestowed on her; she came altered then
 And more inclining to the city-tuck.
 Whom should this piece of transformation visit
 After the common courtesy of frailty
 In our house here? Surely not any servant; 25
 They are not kept so lusty, she so low.
 I'm at a strange stand: love and luck assist me!
 The truth I shall win from him by false play.

    Enter GASPERO.

 He's now returned. [*To Gaspero*] Well, sir, as you were
            saying,
 Go forward with your tale.
Gaspero.   What, I know nothing. 30
Sebastian. The gentlewoman?
Gaspero.   She's gone out at back-door now.
Sebastian. Then farewell she, and you, if that be all.
Gaspero. Come, come, thou shalt have more. I have no power
 To lock myself up from thee.
Sebastian.   So methinks.
Gaspero. You shall not think, trust me, sir, you shall not. 35
 Your ear. She's one o' th' falling family,
 A quean my master keeps; she lies at Rutneys.
Sebastian. Is't possible? I thought I had seen her somewhere.
Gaspero. I tell you truth sincerely. She's been thrice here
 By stealth within these ten days, and departed still 40

With pleasure and with thanks, sir; 'tis her luck.
Surely I think if ever there were man
Bewitched in this world, 'tis my master, sirrah.
Sebastian. Thinkst thou so, Gasper?
Gaspero.   O, sir, too apparent.
Sebastian. [*Aside*] This may prove happy. 'Tis the likeliest means   45
    That fortune yet e'er showed me.

Enter ISABELLA [with a letter.]

Isabella.   You're both here now
    And strangers newly lighted! Where's your attendance?
Sebastian. [*Aside*] I know what makes you waspish. A pox on't,
    She'll every day be angry now at nothing.

Exeunt [GASPERO and SEBASTIAN.]

Isabella. I'll call her stranger ever in my heart.   50
    She's killed the name of sister through base lust
    And fled to shifts. O, how a brother's good thoughts
    May be beguiled in woman! Here's a letter,
    Found in her absence, reports strangely of her
    And speaks her impudence. She's undone herself—   55
    I could not hold from weeping when I read it—
    Abused her brother's house and his good confidence.
    'Twas done not like herself. I blame her much.
    But if she can but keep it from his knowledge
    I will not grieve him first. It shall not come   60
    By my means to his heart.

Enter GASPERO.

                              Now, sir, the news?
Gaspero. You called 'em strangers. 'Tis my master's sister,
                                                    madam.
Isabella. O, is't so? She's welcome. Who's come with her?
Gaspero. I see none but Aberzanes.   [*Exit* GASPERO]
Isabella.   He's enough
    To bring a woman to confusion,   65
    More than a wiser man or a far greater.
    A letter came last week to her brother's hands
    To make way for her coming up again,
    After her shame was lightened; and she writ there,
    The gentleman her mother wished her to,   70
    Taking a violent surfeit at a wedding,
    Died ere she came to see him. What strange cunning
    Sin helps a woman to! Here she comes now.

Enter ABERZANES and FRANCISCA.

Sister, you're welcome home again.
Francisca.   Thanks, sweet sister.
Isabella. You've had good speed.
Francisca.   [*Aside*] What says she?
                    [*To her*] I have made   75
All the best speed I could.
Isabella.   I well believe you.
Sir, we're all much beholding to your kindness.
Aberzanes. My service ever, madam, to a gentlewoman.
I took a bonny mare I keep, and met her
Some ten mile out of town—eleven I think—   80
'Twas at the stump I met you, I remember,
At bottom of the hill.
Francisca.   'Twas there about, sir.
Aberzanes. Full eleven then by the rod, if they were measured.
Isabella. You look ill, methinks. Have you been sick of late?
'Troth, very bleak, doth she not? How think you, sir?   85
Aberzanes. No, no; a little sharp with riding, she's rid sore.
Francisca. I ever look lean after a journey, sister;
One shall do that has travelled, travelled hard.
Aberzanes. Till evening I commend you to yourselves, ladies.
                                        Exit.

Isabella. [*Aside*] And that's best trusting to, if you were hanged.   90
[*To Francisca*] You're well acquainted with his hand went
                                        out now?

Francisca. His hand?
Isabella.   I speak of nothing else. I think 'tis there.

[*Giving letter.*]

Please you to look upon't; and when you've done
If you did weep, it could not be amiss,
A sign you could say grace after a full meal.   95
You had not need look paler, yet you do.
'Twas ill done to abuse yourself and us,
To wrong so good a brother and the thoughts
That we both held of you. I did doubt you much
Before our marriage-day; but then my strangeness   100
And better hope still kept me off from speaking.
Yet may you find a kind and peaceful sister of me,
If you desist here and shake hands with folly,
Which you've more cause to do than I to wish you.
As truly as I bear a love to goodness,   105
Your brother knows not yet on't, nor shall ever
For my part, so you leave his company.

But if I find you impudent in sinning,
I will not keep't an hour, nay prove your enemy
And you know who will aid me. As you've goodness,   110
You may make use of this; I'll leave it with you.   *Exit.*
Francisca. Here's a sweet churching after a woman's labour
And a fine 'Give you joy'! [*Addressing the letter.*]
                                        Why, where the devil
Lay you to be found out? The sudden hurry
Of hastening to prevent shame brought shame forth.   115
That's still the curse of all lascivious stuff:
Misdeeds could never yet be wary enough.
Now must I stand in fear of every look,
Nay, tremble at a whisper. She can keep it secret?
That's very likely and a woman too!   120
I'm sure I could not do't; and I am made
As well as she can be for any purpose.
'Twould never stay with me two days—I have cast it—
The third would be a terrible sick day with me,
Not possible to bear it. Should I then   125
Trust to her strength in't, that lies every night
Whispering the day's news in a husband's ear?
No; and I have thought upon the means. Blest fortune,
I must be quit with her in the same fashion
Or else 'tis nothing. There's no way like it   130
To bring her honesty into question cunningly.
My brother will believe small likelihoods,
Coming from me too. I, lying now i'th' house,
May work things to my will, beyond conceit too.
Disgrace her first, her tale will ne'er be heard;   135
I learned that counsel first of a sound guard.
I do suspect Gasper, my brother's squire there,
Had some hand in this mischief, for he's cunning
And I perhaps may fit him.

                    Enter ANTONIO.

Antonio.   Your sister told me
You were come. Thou'rt welcome.
Francisca.   Where is she?   140
Antonio. Who? My wife?
Francisca.   Ay, sir.
Antonio.   Within.
Francisca. Not within hearing, think you?
Antonio.   Within hearing?
What's thy conceit in that? Why shak'st thy head so?

And lookst so pale and poorly?
Francisca.   I'm a fool indeed
    To take such grief for others—for your fortune, sir.   145
Antonio. My fortune? Worse things yet? Farewell life then!
Francisca. I fear you're much deceived, sir, in this woman.
Antonio. Who? In my wife? Speak low! Come hither, softly,
                                                sister.
Francisca. I love her as a woman you made choice of;
    But when she wrongs you, natural love is touched, brother,   150
    And that will speak you know.
Antonio.   I trust it will.
Francisca. I held a shrewd suspicion of her lightness
    At first, when I went down, which made me haste the sooner,
    But more to make amends; at my return now
    I found apparent signs.
Antonio.   Apparent, sayst thou?   155
Francisca. Ay, and of base lust too; that makes th' affliction.
Antonio. There has been villainy wrought upon me then,
   'Tis too plain now.
Francisca.   Happy are they, I say still,
    That have their sisters living i'th' house with 'em,
    Their mothers or some kindred, a great comfort   160
    To all poor married men. It is not possible
    A young wife can abuse a husband then,
    'Tis found straight. But swear secrecy to this, brother.
Antonio. To this, and all thou wilt have.
Francisca.   Then this follows, sir.

                [*Whispers to him.*]

Antonio. I praise thy counsel well. I'll put't in use straight.   165
    See where she comes herself.   [*Exit* FRANCISCA.]

            Enter ISABELLA.

                Kind, honest lady,
    I must now borrow a whole fortnight's leave of thee.
Isabella. How, sir! A fortnight's?
Antonio. It may be but ten days, I know not yet.
    'Tis business for the state and't must be done.   170
Isabella. I wish good speed to't then.
Antonio.   Why that was well spoke.
    I'll take but a foot-boy. I need no more.
    The rest I'll leave at home to do you service.
Isabella. Use your own pleasure, sir.
Antonio.   Till my return

You'll be good company, my sister and you.   175
Isabella. We shall make shift, sir.
Antonio.   I'm glad now she's come,
    And so the wishes of my love to both.   Exit.
Isabella. And our good prayers with you, sir.

                    Enter SEBASTIAN [as CELIO.]

Sebastian.   [Aside] Now my fortune!
    [To Isabella] By your kind favour, madam.
Isabella.   With me, sir?
Sebastian. The words shall not be many, but the faithfulness   180
    And true respect that is included in 'em
    Is worthy your attention, and may put upon me
    The fair repute of a just, honest servant.
Isabella. What's here to do, sir,
    There's such great preparation toward?   185
Sebastian. In brief, that goodness in you is abused, madam;
    You have the married life but 'tis a strumpet
    That has the joy on't and the fruitfulness;
    There goes away your comfort.
Isabella.   How! A strumpet?
Sebastian. Of five years' cost and upwards: a dear mischief,   190
    As they are all of 'em. His fortnight's journey
    Is to that country, if it be not rudeness
    To speak the truth. I have found it all out, madam.
Isabella. Thou'st found out thine own ruin; for to my knowledge
    Thou dost belie him basely. I dare swear   195
    He's a gentleman as free from that folly
    As ever took religious life upon him.
Sebastian. Be not too confident to your own abuse, madam.
    Since I have begun the truth, neither your frowns—
    The only curses that I have on earth   200
    Because my means depends upon your service—
    Nor all the execration of man's fury
    Shall put me off. Though I be poor, I'm honest,
    And too just in this business. I perceive now
    Too much respect and faithfulness to ladies   205
    May be a wrong to servants.
Isabella.   Art thou yet
    So impudent to stand in't?
Sebastian.   Are you yet so cold, madam,
    In the belief on't? There my wonder's fixed,
    Having such blessed health and youth about you,
    Which makes the injury mighty.

Isabella.   Why, I tell thee   210
    It were too great a fortune for thy lowness
    To find out such a thing! Thou dost not look
    As if thou'rt made for't. By the precious sweets of love
    I would give half my wealth for such a bargain,
    And think 'twere bought too cheap. Thou canst not guess   215
    Thy means and happiness, should I find this true.
    First, I'd prefer thee to the lord, my uncle,
    He's governor of Ravenna; all the advancements
    I'th'kingdom flows from him. What need I boast that
    Which common fame can teach thee?
Sebastian.   Then thus, madam: 220
    Since I presume now on your height of spirit
    And your regard to your own youth and fruitfulness,
    Which every woman naturally loves and covets,
    Accept but of my labour in directions,
    You shall both find your wrongs, which you may right   225
    At your own pleasure, yet not missed tonight
    Here in the house neither. None shall take notice
    Of any absence in you, as I have thought on't.
Isabella. Do this and take my praise and thanks for ever.
Sebastian. As I deserve, I wish 'em and will serve you.   *Exeunt.*   230

[ACT III] SCENE iii

Enter HECATE, [STADLIN, HOPPO, *three other*] Witches *and*
    FIRESTONE [*carrying eggs, herbs, etc.*]

Hecate. The moon's a gallant; see how brisk she rides!
Stadlin. Here's a rich evening, Hecate.
Hecate.   Ay, is't not, wenches,
    To take a journey of five thousand mile?
Hoppo. Ours will be more tonight.
Hecate.   O, 'twill be precious!
    Heard you the owl yet?
Stadlin.   Briefly in the copse   5
    As we came through now.
Hecate.   'Tis high time for us then.
Stadlin. There was a bat hung at my lips three times
    As we came through the woods and drank her fill.
    Old Puckle saw her.
Hecate.   You are fortunate still;
    The very screech-owl lights upon your shoulder   10
    And woos you like a pigeon. Are you furnished?

Have you your ointments?
Stadlin.   All.
Hecate.   Prepare to flight then.
    I'll overtake you swiftly.
Stadlin.   Hie thee, Hecate:
    We shall be up betimes.
Hecate.   I'll reach you quickly.
                        [*Exeunt all the* Witches *except* HECATE.]
Firestone. They're all going a-birding tonight. They talk of fowls   15
    i'th' air that fly by day, I am sure they'll be a company of foul
    sluts there tonight. If we have not mortality after it, I'll be
    hanged, for they are able to putrefy it, to infect a whole region.
    She spies me now.
Hecate.   What, Firestone, our sweet son?
Firestone. [*Aside*] A little sweeter than some of you, or a dunghill   20
    were too good for me.
Hecate. How much hast here?
Firestone.   Nineteen and all brave plump ones,
    Besides six lizard's and three serpentine eggs.
Hecate. Dear and sweet boy; what herbs hast thou?
Firestone. I have some marmartin and mandragon.   25
Hecate. *Marmaritin* and *mandragora* thou wouldst say.
    Here's *panax* too! I thank thee.
Firestone.   My pan aches I am sure
    With kneeling down to cut 'em.
Hecate.   And *selago*,
    Hedge-hyssop too: how near he goes my cuttings!
    Were they all cropped by moonlight?
Firestone.   Every blade of 'em,   30
    Or I am a moon-calf, mother.
Hecate.   Hie thee home with 'em;
    Look well to the house tonight; I am for aloft.
Firestone. [*Aside*] Aloft, quoth you? I would you would break your
    neck once, that I might have all quickly! [*Music in the air.*] [*To
    Hecate*] Hark, hark, mother! They are above the steeple al-   35
    ready, flying over your head with a noise of musicians.
Hecate. They are there indeed. Help, help me! I'm too late else.

                        Song.

[*Voices.*] (*in the air.*) *Come away, come away,*
                        Hecate, Hecate, come away!
Hecate.   *I come, I come, I come, I come,*   40
                        With all the speed I may,
                        With all the speed I may.

	Where's Stadlin?	
[Voice.] *(in the air.)*	Here.	
Hecate.	Where's Puckle?	
[Voices.] *(in the air.)*	Here.	
	And Hoppo too and Hellwain too;	45
	We lack but you, we lack but you;	
	Come away, make up the count.	
Hecate.	I will but 'noint, and then I mount.	

[HECATE *anoints herself.*]

| [Malkin.] *(above)* | There's one comes down to fetch his dues; | |
| | A kiss, a coll, a sip of blood; | 50 |

([MALKIN], *a* Spirit *like a Cat descends.*)

	And why thou stay'st so long	
	I muse, I muse.	
	Since the air's so sweet and good.	
Hecate.	O, art thou come?	
	What news, what news?	55
[Malkin.]	All goes still to our delight,	
	Either come or else	
	Refuse, refuse.	
Hecate.	Now I am furnished for the flight.	

[MALKIN *sings.*]

Firestone. Hark, hark? The cat sings a brave treble in her own   60
language!
Hecate. (Going up [with MALKIN.]) Now I go, now I fly,
Malkin, my sweet spirit, and I.
O, what a dainty pleasure 'tis
To ride in the air   65
When the moon shines fair.
And sing and dance and toy and kiss;
Over woods, high rocks and mountains,
Over seas, our mistress' fountains,
Over steeples, towers and turrets   70
We fly by night, 'mongst troops of spirits;
No ring of bells to our ears sounds,
No howls of wolves, no yelps of hounds.
No, not the noise of water's breach
Or cannon's throat our height can reach.   75
| [Voices.] *(above)* | No ring of bells, etc. |

Firestone. Well, mother, I thank your kindness. You must be gam-
bolling i'th' air, and leave me to walk here like a fool and a
mortal.   *Exit.*

ACT IV

Enter ALMACHILDES.

Almachildes. Though the fates have endued me with a pretty kind
of lightness that I can laugh at the world in a corner on't, and
can make myself merry on fasting-nights to rub out a supper—
which were a precious quality in a young formal student—yet,
let the world know, there is some difference betwixt my jovial   5
condition and the lunary state of madness. I am not quite out of
my wits. I know a bawd from an aqua-vitae shop, a strumpet
from wildfire and a beadle from brimstone. Now shall I try the
honesty of a great woman soundly. She reckoning the duke's
made away, I'll be hanged if I be not the next now. If I trust her   10
as she's a woman, let one of her long hairs wind about my heart,
and be the end of me—which were a piteous lamentable
tragedy and might be entitled *A fair warning for all hair-
bracelets.*
Already there's an insurrection   15
Among the people. They are up in arms
Not out of any reason, but their wills,
Which are in them their saints, sweating and swearing,
Out of their zeal to rudeness, that no stranger,
As they term her, shall govern over them.   20
They say they'll raise a duke among themselves first.

Enter DUCHESS.

Duchess. O, Almachildes, I perceive already
 Our loves are born to crosses. We're beset
 By multitudes; and, which is worse, I fear me
 Unfriended too of any. My chief care   25
 Is for thy sweet youth's safety.
Almachildes.   [*Aside*] He that believes you not
 Goes the right way to heaven, o' my conscience!
Duchess. There is no trusting of 'em. They are all as barren
 In pity as in faith. He that puts confidence
 In them dies openly to the sight of all men,   30
 Not with his friends and neighbours in peace private,
 But as his shame so his cold farewell is
 Public and full of noise. But keep you close, sir,
 Not seen of any, till I see the way
 Plain for your safety. I expect the coming   35

Of the lord governor whom I will flatter
With fair entreaties to appease their wildness,
And before him take a great grief upon me
For the duke's death, his strange and sudden loss;
And when a quiet comes expect thy joys.   40

Almachildes. [*Aside*] I do expect now to be made away
    'Twixt this and Tuesday night; if I live Wednesday
    Say I have been careful and shunned spoon-meat.   *Exit.*

Duchess. This fellow lives too long after the deed,
    I'm weary of his sight. He must die quickly   45
    Or I've small hope of safety. My great aim's
    At the lord governor's love; he is a spirit
    Can sway and countenance; these obey and crouch.
    My guiltiness had need of such a master
    That with a beck can suppress multitudes   50
    And dim misdeeds with radiance of his glory,
    Not to be seen with dazzled, popular eyes.
    And here behold him come.

        Enter L[ORD] GOVERNOR [*attended by* Gentlemen.]

Governor.   Return back to 'em,
    Say we desire 'em to be friends of peace
    Till they hear farther from us.   [*Exeunt* Gentlemen.]

Duchess.   O my lord,   55
    I fly unto the pity of your nobleness,
    The grieved'st lady that was e'er beset
    With storms of sorrows or wild rage of people.
    Never was woman's grief for loss of lord
    Dearer than mine to me.

Governor.   There's no right done   60
    To him now, madam, by wrong done to yourself.
    Your own good wisdom may instruct you so far;
    And for the people's tumult, which oft grows
    From liberty or rankness of long peace,
    I'll labour to restrain as I've begun, madam.   65

Duchess. My thanks and prayers shall ne'er forget you, sir.
    And in time to come, my love.

Governor.   Your love, sweet madam?
    You make my joys too happy. I did covet
    To be the fortunate man that blessing visits,
    Which I'll esteem the crown and full reward   70
    Of service present and deserts to come.
    It is a happiness I'll be bold to sue for
    When I have set a calm upon these spirits

That now are up for ruin.
Duchess.   Sir, my wishes
Are so well met in yours, so fairly answered   75
And nobly recompensed, it makes me suffer
In those extremes that few have ever felt;
To hold two passions in one heart at once
Of gladness and of sorrow.
Governor.   Then as the olive
Is the meek ensign of fair fruitful peace,   80
So is this kiss of yours.   [*Kisses her.*]
Duchess.   Love's power be with you, sir.
Governor. [*Aside*] How she's betrayed her; may I breathe no
                                                        longer
Than to do virtue service, and bring forth
The fruits of noble thoughts, honest and loyal.
This will be worth th'observing; and I'll do't.   *Exit.*   85
Duchess. What a sure happiness confirms joy to me,
Now in the times of my most imminent dangers!
I looked for ruin, and increase of honour
Meets me auspiciously. But my hopes are clogged now
With an unworthy weight: there's the misfortune.   90
What course shall I take now with this young man,
For he must be no hind'rance? I have thought on't.
I'll take some witch's counsel for his end,
That will be sur'st. Mischief is mischief's friend.   *Exit.*

[ACT IV] SCENE ii

Enter SEBASTIAN *and* FERNANDO.

Sebastian. If ever you knew force of love in life, sir,
Give to mine pity.
Fernando.   You do ill to doubt me.
Sebastian. I could make bold with no friend seemlier
Than with yourself because you were in presence
At our vow-making.
Fernando.   I'm a witness to't.   5
Sebastian. Then you best understand of all men living
This is no wrong I offer, no abuse
Either to faith or friendship; for we're registered
Husband and wife in heaven, though there wants that
Which often keeps licentious man in awe   10
From starting from their wedlocks, the knot public.

'Tis in our souls knit fast, and how more precious
The soul is than the body, so much judge
The sacred and celestial tie within us
More than the outward form which calls but witness   15
Here upon earth to what is done in heaven.
Though I must needs confess the least is honourable,
As an ambassador sent from a king
Has honour by the employment, yet there's greater
Dwells in the king that sent him; so in this.   20
Fernando. I approve all you speak and will appear to you
A faithful, pitying friend.

Enter FLORIDA.

Sebastian.   Look, there is she, sir,
One good for nothing but to make use of;
And I'm constrained to employ her to make all things
Plain, easy and probable; for when she comes   25
And finds one here that claims him, as I've taught
Both this to do't and he to compound with her,
'Twill stir belief the more of such a business.
Fernando. I praise the carriage well.
Sebastian.   [*To Florida*] Hark you, sweet mistress,
I shall do you a simple turn in this;   30
For she disgracèd thus, you are in favour
For ever with her husband.
Florida.   That's my hope, sir.
I would not take the pains else. Have you the keys
Of the garden-side that I may get betimes in
Closely and take her lodging?
Sebastian.   Yes, I have thought upon you.   35
Here be the keys.   [*Giving keys.*]
Florida.   Marry and thanks, sweet sir;
Set me a-work so still.
Sebastian.   [*Aside*] Your joys are false ones;
You're like to lie alone; you'll be deceived
Of the bedfellow you look for, else my purpose
Were in an ill case. He's on his fortnight's journey;   40
You'll find cold comfort there. A dream will be
Even the best market you can make tonight.
[*To her*] She'll not be long now; you may lose no time
                                             neither.
If she but take you at the door 'tis enough.
When a suspect doth catch once, it burns mainly.   45
There may you end your business and as cunningly

As if you were i'th' chamber, if you please
To use but the same art.
Florida.   What need you urge that
Which comes so naturally I cannot miss on't?
What makes the devil so greedy of a soul   50
But 'cause he's lost his own, to all joys lost?
So 'tis our trade to set snares for other women
'Cause we were once caught ourselves.   [*Exit.*]
Sebastian.   A sweet allusion!
Hell and a whore it seems are partners then
In one ambition. Yet thou'rt here deceived now.   55
Thou canst set none to hurt or wrong her honour;
It rather makes it perfect.
                    [*Embracing* FERNANDO.] Best of friends,
That ever love's extremities were blessed with,
I feed mine arms with thee and call my peace
The offspring of thy friendship. I will think   60
This night my wedding-night; and with a joy
As reverend as religion can make man's,
I will embrace this blessing. Honest actions
Are laws unto themselves, and that good fear
Which is on others forced, grows kindly there.   65

                    [*Knocking within.*]

Fernando. Hark, hark! One knocks. Away, sir, 'tis she certainly.
                              [*Exit* SEBASTIAN.]
It sounds much like a woman's jealous 'larum.

                    Enter ISABELLA.

Isabella. By your leave, sir.
Fernando.   You're welcome, gentlewoman.
Isabella. [*Aside*] Our ladyship then stands us in no stead now;
          [*To Fernando*] One word in private, sir. [*Whispers to him.*]
Fernando.   No, surely, forsooth,   70
There is no such here; you've mistook the house.
Isabella. O, sir, that have I not. Excuse me there.
I come not with such ignorance; think not so, sir.
'Twas told me at the entering of your house here
By one that knows him too well.
Fernando.   Who should that be?   75
Isabella. Nay, sir, betraying is not my profession.
But here I know he is; and I presume
He would give me admittance if he knew on't,
As one on's nearest friends.

Fernando.   You're not his wife, forsooth?
Isabella. Yes, by my faith, am I.
Fernando.   Cry you mercy then, lady.   80
Isabella. [*Aside*] She goes here by the name on's wife: good stuff!
    But the bold strumpet never told me that.
Fernando. We are so oft deceived that let out lodgings,
    We know not whom to trust. 'Tis such a world,
    There are so many odd tricks now-a-days   85
    Put upon housekeepers.
Isabella.   Why, do you think I'd wrong
    You or the reputation of your house?
    Pray show me the way to him.
Fernando.   He's asleep, lady,
    The curtains drawn about him.
Isabella.   Well, well, sir,
    I'll have that care, I'll not disease him much.   90
    Tread you but lightly. [*Aside*] O, of what gross falsehood
    Is man's heart made of! Had my first love lived
    And returned safe he would have been a light
    To all men's actions, his faith shined so bright.
                         Exit [*with* FERNANDO.]

                Enter SEBASTIAN [*as* CELIO.]

Sebastian. I cannot so deceive her, 'twere too sinful;   95
    There's more religion in my love than so.
    It is not treacherous lust that gives content
    T'an honest mind; and this could prove no better.
    Were it in me a part of manly justice
    That have sought strange hard means to keep her chaste   100
    To her first vow, and I t'abuse her first?
    Better I never knew what comfort were
    In woman's love than wickedly to know it.
    What could the falsehood of one night avail him
    That must enjoy for ever or he's lost?   105
    'Tis the way rather to draw hate upon me;
    For known, 'tis as impossible she should love me
    As youth, in health, to dote upon a grief,
    Or one that's robbed and bound t'affect the thief.
    No, he that would soul's sacred comfort win   110
    Must burn in pure love like a seraphin.

                Enter ISABELLA.

Isabella. Celio?
Sebastian.   Sweet madam?

Isabella.   Thou'st deluded me.
    There's nobody.
Sebastian.   How! I wonder he would miss, madam,
    Having appointed too; 'twere a strange goodness
    If heaven should turn his heart now by the way.   115
Isabella. O never, Celio!
Sebastian.   Yes, I've known the like.
    Man is not at his own disposing, madam;
    The blessed powers have provided better for him
    Or he were miserable. He may come yet.
    'Tis early madam; if you would be pleased   120
    To embrace my counsel, you should see this night over,
    Since you've bestowed this pains.
Isabella.   ʻ   I intend so.
Sebastian [*Aside*] That strumpet would be found else she should
                                                                  go;
    I curse the time now I did e'er make use
    Of such a plague. Sin knows not what it does.   *Exeunt.* 125

                    [ACT IV] SCENE iii

            Enter FRANCISCA *in her chamber* [*above*].

Francisca. 'Tis now my brother's time, even much about it,
 ‚ For, though he dissembled a whole fortnight's absence,
    He comes again tonight. 'Twas so agreed
    Before he went. I must bestir my wits now
    To catch this sister of mine and bring her name   5
    To some disgrace first, to preserve mine own.
    There's profit in that cunning. She cast off
    My company betimes tonight, by tricks and sleights,
    And I was well contented. I am resolved
    There's no hate lost between us, for I know   10
    She does not love me now but painfully,
    Like one that's forced to smile upon a grief
    To bring some purpose forward; and I'll pay her
    In her own metal. They're now all at rest,
    And Gasper there, and all. List! [*Snoring within.*] Fast asleep, 15
    He cries it hither. I must disease you straight, sir.
    For the maid-servants and the girls o'th' house,
    I spiced them lately with a drowsy posset.
    They will not hear in haste. [*Noise within.*] My brother's
                                                              come!
    O, where's this key now for him? Here 'tis happily.   20

But I must wake him first.—Why, Gasper, Gasper!

Enter GASPERO [*below.*]

Gaspero. What a pox gasp you for?
Francisca.   Now I'll throw't down.
Gaspero. Who's that called me now? Somebody called 'Gasper'.
Francisca. O, up, as thou'rt an honest fellow, Gasper.
Gaspero. I shall not rise tonight then. What's the matter?   25
    Who's that? Young mistress?
Francisca.   Ay, up, up, sweet Gasper.
    My sister hath both knocked and called this hour
    And not a maid will stir.
Gaspero.   They'll stir enough sometimes.
Francisca. Hark, hark again, Gasper! O run, run, prithee!
Gaspero. Give me leave to clothe myself.
Francisca.   Standst upon clothing   30
    In an extremity? Hark, hark again!
    She may be dead ere thou com'st. O, in quickly!
                         [*Exit* GASPERO.]

 He's gone. He cannot choose but be took now
    Or met in his return; that will be enough.

Enter ANTONIO [*above.*]

    Brother? Here, take this light.
Antonio.   My careful sister.   35
Francisca. Look first in his own lodging ere you enter.
                         [*Exit* ANTONIO.]
Antonio. [*Within*] O abusèd confidence! Here's nothing of him
    But what betrays him more.
Francisca.   Then 'tis too true, brother.
Antonio. [*Within*] I'll make base lust a terrible example.
    No villainy e'er paid dearer.
[*Florida.*]   [*Within*] Help! Hold, sir!   40
Antonio. [*Within*] I'm deaf to all humanity.
Francisca.   List, list!
    A strange and sudden silence after all.
    I trust he's spoiled 'em both—too dear a happiness!
    O, how I tremble between doubts and joys!
Antonio. [*Within*] There perish both! Down to the house of
                         falsehood   45
    Where perjurous wedlock weeps.

     [*Re-entering below with his sword drawn.*]
                 O, perjurous woman!

She'd took the innocence of sleep upon her
At my approach and would not see me come,
As if she'd lain there like a harmless soul
And never dreamed of mischief. What's all this now?   50
I feel no ease; the burden's not yet off
So long as th'abuse sticks in my knowledge.
O, 'tis a pain of hell to know one's shame!
Had it been hid and done, it'd been done happy;
For he that's ignorant lives long and merry.   55
Francisca. [*Aside*] I shall know all now. [*To Antonio*] Brother!
Antonio.   Come down quickly,
For I must kill thee too.
Francisca.   Me?
Antonio.   Stay not long;
If thou desir'st to die with little pain,
Make haste I'd wish thee, and come willingly.
If I be forced to come I shall be cruel   60
Above a man to thee.
Francisca.   Why, sir! My brother!
Antonio. Talk to thy soul if thou wilt talk at all;
To me thou'rt lost for ever.
Francisca.   This is fearful in you
Beyond all reason, brother. Would you thus
Reward me for my care and truth shown to you?   65
Antonio. A curse upon 'em both and thee for company!
'Tis that too diligent, thankless care of thine
Makes me a murderer and that ruinous truth
That lights me to the knowledge of my shame.
Hadst thou been secret, then had I been happy   70
And had a hope, like man, of joys to come.
Now here I stand, a stain to my creation;
And, which is heavier than all torments to me,
The understanding of this base adultery,
And that thou toldst me first, which thou deserv'st   75
Death worthily for.
Francisca.   If that be the worst, hold, sir!
Hold, brother, I can ease your knowledge straight,
By my soul's hopes, I can. There's no such thing.
Antonio. How?
Francisca.   Bless me but with life, I'll tell you all.
Your bed was never wronged.
Antonio.   What! Never wronged?   80
Francisca. I ask but mercy as I deal with truth now.
'Twas only my deceit, my plot and cunning

    To bring disgrace upon her; by that means
    To keep mine own hid, which none knew but she.
    To speak troth, I had a child by Aberzanes, sir.   85
Antonio. How! Aberzanes?
Francisca.   And my mother's letter
    Was counterfeited to get time and place
    For my delivery.
Antonio.   O, my wrath's redoubled!
Francisca. At my return she could speak all my folly
    And blamed me with good counsel. I, for fear   90
    It should be made known, thus rewarded her,
    Wrought you into suspicion without cause,
    And at your coming raised up Gasper suddenly,
    Sent him but in before you by a falsehood,
    Which, to your kindled jealousy, I knew   95
    Would add enough. What's now confessed is true.
Antonio. The more I hear, the worse it fares with me.
    I've killed 'em now for nothing; yet the shame
    Follows my blood still. Once more, come down.
    Look you, my sword goes up. [*Sheathing sword.*]
                   Call Hermio to me;   100
    Let the new man alone.   [*Exit* FRANCISCA *above.*]
                  He'll wake too soon
    To find his mistress dead and lose a service.
    Already the day breaks upon my guilt.
    I must be brief and sudden. Hermio!

              Enter HERMIO.

Hermio.   Sir?
Antonio. Run, knock up Aberzanes speedily;   105
    Say I desire his company this morning
    To yonder horse-race, tell him; that will fetch him.
    O, hark you, by the way— [*Whispers.*]
Hermio.   Yes, sir.
Antonio.   Use speed now,
    Or I will ne'er use thee more; and perhaps
    I speak in a right hour. My grief o'erflows;   110
    I must in private go and vent my woes.   *Exeunt.*

ACT V

Enter ANTONIO *and* ABERZANES.

Antonio. You are welcome, sir.
Aberzanes.   I think I'm worthy on't,
    For look you, sir, I come untrussed, in troth.
Antonio. The more's the pity—honester men go to't—
    That slaves should 'scape it. What blade have you got there?
Aberzanes. Nay, I know not that, sir. I am not acquainted greatly   5
    with the blade. I am sure 'tis a good scabbard and that
    satisfies me.
Antonio. 'Tis long enough indeed, if that be good.
Aberzanes. I love to wear a long weapon. 'Tis a thing
                                 commendable.
Antonio. I pray draw it, sir.
Aberzanes.   It is not to be drawn.   10
Antonio. Not to be drawn?
Aberzanes. I do not care to see't. To tell you truth, sir, 'tis only a
    holiday thing to wear by a man's side.
Antonio. Draw it, or I'll rip thee down from neck to navel
    Though there's small glory in't.   15
Aberzanes. Are you in earnest, sir?
Antonio.   I'll tell thee that anon.
Aberzanes. Why, what's the matter, sir?
Antonio. [*Aside)* What a base misery is this in life now!
    This slave had so much daring courage in him
    To act a sin would shame whole generations,   20
    But hath not so much honest strength about him
    To draw a sword in way of satisfaction.
    [*To him*] This shows thy great guilt, that thou dar'st not
                                   fight.
Aberzanes. Yes, I dare fight, sir, in an honest cause.
Antonio. Why come then, slave, thou'st made my sister a whore.   25
Aberzanes. Prove that an honest cause and I'll be hanged.
Antonio. So many starting-holes? Can I light no way?
    Go to, you shall have your wish: all honest play.
    [*To Francisca within.*] Come forth, thou fruitful wickedness,
                                  thou seed
    Of shame and murder!

                [*Enter* FRANCISCA.]

                Take to thee in wedlock   30

Baseness and cowardice, a fit match for thee!
Come, sir, along with me.
Aberzanes.   'Las, what to do?
  I am too young to take a wife, in troth.
Antonio. But old enough to take a strumpet though.
  You'd fain get all your children beforehand,   35
  And marry when you've done. That's a strange course, sir.
  This woman I bestow on thee. What dost thou say?
Aberzanes. I would I had such another to bestow on you, sir.
Antonio. Uncharitable slave! Dog! Coward as thou art,
  To wish a plague so great as thine to any.   40
Aberzanes. To my friend, sir, where I think I may be bold.
Antonio. Down, and do't solemnly. [*They kneel.*] Contract
                                                      yourselves
  With truth and zeal, or ne'er rise up again.
  I will not have her die i'th' state of strumpet
  Though she took pride to live one.—Hermio, the wine!   45

                    [*Enter* HERMIO *with wine.*]

Hermio. 'Tis here, sir. [*Aside*] 'Troth, I wonder at some things,
  But I'll keep honest.
Antonio.   So, here's to you both now; [*He drinks.*]
  And to your joys, if't be your luck to find 'em;
  I tell you, you must weep hard if you do.
  Divide it 'twixt you both. [*They drink.*] You shall not need   50
  A strong bill of divorcement after that
  If you mislike your bargain. Go, get in now,
  Kneel and pray heartily to get forgiveness
  Of those two souls whose bodies thou hast murdered.
                    [*Exeunt* ABERZANES *and* FRANCISCA.]
  Spread, subtle poison! Now my shame in her   55
  Will die when I die. There's some comfort yet.
  I do but think how each man's punishment
  Proves still a kind of justice to himself.
  I was the man that told this innocent gentlewoman,
  Whom I did falsely wed and falsely kill,   60
  That he that was her husband first by contract
  Was slain i'th' field; and he's known yet to live.
  So did I cruelly beguile her heart,
  For which I'm well rewarded; so is Gasper,
  Who, to befriend my love, swore fearful oaths   65
  He saw the last breath fly from him. I see now
  'Tis a thing dreadful t'abuse holy vows
  And falls most weighty.

Hermio.   Take comfort, sir,
   You're guilty of no death. They're only hurt,
   And that not mortally.
Antonio.   Thou breath'st untruths.   70

                    Enter GASPERO [*wounded.*]

Hermio. Speak Gasper for me then.
Gaspero.   Your unjust rage, sir,
   Has hurt me without cause.
Antonio.   'Tis changed to grief for't.
   How fares my wife?
Gaspero.   No doubt, sir, she fares well,
   For she ne'er felt your fury. The poor sinner
   That hath this seven year kept herself sound for you,   75
   'Tis your luck to bring her into th' surgeon's hands now.
Antonio. Florida?
Gaspero.   She. I know no other, sir.
   You were ne'er at charge yet but with one light horse.
Antonio. Why, where's your lady? Where's my wife tonight then?
Gaspero. Nay, ask not me, sir; your struck doe within   80
   Tells a strange tale of her.
Antonio.   This is unsufferable!
   Never had man such means to make him mad.
   O that the poison would but spare my life
   Till I had found her out!
Hermio.   Your wish is granted, sir.
   Upon the faithfulness of a pitying servant   85
   I gave you none at all; my heart was kinder.
   Let not conceit abuse you, you're as healthful,
   For any drug, as life yet ever found you.
Antonio. Why here's a happiness wipes off mighty sorrows.
   The benefit of ever-pleasing service   90
   Bless thy profession!

          Enter L[ORD] GOVERNOR [*attended by* Gentlemen].

                    O, my worthy lord,
   I have an ill bargain; never man had worse.
   The woman that, unworthy, wears your blood
   To countenance sin in her—your niece—she's false.
Governor. False?
Antonio.   Impudent, adulterous.
Governor.   You're too loud,   95
   And grow too bold too with her virtuous meekness.

                    Enter FLORIDA [*wounded.*]

Who dare accuse her?
Florida.   Here's one dare and can.
    She lies this night with Celio, her own servant;
    The place Fernando's house.
Governor.   Thou dost amaze us.
Antonio. Why here's but lust translated from one baseness   100
    Into another. Here I thought to have caught 'em
    But lighted wrong by false intelligence
    And made me hurt the innocent. But now
    I'll make my revenge dreadfuller than a tempest;
    An army should not stop me or a sea   105
    Divide 'em from my revenge.   *Exit.*
Governor.   I'll not speak
    To have her spared if she be base and guilty.
    If otherwise, heaven will not see her wronged;
    I need not take care for her. Let that woman
    Be carefully looked to, both for health and sureness.   110
    It is not that mistaken wound thou wear'st
    Shall be thy privilege.
Florida.   You cannot torture me
    Worse than the surgeon does: so long I care not.
                [*Exit* FLORIDA *and* GASPERO *attended.*]
[*Governor.*] If she be adulterous I will never trust
    Virtues in women, they're but veils for lust.   115
                  Exit [*with* Gentlemen.]
Hermio. To what a lasting ruin mischief runs!
    I had thought I had well and happily ended all
    In keeping back the poison, and new rage now
    Spreads a worse venom! My poor lady grieves me;
    'Tis strange to me that her sweet seeming virtues   120
    Should be so meanly overtook with Celio,
    A servant: 'tis not possible.

        Enter ISABELLA *and* SEBASTIAN [*as* CELIO.]

Isabella.   Good morrow, Hermio.
    My sister stirring yet?
Hermio.   How, stirring, forsooth!
    Here has been simple stirring. Are you not hurt, madam?
    Pray speak, we have a surgeon ready.
Isabella.   How! A surgeon?   125
Hermio. Hath been at work these five hours.
Isabella.   How he talks!
Hermio. Did you not meet my master?
Isabella.   How, your master?

Why, came he home tonight?

Hermio.   Then know you nothing.

                                                                                Madam,

Please you but walk in, you shall hear strange business.

Isabella. [*To Sebastian*] I'm much beholding to your truth now,

                                                              am I not?   130

You've served me fair. My credit's stained for ever.

                                                              Exit [*with* HERMIO.]

Sebastian. This is the wicked'st fortune that e'er blew.

We're both undone for nothing. There's no way

Flatters recovery now, the thing's so gross.

Her disgrace grieves me more than a life's loss.   *Exit.*   135

[ACT V] SCENE ii

Enter DUCHESS, HECATE, FIRESTONE. [*A cauldron in the centre.*]

Hecate. What death is't you desire for Almachildes?

Duchess. A sudden and a subtle.

Hecate.   Then I have fitted you.

Here lie the gifts of both sudden and subtle.

His picture made in wax and gently molten

By a blue fire kindled with dead men's eyes   5

Will waste him by degrees.

Duchess.   In what time, 'prithee?

Hecate. Perhaps in a moon's progress.

Duchess.   What? A month?

Out upon pictures if·they be so tedious!

Give me things with some life.

Hecate.   Then seek no farther.

Duchess. This must be done with speed. Dispatched this night   10

If it may possible.

Hecate.   I have it for you;

Here's that will do't. Stay but perfection's time

And that's not five hours hence.

Duchess. Canst thou do this?

Hecate.   Can I?

Duchess.   I mean so closely?

Hecate. So closely do you mean too?

Duchess.   So artfully, so cunningly?   15

Hecate. Worse and worse; doubts and incredulities!

They make me mad. Let scrupulous greatness know:

Cum volui ripis ipsis mirantibus amnes

In fontes rediere suos, concussaque sisto,

Stantia concutio, cantu freta nubila pello,   20
Nubilaque induco, ventos, abigoque vocoque
Viperias rumpo verbis et carmine fauces,
Et siluas moueo, iubeoque tremiscere montes
Et mugire solum, manesque exire sepulchris.
Teque, luna, traho. Can you doubt me then, daughter?   25
That can make mountains tremble, miles of woods walk,
Whole earth's foundation bellow and the spirits
Of the entombed to burst out from their marbles,
Nay, draw yond moon to my involved designs?
Firestone. [*Aside*] I know as well as can be when my mother's mad   30
and our great cat angry: for one spits French then and th'other
spits Latin.
Duchess. I did not doubt you, mother.
Hecate.   No? What did you?
My power's so firm, it is not to be questioned.
Duchess. Forgive what's past; and now I know th' offensiveness   35
That vexes art, I'll shun th' occasion ever.
Hecate. Leave all to me and my five sisters, daughter.
It shall be conveyed in at howlet-time.
Take you no care, my spirits know their moments.
Raven or screech-owl never fly by th' door   40
But they call in—I thank 'em—and they lose not by't.
I give 'em barley soaked in infant's blood.
They shall have *semina cum sanguine*,
Their gorge crammed full, if they come once to our house.
We are no niggard.   45
                          [*Exit* DUCHESS.]

Firestone. They fare but too well when they come hither. They ate
up as much t'other night as would have made me a good conscionable pudding.
Hecate. Give me some lizard's brain. Quickly, Firestone!

        [FIRESTONE *brings the different ingredients for the charm as*
                  HECATE *calls for them.*]

Where's Grannam Stadlin and all the rest o' th' sisters?   50
Firestone. All at hand, forsooth.

        [*Enter* STADLIN, HOPPO, *and the three other* Witches.]

Hecate. Give me marmaritin; some bear-breech. When!
Firestone. Here's bear-breech and lizard's brain, forsooth.
Hecate. Into the vessel;
And fetch three ounces of the red-haired girl   55
I killed last midnight.

Firestone.   Whereabouts, sweet mother?
Hecate. Hip; hip or flank. Where is the *acopus*?
Firestone. You shall have *acopus*, forsooth.
Hecate. Stir, stir about, whilst I begin the charm.

(A charm-song about a vessel.)

> *Black spirits and white; red spirits and grey,*   60
> *Mingle, mingle, mingle, you that mingle may.*
> > *Titty, Tiffin,*
> > *Keep it stiff in;*
> > *Firedrake, Puckey,*
> > *Make it lucky;*   65
> > *Liard, Robin,*
> > *You must bob in.*
> *Round, around, around, about, about!*
> *All ill come running in, all good keep out!*

First Witch. Here's the blood of a bat.
Hecate.   *Put in that, O put in that!*   70
Second Witch. Here's libbard's bane.
Hecate.   *Put in a grain.*
First Witch. The juice of toad, the oil of adder.
Second Witch. Those will make the younker madder.
Hecate. Put in—there's all; and rid the stench.
Firestone. Nay, here's three ounces of the red-haired wench.   75
All [*Witches.*] *Round, around, around, etc.*
Hecate. So, so, enough. Into the vessel with it.
There, 't hath the true perfection. I am so light
At any mischief; there's no villainy
But is a tune methinks.   80
Firestone. [*Aside*] A tune? 'Tis to the tune of damnation then, I
warrant you, and that song hath a villainous burden.
Hecate. Come, my sweet sisters. Let the air strike our tune
Whilst we show reverence to yond peeping moon.
Here they dance The Witches' Dance and exeunt.

[ACT V] SCENE iii

Enter L[ORD] GOVERNOR, ISABELLA, [SEBASTIAN as CELIO],
FLORIDA, FRANCISCA, ABERZANES, GASPERO [and Servants].

Isabella. My lord, I have given you nothing but the truth
Of a most plain and innocent intent.
My wrongs being so apparent in this woman—

A creature that robs wedlock of all comfort
Where'er she fastens—I could do no less   5
But seek means privately to shame his folly.
No farther reached my malice, and it glads me
That none but my base injurer is found
To be my false accuser.

Governor.   This is strange
That he should give the wrongs, yet seek revenge.   10
[*To Sebastian*] But, sirrah, you; you are accused here doubly.
First, by your lady, for a false intelligence
That caused her absence, which much hurts her name
Though her intents were blameless; next, by this woman,
For an adulterous design and plot   15
Practised between you to entrap her honour,
Whilst she, for her hire, should enjoy her husband.
Your answer?

Sebastian.   Part of this is truth, my lord,
To which I'm guilty in a rash intent,
But clear in act; and she most clear in both,   20
Not sanctity more spotless.

[*Enter* HERMIO.]

Hermio.   O, my lord!
Governor. What news breaks there?
Hermio.   Of strange destruction.
Here stands the lady that within this hour
Was made a widow.
Governor.   How!
Hermio.   Your niece, my lord.
A fearful, unexpected accident   25
Brought death to meet his fury. For my lord,
Entering Fernando's house like a raised tempest,
Which nothing heeds but its own violent rage,
Blinded with wrath and jealousy, which scorn guides,
From a false trap-door fell into a depth   30
Exceeds a temple's height, which takes into it
Part of the dungeon that falls threescore fathom
Under the castle.
Governor.   O, you seed of lust,
Wrongs and revenges wrongful, with what terrors
You do present yourselves to wretched man   35
When his soul least expects you!
Isabella.   I forgive him
All his wrongs now and sign it with my pity.

Florida. O, my sweet servant! [*Swoons.*]
Governor.   Look to yond light mistress.
Gaspero. She's in a swoon, my lord.
Governor.   Convey her hence:
    It is a sight would grieve a modest eye   40
    To see a strumpet's soul sink into passion
    For him that was the husband of another.
                      [*Servants remove* FLORIDA.]
    Yet all this clears not you.
Sebastian.   Thanks to heaven
    That I am now of age to clear myself then.

             [*Discovers himself.*]

Governor. Sebastian!
Sebastian.   The same, much wronged, sir.
Isabella.   Am I certain   45
    Of what mine eye takes joy to look upon?
Sebastian. Your service cannot alter me from knowledge.
    I am your servant ever.
Governor.   Welcome to life, sir.
    Gasper, thou swor'st his death.
Gaspero.   I did indeed, my lord,
    And have been since well paid for't. One forsworn mouth   50
    Hath got me two or three more here.
Sebastian.   I was dead, sir,
    Both to my joys and all men's understanding
    Till this my hour of life. For 'twas my fortune
    To make the first of my return to Ravenna
    A witness to that marriage; since which time   55
    I have walked beneath myself and all my comforts,
    Like one on earth whose joys are laid above.
    And though it had been offence small in me
    To enjoy mine own, I left her pure and free.
Governor. The greater and more sacred is thy blessing,   60
    For where heaven's bounty holy ground-work finds,
    'Tis like a sea encompassing chaste minds.
Hermio. The duchess comes, my lord.
Governor.   Be you then all witnesses
    Of an intent most horrid.

             Enter DUCHESS.

Duchess.   [*Aside*] One poor night
    Ends Almachildes now.   65
    Better his meaner fortunes wept than ours

That took the true height of a princess' spirit
To match unto their greatness. Such lives as his
Were only made to break the force of fate
Ere it came at us and receive the venom.   70
'Tis but a usual friendship for a mistress
To lose some forty years' life in hopeful time
And hazard an eternal soul for ever.
As young as he has done't and more desertful.
Governor. Madam.   75
Duchess. My lord?
Governor. This is the hour that I've so long desired.
    The tumult's full appeased. Now may we both
    Exchange embraces with a fortunate arm
    And practise to make love-knots, thus—

[*A curtain is drawn and the*] DUKE *is discovered* [*on a couch as if
                             dead*].

Duchess.   My lord!   80
Governor. Thus, lustful woman and bold murd'ress, thus!
    Blessed powers, to make my loyalty and truth so happy!
    Look thee, thou shame of greatness, stain of honour!
    Behold thy work, and weep before thy death,
    If thou be'st blest with sorrow and a conscience,   85
    Which is a gift from heaven and seldom knocks
    At any murderer's breast with sounds of comfort,
    See this thy worthy and unequalled piece—
    A fair encouragement for another husband!
Duchess. Bestow me upon death, sir; I am guilty,   90
    And of a cruelty above my cause;
    His injury was too low for my revenge.
    Perform a justice that may light all others
    To noble actions. Life is hateful to me,
    Beholding my dead lord. Make us an one   95
    In death, whom marriage made one of two living,
    Till cursèd fury parted us. My lord,
    I covet to be like him.
Governor.   No, my sword
    Shall never stain the virgin brightness on't
    With blood of an adult'ress.
Duchess.   There, my lord,   100
    I dare my accuser and defy the world,
    Death, shame and torment. Blood I am guilty of
    But not adultery, not the breach of honour.
Governor. No? Come forth, Almachildes!

Duchess.   Almachildes?

Enter ALMACHILDES.

Hath time brought him about to save himself   105
By my destruction? I am justly doomed.
Governor. Do you know this woman?
Almachildes. I have known her better, sir, than at this time.
Governor. But she defies you there.
Almachildes.   That's the common trick of them all.
Duchess. Nay, since I am touched so near, before my death,   110
Then in right of honour's innocence, I am bold
To call heaven and my woman here to witness.

Enter AMORETTA.

My lord, let her speak truth, or may she perish!
Amoretta. Then, sir, by all the hopes of a maid's comfort
Either in faithful service or blessed marriage,   115
The woman that his blinded folly knew
Was only a hired strumpet, a professor
Of lust and impudence, which here is ready
To approve what I have spoken.
Almachildes.   A common strumpet?
This comes of scarves! I'll never more wear   120
An haberdasher's shop before mine eyes again.
Governor. My sword is proud thou art lightened of that sin.
Die then a murd'ress only.
Duke. [*Rising and embracing her.*] Live a duchess!
Better than ever loved, embraced and honoured.
Duchess. [*Kneels.*] My lord!
Duke.   Nay, since in honour thou canst justly rise,   125
Vanish all wrongs. Thy former practice dies.
I thank thee, Almachildes, for my life,
This lord for truth, and heaven for such a wife,
Who, though her intent sinned, yet she makes amends
With grief and honour, virtue's noblest ends.   130
What grieved you then shall never more offend you:
Your father's skull with honour we'll inter
And give the peace due to the sepulchre;
And in all times may this day ever prove
A day of triumph, joy and honest love.   *Exeunt.*   135

WILLIAM ROWLEY, THOMAS DEKKER, JOHN FORD, & c

THE WITCH OF EDMONTON

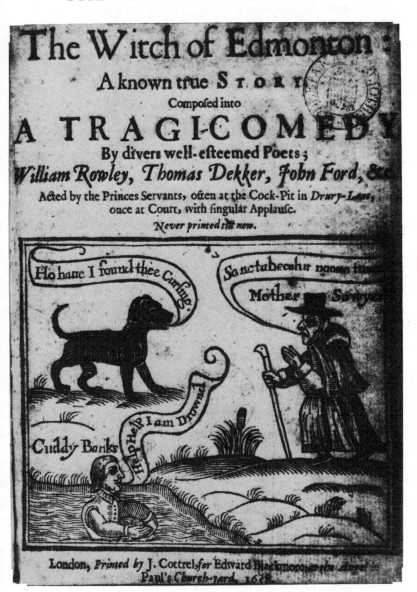

The Witch of Edmonton :
A known true S T O R Y
Composed into
A TRAGI-COMEDY
By divers well-esteemed Poets;
William Rowley, Thomas Dekker, John Ford, &c.
Acted by the Princes Servants, often at the Cock-Pit in Drury-Lane,
once at Court, with singular Applause.
Never printed till now.

Ho have I found thee Curfing.

Sanctabecetur nomen tuum

Mother Sawyer

Help Help I am Drown'd

Cuddy Banks

London, Printed by J. Cottrel, for Edward Blackmore, at the Angel in
Paul's Church-yard, 1658.

ACTORS' NAMES

SIR ARTHUR CLARINGTON.
OLD THORNEY, *a gentleman.*
OLD CARTER, *a rich yeoman.*
OLD BANKS, *a countryman.*
W. MAGO, ⎫ *two countrymen.*   5
W. HAMLUC, ⎭
Three other Countrymen.
WARBECK, ⎫ *suitors to* [Old] *Carter's daughters.*
SOMERTON, ⎭
FRANK [THORNEY], *Thorney's son.*   10
YOUNG CUDDY BANKS, *the Clown.*
Four Morris Dancers.
OLD RATCLIFFE.
SAWGUT, *an old fiddler.*
POLDAVIS, *a barber's boy.*   15
JUSTICE.
Constable.
Officers.
Servingmen.
DOG, *a Familiar.*   20
A Spirit.

WOMEN

MOTHER [ELIZABETH] SAWYER, *the Witch.*
ANNE, [Old] *Ratcliffe's wife.*
SUSAN,   ⎫ [Old] *Carter's daughters.*
KATHERINE,⎭   25
WINNIFRIDE, *Sir Arthur* [Clarington]*'s maid.*
[JANE, a maid].

The whole argument is this distich.

Forced marriage, murder; murder blood requires.
Reproach, revenge; revenge hell's help desires.

PROLOGUE

The town of Edmonton hath lent the stage
A Devil and a Witch, both in an age.
To make comparisons it were uncivil
Between so even a pair, a Witch and Devil.
But as the year doth with his plenty bring   5
As well a latter as a former spring,
So has this Witch enjoyed the first, and reason
Presumes she may partake the other season.
In acts deserving name, the proverb says,
Once good, and ever; why not so in plays?   10
Why not in this? Since, Gentlemen, we flatter
No expectation, here is mirth and matter.

                              Master Bird.

ACT I

Enter FRANK THORNEY [*and*] WINNIFRIDE *with child.*

Frank Thorney. Come, wench, why here's a business soon
                                      dispatched.
  Thy heart, I know, is now at ease. Thou needst not
  Fear what the tattling gossips in their cups
  Can speak against thy fame. Thy child shall know
  Who to call dad now.
Winnifride.   You have discharged   5
  The true part of an honest man; I cannot
  Request a fuller satisfaction
  Than you have freely granted. Yet methinks
  'Tis an hard case, being lawful man and wife,
  We should not live together.
Frank Thorney.   Had I failed   10
  In promise of my truth to thee, we must
  Have then been ever sundered. Now the longest
  Of our forbearing either's company
  Is only but to gain a little time
  For our continuing thrift, that so hereafter   15
  The heir that shall be born may not have cause
  To curse his hour of birth, which made him feel
  The misery of beggary and want,
  Two devils that are occasions to enforce
  A shameful end. My plots aim but to keep   20
  My father's love.
Winnifride.   And that will be as difficult
  To be preserved when he shall understand
  How you are married, as it will be now,
  Should you confess it to him.
Frank Thorney.   Fathers are
  Won by degrees, not bluntly, as our masters   25
  Or wrongèd friends are. And besides, I'll use
  Such dutiful and ready means, that ere
  He can have notice of what's past, th'inheritance,
  To which I am born heir, shall be assured.
  That done, why, let him know it. If he like it not,   30
  Yet he shall have no power in him left

To cross the thriving of it.
Winnifride.　　　　　　　　You, who had
　The conquest of my maiden-love, may easily
　Conquer the fears of my distrust. And whither
　Must I be hurried?
Frank Thorney.　　　　　Prithee do not use　　　　　　35
　A word so much unsuitable to the constant
　Affections of thy husband. Thou shalt live
　Near Waltham Abbey with thy Uncle Selman.
　I have acquainted him with all at large.
　He'll use thee kindly. Thou shalt want no pleasures,　　40
　Nor any other fit supplies whatever
　Thou canst in heart desire.
Winnifride.　　　　　　　　All these are nothing
　Without your company.
Frank Thorney.　　　　　Which thou shalt have
　Once every month at least.
Winnifride.　　　　　　　　Once every month!
　Is this to have an husband?
Frank Thorney.　　　　　　Perhaps oftener;　　　　　　45
　That's as occasion serves.
Winnifride.　　　　　　　Ay, ay; in case
　No other beauty tempt your eye whom you
　Like better, I may chance to be remembered,
　And see you now and then. Faith, I did hope
　You'd not have used me so. 'Tis but my fortune.　　　　50
　And yet, if not for my sake, have some pity
　Upon the child I go with that's your own.
　And, 'less you'll be a cruel-hearted father,
　You cannot but remember that.
　Heaven knows how—
Frank Thorney.　　　　　To quit which fear at once,　　55
　As by the ceremony late performed,
　I plighted thee a faith as free from challenge
　As any double thought, once more in hearing
　Of heaven and thee, I vow that never henceforth
　Disgrace, reproof, lawless affections, threats,　　　　60
　Or what can be suggested 'gainst our marriage
　Shall cause me falsify that bridal oath
　That binds me thine. And, Winnifride, whenever
　The wanton heat of youth by subtle baits
　Of beauty, or what woman's art can practise,　　　　65
　Draw me from only loving thee, let heaven
　Inflict upon my life some fearful ruin.

I hope thou dost believe me.
Winnifride.   Swear no more.
   I am confirmed, and will resolve to do
   What you think most behoveful for us.
Frank Thorney.   Thus then: 70
   Make thyself ready, at the furthest house
   Upon the green, without the town, your uncle
   Expects you. For a little time, farewell.
Winnifride.   Sweet,
   We shall meet again as soon as thou canst possibly?
Frank Thorney. We shall. One kiss. [*Kisses her.*] Away.

                                 [*Exit* WINNIFRIDE.]

         Enter SIR ARTHUR CLARINGTON.

Sir Arthur.   Frank Thorney.
Frank Thorney.   Here, sir.   75
Sir Arthur. Alone? Then must I tell thee in plain terms
   Thou hast wronged thy master's house basely and lewdly.
Frank Thorney. Your house, sir?
Sir Arthur.   Yes, sir. If the nimble devil
   That wantoned in your blood rebelled against
   All rules of honest duty, you might, sir,   80
   Have found out some more fitting place than here
   To have built a stews in. All the country whispers
   How shamefully thou hast undone a maid
   Approved for modest life, for civil carriage,
   Till thy prevailing perjuries enticed her   85
   To forfeit shame. Will you be honest yet,
   Make her amends and marry her?
Frank Thorney.   So, sir,
   I might bring both myself and her to beggary,
   And that would be a shame worse than the other.
Sir Arthur. You should have thought on this before, and then   90
   Your reason would have overswayed the passion
   Of your unruly lust. But that you may
   Be left without excuse, to salve the infamy
   Of my disgracèd house, and 'cause you are
   A gentleman and both of you my servants,   95
   I'll make the maid a portion.
Frank Thorney.   So you promised me
   Before, in case I married her. I know
   Sir Arthur Clarington deserves the credit
   Report hath lent him, and presume you are
   A debtor to your promise. But upon   100

What certainty shall I resolve? Excuse me
  For being somewhat rude.
Sir Arthur.   'Tis but reason.
  Well, Frank, what thinkst thou of two hundred pound
  And a continual friend?
Frank Thorney.   Though my poor fortunes
  Might happily prefer me to a choice   105
  Of a far greater portion, yet, to right
  A wrongèd maid and to preserve your favour,
  I am content to accept your proffer.
Sir Arthur.   Art thou?
Frank Thorney. Sir, we shall every day have need to employ
  The use of what you please to give.
Sir Arthur.   Thou shalt have't.   110
Frank Thorney. Then I claim your promise. We are man and
                                                      wife.
Sir Arthur. Already?
Frank Thorney.   And more than so; I have promised her
  Free entertainment in her uncle's house
  Near Waltham Abbey, where she may securely
  Sojourn, till time and my endeavours work   115
  My father's love and liking.
Sir Arthur.   Honest Frank!
Frank Thorney. I hope, sir, you will think I cannot keep her
  Without a daily charge.
Sir Arthur.   As for the money,
  'Tis all thine own, and though I cannot make thee
  A present payment, yet thou shalt be sure   120
  I will not fail thee.
Frank Thorney.   But our occasions—
Sir Arthur.   Nay, nay,
  Talk not of your occasions. Trust my bounty,
  It shall not sleep. Hast married her, i'faith, Frank?
  'Tis well, 'tis passing well. [*Aside*] Then, Winnifride,
  Once more thou art an honest woman. [*To Frank*] Frank,   125
  Thou hast a jewel. Love her, she'll deserve it.
  And when to Waltham?
Frank Thorney.   She is making ready.
  Her uncle stays for her.
Sir Arthur.   Most provident speed.
  Frank, I will be thy friend, and such a friend.
  Thou'lt bring her thither?
Frank Thorney.   Sir, I cannot. Newly   130
  My father sent me word I should come to him.

Sir Arthur. Marry, and do. I know thou hast a wit
     To handle him.
Frank Thorney.   I have a suit t'ye.
Sir Arthur.   What is't?
     Anything, Frank, command it.
Frank Thorney.   That you'll please
     By letters to assure my father that   135
     I am not married.
Sir Arthur.   How?
Frank Thorney.   Some one or other
     Hath certainly informed him that I purposed
     To marry Winnifride, on which he threatened
     To disinherit me. To prevent it,
     Lowly I crave your letters, which he seeing   140
     Will credit. And I hope, ere I return,
     On such conditions as I'll frame, his lands
     Shall be assured.
Sir Arthur.   But what is there to quit
     My knowledge of the marriage?
Frank Thorney.   Why, you were not
     A witness to it.
Sir Arthur.   I conceive; and then,   145
     His land confirmed, thou wilt acquaint him thoroughly
     With all that's passed.
Frank Thorney.   I mean no less.
Sir Arthur.   Provided
     I never was made privy to it.
Frank Thorney.   Alas, sir,
     Am I a talker?
Sir Arthur.   Draw thyself the letter,
     I'll put my hand to it. I commend thy policy.   150
     Thou'rt witty, witty Frank. Nay, nay, 'tis fit,
     Dispatch it.
Frank Thorney. I shall write effectually.   *Exit.*
Sir Arthur. Go thy way, cuckoo. Have I caught the young man?
     One trouble then is freed. He that will feast
     At others' cost must be a bold-faced guest.   155

Enter WINNIFRIDE *in a riding suit.*

Winnifride. I have heard the news. All now is safe,
     The worst is past.
Sir Arthur.   Thy lip, wench. [*Kisses her.*] I must bid
     Farewell for fashion's sake, but I will visit thee
     Suddenly, girl. This was cleanly carried,

Ha, was't not, Win?
Winnifride.   Then were my happiness   160
   That I in heart repent I did not bring him
   The dower of a virginity. Sir, forgive me,
   I have been much to blame. Had not my lewdness
   Given way to your immoderate waste of virtue,
   You had not with such eagerness pursued   165
   The error of your goodness.
Sir Arthur.   Dear, dear Win,
   I hug this art of thine. It shows how cleanly
   Thou canst beguile, in case occasion serve,
   To practise. It becomes thee. Now we share
   Free scope enough, without control or fear,   170
   To interchange our pleasures. We will surfeit
   In our embraces, wench. Come, tell me, when
   Wilt thou appoint a meeting?
Winnifride.   What to do?
Sir Arthur. Good, good, to con the lesson of our loves,
   Our secret game.
Winnifride.   O, blush to speak it further!   175
   As you're a noble gentleman, forget
   A sin so monstrous. 'Tis not gently done
   To open a cured wound. I know you speak
   For trial. 'Troth, you need not.
Sir Arthur.   I for trial?
   Not I, by this good sunshine!
Winnifride.   Can you name   180
   That syllable of good and yet not tremble
   To think to what a foul and black intent
   You use it for an oath? Let me resolve you.
   If you appear in any visitation
   That brings not with it pity for the wrongs   185
   Done to abusèd Thorney, my kind husband;
   If you infect mine ear with any breath
   That is not thoroughly perfumed with sighs
   For former deeds of lust, may I be cursed,
   Even in my prayers, when I vouchsafe   190
   To see or hear you! I will change my life
   From a loose whore to a repentant wife.
Sir Arthur. Wilt thou turn monster now? Art not ashamed
   After so many months to be honest at last?
   Away, away! Fie on't!
Winnifride.   My resolution   195
   Is built upon a rock. This very day

Young Thorney vowed, with oaths not to be doubted,
That never any change of love should cancel
The bonds in which we are to either bound
Of lasting truth. And shall I then, for my part,   200
Unfile the sacred oath set on record
In heaven's book? Sir Arthur, do not study
To add to your lascivious lust the sin
Of sacrilege; for if you but endeavour
By any unchaste word to tempt my constancy   205
You strive as much as in you lies to ruin
A temple hallowed to the purity
Of holy marriage. I have said enough.
You may believe me.
Sir Arthur.   Get you to your nunnery,
There freeze in your cold cloister. This is fine!   210
Winnifride. Good angels guide me! Sir, you'll give me leave
To weep and pray for your conversion?
Sir Arthur.   Yes.
Away to Waltham! Pox on your honesty!
Had you no other trick to fool me? Well,
You may want money yet.
Winnifride.   None that I'll send for   215
To you for hire of a damnation.
When I am gone think on my just complaint:
I was your devil; O, be you my saint!   *Exit.*
Sir Arthur. Go, go thy ways, as changeable a baggage
As ever cozened knight..I'm glad I'm rid of her.   220
Honest? Marry, hang her! Thorney is my debtor,
I thought to have paid him too, but fools have fortune. *Exit.*

[ACT I] SCENE ii

Enter OLD THORNEY *and* OLD CARTER.

Old Thorney. You offer, Master Carter, like a gentleman;
I cannot find fault with it, 'tis so fair.
Old Carter. No gentleman I, Master Thorney; spare the Master-
ship, call me by my name, John Carter. Master is a title my
father, nor his before him, were acquainted with. Honest Hert-   5
fordshire yeomen, such an one am I. My word and my deed
shall be proved one at all times. I mean to give you no security
for the marriage-money.
Old Thorney. How! No security?

Although it need not so long as you live,   10
Yet who is he has surety of his life one hour?
Men, the proverb says, are mortal, else, for my part,
I distrust you not, were the sum double.

Old Carter. Double, treble, more or less, I tell you, Master Thorney, I'll give no security. Bonds and bills are but tarriers to catch   15
fools and keep lazy knaves busy. My security shall be present
payment. And we here about Edmonton hold present payment
as sure as an alderman's bond in London, Master Thorney.

Old Thorney. I cry you mercy, sir, I understood you not.

Old Carter. I like young Frank well, so does my Susan too. The girl   20
has a fancy to him, which makes me ready in my purse. There
be other suitors within, that make much noise to little purpose.
If Frank love Sue, Sue shall have none but Frank. 'Tis a manner-
ly girl, Master Thorney, though but an homely man's daughter.
There have worse faces looked out of black bags, man.   25

Old Thorney. You speak your mind freely and honestly. I marvel
my son comes not. I am sure he will be here sometime today.

Old Carter. Today or tomorrow, when he comes he shall be
welcome to bread, beer and beef—yeoman's fare, we have no
kickshaws; full dishes, whole bellyfulls. Should I diet three days   30
at one of the slender city-suppers, you might send me to Barber-
Surgeons' Hall the fourth day to hang up for an anatomy. Here
come they that—

> *Enter* WARBECK *with* SUSAN, SOMERTON *with* KATHERINE.

How now, girls! Every day play-day with you? Valentine's day
too, all by couples? Thus will young folks do when we are laid   35
in our graves, Master Thorney. Here's all the care they take.
And how do you find the wenches, gentlemen? Have they any
mind to a loose gown and a straight shoe? Win 'em and wear
'em. They shall choose for themselves by my consent.

Warbeck. You speak like a kind father. Sue, thou hearest   40
The liberty that's granted thee. What sayest thou?
Wilt thou be mine?

Susan.   Your what, sir? I dare swear,
Never your wife.

Warbeck.   Canst thou be so unkind,
Considering how dearly I affect thee,
Nay, dote on thy perfections?

Susan.   You are studied   45
Too scholar-like in words I understand not.
I am too coarse for such a gallant's love
As you are.

Warbeck.   By the honour of gentility—
Susan. Good sir, no swearing. Yea and nay with us
     Prevails above all oaths you can invent.   50
Warbeck. By this white hand of thine—
Susan.   Take a false oath?
     Fie, fie! Flatter the wise, fools not regard it,
     And one of these am I.
Warbeck.   Dost thou despise me?
Old Carter. Let 'em talk on, Master Thorney. I know Sue's mind.
     The fly may buzz about the candle; he shall but singe his wings   55
     when all's done. Frank, Frank is he has her heart.
Somerton. But shall I live in hope, Kate?
Katherine. Better so than be a desperate man.
Somerton. Perhaps thou thinkst it is thy portion
     I level at? Wert thou as poor in fortunes   60
     As thou art rich in goodness, I would rather
     Be suitor for the dower of thy virtues
     Than twice thy father's whole estate. And, prithee,
     Be thou resolvèd so.
Katherine.   Master Somerton,
     It is an easy labour to deceive   65
     A maid that will believe men's subtle promises,
     Yet I conceive of you as worthily
     As I presume you do deserve.
Somerton.   Which is
     As worthily in loving thee sincerely
     As thou art worthy to be so beloved.   70
Katherine. I shall find time to try you.
Somerton.   Do, Kate, do.
     And when I fail, may all my joys forsake me.
Old Carter. Warbeck and Sue are at it still. I laugh to myself, Master
     Thorney, to see how earnestly he beats the bush while the bird
     is flown into another's bosom. A very unthrift, Master Thor-   75
     ney, one of the country roaring-lads. We have such as well as
     the city, and as arrant rake-hells as they are, though not so
     nimble at their prizes of wit. Sue knows the rascal to an hair's
     breadth, and will fit him accordingly.
Old Thorney. What is the other gentleman?   80
Old Carter. One Somerton, the honester man of the two by five
     pound in every stone-weight. A civil fellow, he has a fine conve-
     nient estate of land in West Ham, by Essex. Master Ranges,
     that dwells by Enfield, sent him hither. He likes Kate well. I may
     tell you I think she likes him as well. If they agree, I'll not hinder 85
     the match for my part. But that Warbeck is such another—I use

him kindly for Master Somerton's sake, for he came hither first
as a companion of his. Honest men, Master Thorney, may fall
into knaves' company now and then.

Warbeck. Three hundred a year jointure, Sue.   90
Susan. Where lies it, by sea or by land? I think by sea.
Warbeck. Do I look a captain?
Susan.   Not a whit, sir.
Should all that use the seas be reckoned captains,
There's not a ship should have a scullion in her
To keep her clean.
Warbeck.   Do you scorn me, Mistress Susan?   95
Am I a subject to be jeered at?
Susan.   Neither
Am I a property for you to use
As stale to your fond wanton loose discourse.
Pray, sir, be civil.
Warbeck.   Wilt be angry, wasp?
Old Carter. God-a-mercy, Sue! She'll firk him, on my life, if he 100
fumble with her.

            Enter FRANK [THORNEY].

Master Francis Thorney, you are welcome indeed. Your father
expected your coming. How does the right worshipful knight,
Sir Arthur Clarington, your master?
Frank Thorney. In health this morning. Sir, my duty.
Old Thorney.   Now   105
You come as I could wish.
Warbeck.   Frank Thorney, ha!
Susan. You must excuse me.
Frank Thorney.   Virtuous Mistress Susan.
Kind Mistress Katherine.

            Salutes them.

                Gentlemen, to both
Good time o'th'day.
Somerton.   The like to you.
Warbeck.   'Tis he.
A word, friend. [*To Somerton.*] On my life, this is the man   110
Stands fair in crossing Susan's love to me.
Somerton. [*To Warbeck.*] I think no less. Be wise, and take no
                                        notice on't.
He that can win her best deserves her.
Warbeck.   [*To Somerton.*] Marry
A serving-man? Mew!

Somerton.   [*To Warbeck.*] Prithee, friend,
                                              no more.
Old Carter. Gentlemen all, there's within a slight dinner ready, if   115
    you please to taste of it, Master Thorney, Master Francis,
    Master Somerton—Why, girls! What, huswives! Will you
    spend all your forenoon in tittle-tattles? Away! It's well,
    i'faith.—Will you go in, gentlemen?
Old Thorney. We'll follow presently. My son and I   120
    Have a few words of business.
Old Carter.   At your pleasure.
                                              Exeunt the rest.
Old Thorney. I think you guess the reason, Frank, for which
    I sent for you.
Frank Thorney.   Yes, sir.
Old Thorney.   I need not tell you
    With what a labyrinth of dangers daily
    The best part of my whole estate's encumbered.   125
    Nor have I any clew to wind it out
    But what occasion proffers me. Wherein
    If you should falter I shall have the shame,
    And you the loss. On these two points rely
    Our happiness or ruin. If you marry   130
    With wealthy Carter's daughter there's a portion
    Will free my land, all which I will instate
    Upon the marriage to you. Otherwise
    I must be of necessity enforced
    To make a present sale of all, and yet,   135
    For ought I know, live in as poor distress,
    Or worse, than now I do. You hear the sum?
    I told you thus before. Have you consider'd on't?
Frank Thorney. I have, sir. And however I could wish
    To enjoy the benefit of single freedom,   140
    For that I find no disposition in me
    To undergo the burden of that care
    That marriage brings with it, yet to secure
    And settle the continuance of your credit,
    I humbly yield to be directed by you   145
    In all commands.
Old Thorney.   You have already used
    Such thriving protestations to the maid
    That she is wholly yours. And, speak the truth,
    You love her, do you not?
Frank Thorney.   'Twere pity, sir,
    I should deceive her.

Old Thorney.   Better you'd been unborn.   150
    But is your love so steady that you mean,
    Nay, more, desire to make her your wife?
Frank Thorney.   Else, sir,
    It were a wrong not to be righted.
Old Thorney.   True,
    It were. And you will marry her?
Frank Thorney.   Heaven prosper it!
    I do intend it.
Old Thorney.   O, thou art a villain!   155
    A devil like a man! Wherein have I
    Offended all the powers so much, to be
    Father to such a graceless, godless son?
Frank Thorney. To me, sir, this? O my cleft heart!
Old Thorney.   To thee,
    Son of my curse. Speak truth and blush, thou monster.   160
    Hast thou not married Winnifride, a maid
    Was fellow-servant with thee?
Frank Thorney.   [*Aside*] Some swift spirit
    Has blown this news abroad. I must outface it.
Old Thorney. D'you study for excuse? Why all the country
    Is full on't.
Frank Thorney. With your licence, 'tis not charitable,   165
    I am sure it is not fatherly, so much
    To be o'erswayed with credulous conceit
    Of mere impossibilities. But fathers
    Are privileged to think and talk at pleasure.
Old Thorney. Why, canst thou yet deny thou hast no wife?   170
Frank Thorney. What do you take me for? An atheist?
    One that nor hopes the blessedness of life
    Hereafter, neither fears the vengeance due
    To such as make the marriage-bed an inn
    Which travellers day and night,   175
    After a toilsome lodging, leave at pleasure?
    Am I become so insensible of losing
    The glory of creation's work, my soul?
    O, I have lived too long!
Old Thorney.   Thou hast, dissembler.
    Darest thou persèver yet, and pull down wrath   180
    As hot as flames of hell to strike thee quick
    Into the grave of horror? I believe thee not.
    Get from my sight!
Frank Thorney.   Sir, though mine innocence
    Needs not a stronger witness than the clearness

Of an unperished conscience, yet, for that   185
I was informed how mainly you had been
Possessed of this untruth, to quit all scruple
Please you peruse this letter. 'Tis to you.
Old Thorney. From whom?
Frank Thorney.   Sir Arthur Clarington, my master.
Old Thorney. Well, sir. [*Reads the letter.*]
Frank Thorney.   [*Aside*] On every side I am distracted,   190
Am waded deeper into mischief
Than virtue can avoid. But on I must.
Fate leads me, I will follow. [*To him*] There you read
What may confirm you.
Old Thorney.   Yes, and wonder at it.
Forgive me, Frank. Credulity abused me.   195
My tears express my joy, and I am sorry
I injured innocence.
Frank Thorney.   Alas! I knew
Your rage and grief proceeded from your love
To me. So I conceived it.
Old Thorney.   My good son.
I'll bear with many faults in thee hereafter;   200
Bear thou with mine.
Frank Thorney.   The peace is soon concluded.

Enter OLD CARTER [*and* SUSAN].

Old Carter. Why, Master Thorney, d'ye mean to talk out your din-
ner? The company attends your coming. What must it be,
Master Frank, or son Frank? I am plain Dunstable.
Old Thorney. Son, brother, if your daughter like to have it so.   205
Frank Thorney. I dare be confident she's not altered
From what I left her at our parting last.
Are you, fair maid?
Susan.   You took too sure possession
Of an engaged heart.
Frank Thorney.   Which now I challenge.
Old Carter. Marry, and much good may it do thee, son. Take her   210
to thee. Get me a brace of boys at a burden, Frank. The nursing
shall not stand thee in a pennyworth of milk. Reach her home
and spare not. When's the day?
Old Thorney. Tomorrow, if you please. To use ceremony
Of charge and custom were to little purpose,   215
Their loves are married fast enough already.
Old Carter. A good motion. We'll e'en have an household dinner,
and let the fiddlers go scrape. Let the bride and bridegroom

dance at night together, no matter for the guests. Tomorrow,
Sue, tomorrow.—Shall's to dinner now?   220
Old Thorney. We are on all sides pleased, I hope.
Susan. Pray heaven I may deserve the blessing sent me.
Now my heart is settled.
Frank Thorney.   So is mine.
Old Carter. Your marriage-money shall be received before your
wedding-shoes can be pulled on. Blessing on you both!   225
Frank Thorney [*Aside*] No man can hide his shame from heaven
that views him.
In vain he flees whose destiny pursues him.   *Exeunt.*

ACT II

SCENE i

Enter ELIZABETH SAWYER *gathering sticks.*

Elizabeth Sawyer. And why on me? Why should the envious world
Throw all their scandalous malice upon me?
'Cause I am poor, deformed and ignorant,
And like a bow buckled and bent together
By some more strong in mischiefs than myself,   5
Must I for that be made a common sink
For all the filth and rubbish of men's tongues
To fall and run into? Some call me witch,
And, being ignorant of myself, they go
About to teach me how to be one, urging   10
That my bad tongue, by their bad usage made so,
Forspeaks their cattle, doth bewitch their corn,
Themselves, their servants and their babes at nurse.

Enter OLD BANKS.

This they enforce upon me, and in part
Make me to credit it. And here comes one   15
Of my chief adversaries.
Old Banks. Out, out upon thee, witch!
Elizabeth Sawyer.   Dost call me witch?
Old Banks. I do, witch, I do; and worse I would, knew I a name
more hateful. What makest thou upon my ground?
Elizabeth Sawyer. Gather a few rotten sticks to warm me.   20
Old Banks. Down with them when I bid thee, quickly. I'll make

thy bones rattle in thy skin else.

Elizabeth Sawyer. You won't, churl, cut-throat, miser! [*Throws
    down sticks.*] There they be. Would they stuck 'cross thy
    throat, thy bowels, thy maw, thy midriff.   25

Old Banks. Sayest thou me so? Hag, out of my ground!

                    [*Beats her.*]

Elizabeth Sawyer. Dost strike me, slave, curmudgeon! Now thy
    bones ache, thy joints cramp, and convulsions stretch and
    crack thy sinews!

Old Banks. Cursing, thou hag! Take that and that.   30

                [Beats her and] exit.

Elizabeth Sawyer. Strike, do, and withered may that hand and
                                                                     arm
    Whose blows have lamed me drop from the rotten trunk.
    Abuse me! Beat me! Call me hag and witch!
    What is the name? Where and by what art learned?
    What spells, what charms or invocations   35
    May the thing called Familiar be purchased?

    Enter YOUNG BANKS *and three or four more* [*Morris Dancers*].

Young Banks. A new head for the tabor, and silver tipping for the
    pipe. Remember that, and forget not five leash of new bells.

First Dancer. Double bells! Crooked Lane, ye shall have 'em
    straight in Crooked Lane. Double bells all if it be possible.   40

Young Banks. Double bells? Double coxcombs! Trebles, buy me
    trebles, all trebles, for our purpose is to be in the altitudes.

Second Dancer. All trebles? Not a mean?

Young Banks. Not one. The morris is so cast we'll have neither
    mean nor base in our company, fellow Rowland.   45

Third Dancer. What! Nor a counter?

Young Banks. By no means, no hunting counter. Leave that to
    Enville Chase men. All trebles, all in the altitudes. Now for the
    disposing of parts in the morris, little or no labour will serve.

Second Dancer. If you that be minded to follow your leader, know   50
    me, an ancient honour belonging to our house, for a fore-horse
    in a team and fore-gallant in a morris. My father's stable is not
    unfurnished.

Third Dancer. So much for the fore-horse, but how for a good
    hobby-horse?   55

Young Banks. For a hobby-horse? Let me see an almanac. [*Consults
    almanac.*] Midsummer-moon, let me see ye. 'When the moon's
    in the full, then's wit in the wane.' No more. Use your best skill;

your morris will suffer an eclipse.

First Dancer. An eclipse?   60

Young Banks. A strange one.

Second Dancer. Strange?

Young Banks. Yes, and most sudden. Remember the fore-gallant
     and forget the hobby-horse. The whole body of your morris
     will be darkened. There be of us—but 'tis no matter. Forget the   65
     hobby-horse.

First Dancer. Cuddy Banks, have you forgot since he paced it from
     Enville Chase to Edmonton? Cuddy, honest Cuddy, cast thy
     stuff.

Young Banks. Suffer may ye all. It shall be known I can take mine   70
     ease as well as another man. Seek your hobby-horse where you
     can get him.

First Dancer. Cuddy, honest Cuddy, we confess and are sorry for
     our neglect.

Second Dancer. The old horse shall have a new bridle.   75

Third Dancer. The caparisons new painted.

Fourth Dancer. The tail repaired.

First Dancer. The snaffle and the bosses new saffroned o'er. Kind,—

Second Dancer. Honest,—

Third Dancer. Loving, ingenious,—   80

Fourth Dancer. Affable Cuddy.

Young Banks. To show I am not flint but affable, as you say, very
     well stuffed, a kind of warm dough or puff-paste, I relent, I
     connive, most affable Jack. Let the hobby-horse provide a
     strong back. He shall not want a belly when I am in 'em.   85

     [*Sees* ELIZABETH SAWYER.]

But 'uds me, Mother Sawyer!

First Dancer. The old Witch of Edmonton! If our mirth be not
     crossed—

Second Dancer. Bless us, Cuddy, and let her curse her tother eye
     out. What dost now?   90

Young Banks. Ungirt, unblessed, says the proverb; but my girdle
     shall serve a riding knot, and a fig for all the witches in Chris-
     tendom! What wouldst thou?

First Dancer. The devil cannot abide to be crossed.

Second Dancer. And scorns to come at any man's whistle.   95

Third Dancer. Away—

Fourth Dancer. With the witch!

All. Away with the Witch of Edmonton!

                         Ex[eunt] in strange postur[es].

Elizabeth Sawyer. Still vexed! Still tortured! That curmudgeon
                                                    Banks
    Is ground of all my scandal. I am shunned   100
    And hated like a sickness, made a scorn
    To all degrees and sexes. I have heard old beldams
    Talk of familiars in the shape of mice,
    Rats, ferrets, weasels and I wot not what,
    That have appeared and sucked, some say, their blood.   105
    But by what means they came acquainted with them
    I'm now ignorant. Would some power, good or bad,
    Instruct me which way I might be revenged
    Upon this churl, I'd go out of myself
    And give this fury leave to dwell within   110
    This ruined cottage ready to fall with age,
    Abjure all goodness, be at hate with prayer,
    And study curses, imprecations,
    Blasphemous speeches, oaths, detested oaths,
    Or anything that's ill; so I might work   115
    Revenge upon this miser, this black cur
    That barks and bites, and sucks the very blood
    Of me and of my credit. 'Tis all one
    To be a witch as to be counted one.
    Vengeance, shame, ruin light upon that canker!   120

Enter DOG.

Dog. Ho! Have I found thee cursing? Now thou art mine own.
Elizabeth Sawyer. Thine? What art thou?
Dog.   He thou hast so often
    Importuned to appear to thee, the devil.
Elizabeth Sawyer.   Bless me! The devil?
Dog. Come, do not fear, I love thee much too well
    To hurt or fright thee. If I seem terrible,   125
    It is to such as hate me. I have found
    Thy love unfeigned, have seen and pitied
    Thy open wrongs, and come, out of my love,
    To give thee just revenge against thy foes.
Elizabeth Sawyer. May I believe thee?
Dog.   To confirm't, command me   130
    Do any mischief unto man or beast,
    And I'll effect it, on condition
    That, uncompelled, thou make a deed of gift
    Of soul and body to me.
Elizabeth Sawyer.   Out, alas!
    My soul and body?

[handwritten margin note:] Same thing the devil says to Faustus

Dog.   And that instantly,   135
    And seal it with thy blood. If thou deniest
    I'll tear thy body in a thousand pieces.
Elizabeth Sawyer. I know not where to seek relief. But shall I,
    After such covenants sealed, see full revenge
    On all that wrong me?
Dog.   Ha, ha! Silly woman!   140
    The devil is no liar to such as he loves.
    Didst ever know or hear the devil a liar
    To such as he affects?
Elizabeth Sawyer. Then I am thine, at least so much of me
    As I can call mine own.
Dog.   Equivocations?   145
    Art mine or no? Speak or I'll tear—
Elizabeth Sawyer.   All thine.
Dog. Seal't with thy blood.

        Sucks her arm, thunder and lightning.

        See, now I dare call thee mine.
    For proof, command me. Instantly I'll run
    To any mischief; goodness can I none.
Elizabeth Sawyer. And I desire as little. There's an old churl,   150
    One Banks—
Dog.   That wronged thee. He lamed thee, called thee
                               witch.
Elizabeth Sawyer. The same; first upon him I'd be revenged.
Dog. Thou shalt. Do but name how.
Elizabeth Sawyer.   Go touch his life.
Dog. I cannot.
Elizabeth Sawyer. Hast thou not vowed? Go kill the slave.
Dog. I wonnot.
Elizabeth Sawyer. I'll cancel then my gift.
Dog.   Ha, ha!
Elizabeth Sawyer.   Dost laugh?   155
    Why wilt not kill him?
Dog.   Fool, because I cannot.
    Though we have power, know it is circumscribed
    And tied in limits. Though he be curst to thee,
    Yet of himself he is loving to the world
    And charitable to the poor. Now men   160
    That, as he, love goodness, though in smallest measure,
    Live without compass of our reach. His cattle
    And corn I'll kill and mildew, but his life,

Until I take him as I late found thee,
Cursing and swearing, I have no power to touch.   165
Elizabeth Sawyer. Work on his corn and cattle then.
Dog.   I shall.
The Witch of Edmonton shall see his fall
If she at least put credit in my power,
And in mine only, make orisons to me,
And none but me.
Elizabeth Sawyer.   Say how, and in what manner.   170
Dog. I'll tell thee. When thou wishest ill,
Corn, man or beast would spoil or kill,
Turn thy back against the sun
And mumble this short orison:
If thou to death or shame pursue 'em,   175
Sanctibicetur nomen tuum.
Elizabeth Sawyer. If thou to death or shame pursue 'em
Sanctibecetur nomen tuum.
Dog. Perfect. Farewell. Our first-made promises
We'll put in execution against Banks.   *Exit.*   180
Elizabeth Sawyer. Contaminetur nomen tuum. I'm an expert
                                                    scholar,
Speak Latin, or I know not well what language,
As well as the best of 'em. But who comes here?

Enter YOUNG BANKS.

The son of my worst foe. *To death pursue 'em*
Et sanctabecetur nomen tuum.   185
Young Banks. What's that she mumbles? The devil's *pater noster?*
Would it were else! Mother Sawyer, good morrow.
Elizabeth Sawyer. Ill morrow to thee, and all the world that flout a
poor old woman. *To death pursue 'em, and sanctabacetur*
nomen tuum.   190
Young Banks. Nay, good Gammer Sawyer, whate'er it please my
father to call you, I know you are—
Elizabeth Sawyer. A witch.
Young Banks. A witch? Would you were else i'faith!
Elizabeth Sawyer. Your father knows I am by this.   195
Young Banks. I would he did.
Elizabeth Sawyer. And so in time may you.
Young Banks. I would I might else. But, witch or no witch, you are a
motherly woman, and though my father be a kind of God-bless-
us, as they say, I have an earnest suit to you. And if you'll be so   200
kind to ka me one good turn, I'll be so courteous as to kob you
another.

Elizabeth Sawyer. What's that? To spurn, beat me and call me
    witch, as your kind father doth?
Young Banks. My father? I am ashamed to own him. If he has hurt   205
    the head of thy credit there's money to buy thee a plaster. [*Gives
    her money.*] And a small courtesy I would require at thy hands.
Elizabeth Sawyer. You seem a good young man, [*Aside*] and I must
    dissemble the better to accomplish my revenge. [*To him*] But
    for this silver, what wouldst have me do? Bewitch thee?   210
Young Banks. No, by no means, I am bewitched already. I would
    have thee so good as to unwitch me, or witch another with me
    for company.
Elizabeth Sawyer. I understand thee not. Be plain, my son.
Young Banks. As a pike-staff, mother. You know Kate Carter?   215
Elizabeth Sawyer. The wealthy yeoman's daughter. What of her?
Young Banks. That same party hath bewitched me.
Elizabeth Sawyer. Bewitched thee?
Young Banks. Bewitched me, *hisce auribus.* I saw a little devil fly
    out of her eye like a burbolt, which sticks at this hour up to the   220
    feathers in my heart. Now my request is to send one of thy
    what-d'ye-call-'ems, either to pluck that out, or stick another as
    fast in hers. Do, and here's my hand, I am thine for three lives.
Elizabeth Sawyer. [*Aside*] We shall have sport. [*To him*] Thou art
    in love with her?   225
Young Banks. Up to the very hilts, mother.
Elizabeth Sawyer. And thou'dst have me make her love thee too?
Young Banks. [*Aside*] I think she'll prove a witch in earnest. [*To
    her*] Yes, I could find in my heart to strike her three quarters
    deep in love with me too.   230
Elizabeth Sawyer. But dost thou think that I can do't, and I alone?
Young Banks. Truly, Mother Witch, I do verily believe so and,
    when I see it done, I shall be half persuaded so too.
Elizabeth Sawyer. It's enough. What art can do, be sure of. Turn to
    the west, and whatsoe'er thou hearest or seest, stand silent and   235
    be not afraid.

    She stamps. Enter the DOG; *he fawns and leaps upon her.*

Young Banks. Afraid, Mother Witch? Turn my face to the west? I
    said I should always have a back-friend of her, and now it's out.
    An her little devil should be hungry, come sneaking behind me
    like a cowardly catchpole and clap his talons on my haunches!   240
    'Tis woundy cold sure. I dudder and shake like an aspen-leaf
    every joint of me.
Elizabeth Sawyer. *To scandal and disgrace pursue 'em
    Et sanctabicetur nomen tuum.*

How now, my son, how is't?   245

Exit DOG.

Young Banks. Scarce in a clean life, Mother Witch. But did your
   goblin and you spout Latin together?

Elizabeth Sawyer. A kind of charm I work by. Didst thou hear me?

Young Banks. I heard I know not the devil what mumble in a scurvy
   base tone, like a drum that had taken cold in the head the last   250
   muster. Very comfortable words. What were they? And who
   taught them you?

Elizabeth Sawyer. A great learned man.

Young Banks. Learned man! Learned devil it was as soon! But what,
   what comfortable news about the party?   255

Elizabeth Sawyer. Who? Kate Carter? I'll tell thee. Thou knowst the
   stile at the west end of thy father's peas-field. Be there tomorrow night after sunset and the first live thing thou seest be sure
   to follow, and that shall bring thee to thy love.

Young Banks. In the peas-field? Has she a mind to codlings already? 260
   The first living thing I meet, you say, shall bring me to her?

Elizabeth Sawyer. To a sight of her, I mean. She will seem wantonly
   coy and flee thee, but follow her close and boldly. Do but embrace her in thy arms once and she is thine own.

Young Banks. At the stile at the west end of my father's peas-land, 265
   the first live thing I see, follow and embrace her and she shall be
   thine. Nay, an I come to embracing once she shall be mine. I'll
   go near to make at eaglet else.   *Exit.*

Elizabeth Sawyer. A ball well bandied! Now the set's half won.
   The father's wrong I'll wreak upon the son.   *Exit.* 270

[ACT II] SCENE ii

Enter [OLD] CARTER, WARBECK [*and*] SOMERTON.

Old Carter. How now, gentlemen! Cloudy? I know, Master
   Warbeck, you are in a fog about my daughter's marriage.

Warbeck. And can you blame me, sir?

Old Carter. Nor you me justly. Wedding and hanging are tied up
   both in a proverb, and destiny is the juggler that unties the knot.   5
   My hope is you are reserved to a richer fortune than my poor
   daughter.

Warbeck. However, your promise—

Old Carter. Is a kind of debt, I confess it.

Warbeck. Which honest men should pay.   10

Old Carter. Yet some gentlemen break in that point now and then,
   by your leave, sir.

Somerton. I confess thou hast had a little wrong in the wench, but
    patience is the only salve to cure it. Since Thorney has won the
    wench, he has most reason to wear her.   15
Warbeck. Love in this kind admits no reason to wear her.
Old Carter. Then love's a fool, and what wise man will take
    exception?
Somerton. Come, frolic, Ned. Were every man master of his own
    fortune, Fate might pick straws and Destiny go a-wool   20
    -gathering.
Warbeck. You hold yours in a string, though. 'Tis well, but if there
    be any equity, look thou to meet the like usage ere long.
Somerton. In my love to her sister Katherine? Indeed, they are a pair
    of arrows drawn out of one quiver and should fly at an even   25
    length. If she do run after her sister—
Warbeck. Look for the same mercy at my hands as I have received at
    thine.
Somerton. She'll keep a surer compass. I have too strong a con-
    fidence to mistrust her.   30
Warbeck. And that confidence is a wind that has blown many a
    married man ashore at Cuckold's Haven, I can tell you. I wish
    yours more prosperous though.
Old Carter. Whate'er you wish, I'll master my promise to him.
Warbeck. Yes, as you did to me.   35
Old Carter. No more of that, if you love me. But for the more
    assurance, the next offered occasion shall consummate the mar-
    riage, and that once sealed—

        Enter YOUNG [FRANK] THORNEY *and* SUSAN.

Somerton. Leave the manage of the rest to my care. But see, the
    bridegroom and bride come, the new pair of Sheffield knives   40
    fitted both to one sheath.
Warbeck. The sheath might have been better fitted if somebody had
    their due. But—
Somerton. No harsh language, if thou lovest me. Frank Thorney
    has done—   45
Warbeck. No more than I, or thou, or any man, things so standing,
    would have attempted.
Somerton. Good-morrow, Master Bridegroom.
Warbeck.   Come, give thee joy.
    Mayst thou live long and happy in thy fair choice.
Frank Thorney. I thank ye, gentlemen.   50
    Kind Master Warbeck, I find you loving.
Warbeck. Thorney, that creature, [*Aside*] much good do thee
                                      with her,

[*To him*] Virtue and beauty hold fair mixture in her.
She's rich, no doubt, in both. Yet were she fairer
Thou art right worthy of her. Love her, Thorney;   55
'Tis nobleness in thee, in her but duty.
The match is fair and equal, the success
I leave to censure. Farewell, Mistress Bride:
Till now elected, thy old scorn deride.   *Exit.*
Somerton. Good Master Thorney.   [*Exit.*]   60
Old Carter. Nay, you shall not part till you see the barrels run a-tilt,
    gentlemen.   *Exit*
Susan. Why change you your face, sweetheart?
Frank Thorney.   Who? I?
    For nothing.
Susan.   Dear, say not so. A spirit of your
    Constancy cannot endure this change for nothing.   65
    I have observed strange variations in you.
Frank Thorney. In me?
Susan.   In you, sir. Awake, you seem to dream
    And in your sleep you utter sudden and
    Distracted accents, like one at enmity
    With peace. Dear loving husband, if I may dare   70
    To challenge any interest in you,
    Give me the reason fully. You may trust
    My breast as safely as your own.
Frank Thorney.   With what?
    You half amaze me. Prithee—
Susan.   Come, you shall not,
    Indeed, you shall not shut me from partaking   75
    The least dislike that grieves you. I am all yours.
Frank Thorney. And I all thine.
Susan.   You are not, if you keep
    The least grief from me; but I find the cause,
    It grew from me.
Frank Thorney.   From you?
Susan.   From some distaste
    In me or my behaviour. You are not kind   80
    In the concealment. 'Las, sir, I am young,
    Silly and plain; more, strange to those contents
    A wife should offer. Say but in what I fail,
    I'll study satisfaction.
Frank Thorney.   Come, in nothing.
Susan. I know I do. Knew I as well in what,   85
    You should not long be sullen. Prithee, love,
    If I have been immodest or too bold,

Speak't in a frown; if peevishly too nice,
Show't in a smile. Thy liking is the glass
By which I'll habit my behaviour.   90
Frank Thorney. Wherefore dost weep now?
Susan.   You, sweet, have the power
To make me passionate as an April day;
Now smile, then weep; now pale, then crimson red.
You are the powerful moon of my blood's sea,
To make it ebb or flow into my face   95
As your looks change.
Frank Thorney.   Change thy conceit, I prithee.
Thou art all perfection. Diana herself
Swells in thy thoughts and moderates thy beauty.
Within thy left eye amorous Cupid sits
Feathering love-shafts, whose golden heads he dipped   100
In thy chaste breast. In the other lies
Blushing Adonis scarfed in modesties.
And still as wanton Cupid blows love-fires,
Adonis quenches out unchaste desires.
And from these two I briefly do imply   105
A perfect emblem of thy modesty.
Then, prithee, dear, maintain no more dispute,
For when thou speakst, it's fit all tongues be mute.
Susan. Come, come, those golden strings of flattery
Shall not tie up my speech, sir. I must know   110
The ground of your disturbance.
Frank Thorney.   Then look here,
For here, here is the fen in which this Hydra
Of discontent grows rank.
Susan.   Heaven shield it! Where?
Frank Thorney. In mine own bosom, here the cause has root.
The poisoned leeches twist about my heart,   115
And will, I hope, confound me.
Susan.   You speak riddles.
Frank Thorney. Take't plainly then. 'Twas told me by a woman,
Known and approved in palmistry,
I should have two wives.
Susan.   Two wives? Sir, I take it
Exceeding likely. But let not conceit hurt you.   120
You are afraid to bury me?
Frank Thorney.   No, no, my Winnifride.
Susan. How say you? Winnifride? You forget me.
Frank Thorney. No, I forget myself, Susan.
Susan.   In what?

Frank Thorney. Talking of wives I pretend Winnifride,
    A maid that at my mother's waited on me   125
    Before thyself.
Susan.   I hope, sir, she may live
    To take my place. But why should all this move you?
Frank Thorney. [*Aside*] The poor girl! She has't before thee,
    And that's the fiend torments me.
Susan.   Yet why should this
    Raise mutiny within you? Such presages   130
    Prove often false, or say it should be true?
Frank Thorney. That I should have another wife?
Susan.   Yes, many;
    If they be good, the better.
Frank Thorney.   Never any equal
    To thee in goodness.
Susan.   Sir, I could wish I were
    Much better for you. Yet if I knew your fate   135
    Ordained you for another, I could wish,
    So well I love you and your hopeful pleasure,
    Me in my grave, and my poor virtues added
    To my successor.
Frank Thorney.   Prithee, prithee, talk not
    Of death or graves. Thou art so rare a goodness   140
    As death would rather put itself to death
    Than murder thee. But we, as all things else,
    Are mutable and changing.
Susan.   Yet you still move
    In your first sphere of discontent. Sweet, chase
    Those clouds of sorrow, and shine clearly on me.   145
Frank Thorney. At my return I will.
Susan.   Return? Ah me!
    Will you then leave me?
Frank Thorney.   For a time I must.
    But how? As birds their young, or loving bees
    Their hives, to fetch home richer dainties.
Susan.   Leave me?
    Now has my fear met its effect. You shall not,   150
    Cost it my life, you shall not.
Frank Thorney.   Why? Your reason?
Susan. Like to the lapwing have you all this while
    With your false love deluded me, pretending
    Counterfeit senses for your discontent,
    And now at last it is by chance stole from you.   155
Frank Thorney. What! What by chance?

Susan.   Your pre-appointed meeting
     Of single combat with young Warbeck.
Frank Thorney.   Ha!
Susan. Even so! Dissemble not, 'tis too apparent.
     Then in his look I read it. Deny it not,
     I see't apparent. Cost it my undoing,   160
     And unto that my life, I will not leave you.
Frank Thorney. Not until when?
Susan.   Till he and you be friends.
     Was this your cunning, and then flam me off
     With an old witch, two wives and Winnifride?
     You're not so kind indeed as I imagined.   165
Frank Thorney. And you more fond by far than I expected.
     It is a virtue that attends thy kind.
     But of our business within; and by this kiss
     I'll anger thee no more, 'troth, chuck, I will not.

                    [*Kisses her.*]

Susan. You shall have no just cause.
Frank Thorney.   Dear Sue, I shall not. *Exeunt.* 170

ACT III

SCENE i

Enter [YOUNG] CUDDY BANKS *and Morris-dancers.*

First Dancer. Nay, Cuddy, prithee do not leave us now. If we part
     all this night, we shall not meet before day.
Second Dancer. I prithee, Banks, let's keep together now.
Young Banks. If you were wise, a word would serve; but as you are,
     I must be forced to tell you again I have a little private business,   5
     an hour's work; it may prove but an half hour's, as luck may
     serve, and then I take horse and along with you. Have we e'er a
     witch in the morris?
First Dancer. No, no; no woman's part but Maid Marian and the
     hobby-horse.   10
Young Banks. I'll have a witch. I love a witch.
First Dancer. 'Faith, witches themselves are so common now-a-
     days that the counterfeit will not be regarded. They say we have
     three or four in Edmonton besides Mother Sawyer.
Second Dancer. I would she would dance her part with us.   15

Third Dancer. So would not I, for, if she comes, the devil and all
   comes along with her.
Young Banks. Well, I'll have a witch. I have loved a witch ever since
   I played at cherry-pit. Leave me and get my horse dressed. Give
   him oats, but water him not till I come. Whither do we foot it   20
   first?
Second Dancer. To Sir Arthur Clarington's first, then whither thou
   wilt.
Young Banks. Well, I am content. But we must up to Carter's, the
   rich yeoman. I must be seen on hobby-horse there.   25
First Dancer. O, I smell him now. I'll lay my ears Banks is in love
   and that's the reason he would walk melancholy by himself.
Young Banks. Ha! Who was that said I was in love?
First Dancer. Not I.
Second Dancer. Not I.   30
Young Banks. Go to, no more of that. When I understand what you
   speak, I know what you say. Believe that.
First Dancer. Well, 'twas I, I'll not deny it. I meant no hurt in't. I
   have seen you walk up to Carter's of Chessum. Banks, were not
   you there last Shrovetide?   35
Young Banks. Yes, I was ten days together there the last Shrovetide.
Second Dancer. How could that be when there are but seven days in
   the week?
Young Banks. Prithee peace! I reckon *stila nova* as a traveller. Thou
   understandest as a fresh-water farmer that never sawest a week   40
   beyond sea. Ask any soldier that ever received his pay but in the
   Low Countries, and he'll tell thee there are eight days in the
   week there hard by. How dost thou think they rise in High
   Germany, Italy and those remoter places?
Third Dancer. Ay, but simply there are but seven days in the week   45
   yet.
Young Banks. No, simply as thou understandest. Prithee, look but
   in the lover's almanac. When he has been but three days absent,
   'O', says he, 'I have not seen my love these seven years. There's
   a long cut.' When he comes to her again, and embraces her, 'O',   50
   says he, 'now methinks I am in heaven', and that's a pretty step.
   He that can get up to heaven in ten days need not repent his
   journey. You may ride a hundred days in a caroche, and be
   further off than when you set forth. But, I pray you, good
   morris-mates, now leave me. I will be with you by midnight.   55
First Dancer. Well, since he will be alone, we'll back again and
   trouble him no more.
All. But remember, Banks.
Young Banks. The hobby-horse shall be remembered. But hark

you, get Poldavis, the barber's boy, for the witch, because he   60
can show his art better than another.

         Exeunt [all but YOUNG BANKS].

Well, now to my walk. I am near the place where I should meet I
know not what. Say I meet a thief, I must follow him, if to the
gallows. Say I meet a horse, or hare, or hound, still I must
follow. Some slow-paced beast, I hope; yet love is full of light-   65
ness in the heaviest lovers.

        [*Enter* DOG.]

Ha! My guide is come. A water-dog. I am thy first man, Sculler.
I go with thee. Ply no other but myself. Away with the boat.
Land me but at Katherine's Dock, my sweet Katherine's Dock,
and I'll be a fare to thee. [DOG *leads*.] That way? Nay, which   70
way thou wilt, thou knowst the way better than I. [*Aside*] Fine
gentle cur it is, and well brought up I warrant him. [*To Dog*]
We go a-ducking, spaniel; thou shalt fetch me the ducks, pretty
kind rascal.

    Enter [a] SPIRIT *in shape of* KATHERINE,
      vizarded, and takes it off.

Spirit. [*Aside*] Thus throw I off mine own essential horror,   75
  And take the shape of a sweet lovely maid
  Whom this fool dotes on. We can meet his folly,
  But from his virtues must be runaways.
  We'll sport with him, but when we reckoning call,
  We know where to receive. Th' witch pays for all.   80

       DOG *barks.*

Young Banks. Ay? Is that the watchword? She's come. Well, if ever
  we be married, it shall be at Barking Church in memory of thee.
  Now come behind, kind cur.
    And have I met thee, sweet Kate?
    I will teach thee to walk so late.   85
  O, see, we meet in metre. What? Dost thou trip from me? O
  that I were upon my hobby-horse, I would mount after thee
  so nimble.
    'Stay, nymph, stay, nymph,' singed Apollo.
    Tarry and kiss me, sweet nymph, stay.   90
    Tarry and kiss me, sweet.
    We will to Chessum Street,
    And then to the house stands in the highway.
  Nay, by your leave, I must embrace you.

       [*Exeunt* SPIRIT *and* YOUNG BANKS.]

[*Within*] O, help, help! I am drowned, I am drowned!   95
Dog. Ha, ha, ha, ha!

Enter [YOUNG BANKS] *wet.*

Young Banks. This was an ill night to go a-wooing in; I find it now
in Pond's almanac. Thinking to land at Katherine's Dock, I was
almost at Gravesend. I'll never go to a wench in the dog-days
again. Yet 'tis cool enough. Had you never a paw in this dog-   100
trick? A mangie take that black hide of yours! I'll throw you in
at Limehouse in some tanner's pit or other.
Dog. Ha, ha, ha, ha!
Young Banks. How now! Who's that laughs at me? Hist to him.

DOG *barks.*

Peace, peace! Thou didst but thy kind neither. 'Twas my own   105
fault.
Dog. Take heed how thou trustest the devil another time.
Young Banks. How now! Who's that speaks? I hope you have not
your reading tongue about you?
Dog. Yes, I can speak.   110
Young Banks. The devil you can! You have read Aesop's fables,
then. I have played one of your parts then, the dog that catched
at the shadow in the water. Pray you, let me catechise you a
little. What might one call your name, dog?
Dog. My dame calls me Tom.   115
Young Banks. 'Tis well, and she may call me Ass, so there's an
whole one betwixt us, Tom-Ass. She said I should follow you,
indeed. Well, Tom, give me thy fist, we are friends. You shall be
mine ingle. I love you, but I pray you let's have no more of these
ducking devices.   120
Dog. Not, if you love me. Dogs love where they are beloved. Cher-
ish me, and I'll do anything for thee.
Young Banks. Well, you shall have jowls and livers. I have butchers
to my friends that shall bestow 'em, and I will keep crusts and
bones for you, if you'll be a kind dog, Tom.   125
Dog. Anything. I'll help thee to thy love.
Young Banks. Wilt thou? That promise shall cost me a brown loaf,
though I steal it out of my father's cupboard. You'll eat stolen
goods, Tom, will you not?
Dog. O, best of all. The sweetest bits, those.   130
Young Banks. You shall not starve, Ningle Tom, believe that. If you
love fish, I'll help you to maids and soles. I'm acquainted with a
fishmonger.
Dog. Maids and soles? O, sweet bits! Banqueting stuff, those.

Young Banks. One thing I would request you, Ningle, as you have   135
    played the knavish cur with me a little, that you would mingle
    amongst our morris-dancers in the morning. You can dance?
Dog. Yes, yes, anything. I'll be there, but unseen to any but thyself.
    Get thee gone before. Fear not my presence. I have work
    tonight. I serve more masters, more dames, than one.   140
Young Banks. [*Aside*] He can serve Mammon and the Devil too!
Dog. It shall concern thee and thy love's purchase.
    There's a gallant rival loves the maid,
    And likely is to have her. Mark what a mischief,
    Before the morris ends, shall light on him.   145
Young Banks. O, sweet Ningle, thy neuf once again. Friends must
    part for a time. Farewell, with this remembrance, shalt have
    bread too when we meet again. If ever there were an honest
    devil, 'twill be the Devil of Edmonton, I see. Farewell, Tom. I
    prithee dog me as soon as thou canst.   *Exit* [YOUNG] BANKS.   150
Dog. I'll not miss thee, and be merry with thee.
    Those that are joys denied must take delight
    In sins and mischiefs; 'tis the devil's right.   *Exit* DOG.

[ACT III, SCENE ii]

Enter YOUNG [FRANK] THORNEY, WINNIFRIDE *as a boy,*
[*weeping.*]

Frank Thorney. Prithee no more. Those tears give nourishment
    To weeds and briers in me, which shortly will
    O'ergrow and top my head. My shame will sit
    And cover all that can be seen of me.
Winnifride. I have not shown this cheek in company,   5
    Pardon me now. Thus singled with yourself,
    It calls a thousand sorrows round about;
    Some going before and some on either side,
    But infinite behind; all chained together.
    Your second adulterous marriage leads,   10
    That's the sad eclipse: the effects must follow
    As plagues of shame, spite, scorn and obloquy.
Frank Thorney. Why? Hast thou not left one hour's patience
    To add to all the rest? One hour bears us
    Beyond the reach of all these enemies.   15
    Are we not now set forward in the flight,
    Provided with the dowry of my sin
    To keep us in some other nation?

> While we together are, we are at home
> In any place.

Winnifride.   'Tis foul ill-gotten coin,   20
> Far worse than usury or extortion.

Frank Thorney. Let my father then make the restitution,
> Who forced me take the bribe. It is his gift
> And patrimony to me; so I receive it.
> He would not bless, nor look a father on me,   25
> Until I satisfied his angry will.
> When I was sold, I sold myself again—
> Some knaves have done't in lands, and I in body—
> For money, and I have the hire. But, sweet, no more,
> 'Tis hazard of discovery, our discourse,   30
> And then prevention takes off all our hopes.
> For only but to take her leave of me
> My wife is coming.

Winnifride.   Who coming? Your wife!

Frank Thorney. No, no, thou art her. The woman, I knew
> Not how to call her now, but after this day   35
> She shall be quite forgot and have no name
> In my remembrance. See, see, she's come.

Enter SUSAN.

>   Go lead
> The horses to the hill's top, there I'll meet thee.

Susan. Nay, with your favour, let him stay a little.
> I would part with him too, because he is   40
> Your sole companion, and I'll begin with him,
> Reserving you the last.

Frank Thorney.   Ay, with all my heart.

Susan. You may hear, if it please you, sir.

Frank Thorney.   No, 'tis not fit.
> Some rudiments, I conceive, they must be,
> To overlook my slippery footings. And so—   45

Susan. No, indeed, sir.

Frank Thorney.   Tush, I know it must be so
> And 'tis necessary. On, but be brief.   [*Walks aside.*]

Winnifride. What charge soe'er you lay upon me, mistress,
> I shall support it faithfully, being honest,
> To my best strength.   50

Susan. Believe't shall be no other. I know you were
> Commended to my husband by a noble knight.

Winnifride. O, gods! O, mine eyes!

Susan.   How now? What ail'st thou, lad?

Winnifride. Something hit mine eye, it makes it water still,
 Even as you said 'commended to my husband'.   55
 Some dor I think it was. I was, forsooth,
 Commended to him by Sir Arthur Clarington.
Susan. Whose servant once my Thorney was himself.
 That title, methinks, should make you almost fellows,
 Or at the least much more than a servant,   60
 And I am sure he will respect you so.
 Your love to him, then, needs no spur from me,
 And what for my sake you will ever do,
 'Tis fit it should be bought with something more
 Than fair entreats. Look! Here's a jewel for thee, 65
 A pretty wanton label for thine ear,
 And I would have it hang there, still to whisper
 These words to thee, 'Thou hast my jewel with thee'.
 It is but earnest of a larger bounty
 When thou returnest with praises of thy service, 70
 Which I am confident thou wilt deserve.
 Why, thou art many now besides thyself.
 Thou mayst be servant, friend and wife to him.
 A good wife is them all. A friend can play
 The wife and servant's part, and shift enough, 75
 No less the servant can the friend and wife.
 'Tis all but sweet society, good counsel,
 Interchanged loves, yes, and counsel-keeping.
Frank Thorney. Not done yet?
Susan. Even now, sir.   80
Winnifride. Mistress, believe my vow. Your severe eye,
 Were it present to command, your bounteous hand,
 Were it then by to buy or bribe my service,
 Shall not make me more dear or near unto him,
 Than I shall voluntary. I'll be all your charge, 85
 Servant, friend, wife to him.
Susan.   Wilt thou?
 Now blessings go with thee for't! Courtesies
 Shall meet thee coming home.
Winnifride.   Pray you, say plainly,
 Mistress, are you jealous of him? If you be,
 I'll look to him that way too.
Susan.   Sayst thou so?   90
 I would thou hadst a woman's bosom now.
 We have weak thoughts within us. Alas,
 There's nothing so strong in us as suspicion.
 But I dare not, nay, I will not think

So hardly of my Thorney.
Winnifride.   Believe it, mistress,   95
I'll be no pander to him, and if I find
Any loose lubric scapes in him, I'll watch him,
And at my return protest I'll show you all.
He shall hardly offend without my knowledge.
Susan. Thine own diligence is that I press,   100
And not the curious eye over his faults.
Farewell. If I should never see thee more,
Take it forever.
Frank Thorney. Prithee take that along with thee,

Gives his sword.

and haste thee
To the hill's top. I'll be there instantly.   105
Susan. No haste, I prithee, slowly as thou canst.

Exit WINNIFRIDE.

Pray let him obey me now; 'tis happily
His last service to me. My power is e'en
A-going out of sight.
Frank Thorney.   Why would you delay?
We have no other business now but to part.   110
Susan. And will not that, sweetheart, ask a long time?
Methinks it is the hardest piece of work
That e'er I took in hand.
Frank Thorney.   Fie, fie! Why look,
I'll make it plain and easy to you. Farewell.

Kisses [her].

Susan. Ah, 'las! I am not half perfect in it yet.   115
I must have it read over an hundred times.
Pray you take some pains, I confess my dullness.
Frank Thorney. [Aside] What a thorn this rose grows on! Parting
were sweet,
But what a trouble 'twill be to obtain it!
[*To her*] Come.

Kisses [her].

Again and again. Farewell. Yet wilt return?   120
All questions of my journey, my stay, employment
And revisitation, fully I have answered all.
There's nothing now behind, but nothing.
Susan. And that nothing is more hard than anything,
Than all the everythings. This request—

Frank Thorney.   What is it?   125
Susan. That I may bring you through one pasture more
            Up to yon knot of trees. Amongst those shadows
            I'll vanish from you, they shall teach me how.
Frank Thorney. Why, 'tis granted. Come, walk then.
Susan.   Nay, not too fast.
            They say slow things have best perfection;   130
            The gentle shower wets to fertility,
            The churlish storm may mischief with his bounty;
            The baser beasts take strength, even from the womb,
            But the lord lion's whelp is feeble long.   *Exeunt.*

                    [ACT III, SCENE iii]

                        Enter DOG.

Dog. Now for an early mischief and a sudden.
            The mind's about it now. One touch from me
            Soon sets the body forward.

            Enter YOUNG [FRANK] THORNEY [*and*] SUSAN.

Frank Thorney. Your request is out. Yet will you leave me?
Susan.   What?
            So churlishly? You'll make me stay for ever,   5
            Rather than part with such a sound from you.
Frank Thorney. Why, you almost anger me. Pray you, be gone.
            You have no company, and 'tis very early;
            Some hurt may betide you homewards.
Susan.   Tush! I fear none.
            To leave you is the greatest hurt I can suffer.   10
            Besides, I expect your father and mine own
            To meet me back, or overtake me with you.
            They began to stir when I came after you;
            I know they'll not be long.
Frank Thorney.   [*Aside*] So, I shall have more trouble.

                        DOG *rubs him.*

            Thank you for that. Then I'll ease all at once.   15
            'Tis done now, what I ne'er thought on. [*To her*]
                                        You shall not go back.
Susan. Why? Shall I go along with thee? Sweet music!
Frank Thorney. No, to a better place.
Susan.   Any place, I.

I'm there at home where thou pleasest to have me.
Frank Thorney. At home? I'll leave you in your last lodging.   20
    I must kill you.
Susan.   O, fine! You'd fright me from you.
Frank Thorney. You see I had no purpose, I'm unarmed.
    'Tis this minute's decree, and it must be.
    Look, this will serve your turn.

[Draws a knife.]

Susan.   I'll not turn from it
    If you be earnest, sir. Yet you may tell me   25
    Wherefore you'll kill me.
Frank Thorney.   Because you are a whore.
Susan. There's one deep wound already—a whore?
    'Twas ever further from me than the thought
    Of this black hour. A whore?
Frank Thorney.   Yes, I'll prove it,
    And you shall confess it. You are my whore.   30
    No wife of mine. The word admits no second.
    I was before wedded to another, have her still.
    I do not lay the sin unto your charge,
    'Tis all mine own. Your marriage was my theft,
    For I espoused your dowry, and I have it.   35
    I did not purpose to have added murder;
    The devil did not prompt me. Till this minute
    You might have safe returned; now you cannot.
    You have dogged your own death.

Stabs her.

Susan.   And I deserve it.
    I'm glad my fate was so intelligent.   40
    'Twas some good spirit's motion. Die? O, 'twas time!
    How many years might I have slept in sin?
    Sin of my most hatred too, adultery!
Frank Thorney. Nay, sure, 'twas likely that the most was past,
    For I meant never to return to you   45
    After this parting.
Susan.   Why, then I thank you more.
    You have done lovingly, leaving yourself,
    That you would thus bestow me on another.
    Thou art my husband, Death, and I embrace thee
    With all the love I have. Forget the stain   50
    Of my unwitting sin, and then I come
    A crystal virgin to thee. My soul's purity

Shall with bold wings ascend the doors of Mercy,
For Innocence is ever her companion.
Frank Thorney. Not yet mortal? I would not linger you,   55
Or leave you a tongue to blab.

[Stabs her again.]

Susan. Now Heaven reward you ne'er the worse for me!
I did not think that death had been so sweet,
Nor I so apt to love him. I could ne'er die better
Had I stayed forty years for preparation,   60
For I'm in charity with all the world.
Let me for once be thine example, Heaven.
Do to this man as I him free forgive,
And may he better die and better live.

She dies.

Frank Thorney. 'Tis done, and I am in! Once past our height,   65
We scorn the deep'st abyss. This follows now,
To heal her wounds by dressing of the weapon.
Arms, thighs, hands, any place, we must not fail

Wounds himself.

Light scratches, giving such deep ones. The best I can
To bind myself to this tree. Now's the storm,   70
Which, if blown o'er, many fair days may follow.

DOG *ties him.*

So, so, I'm fast. I did not think I could
Have done so well behind me. How prosperous
And effectual mischief sometimes is. Help! Help!
Murder, murder, murder!   *Exit* DOG.   75

Enter [OLD] CARTER *and* OLD THORNEY.

Old Carter. Ha! Whom tolls the bell for?
Frank Thorney.   O! O!
Old Thorney.   Ah me!
The cause appears too soon; my child, my son!
Old Carter. Susan, girl, child! Not speak to thy father? Ha!
Frank Thorney. O lend me some assistance to o'ertake
This hapless woman.
Old Thorney.   Let's o'ertake the murderers.   80
Speak whilst thou canst, anon may be too late.
I fear thou hast death's mark upon thee too.
Frank Thorney. I know them both, yet such an oath is passed

As pulls damnation up if it be broke.
I dare not name 'em. Think what forced men do.   85
Old Thorney. Keep oath with murderers! That were a conscience
To hold the devil in.
Frank Thorney.   Nay, sir, I can describe 'em;
Shall show them as familiar as their names.
The taller of the two at this time wears
His satin doublet white but crimson lined,   90
Hose of black satin, cloak of scarlet—
Old Thorney. Warbeck, Warbeck, Warbeck! Do you list to this,
sir?
Old Carter. Yes, yes, I listen you. Here's nothing to be heard.
Frank Thorney. Th'other's cloak branched velvet, black,
velvet-lined
His suit.
Old Thorney. I have 'em already; Somerton, Somerton!   95
Binal revenge all this. Come, sir, the first work
Is to pursue the murderers, when we have removed
These mangled bodies hence.
Old Carter. Sir, take that carcass there, and give me this.
I'll not own her now, she's none of mine.   100
Bob me off with a dumb-show? No, I'll have life.
This is my son too, and while there's life in him,
'Tis half mine. Take you half that silence for't.
When I speak I look to be spoken to.
Forgetful slut!
Old Thorney.   Alas, what grief may do now!   105
Look, sir, I'll take this load of sorrow with me.
Old Carter. Ay, do, and I'll have this. How do you, sir?
Frank Thorney. O, very ill, sir.
Old Carter. Yes, I think so, but 'tis well you can speak yet.
There's no music but in sound, sound it must be.   110
I have not wept these twenty years before,
And that I guess was ere that girl was born.
Yet now methinks, if I but knew the way,
My heart's so full, I could weep night and day.   *Exeunt.*

[ACT III, SCENE iv]

Enter SIR ARTHUR CLARINGTON, WARBECK [*and*] SOMERTON.

Sir Arthur. Come, gentlemen, we must all help to grace
The nimble-footed youth of Edmonton,

That are so kind to call us up today
With an high morris.
Warbeck. I could wish it for the best it were the worst now.   5
Absurdity's in my opinion ever the best dancer in a morris.
Somerton. I could rather sleep than see 'em.
Sir Arthur. Not well, sir?
Somerton. 'Faith not ever thus leaden, yet I know no cause for't.
Warbeck. Now am I beyond mine own condition highly disposed to   10
mirth.
Sir Arthur. Well, you may have yet a morris to help both;
To strike you in a dump, and make him merry.

Enter [SAWGUT *the*] *fiddler and* [*the*] *Morris; all but* [YOUNG]
BANKS.

Sawgut. Come, will you set yourselves in morris-ray? The fore-bell,
second-bell, tenor and great-bell; Maid Marian for the same   15
bell. But where's the weather-cock now? The hobby-horse?
First Dancer. Is not Banks come yet? What a spite 'tis!
Sir Arthur. When set you forward, gentlemen?
Second Dancer. We stay but for the hobby-horse, sir. All our foot-
men are ready.   20
Somerton. 'Tis marvel your horse should be behind your foot.
Second Dancer. Yes, sir, he goes further about. We can come in at
the wicket, but the broad gate must be opened for him.

Enter [YOUNG] BANKS, [*as*] Hobby-Horse, *and* DOG.

Sir Arthur. O, we stayed for you, sir.
Young Banks. Only my horse wanted a shoe, sir, but we shall   25
make you amends ere we part.
Sir Arthur. Ay? Well said. Make 'em drink ere th·y begin.

Enter Servants *with beer.*

Young Banks. A bowl, I prithee, and a little for my horse; he'll
mount the better. Nay, give me. I must drink to him, he'll not
pledge else. [*Drinks.*] Here, Hobby.   30

Holds him the bowl.

I pray you. No? Not drink? You see, gentlemen, we can but
bring our horse to the water; he may choose whether he'll drink
or no.
Somerton. A good moral made plain by history.
Second Dancer. Strike up, Father Sawgut, strike up.   35
Sawgut. E'en when you will, children. Now in the name of the best

foot forward. How now! Not a word in thy guts? I think, children, my instrument has caught cold on the sudden.
Young Banks. [*Aside*] My ningle's knavery; Black Tom's doing.
All. Why, what mean you, Father Sawgut?   40
Young Banks. Why, what would you have him do? You hear his
fiddle is speechless.
Sawgut. I'll lay mine ear to my instrument that my poor fiddle is
bewitched. I played 'The Flowers in May' e'en now as sweet as
a violet. Now 'twill not go against the hair. You see, I can make   45
no more music than a beetle of a cow-turd.
Young Banks. Let me see, Father Sawgut. Say once you had a brave
hobby-horse that you were beholding to. I'll play and dance
too. [*Aside*] Ningle, away with it.
All. Ay, marry, sir.   50

> DOG *plays the morris;* [*the dancers give their morris;*] *which
> ended, enter a* Constable *and* Officers.

Constable. Away with jollity! 'Tis too sad an hour.
     Sir Arthur Clarington, your own assistance,
     In the King's name, I charge, for apprehension
     Of these two murderers, Warbeck and Somerton.
Sir Arthur. Ha! Flat murderers?   55
Somerton. Ha, ha, ha! This has awakened my melancholy.
Warbeck. And struck my mirth down flat. Murderers?
Constable. The accusation is flat against you, gentlemen.
     Sir, you may be satisfied with this.

> [*Shows his warrant.*]

     I hope you'll quietly obey my power;   60
     'Twill make your cause the fairer.
Somerton and Warbeck. O, with all our hearts, sir.
Young Banks. [*Aside*] There's my rival taken up for hangman's
     meat. Tom told me he was about a piece of villainy.—Mates
     and morris-men, you see here's no longer piping, no longer
     dancing. This news of murder has slain the morris. You that
     go the footway, fare ye well. I am for a gallop. Come, Ningle.
                         Exe[*unt* YOUNG BANKS *and* DOG].
Sawgut. (*Strikes his fiddle.*) Ay? Nay, an my fiddle be come to him-
     self again, I care not. I think the devil has been abroad amongst
     us today. I'll keep thee out of thy fit now, if I can.   70
                         Exeunt [SAWGUT *and* Morris-Dancers.]
Sir Arthur. These things are full of horror, full of pity.
     But if this time be constant to the proof,
     The guilt of both these gentlemen I dare take

Upon mine own danger. Yet, howsoever, sir,
Your power must be obeyed.
Warbeck.   O, most willingly, sir.   75
'Tis a most sweet affliction! I could not meet
A joy in the best shape with better will.
Come, fear not, sir. Nor judge, nor evidence
Can bind him o'er who's freed by conscience.
Somerton. Mine stands so upright to the middle zone   80
It takes no shadow to't, it goes alone.   *Exeunt.*

ACT IV

SCENE i

Enter OLD BANKS *and two or three* Countrymen.

Old Banks. My horse this morning runs most piteously of the glanders, whose nose yesternight was as clean as any man's here
now coming from the barber's. And this, I'll take my death
upon't, is long of this jadish witch, Mother Sawyer.
First Countryman. I took my wife and a servingman in our town of   5
Edmonton thrashing in my barn together such corn as country
wenches carry to market. And examining my polecat why she
did so, she swore in her conscience she was bewitched, and
what witch have we about us but Mother Sawyer?
Second Countryman. Rid the town of her, else all our wives will do   10
nothing else but dance about other country maypoles.
Third Countryman. Our cattle fall, our wives fall, our daughters
fall and maidservants fall; and we ourselves shall not be able to
stand if this beast be suffered to graze amongst us.

Enter W. HAMLUC, *with thatch and link.*

Hamluc. Burn the witch, the witch, the witch, the witch!   15
All. What hast got there?
Hamluc. A handful of thatch plucked off a hovel of hers; and they
say, when 'tis burning, if she be a witch she'll come running in.
Old Banks. Fire it, fire it! I'll stand between thee and home for any   20
danger.

As that burns, enter the Witch [ELIZABETH SAWYER.]

Elizabeth Sawyer. Diseases, plagues, the curse of an old woman
follow and fall upon you!

All. Are you come, you old trot?

Old Banks. You hot whore, must we fetch you with fire in your tail?

First Countryman. This thatch is as good as a jury to prove she is a   25
witch.

All. Out, witch! Beat her, kick her, set fire on her!

Elizabeth Sawyer. Shall I be murdered by a bed of serpents? Help,
help!

Enter SIR ARTHUR CLARINGTON and a Justice.

All. Hang her, beat her, kill her!   30

Justice. How now? Forbear this violence!

Elizabeth Sawyer. A crew of villains, a knot of bloody hangmen set
to torment me, I know not why.

Justice. Alas, neighbour Banks, are you a ringleader in mischief?
Fie! To abuse an aged woman!   35

Old Banks. Woman? A she-hellcat, a witch! To prove her one, we
no sooner set fire on the thatch of her house, but in she came
running as if the devil had sent her in a barrel of gunpowder;
which trick as surely proves her a witch as the pox in a snuffling
nose is a sign a man is a whore-master.   40

Justice. Come, come. Firing her thatch? Ridiculous! Take heed, sirs,
what you do. Unless your proofs come better armed, instead of
turning her into a witch, you'll prove yourselves stark fools.

All. Fools?

Justice. Arrant fools.   45

Old Banks. Pray, Master Justice What-do-you-call-'um, hear me
but in one thing. This grumbling devil owes me, I know, no
good will ever since I fell out with her.

Elizabeth Sawyer. And breakest my back with beating me.

Old Banks. I'll break it worse.   50

Elizabeth Sawyer. Wilt thou?

Justice. You must not threaten her; 'tis against law. Go on.

Old Banks. So, sir, ever since, having a dun cow tied up in my back-
side, let me go thither, or but cast mine eye at her and if I should
be hanged, I cannot choose, though it be ten times in an hour,   55
but run to the cow and taking up her tail kiss, saving your
worship's reverence, my cow behind, that the whole town of
Edmonton has been ready to bepiss themselves with laughing
me to scorn.

Justice. And this is long of her?   60

Old Banks. Who the devil else? For is any man such an ass to be such
a baby if he were not bewitched?

Sir Arthur. Nay, if she be a witch, and the harms she does end in
such sports, she may 'scape burning.

Justice. Go, go; pray vex her not. She is a subject, and you must not   65
  be judges of the law to strike her as you please.
All. No, no, we'll find cudgel enough to strike her.
Old Banks. Ay, no lips to kiss but my cow's—!

                                Exeunt [OLD BANKS *and* Countrymen.]

Elizabeth Sawyer. Rots and foul maladies eat up thee and thine!
Justice. Here's none now, Mother Sawyer, but this gentleman, my-   70
  self and you. Let us to some mild questions; have you mild
  answers? Tell us honestly and with a free confession, we'll do
  our best to wean you from it, are you a witch or no?
Elizabeth Sawyer. I am none!
Justice. Be not so furious.   75
Elizabeth Sawyer. I am none. None but base curs so bark at me. I am
  none. Or would I were! If every poor old woman be trod on thus
  by slaves, reviled, kicked, beaten, as I am daily, she, to be revenged, had need turn witch.
Sir Arthur. And you to be revenged have sold your soul to th' devil.   80
Elizabeth Sawyer. Keep thine own from him.
Justice. You are too saucy and too bitter.
Elizabeth Sawyer. Saucy? By what commission can he send my soul
  on the devil's errand more than I can his? Is he a landlord of my
  soul to thrust it, when he list, out of door?   85
Justice. Know whom you speak to?
Elizabeth Sawyer. A man; perhaps no man. Men in gay clothes,
  whose backs are laden with titles and honours, are within far
  more crooked than I am, and if I be a witch, more witch-like.
Sir Arthur. You're a base hell-hound. And now, sir, let me tell you,   90
  far and near she's bruited for a woman that maintains a spirit
  that sucks her.
Elizabeth Sawyer. I defy thee.
Sir Arthur. Go, go. I can, if need be, bring an hundred voices, e'en
  here in Edmonton, that shall loud proclaim thee for a secret and   95
  pernicious witch.
Elizabeth Sawyer. Ha, ha!
Justice. Do you laugh? Why laugh you?
Elizabeth Sawyer. At my name, the brave name this knight gives
  me—witch!   100
Justice. Is the name of witch so pleasing to thine ear?
Sir Arthur. Pray, sir, give way, and let her tongue gallop on.
Elizabeth Sawyer. A witch! Who is not?
  Hold not that universal name in scorn then.
  What are your painted things in princes' courts,   105
  Upon whose eyelids lust sits, blowing fires
  To burn men's souls in sensual hot desires,

Upon whose naked paps a lecher's thought
Acts sin in fouler shapes than can be wrought?
Justice. But those work not as you do.
Elizabeth Sawyer.   No, but far worse.   110
  These by enchantments can whole lordships change
  To trunks of rich attire, turn ploughs and teams
  To Flanders mares and coaches, and huge trains
  Of servitors to a French butterfly.
  Have you not city-witches who can turn   115
  Their husbands' wares, whole standing shops of wares,
  To sumptuous tables, gardens of stol'n sin;
  In one year wasting what scarce twenty win?
  Are not these witches?
Justice.   Yes, yes; but the law
  Casts not an eye on these.
Elizabeth Sawyer.   Why then on me   120
  Or any lean old beldam? Reverence once
  Had wont to wait on age. Now an old woman
  Ill-favoured grown with years, if she be poor
  Must be called bawd or witch. Such so abused
  Are the coarse witches, t'other are the fine,   125
  Spun for the devil's own wearing.
Sir Arthur.   And so is thine.
Elizabeth Sawyer. She on whose tongue a whirlwind sits to blow
  A man out of himself, from his soft pillow
  To lean his head on rocks and fighting waves,
  Is not that scold a witch? The man of law   130
  Whose honeyed hopes the credulous client draws,
  As bees by tinkling basins, to swarm to him
  From his own hive to work the wax in his;
  He is no witch, not he!
Sir Arthur.   But these men-witches
  Are not in trading with hell's merchandise   135
  Like such as you are, that for a word, a look,
  Denial of a coal of fire, kill men,
  Children and cattle.
Elizabeth Sawyer.   Tell them, sir, that do so.
  Am I accused for such an one?
Sir Arthur.   Yes, 'twill be sworn.
Elizabeth Sawyer. Dare any swear I ever tempted maiden,   140
  With golden hooks flung at her chastity,
  To come and lose her honour, and being lost,
  To pay not a denier for't? Some slaves have done it.
  Men-witches can, without the fangs of law

Drawing once one drop of blood, put counterfeit pieces   145
Away for true gold.
Sir Arthur.   By one thing she speaks
I know now she's a witch, and dare no longer
Hold conference with the fury.
Justice.   Let's then away.
Old woman, mend thy life, get home and pray.
                    Exeunt [SIR ARTHUR CLARINGTON *and* Justice]
Elizabeth Sawyer. For his confusion.

                    Enter DOG.

                                        My dear Tom-boy, welcome!   150
I am torn in pieces by a pack of curs
Clapped all upon me, and for want of thee.
Comfort me; thou shalt have the teat anon.
Dog. Bow, wow! I'll have it now.
Elizabeth Sawyer.   I am dried up
With cursing and with madness, and have yet   155
No blood to moisten these sweet lips of thine.
Stand on thy hind-legs up. Kiss me, my Tommy,
And rub away some wrinkles on my brow
By making my old ribs to shrug for joy
Of thy fine tricks. What hast thou done? Let's tickle.   160

                    [*They embrace.*]

Hast thou struck the horse lame as I bid thee?
Dog. Yes, and nipped the sucking child.
Elizabeth Sawyer.   Ho, ho, my dainty,
My little Pearl! No lady loves her hound,
Monkey or parakeet, as I do thee.
Dog. The maid has been churning butter nine hours, but it shall not   165
come.
Elizabeth Sawyer. Let 'em eat cheese and choke.
Dog.   I had rare sport
Among the clowns i'th' morris.
Elizabeth Sawyer.   I could dance
Out of my skin to hear thee. But, my curl-pate,
That jade, that foul-tongued whore, Nan Ratcliffe,   170
Who, for a little soap licked by my sow,
Struck and almost had lamed it; did not I charge thee
To pinch that quean to th' heart?
Dog. Bow, wow, wow! Look here else.

                    Enter ANNE RATCLIFFE *mad.*

Anne Ratcliffe. See, see, see! The Man i'th' Moon has built a new   175
     windmill, and what running there's from all quarters of the city
     to learn the art of grinding.
Elizabeth Sawyer. Ho, ho, ho! I thank thee, my sweet mongrel.
Anne Ratcliffe. Hoyda! A pox of the devil's false hopper! All the
     golden meal runs into the rich knaves' purses, and the poor   180
     have nothing but bran. Hey derry down! Are not you Mother
     Sawyer?
Elizabeth Sawyer. No, I am a lawyer.
Anne Ratcliffe. Art thou! I prithee let me scratch thy face, for thy
     pen has flayed off a great many men's skins. You'll have brave   185
     doings in the vacation, for knaves and fools are at variance in
     every village. I'll sue Mother Sawyer, and her own sow shall
     give in evidence against her.
Elizabeth Sawyer. [*To Dog*] Touch her.

                    [DOG *rubs against* ANNE RATCLIFFE.]

Anne Ratcliffe. O, my ribs are made of a paned hose, and they   190
     break. There's a Lancashire hornpipe in my throat. Hark how it
     tickles it, with doodle, doodle, doodle, doodle! Welcome,
     sergeants! Welcome, devil! Hands, hands! Hold hands and
     dance around, around, around.

          Enter OLD BANKS, *his son* [YOUNG BANKS] *the Clown,* OLD
                    RATCLIFFE [*and*] Country-fellows.

Old Ratcliffe. She's here. Alas, my poor wife is here!   195
Old Banks. Catch her fast, and have her into some close chamber,
     do, for she's as many wives are, stark mad.
Young Banks. The witch, Mother Sawyer! The witch, the devil!
Old Ratcliffe. O, my dear wife! Help, sirs!

          [OLD RATCLIFFE *and the* Country-fellows] *carry her off.*

Old Banks. You see your work, Mother Bumby.   200
Elizabeth Sawyer. My work? Should she and all you here run mad,
     is the work mine?
Young Banks. No, on my conscience, she would not hurt a devil of
     two years old.

               Enter OLD RATCLIFFE *and the rest.*

     How now! What's become of her?   205
Old Ratcliffe. Nothing. She's become nothing but the miserable
     trunk of a wretched woman. We were in her hands as reeds in a
     mighty tempest. Spite of our strengths away she brake, and
     nothing in her mouth being heard but 'the devil, the witch, the

witch, the devil', she beat out her own brains, and so died.   210
Young Banks. It's any man's case, be he never so wise, to die when
    his brains go a-wool-gathering.
Old Banks. Masters, be ruled by me, let's all to a justice. Hag, thou
    hast done this, and thou shalt answer it.
Elizabeth Sawyer. Banks, I defy thee.   215
Old Banks. Get a warrant first to examine her, then ship her to
    Newgate. Here's enough, if all her other villainies were par-
    doned, to burn her for a witch. You have a spirit, they say,
    comes to you in the likeness of a dog; we shall see your cur at
    one time or other. If we do, unless it be the devil himself, he   220
    shall go howling to the gaol in one chain, and thou in another.
Elizabeth Sawyer. Be hanged thou in a third, and do thy worst!
Young Banks. How, father! You send the poor dumb thing howling
    to th' gaol? He that makes him howl makes me roar.
Old Banks. Why, foolish boy, dost thou know him?   225
Young Banks. No matter if I do or not. He's bailable, I am sure, by
    law. But if the dog's word will not be taken, mine shall.
Old Banks. Thou bail for a dog?
Young Banks. Yes, or a bitch either, being my friend. I'll lie by the
    heels myself before Puppison shall; his dog-days are not come   230
    yet, I hope.
Old Banks. What manner of dog is it? Didst ever see him?
Young Banks. See him? Yes, and given him a bone to gnaw twenty
    times. The dog is no court-foisting hound that fills his belly full
    by base wagging his tail. Neither is it a citizen's water-spaniel, 235
    enticing his master to go a-ducking twice or thrice a week
    whilst his wife makes ducks and drakes at home. This is no
    Paris-garden bandog neither, that keeps a bow-wow-wowing
    to have butchers bring their curs thither, and when all comes to
    all they run away like sheep. Neither is this the Black Dog of   240
    Newgate.
Old Banks. No, Goodman Son-fool, but the dog of hell-gate.
Young Banks. I say, Goodman Father-fool, it's a lie.
All. He's bewitched.
Young Banks. A gross lie as big as myself. The devil in St Dunstan's 245
    will as soon drink with this poor cur as with any Temple-bar
    laundress that washes and wrings lawyers.
Dog. Bow, wow, wow, wow!
All. O, the dog's here, the dog's here!
Old Banks. It was the voice of a dog.   250
Young Banks. The voice of a dog? If that voice were a dog's, what
    voice had my mother? So am I a dog; bow, wow, wow! It was I
    that barked so, father, to make coxcombs of these clowns.

Old Banks. However, we'll be coxcombed no longer; away, there-
    fore, to th' justice for a warrant, and then, Gammer Gurton, 255
    have at your needle of witchcraft!
Elizabeth Sawyer. And prick thine own eyes out. Go, peevish fools!
        Exeunt [OLD BANKS, OLD RATCLIFFE *and* Countrymen.]
Young Banks. Ningle, you had like to have spoiled all with your
    bowings. I was glad to put 'em off with one of my dog-tricks on
    a sudden. I am bewitched, little cost-me-nought, to love thee— 260
    a pox, that morris makes me spit in thy mouth. I dare not stay.
    Farewell, Ningle, you whoreson dog's nose. Farewell, witch.
                                                       Exit.

Dog. Bow, wow, wow, wow.
Elizabeth Sawyer. Mind him not, he's not worth thy worrying. Run
    at a fairer game, that foul-mouthed knight, scurvy Sir Arthur. 265
    Fly at him, my Tommy, and pluck out's throat.
Dog. No, there's a dog already biting's conscience.
Elizabeth Sawyer. That's a sure bloodhound. Come, let's home
                                             and play.
    Our black work ended, we'll make holiday.   *Exeunt.*

[ACT IV] SCENE ii

Enter KATHERINE: *a bed thrust forth, on it* FRANK [THORNEY] *in
a slumber.*

Katherine. Brother, brother! So sound asleep? That's well.
Frank Thorney. No, not I, sister. He that's wounded here,
    As I am; all my other hurts are bitings
    Of a poor flea; but he that here once bleeds
    Is maimed incurably.
Katherine.   My good sweet brother, 5
    For now my sister must grow up in you,
    Though her loss strikes you through, and that I feel
    The blow as deep, I pray thee be not cruel
    To kill me too by seeing you cast away
    In your own helpless sorrow. Good love, sit up, 10
    And if you can give physic to yourself,
    I shall be well.
Frank Thorney.   I'll do my best.
Katherine.   I thank you.
    What do you look about for?
Frank Thorney.   Nothing, nothing;

　　　But I was thinking, sister.
Katherine.　　　　　　　Dear heart, what?
Frank Thorney. Who but a fool would thus be bound to a bed   15
　　　Having this room to walk in?
Katherine.　　　　　　　Why do you talk so?
　　　Would you were fast asleep.
Frank Thorney.　　　　　No, no; I'm not idle.
　　　But here's my meaning: being robbed as I am,
　　　Why should my soul, which married was to hers,
　　　Live in divorce, and not fly after her?   20
　　　Why should not I walk hand in hand with death
　　　To find my love out?
Katherine.　　　　　That were well, indeed,
　　　Your time being come. When death is sent to call you,
　　　No doubt you shall meet her.
Frank Thorney.　　　　　Why should not I go
　　　Without calling?
Katherine.　　　　Yes, brother, so you might,   25
　　　Were there no place to go to when you're gone
　　　But only this.
Frank Thorney.　　'Troth, sister, thou sayst true,
　　　For when a man has been an hundred years
　　　Hard travelling o'er the tottering bridge of age,
　　　He's not the thousand part upon his way.   30
　　　All life is but a wandering to find home.
　　　When we are gone, we are there. Happy were man
　　　Could here his voyage end; he should not then
　　　Answer how well or ill he steered his soul
　　　By heaven's or by hell's compass; how he put in,   35
　　　Losing blessed goodness' shore, at such a sin;
　　　Nor how life's dear provision he has spent;
　　　Nor how far he in's navigation went
　　　Beyond commission. This were a fine reign;
　　　To do ill and not hear of it again.   40
　　　Yet then were man more wretched than a beast,
　　　For, sister, our dead pay is sure the best.
Katherine. 'Tis so, the best or worst, and I wish heaven
　　　To pay, and so I know it will, that traitor,
　　　That devil Somerton, who stood in mine eye   45
　　　Once as an angel, home to his deservings.
　　　What villain but himself, once loving me,
　　　With Warbeck's soul would pawn his own to hell
　　　To be revenged on my poor sister?
Frank Thorney.　　　　　Slaves!

A pair of merciless slaves! Speak no more of them.   50
Katherine. I think this talking hurts you.
Frank Thorney.   Does me no good, I'm sure.
    I pay for't everywhere.
Katherine.   I have done then.
    Eat, if you cannot sleep. You have these two days
    Not tasted any food. Jane, is it ready?
Frank Thorney. What's ready? What's ready?   55

[Enter a Maid *with chicken.]*

Katherine. I have made ready a roasted chicken for you.
    Sweet, wilt thou eat?
Frank Thorney.   A pretty stomach on a sudden; yes—
    There's one in the house can play upon a lute,
    Good girl, let's hear him too.
Katherine.   You shall, dear brother.
                          [Exit Maid.]
    Would I were a musician, you should hear   60
    How I would feast your ear.

Lute plays.

                Stay, mend your pillow
    And raise you higher.
Frank Thorney.   I am up too high,
    Am I not, sister, now?
Katherine.   No, no, 'tis well.
    Fall to, fall to.—A knife. Here's never a knife,
    Brother, I'll look out yours. *[She picks up his coat.]*

Enter DOG, *shrugging as it were for joy, and dances.*

Frank Thorney.   Sister, O, sister,   65
    I am ill upon a sudden and can eat nothing.
Katherine. In very deed you shall. The want of food
    Makes you so faint. *[Discovers knife.]* Ha! Here's none in
                          your pocket.
    I'll go fetch a knife.   *Exit.*
Frank Thorney.   Will you? 'Tis well, all's well.

*She gone, he searches first one, then the other pocket. Knife
found.* DOG *runs off. He lies on one side. The* Spirit *of* SUSAN *his
second wife comes to the bed-side. He stares at it, and turning
to the other side, it's there too. In the meantime,* WINNIFRIDE *as
a page comes in, stands at his bed's feet sadly. He frighted, sits
upright. The* Spirit *vanishes.*

Frank Thorney. What art thou?

Winnifride. A lost creature.

Frank Thorney. So am I too.— 70
 Win? Ah, my she-page!

Winnifride. For your sake I put on
 A shape that's false, yet do I wear a heart
 True to you as your own.

Frank Thorney. Would mine and thine
 Were fellows in one house. Kneel by me here.
 On this side now! How dar'st thou come to mock me 75
 On both sides of my bed?

Winnifride. When?

Frank Thorney. But just now;
 Outface me, stare upon me with strange postures,
 Turn my soul wild by a face in which were drawn
 A thousand ghosts leapt newly from their graves
 To pluck me into a winding-sheet.

Winnifride. Believe it, 80
 I came no nearer to you than yon place
 At your bed's feet, and of the house had leave,
 Calling myself your horse-boy, in to come
 And visit my sick master.

Frank Thorney. Then 'twas my fancy.
 Some windmill in my brains for want of sleep. 85

Winnifride. Would I might never sleep so you could rest.
 But you have plucked a thunder on your head,
 Whose noise cannot cease suddenly. Why should you
 Dance at the wedding of a second wife,
 When scarce the music which you heard at mine 90
 Had ta'en a farewell of you? O this was ill!
 And they who thus can give both hands away
 In th'end shall want their best limbs.

Frank Thorney. Winnifride,
 The chamber-door fast?

Winnifride. Yes.

Frank Thorney. Sit thee then down,
 And when thou'st heard me speak, melt into tears. 95
 Yet I, to save those eyes of thine from weeping,
 Being to write a story of us two,
 Instead of ink, dipped my sad pen in blood,
 When of thee I took leave, I went abroad
 Only for pillage, as a freebooter, 100
 What gold soe'er I got to make it thine.
 To please a father I have heaven displeased.

Striving to cast two wedding rings in one,
Through my bad workmanship I now have none;
I have lost her and thee.

Winnifride.   I know she's dead,   105
But you have me still.

Frank Thorney.   Nay, her this hand
Murdered, and so I lose thee too.

Winnifride.   O, me!

Frank Thorney. Be quiet, for thou my evidence art,
Jury and judge. Sit quiet and I'll tell all.

> *As they whisper, enter at one end of the stage* OLD CARTER *and*
> KATHERINE, DOG *at the other, pawing softly at* FRANK
> [THORNEY].

Katherine. I have run madding up and down to find you,   110
Being laden with the heaviest news that ever
Poor daughter carried.

Old Carter.   Why? Is the boy dead?

Katherine. Dead, sir! O, father, we are cozened. You are told
The murderer sings in prison, and he laughs here.
This villain killed my sister. See else, see,   115

> [*Showing the knife in* FRANK THORNEY'S *coat-pocket.*]

A bloody knife in's pocket.

Old Carter.   Bless me, patience!

Frank Thorney. The knife, the knife, the knife!

Katherine. What knife?   *Exit* DOG.

Frank Thorney.   To cut my chicken up, my chicken.
Be you my carver, father.

Old Carter.   That I will.

Katherine. [*Aside*] How the devil steels our brows after doing ill!   120

Frank Thorney. My stomach and my sight are taken from me;
All is not well within me.

Old Carter. I believe thee, boy; I that have seen so many moons clap
their horns on other men's foreheads to strike them sick, yet
mine to 'scape and be well; I that never cast away a fee upon   125
urinals, but am as sound as an honest man's conscience when
he's dying, I should cry out as thou dost, 'All is not well within
me', felt I but the bag of thy imposthumes. Ah, poor villain! Ah,
my wounded rascal! All my grief is, I have now small hope of
thee.   130

Frank Thorney. Do the surgeons say my wounds are dangerous
then?

Old Carter. Yes, yes and there's no way with thee but one.

Frank Thorney. Would he were to open them.

Old Carter. I'll go to fetch him. I'll make an holiday to see thee as I
    wish.   *Exit to fetch* Officers.   135

Frank Thorney. A wondrous kind old man.

Winnifride. [*Aside*] Your sin's the blacker so to abuse his
                                           goodness.

    [*Aloud.*] Master, how do you?

Frank Thorney.   Pretty well now, boy.
    I have such odd qualms come 'cross my stomach.
    I'll fall to. Boy, cut me.

Winnifride.   [*Aside*] You have cut me, I'm sure.   140
    [*Aloud.*] A leg or wing, sir.

Frank Thorney.   No, no, no; a wing.
    [*Aside*] Would I had wings but to soar up yon tower.
    But here's a clog that hinders me.

    [*Enter*] *Father* [OLD CARTER] *with her* [SUSAN'S *body*] *in a coffin*
          [*carried by two* Servants.]

                  What's that?

Old Carter. That? What? O, now I see her; 'tis a young wench, my
    daughter, sirrah, sick to the death, and hearing thee to be an   145
    excellent rascal for letting blood, she looks out at a casement
    and cries, 'Help, help! Stay that man! Him I must have, or
    none'.

Frank Thorney. For pity's sake, remove her. See, she stares
    With one broad open eye still in my face.   150

Old Carter. Thou puttest both her's out, like a villain as thou art.
    Yet see, she is willing to lend thee one again to find out the
    murderer, and that's thyself.

Frank Thorney. Old man, thou liest!

Old Carter. So shalt thou, i'th' gaol. Run for officers.   155

Katherine. O, thou merciless slave!
    She was, though yet above ground, in her grave
    To me; but thou hast torn it up again.
    Mine eyes too much drowned, now must feel more rain.

Old Carter. Fetch officers.   160

                            Exit KATHERINE.

Frank Thorney. For whom?

Old Carter. For thee, sirrah, sirrah! Some knives have foolish posies
    upon them, but thine has a villainous one. Look! O, it is enamel-
    led with the heart-blood of thy hated wife, my beloved daugh-
    ter. What sayst thou to this evidence? Is't not sharp? Dos't not   165
    strike home? Thou canst not answer honestly and without a
    trembling heart to this one point, this terrible bloody point.

Winnifride. I beseech you, sir,
　　Strike him no more; you see he's dead already.
Old Carter. O, sir, you held his horses. You are as arrant a rogue as　170
　　he. Up, go you too.
Frank Thorney. As you're a man, throw not upon that woman
　　Your loads of tyranny, for she's innocent.
Old Carter. How! How! A woman? Is't grown to a fashion for
　　women in all countries to wear the breeches?　　　　　175
Winnifride. I am not as my disguise speaks me, sir, his page,
　　But his first, only wife, his lawful wife.
Old Carter. How! How! More fire i'th' bedstraw!
Winnifride. The wrongs which singly fell upon your daughter,
　　On me are multiplied. She lost a life,　　　　　180
　　But I an husband and myself must lose
　　If you call him to a bar for what he has done.
Old Carter. He has done it then?
Winnifride. Yes, 'tis confessed to me.
Frank Thorney.　　　　　　　　Dost thou betray me?
Winnifride. O, pardon me, dear heart! I am mad to lose thee,　185
　　And know not what I speak; but if thou didst,
　　I must arraign this father for two sins,
　　Adultery and murder.

　　　　　　　　　Enter KATHERINE.

Katherine.　　　　　　　　Sir, they are come.
Old Carter. Arraign me for what thou wilt, all Middlesex knows me
　　better for an honest man than the middle of a market-place　190
　　knows thee for an honest woman. Rise, sirrah, and don your
　　tacklings; rig yourself for the gallows, or I'll carry thee thither
　　on my back. Your trull shall to the gaol go with you. There be
　　as fine Newgate birds as she that can draw him in. Pox on's
　　wounds!　　　　　　　　195
Frank Thorney. I have served thee, and my wages now are paid,
　　Yet my worst punishment shall, I hope, be stayed.　　*Exeunt.*

ACT V

SCENE i

　　　Enter MOTHER [ELIZABETH] SAWYER *alone.*

Elizabeth Sawyer. Still wronged by every slave, and not a dog
　　Bark in his dame's defence? I am called witch,

Yet am myself bewitched from doing harm.
Have I given up myself to thy black lust
Thus to be scorned? Not see me in three days!   5
I'm lost without my Tomalin. Prithee come.
Revenge to me is sweeter far than life;
Thou art my raven on whose coal-black wings
Revenge comes flying to me. O my best love!
I am on fire, even in the midst of ice,   10
Raking my blood up till my shrunk knees feel
Thy curled head leaning on them. Come then, my darling.
If in the air thou hover'st, fall upon me
In some dark cloud; and as I oft have seen
Dragons and serpents in the elements,   15
Appear thou now so to me. Art thou i'th' sea?
Muster up all the monsters from the deep,
And be the ugliest of them. So that my bulch
Show but his swart cheek to me, let earth cleave
And break from hell, I care not! Could I run   20
Like a swift powder-mine beneath the world,
Up would I blow it all to find out thee,
Though I lay ruined in it. Not yet come!
I must then fall to my old prayer,
Sanctibiceter nomen tuum.   25
Not yet come! Worrying of wolves, biting of mad dogs, the
manges and the—

Enter DOG [*now white*].

Dog. How now! Whom art thou cursing?
Elizabeth Sawyer. Thee! Ha! No, 'tis my black cur I am cursing for
   not attending on me.   30
Dog. I am that cur.
Elizabeth Sawyer. Thou liest. Hence, come not nigh me.
Dog. Bow, wow!
Elizabeth Sawyer. Why dost thou thus appear to me in white,
   As if thou wert the ghost of my dear love?   35
Dog. I am dogged, list not to tell thee. Yet, to torment thee, my
   whiteness puts thee in mind of thy winding sheet.
Elizabeth Sawyer. Am I near death?
Dog. Yes, if the dog of hell be near thee. When the devil comes to
   thee as a lamb, have at thy throat!   40
Elizabeth Sawyer. Off, cur!
Dog. He has the back of a sheep, but the belly of an otter; devours
   by sea and land. Why am I in white? Didst thou not pray to me?
Elizabeth Sawyer. Yes, thou dissembling hell-hound!

Why now in white more than at other times?   45
Dog. Be blasted with the news! Whiteness is day's foot-boy, a fore-
runner to light which shows thy old rivelled face. Villains are
stripped naked; the witch must be beaten out of her cockpit.
Elizabeth Sawyer. Must she? She shall not! Thou art a lying
                                                                 spirit.
Why to mine eyes art thou a flag of truce?   50
I am at peace with none; 'tis the black colour,
Or none, which I fight under. I do not like
Thy puritan paleness; glowing furnaces
Are far more hot than they which flame outright.
If thou my old dog art, go and bite such   55
As I shall set thee on.
Dog. I will not.
Elizabeth Sawyer. I'll sell my self to twenty thousand fiends
To have thee torn in pieces then.
Dog. Thou canst not. Thou art so ripe to fall into hell, that no more 60
of my kennel will so much as bark at him that hangs thee.
Elizabeth Sawyer. I shall run mad.
Dog. Do so. Thy time is come to curse, and rave, and die. The
glass of thy sins is full, and it must run out at gallows.
Elizabeth Sawyer. It cannot, ugly cur. I'll confess nothing,   65
And not confessing, who dare come and swear
I have bewitched them? I'll not confess one mouthful.
Dog. Choose, and be hanged or burned.
Elizabeth Sawyer. Spite of the devil and thee, I'll muzzle up my
tongue from telling tales.   70
Dog. Spite of thee and the devil, thou'lt be condemned.
Elizabeth Sawyer. Yes! When?
Dog. And ere the executioner catch thee full in's claws, thou'lt
confess all.
Elizabeth Sawyer. Out, dog!
Dog.   Out, witch! Thy trial is at hand.   75
Our prey being had, the devil does laughing stand.

        The DOG *stands aloof. Enter* OLD BANKS, RATCLIFFE *and*
                            Countrymen.

Old Banks. She's here; attach her. Witch, you must go with us.
Elizabeth Sawyer. Whither? To hell?
Old Banks. No, no, no, old crone. Your mittimus shall be made
thither, but your own jailors shall receive you. Away with her!   80

                        [*They seize her.*]

Elizabeth Sawyer. My Tommy! My sweet Tom-boy! O thou dog!

Dost thou now fly to thy kennel and forsake me?
Plagues and consumptions—

                                   Exeunt [all but DOG.]

Dog.   Ha, ha, ha, ha!
    Let not the world witches or devils condemn;
    They follow us, and then we follow them.   85

            [*Enter*] YOUNG BANKS *to thẹ* DOG.

Young Banks. I would fain meet with mine ingle once more. He has
    had a claw amongst 'em. My rival, that loved my wench, is like
    to be hanged like an innocent. A kind cur where he takes, but
    where he takes not, a dogged rascal. I know the villain loves me.

                    [DOG] *barks.*

    No! Art thou there? That's Tom's voice, but 'tis not he. This is a   90
    dog of another hair, this. Bark and not speak to me? Not Tom
    then. There's as much difference betwixt Tom and this as be-
    twixt white and black.
Dog. Hast thou forgot me?

                    [DOG *barks.*]

Young Banks. That's Tom again. Prithee, ningle, speak. Is thy name   95
    Tom?
Dog. Whilst I served my old Dame Sawyer 'twas. I'm gone from her
    now.
Young Banks. Gone? Away with the witch then, too! She'll never
    thrive if thou leavest her. She knows no more how to kill a cow,   100
    or a horse, or a sow without thee, than she does to kill a goose.
Dog. No, she has done killing now, but must be killed for what she
    has done. She's shortly to be hanged.
Young Banks. Is she? In my conscience, if she be, 'tis thou hast
    brought her to the gallows, Tom.   105
Dog. Right; I served her to that purpose. 'Twas part of my wages.
Young Banks. This was no honest servant's part, by your leave,
    Tom. This remember, I pray you, between you and I, I enter-
    tained you ever as a dog, not as a devil.
Dog. True, and so I used thee doggedly, not devilishly. I have de-   110
    luded thee for sport to laugh at. The wench thou seekst after
    thou never spakst with, but a spirit in her form, habit and
    likeness. Ha, ha!
Young Banks. I do not then wonder at the change of your garments,
    if you can enter into shapes of women too.   115
Dog. Any shape to blind such silly eyes as thine, but chiefly those
    coarse creatures, dog or cat, hare, ferret, frog, toad.

Young Banks. Louse or flea?

Dog. Any poor vermin.

Young Banks. It seems you devils have poor thin souls that you can   120
bestow yourselves in such small bodies. But pray you, Tom, one
question at parting—I think I shall never see you more—where
do you borrow those bodies that are none of your own? The
garment-shape you may hire at broker's.

Dog. Why wouldst thou know that, fool? It avails thee not.   125

Young Banks. Only for my mind's sake, Tom, and to tell some of
my friends.

Dog. I'll thus much tell thee. Thou never art so distant
From an evil spirit but that thy oaths,
Curses and blasphemies pull him to thine elbow.   130
Thou never tellst a lie but that a devil
Is within hearing it; thy evil purposes
Are ever haunted. But when they come to act,
As thy tongue slandering, bearing false witness,
Thy hand stabbing, stealing, cosening, cheating,   135
He's then within thee. Thou playst, he bets upon thy part.
Although thou lose, yet he will gain by thee.

Young Banks. Ay? Then he comes in the shape of a rook?

Dog. The old cadaver of some self-strangled wretch
We sometimes borrow, and appear human.   140
The carcass of some disease-slain strumpet
We varnish fresh, and wear as her first beauty.
Didst never hear? If not, it has been done.
An hot luxurious lecher in his twines,
When he has thought to clip his dalliance,   145
There has provided been for his embrace
A fine hot flaming devil in her place.

Young Banks. Yes, I am partly a witness to this, but I never could
embrace her. I thank thee for that, Tom. Well again I thank
thee, Tom, for all this counsel; without a fee too. There's few   150
lawyers of thy mind now. Certainly, Tom, I begin to pity thee.

Dog. Pity me! For what?

Young Banks. Were it not possible for thee to become an honest dog
yet? 'Tis a base life that you lead, Tom, to serve witches, to kill
innocent children, to kill harmless cattle, to stroy corn and   155
fruit, etc. 'Twere better yet to be a butcher and kill for yourself.

Dog. Why? These are all my delights, my pleasures, fool.

Young Banks. Or, Tom, if you could give your mind to ducking, I
know you can swim, fetch and carry, some shop-keeper in
London would take great delight in you and be a tender master   160
over you. Or if you have a mind to the game either at bull or

bear, I think I could prefer you to Moll Cutpurse.

Dog. Ha, ha! I should kill all the game, bulls, bears, dogs, and all,
    not a cub to be left.

Young Banks. You could do, Tom, but you must play fair; you   165
    should be staved off else. Or, if your stomach did better like to
    serve in some nobleman's, knight's, or gentleman's kitchen, if
    you could brook the wheel and turn the spit—your labour
    could not be much—when they have roast meat, that's but once
    or twice in the week at most; here you might lick your own toes   170
    very well. Or if you could translate yourself into a lady's arming
    puppy, there you might lick sweet lips and do many pretty
    offices; but to creep under an old witch's coats and suck like a
    great puppy! Fie upon't! I have heard beastly things of you,
    Tom.   175

Dog. Ha, ha! The worse thou heardst of me the better 'tis.
    Shall I serve thee, fool, at the self-same rate?

Young Banks. No, I'll see thee hanged, thou shalt be damned first! I
    know thy qualities too well. I'll give no suck to such whelps,
    therefore henceforth I defy thee. Out and avaunt!   180

Dog. Nor will I serve for such a silly soul.
    I am for greatness now, corrupted greatness.
    There I'll shug in, and get a noble countenance;
    Serve some Briarean footcloth-strider
    That has an hundred hands to catch at bribes,   185
    But not a finger's nail of charity.
    Such, like the dragon's tail, shall pull down hundreds
    To drop and sink with him. I'll stretch myself
    And draw this bulk small as a silver wire,
    Enter at the least pore tobacco fume   190
    Can make a breach for. Hence, silly fool!
    I scorn to prey on such an atom soul.

Young Banks. Come out, come out, you cur! I will beat thee out of
    the bounds of Edmonton, and tomorrow we go in procession,
    and after thou shalt never come in again. If thou goest to   195
    London I'll make thee go about by Tyburn, stealing in by
    Thieving Lane. If thou canst rub thy shoulder against a lawyer's
    gown as thou passest by Westminster Hall, do; if not, to the
    stairs amongst the bandogs, take water, and the devil go with
    thee.   200

                  Exeunt YOUNG BANKS, DOG *barking.*

[ACT V, SCENE ii]

Enter JUSTICE, SIR ARTHUR [CLARINGTON], WARBECK,
[SOMERTON, OLD] CARTER [*and*] KATHERINE.

Justice. Sir Arthur, though the bench hath mildly censured your
errors, yet you have indeed been the instrument that wrought
all their misfortunes. I would wish you paid down your fine
speedily and willingly.
Sir Arthur. I'll need no urging to it.   5
Old Carter. If you should 'twere a shame to you, for, if I should
speak my conscience, you are worthier to be hanged of the two,
all things considered; and now make what you can of it. But I
am glad these gentlemen are freed.
Warbeck. We knew our innocence.
Somerton.   And therefore feared it not.   10
Katherine. But I am glad that I have you safe.

Noise within.

Justice. How now! What noise is that?
Old Carter. Young Frank is going the wrong way. Alas, poor
youth! Now I begin to pity him.   [*Exeunt.*]

[ACT V, SCENE iii]

Enter YOUNG [FRANK] THORNEY *and* [Officers *with*] halberds
[*and exeunt.*]

Enter as to see the execution OLD CARTER, OLD THORNEY,
KATHERINE, [*and*] WINNIFRIDE *weeping.*

Old Thorney. Here let our sorrows wait him. To press nearer
The place of his sad death, some apprehensions
May tempt our grief too much, at height already.
Daughter, be comforted.
Winnifride.   Comfort and I
Are too far separated to be joined   5
But in eternity. I share too much
Of him that's going thither.
Old Carter.   Poor woman,
'Twas not thy fault. I grieve to see thee weep
For him that hath my pity too.
Winnifride. My fault was lust, my punishment was shame.   10
Yet I am happy that my soul is free
Both from consent, foreknowledge, and intent

204

Of any murder but of mine own honour.
Restored again by a fair satisfaction,
And since not to be wounded.
Old Thorney.   Daughter, grieve not   15
For what necessity forceth; rather resolve
To conquer it with patience.
Alas, she faints!
Winnifride.   My griefs are strong upon me.
My weakness scarce can bear them.
[*Voices.*] (*Within*) Away with her! Hang her! Witch!   20

    Enter [ELIZABETH] SAWYER *to execution*, Officers *with*
    halberds, [*and*] Country-people.

Old Carter. The witch, that instrument of mischief! Did not she
    witch the devil into my son-in-law when he killed my poor
    daughter? Do you hear, Mother Sawyer?
Elizabeth Sawyer. What would you have? Cannot a poor old
                                   woman
    Have your leave to die without vexation?   25
Old Carter. Did you not bewitch Frank to kill his wife? He could
    never have done't without the devil.
Elizabeth Sawyer. Who doubts it? But is every devil mine?
    Would I had one now whom I might command
    To tear you all in pieces. Tom would have done't   30
    Before he left me.
Old Carter. Thou didst bewitch Anne Ratcliffe to kill herself.
Elizabeth Sawyer. Churl, thou liest, I never did her hurt.
    Would you were all as near your ends as I am,
    That gave evidence against me for it.   35
First Countryman. I'll be sworn, Master Carter, she bewitched
    Gammer Washbowl's sow to cast her pigs a day before she
    would have farrowed, yet they were sent up to London, and
    sold for as good Westminster dog-pigs at Bartholomew Fair as
    ever great-bellied ale-wife longed for.   40
Elizabeth Sawyer. These dogs will mad me. I was well resolved
    To die in my repentance. Though 'tis true
    I would live longer if I might, yet since
    I cannot, pray torment me not, my conscience
    Is settled as it shall be. All take heed   45
    How they believe the devil; at last he'll cheat you.
Old Carter. Thou'dst best confess all truly.
Elizabeth Sawyer.   Yet again?
    Have I scarce breath enough to say my prayers,
    And would you force me to spend that in bawling?

Bear witness. I repent all former evil;   50
There is no damnèd conjuror like the devil.
All. Away with her! Away!

> [*Exeunt* ELIZABETH SAWYER *with* Officers.]

> *Enter* FRANK [THORNEY] *to execution,* Officers, JUSTICE,
> SIR ARTHUR [CLARINGTON], WARBECK [*and*] SOMERTON.

Old Thorney. Here's the sad object which I yet must meet
    With hope of comfort, if a repentant end
    Make him more happy than misfortune would   55
    Suffer him here to be.
Frank Thorney.   Good sirs, turn from me.
    You will revive affliction almost killed
    With my continual sorrow.
Old Thorney.   O Frank, Frank!
    Would I had sunk in mine own wants, or died
    But one bare minute ere thy fault was acted.   60
Frank Thorney. To look upon your sorrows executes me
    Before my execution.
Winnifride.   Let me pray you, sir—
Frank Thorney. Thou much wronged woman, I must sigh for
                        thee
    As he that's only loath to leave the world
    For that he leaves thee in it unprovided,   65
    Unfriended; and for me to beg a pity
    From any man to thee when I am gone
    Is more than I can hope; nor, to say truth,
    Have I deserved it. But there is payment
    Belongs to goodness from the great exchequer   70
    Above; it will not fail thee, Winnifride.
    Be that thy comfort.
Old Thorney.   Let it be thine too,
    Untimely-lost young man.
Frank Thorney.   He is not lost
    Who bears his peace within him. Had I spun
    My web of life out at full length, and dreamed   75
    Away my many years in lusts, in surfeits,
    Murders of reputations, gallant sins
    Commended or approved; then, though I had
    Died easily, as great and rich men do,
    Upon my own bed, not compelled by justice,   80
    You might have mourned for me indeed; my miseries
    Had been as everlasting, as remediless.
    But now the law hath not arraigned, condemned

With greater rigour my unhappy fact
Than I myself have every little sin   85
My memory can reckon from my childhood.
A court hath been kept here where I am found
Guilty; the difference is, my impartial judge
Is much more gracious than my faults
Are monstrous to be named, yet they are monstrous.   90
Old Thorney. Here's comfort in this penitence.
Winnifride.   It speaks
How truly you are reconciled, and quickens
My dying comfort that was near expiring
With my last breath. Now this repentance makes thee
As white as innocence, and my first sin with thee,   95
Since which I knew none like it, by my sorrow
Is clearly cancelled. Might our souls together
Climb to the height of their eternity,
And there enjoy what earth denied us, happiness.
But since I must survive and be the monument   100
Of thy loved memory, I will preserve it
With a religious care, and pay thy ashes
A widow's duty, calling that end best
Which, though it stain the name, makes the soul blest.
Frank Thorney. Give me thy hand, poor woman.
                              [*Takes her hand.*] Do not weep.   105
Farewell. Thou dost forgive me?
Winnifride.   'Tis my part
To use that language.
Frank Thorney.   O, that my example
Might teach the world hereafter what a curse
Hangs on their heads who rather choose to marry
A goodly portion than a dower of virtues!   110.
Are you there, gentlemen? There is not one
Amongst you whom I have not wronged; you most.
I robbed you of a daughter, but she is
In heaven, and I must suffer for it willingly.
Old Carter. Ay, ay, she's in heaven, and I am glad to see thee so well   115
prepared to follow her. I forgive thee with all my heart. If thou
hadst not had ill counsel thou wouldst not have done as thou
didst; the more shame for them.
Somerton. Spare your excuse to me, I do conceive
What you would speak. I would you could as easily   120
Make satisfaction to the law as to my wrongs.
I am sorry for you.
Warbeck.   And so am I,

And heartily forgive you.

Katherine.   I will pray for you

For her sake, who I am sure did love you dearly.

Sir Arthur. Let us part friendly too. I am ashamed   125

Of my part in thy wrongs.

Frank Thorney.   You are all merciful,

And send me to my grave in peace. Sir Arthur,

Heavens send you a new heart! Lastly to you, sir;

And though I have deserved not to be called

Your son, yet give me leave upon my knees   130

To beg a blessing. [*Kneels.*]

Old Thorney.   Take it. Let me wet

Thy cheeks with the last tears my griefs have left me.

O Frank, Frank, Frank!

Frank Thorney.   Let me beseech you, gentlemen,

To comfort my old father. Keep him with ye;

Love this distressèd widow, and as often   135

As you remember what a graceless man

I was, remember likewise that these are

Both free, both worthy of a better fate

Than such a son or husband as I have been.

All help me with your prayers. On, on, 'tis just   140

That law should purge the guilt of blood and lust.

Exit [*with* Officers.]

Old Carter. Go thy ways. I did not think to have shed one tear for
thee, but thou hast made me water my plants spite of my heart.
Master Thorney, cheer up, man. Whilst I can stand by you, you
shall not want help to keep you from falling. We have lost our   145
children, both on's the wrong way, but we cannot help it. Better
or worse, 'tis now as 'tis.

Old Thorney. I thank you, sir. You are more kind than I

Have cause to hope or look for.

Old Carter. Master Somerton, is Kate yours or no?   150

Somerton. We are agreed.

Katherine.   And but my faith is passed,

I should fear to be married. Husbands are

So cruelly unkind. Excuse me that

I am thus troubled.

Somerton.   Thou shalt have no cause.

Justice. Take comfort, Mistress Winnifride. Sir Arthur,   155

For his abuse to you and to your husband,

Is by the bench enjoined to pay you down

A thousand marks.

Sir Arthur.   Which I will soon discharge.

Winnifride. Sir, 'tis too great a sum to be employed
    Upon my funeral.   160
Old Carter. Come, come. If luck had served, Sir Arthur, and every
    man had his due, somebody might have tottered ere this with-
    out paying fines, like it as you list. Come to me, Winnifride;
    shalt be welcome. Make much of her, Kate, I charge you. I do
    not think but she's a good wench and hath had wrong as well as   165
    we. So, let's every man home to Edmonton with heavy hearts,
    yet as merry as we can, though not as we would.
Justice. Join, friends, in sorrow, make of all the best.
    Harms past may be lamented, not redressed.   *Exeunt.*

EPILOGUE

Winnifride. I am a widow still, and must not sort
    A second choice without a good report,
    Which though some widows find, and few deserve,
    Yet I dare not presume, but will not swerve
    From modest hopes. All noble tongues are free;   5
    The gentle may speak one kind word for me.
                                     PHEN.

FINIS.

COMMENTARY

THE TRAGEDY OF SOPHONISBA

To the General Reader
1–5. *Know ... studies*] a hit at Jonson's dramatic practice in *Sejanus*, published in quarto in 1605. The play had been hissed from the stage when first presented at the Globe in 1603.

Argument
1. *height*] loftiness of mind or magnanimity. The reference is to Massinissa.
2. *worthy*] deserved.

Interlocutors
INTERLOCUTORS] speakers, *dramatis personae*. Massinissa, Syphax, Asdrubal (Hasdrubal), Scipio (Africanus) and Sophonisba are historical figures drawn from Appian's *Roman History*, Bk. VIII. Gisco's name also derives from Appian, for it is the name of Hasdrubal's father. Erictho is taken from Lucan's *Pharsalia*, Bk. VI. Historically, it is likely that Massinissa, as a prince of the Massyllian tribe, and Syphax, as a Numidian, would have been black, although Marston makes no reference to this and it is unlikely that they were played as such.

Prologus
SD] Such elaborate and formalised stage business is characteristic of the text, as is the frequent use of music and song for which the Boys' Companies were noted; see Introduction, pp. 9–11.
0.6 targets] light shields.
5. *feodars*] vassals, owing homage and service (Wo., not recorded in *OED*).
6. *Hannibal*] the Carthaginian general who led his army across the Alps to attack Rome and its provinces (218 B.C.). He reached the gates of Rome in 211 B.C. but was unable to take the city. Hannibal was recalled to Carthage in 203 B.C. The events

of the play took place between 205 and 203 B.C.
13. *doubtful*] uncertain.
16. *Apollo*] the god of poetry and music. *Hymen*] the god of marriage.
17. *Juno*] the queen of heaven, sister and wife of Jupiter; guardian of women and protectress of marriage.
18. *Venus*] the goddess of love, especially sensual love.
29. Nec ... extra] a modification of Perseus, *Satires*, I, 7: '*Nec te quaesiveris extra*'. Marston's version is characteristically aggressive, 'Nor does he seek any advice but his own'.

I.i.
9. *addictions*] inclinations.
14. *gall*] bitterness of spirit.
35. *two-necked eagles*] an anachronism. The Roman eagle emblem was single-headed.
38. *ooze*] mud-bank.
40–2. *O ... drunk*] Gnaeus Cornelius Scipio and Publius Cornelius Scipio were both killed in Spain campaigning against the Carthaginians under Hasdrubal in 212 B.C.; see Appian, Bk. VI, Ch. iii, 16.
42. *three ... hundred*] Wo's expansion of Q's '30000' is metrically preferable to the alternative 'thirty thousand'.
49. *vengeance*] trisyllabic as in *AR*, III.ii.36, 39, 41.
52. *yield*] submit to, owe service to.
63. *mix ... arms*] i.e. join us both in friendship and military alliance.
69. *heap*] great company.
74–6. *No reason ... might*] Syphax early demonstrates the power of passion and unreason over his actions and attitudes.

I.ii.
4. *You ... undone*] the sexual quibble on 'undone' is one of the few examples of bawdy in the play.

5. *Humblest service*] i.e. 'your humble
servant'; Zanthia, fearing she has gone too
far, turns formally obsequious (Wo.).

7. *such ceremony*] the ceremony of which
Sophonisba complains is that of the
Elizabethan and Jacobean 'bedding' of the
bride; see Puttenham, *Art of English
Poesie*, Ch. XXVI.

shape] manner, arrangement (*OED* 3).

11. *figures . . . locution*] patterns or
conventions of speech.

12. *about-phrases*] statements which are
opposite to one's inclinations and feelings.
Sophonisba seems to resent conventional
bridal modesty; cf. Crispinella in *The
Dutch Courtesan*.

22. *shuttlecock*] a game similar to
badminton but carrying a primary bawdy
meaning.

23. *respective*] courteous or fitting.

24. *complement*] a completing accessory
or adjunct.

31. *You go very high*] Zanthia refers to
the height of Sophonisba's chopines, shoes
constructed of a base of leather and fitted
to a column of cork sometimes up to
eighteen inches high.

32.2 *whilst . . . enters*] Q's stage direction
anticipates Massinissa's entry at line 35.2.

35. *Fair . . . lady*] i.e. may the performance
of your marital duties be successful.

35.1 *antiquely*] in an ancient manner (cf.
AR, IV.v.72); Bu.'s reading 'anticly' is
worth consideration in view of the
'fantastic' manner of the dance. Ingram, p.
155, suggests that the 'dainty mock-
fighting' of the boys here prepares for the
contrasting real fight which ensues with
the entry of Carthalo at l. 62ff.

40. a white ribbon] 'The maiden girdle
worn by unmarried women. It was loosed
by the bridegroom on the marriage night'
(Bu.).

42. Io to Hymen!] Praise to the wedding
god (cf. *AR*, V.iv.19). Q's italics suggest
that this phrase was sung each time.

46. *virtue . . . her*] who pretends to, but
does not possess virtue (Wo.).

56. *Atlas*] son of Titan. As a punishment
for his part in the revolt of the Titans he
was forced to support the heavens with his
head and hands.

59. *stems*] off-spring.

61. *divining*] prophecy.

62.2 darts] arrows.

65. *Resolve*] dispel fear or doubt.

66. *The . . . doubt*] For comment on the
frequently italicised *sententiae* in Q see
Introduction, p. 8.

69. *Utica*] an important neighbouring city.

72–4. *Upon . . . breath*] Bradley,
Shakespearian Tragedy, p. 471, sees an
echo of *Macbeth*, 'the Norweyan banners
flout the sky, / And fan our people cold'
(I.ii.50–1).

76. *our anchor . . . back*] Bu.'s emendation
is also possible, 'our rancorous hatred of
the Romans has recoiled on our own
heads'.

slight] K's 'flight' appears to be a mis-
reading of Q's long 's' since he provides no
collation.

78. *quit*] set free, rid.

81. *cast*] reckon, calculate.

83–4. *Desire . . . beyond*] cf. Montaigne,
I.iii, 'We are never in ourselves, but
beyond. Feare, desire, and hope, draw us
ever towards that which is to come, and
remove our sense and consideration from
that which is . . . *A minde in suspense what
is to come, is in a pittifull case*' (p. 25).

90. *barred*] The entrance to Carthage's
harbours could be closed by iron chains to
prevent surprise attack. See Appian,
VIII.xiv.

119. *damp*] fatal choke-damp, or
suffocating damp, resulting from carbonic
acid gas in mines.

125. *damped*] stifled.

129. *trains*] traps, stratagems.

amain] with full speed.

133. *Old . . . hairs*] cf. Montaigne, I.iv,
'And the Philosopher *Byron* was very
pleasant with the king, that for griefe tore
his haire, when he said, *Doth this man
thinke, that baldnesse will asswage his
griefe?*' (p. 34).

137. *charge*] mandate, order.

145. *Massulians*] Massinissa collected 'a
body of cavalry who were trained to hurl
the javelin, advancing and retreating and
advancing again, either by day or night.
For their only method of fighting was flight
and pursuit' (Appian, VIII.iii.11).

149. *cask*] helmet.

151. *Gods . . . arms*] Gods are not true
gods if they do not aid bold and just arms.

161. *glossful*] glossy.

163. *I . . . ignorant*] i.e. 'I must not be, nor
am I ignorant that': Sophonisba is referring
to her choice of Massinissa as husband
rather than Syphax.

169. *quit*] acquit, prove.

170. *I . . . him*] i.e. I will not claim to consummate our marriage.

171. *As . . . princes*] cf. Machiavelli, *The Discourses*, III.vi, 'There is, in fact, a golden saying voiced by Cornelius Tacitus, who says that men have to respect the past but submit to the present, and, while they should be desirous of having good princes, should put up with them of whatever sort they may turn out to be' (p. 399).

179. *Repined*] felt discontented, complained.

182.2 cap-a-pie] head to foot.

187. *pressed to satisfaction*] ready to repay (Wo.).

191. *hull*] float or drift by the force of the wind or current acting on the hull alone.

200–01. *Virtue . . . wise*] i.e. forced virtue has no value, but he who freely acts virtuously demonstrates true wisdom.

210.] H's emendation suggests that Sophonisba addresses Massinissa directly whereas Q's pointing allows a general address to the company. Sophonisba perhaps addresses Massinissa directly from l. 213.

215–16. *the oft . . . children*] cf. Montaigne, III.ix, 'Children are in the number of things, that need not greatly bee desired; especially in these corrupted daies, wherein it would be so hard a matter to make them good' (p. 249).

221. *Best . . . thee!*] May heaven's strongest influences go with you.

229. *Carthage Palladium*] an allusion to the image of Pallas in Troy on which the safety of the city depended for it was thought that Troy could not be captured while it contained this image.

233.3 full music] presumably *tutti*; cf. III.i.117.1, the cornets in particular making the transition to the battle of the second act (see Ingram, p. 155,); but 'full' may carry the sense 'serious' as elsewhere in Marston (see *The Fawne*, Revels ed, p. 70n.).

for the Act] Music between the acts was a regular feature of Boys' Company performance. Marston uses this convention to prepare for transitions of mood and to accompany the introductory dumb show to the opening of the next act as here (cf. Blostein's note to *The Fawne*, V.i.o.1–3, Revels ed.).

II.i.

SD 0.3. impoisoner] Here Marston alters his source for Appian relates that Hasdrubal, still formally allied to Massinissa, 'sent a cavalry escort with him and told them to put him to death secretly in whatever way they could' (Appian, VIII.ii.10).

2. *wood*] distracted, mad. K asserts, without supporting evidence, that the correct reading is 'wooed'. Both the stage-direction and Gelosso's dialogue, however, suggest that he behaves in an excitable and intemperate manner.

11. *greater*] i.e. greater in power or importance.

12. *side*] possibly pride, spirit. The context would suggest 'support'; although OED records no such usage, *side*, v.3. is given as 'to support or countenance'.

14. Profit . . . state] O's 'correction' 'violates the very point he [Hanno] is making—that value judgements ought to be entirely pragmatic' (K). Massinissa's sense of honour is continually contrasted with his enemies' cynical subordination of means to ends, and most especially in this scene.

33–4. *Prosperous . . . story*] cf. Machiavelli, *The Prince*, Ch. XVIII, 'in the actions of men, and especially of princes, from which there is no appeal, the end justifies the means. Let a prince therefore aim at conquering and maintaining the state, and the means will always be judged honourable and praised by every one, for the vulgar is always taken by appearances and the issue of the event' (p. 79).

37. *nice*] fastidious.

41. *engineer*] plotter, layer of snares.

43–8.] Q's extended italics perhaps indicate the rhetorical weight that Carthalo strives for here.

49. *Politic*] scheming, cunning. 'An excellent example of the use of the word in its Machiavellian sense of unscrupulous' (Wo.).

51.] Wo's conjecture happily strengthens the force of Gelosso's claim whilst avoiding Q's unconvincing repetition of 'marble'.

56. *inutility*] uselessness, unprofitableness. Cf. Montaigne, III.i, 'yet is there nothing in nature unserviceable, no not inutility it selfe'.

60–3. *soldered up . . . purges*] Cf.

Montaigne, III.i, 'some necessary functions are not onely base, but faulty: vices finde therein a seate, and employ themselves in the stitching up of our frame; as poysons in the preservations of our health' (p. 8).

68. *stick too nice*] scruple too precisely. Cf. Machiavelli, *Discourses*, III.xli, 'For when the safety of one's country wholly depends on the decision to be taken, no attention should be paid either to justice or injustice, to kindness or cruelty, or to its being praiseworthy or ignominious' (p. 515).

70. *Beware . . . live*] Cf. Machiavelli, *The Prince*, III, 'For it must be noted, that men must either be caressed or else annihilated; they will revenge themselves for small injuries, but cannot do so for great ones; the injury therefore that we do to a man must be such that we need not fear his vengeance' (p. 8).

77–84. *he . . . self*] Cf. Montaigne, III.i, 'I answered not long since, that hardly could I betray my Prince for a particular man, who should be very sory to betray a particular man for my Prince' (pp. 8–9).

107. *entertained*] accepted.

110. *O very woman!*] The changeableness of women was proverbial; cf. 'Women are as wavering as the wind' (W698). Gelosso here assumes that Sophonisba has capitulated.

118–19. *Speech . . . words*] It was a general belief that language divided man from the animal kingdom. Thus Sophonisba's comments imply that the conspirators are motivated by appetite rather than rational propriety. Cf. Montaigne, I.ix, 'Nothing makes us men, and no other meanes keeps us bound one to another, but our word' (p. 47).

119. *equal*] fair, just.

122. *breath*] i.e. consent to the decree.

128. *troops*] crowds.

136. *affected*] tainted.

139. *void*] destitute or deprived of.

142. *Cirta*] Constantine, Syphax's capital, some 200 miles south-west of Carthage.

151. *Neptune*] the god of the sea, here, figuratively, the sea.

153.2 [GISCO . . . separately]] No specific exit is provided for Gisco in Q. It is difficult to see where else he could exit, but it seems inappropriate that he should exit with the Senators.

155. *Ops . . . head*] i.e. let the world be

turned upside-down; although presented in O as masculine, Ops was an earth-goddess with specific responsibilities for the wealth of the harvest.

156. *Saturn*] the husband of Ops and god of agriculture, but here the planet Saturn which, in astrological terms, governed old age and was considered cold and morose.

158. *Jove*] chief of the gods and especially regarded as the ruler of storms, thunder and lightning.

160. *contemning*] scorning, disdaining.

166. *For . . . dry!*] the world having witnessed the perfection of woman in Sophonisba is now ready for complete destruction and, being tinder dry, is vulnerable to Jove's fire.

169. *Phoebus . . . great*] Phoebus Apollo, the god of prophecy and oracles is strong within me.

II.ii.

0.1. *gorget*] a piece of armour for the throat.

0.3. *cuirass*] a piece of body armour consisting of a breast-plate and a back-plate.

10. *To . . . Syphax*] 'One of the vital points of difference between Livy's account and Appian's' (Wo.). In Livy's account Massinissa first meets Sophonisba, Syphax's wife, after her husband's capture and the fall of Cirta. Taken by her beauty and moved by her pleas, he then marries her in order to prevent her humiliation at the hands of Scipio. See Livy, XXX.12.633.

20. *may let a*] Q's variant reading is also possible here.

21. *Too forward bleed*] i.e. bleed too profusely, or possibly 'too forward' goes with 'noble heart'.

23. *ungrate*] ungrateful.

29. *balsam*] aromatic balm for healing wounds.

32. *looks off*] turns its eyes away; i.e. Carthage has lost the battle.

40. *Apollo Pythian*] Apollo was named Pythian from his destruction of the dragon Python, the guardian of Delphi, a deed for which he gained expiation by exile and purification.

41. *statist*] a politician, here in the Machiavellian sense.

41.2. *dressed*] i.e. his wound to be dressed.

42–58. Wo. conjectures that this incident

may owe something to Montaigne (I.xxiii) who relates how a French prince confronted his intended assassin and forgave him. Appian records an attempt by Syphax to bribe one of Massinissa's servants to kill him. The servant took the money to Massinissa and exposed the giver. See Appian, VIII.iii.17.

43. *only*] unique, peerless.

44.1: draw] It is difficult to be sure what Massinissa does at this point. He might draw his sword, or prepare to remove the arrow from his arm. *Q*'s variant 'drane' adds perhaps to the richness of possibilities here for it might imply that Massinissa drains off his wound with a handkerchief (cf. *R3*, IV.iv.276).

47. *stand ... battalia*] form square in battle array.

48. *Entirely of themselves*] i.e. entirely by themselves, thus preventing any possibility of betrayal by the Carthaginians.

54.] K conjectures that *Q*'s empty parenthesis must be for a stage-direction omitted from the manuscript, presumably indicating Massinissa's physical restraint of Gisco's suicide attempt.

71. *over*] *Q*'s 'O' seems to have been caught up from the line above.

90. *action*] play on two meanings— 'valour' and 'stage-performance'.

93. *Stoop*] descend.

II.iii.

7. *Iphigenia*] i.e. 'consider, for example, the story of Iphigenia' (Wo.). Iphigenia was a daughter of Agamemnon and Clytemnestra who, in Euripides's tragedy, was sacrificed in order to ensure a successful passage of the Greek fleet to Troy.

10. *Immense*] boundless, infinite.

11. *Round*] encompassed, *OED* v. 11.

13. *shield of Telamon*] Achilles's shield which was awarded to Ulysses, as a consequence of which Ajax Telamon, in disappointment, went mad and slew himself; cf. *Ant.*, IV.xiii.2.

18. *mazed*] confused, bewildered.

19. *Some ... fall*] Cf. Machiavelli, *Discourses*, III.vi, 'Such is the majesty and the respect inspired by the presence of a prince that he may easily damp the resolution of an operative (i.e. a conspirator) or terrify him' (p. 413).

21. *touch of blood*] humanity.

27. *Assured*] *Q*'s reading is possible here and would imply even greater cynicism in Asdrubal's attitude.

36. *By ... grow*] Bu. conjectures that Marston is alluding to Plutarch's *De Hide et Osiride* (*Marston*, II, 266). Dried blood which is rich in nitrogen is still used as a fertiliser.

39–40. *'Tis ... hate*] Cf. Machiavelli, *The Prince*, XVIII, 'But it is necessary to be able to disguise this character [faithlessness] well and to be a great feigner and dissembler: and men are so simple and so ready to obey present necessities that one who deceives will always find those who allow themselves to be deceived' (p. 78).

40. *close*] secret.

41. *routs*] disorderly or disreputable crowds of people.

56. *train*] plot.

63. *rest*] remain.

69. *look as when*] just as when.

94. *force*] overpower, storm.

96. *He ... it*] Cf. Seneca, *Troades*, l. 291, '*qui non vetat peccare, cum possit, iubet*', 'he who, when he may, forbids not sin, commands it'.

101. *place*] high rank, position.

107–8. *he ... it*] Cf. Seneca, *Medea*, ll. 500–1, '*cui prodest scelus / id fecit*'; 'who profits by a sin has done the sin'.

108. *Brook*] tolerate. Wo. suggests that the whole speech is (deliberately) disordered and garbled. Certainly Asdrubal is panic-stricken and his comment may be directed to his fellow conspirators or be designed to reinforce his own courage.

110. *some*] K suggests that 'some' is a pronoun referring to his quarrelling confederates; he adds 'The sense is marginal anyway, because Asdrubal is raving'.

heat] inspire eagerness, inflame with passion.

hold] maintain position, hold ground.

III.i.

0.1 Organ ... act] Ingram, p. 155, suggests that the musical introduction serves to emphasise 'Sophonisba's steadfastness as well as providing contrast to Syphax's lustfulness'.

0.2 twined] i.e. her hair wound around the dagger.

0.2–3 nightgown-petticoat] The exact nature of Sophonisba's dress is obscure. A nightgown was an ankle-length gown with long sleeves and was for general use, not only for night wear in one's chamber. The 'nightgown-petticoat' suggests a specific petticoat designed to be worn beneath a particular nightgown. (See Linthicum, pp. 184–5, 187–8.)

19. *Be . . . beast*] be only a beast, i.e. show the sensitivity which animals possess.

25. *fame*] reputation.

27. *Achilles*] Greek hero in the Trojan war. Syphax may be referring to Achilles's grief after slaying Penthesilia, the queen of the Amazons.

bear out] withstand or stand the strain of.

31. *We not affect*] i.e. we do not respond to.

35. *rude*] uncultured, unmannerly.

38. *noble*] Bu.'s conjecture captures the tone of Sophonisba's speech well here, but Q's reading makes adequate sense.

44. *clip*] embrace.

62. *foul*] ugly.

64. *maids*] Deighton's emendation makes good sense in terms of Syphax's attempts to render Zanthia compliant. However Q's 'vails' (i.e. gifts, bribes) is a possible, if difficult, reading, as Bu. argues: 'If the text is not corrupt, we must suppose that a sentence breaks off at the word "their". Marston is fond of employing the horrid figure *aposiopesis*. "Vails" is intelligible on the supposition that Syphax is feeing the waiting-woman.'

68. *however*] in all circumstances.

88. *Weak . . . nice*] i.e. only weak, over-hopeful fools are scrupulous in pursuing their own advantage.

100. *but—*] It is left to the actor's gesture to indicate Syphax's nothingness.

102. *with one hand*] The meaning here is obscure. It is possible that some ritual gesture of giving and receiving is intended or that Sophonisba retains one hand undefiled by contact for the sacrifice.

108. *Humour*] whim, mood.

117.1. full music] see I.ii.233.3n.

117.1–2. solemnity of a sacrifice] The stage directions offer an opportunity for elaborate stage business with emphasis on musical accompaniment, a noted strength of the Children's Companies. Chambers

suggests that the altar would be trapped (*ES*, III, 148).

121. *Mercury*] (as god of persuasive eloquence).

123. *Phoebe*] Diana, as goddess of the moon.

fit] accord, agree with.

143.1. a carouse] a full draught of liquor prepared as a toast.

148. *slip*] i.e. fall into the vault; the vault would no doubt be a trap.

163.1. curtains] i.e. the bed-curtains.

167. *Straight . . . king*] presumably Sophonisba bids Zanthia prepare for the king's imminent entry.

178. *by steps*] Cf. Montaigne, III.v, '*The more steps and degrees there are: the more delight and honour is there on the top*' (p. 110).

184. *Let . . . wanting*] i.e. let not your sexual powers be found wanting.

190. *particular faith*] personal loyalty.

203–4. *And . . . crocodile*] Bu. notes that 'Dogs on the banks of the Nile were supposed to drink by snatches, running, from fear of the crocodiles (*Aelian, Var. Hist.* I.4)'.

208. *seven-walled Babel*] Babel and Babylon were frequently confused and it may be that Syphax's allusion to seven walls is figurative rather than literal on the analogy of the seven gates of Thebes and the seven hills of Rome. Babylon was in fact fortified with three walls when Cyrus marched on it in 539 BC; see W. R. Gair's note to the Revels ed. *AR*, II.ii.76–7, 'Hadst thou a jail / With treble walls like antique Babylon'. Thus the phrase denotes an impregnable barrier.

III.ii.

0.2. compliments] ceremonial acts appropriate to a Roman general which provide opportunity for spectacle and elaborate dumb-show consistent with the rest of the play.

9. *fees*] rewards.

thee] Q's 'these' might perhaps refer to the Carthaginians as suggested by K, but Massinissa is here addressing Scipio.

31. *short time man*] i.e. for a while to feel human passions.

Stay prince] i.e. retain your princely nature.

38. *with*] Bu.'s emendation is supported by the repetition of Massinissa's oath at

V.iii.63–66. Wo. retains *worth* arguing for
the sense 'worthy of'.

50. *And ... god*] Cf. Montaigne, III.v,
'Nor is it meet, that we with Gods /
Should be compar'd, there is such ods'
from Catullus, *Elegy*, IV.141 (p. 90).

54–61. *But ... gods*] Massinissa
demonstrates his admiration for those
stoical virtues which enable a man to
withstand misfortune and reject ambition,
pleasure and wealth.

56. *holds*] withstands.

60. *beggars*] makes valueless.

63. *admiration*] his wonder mingled with
reverence for Sophonisba.

72. *amaze*] bewilderment, mental
confusion.

74. *Boldness ... victories*] Cf. Appian,
VIII.iv.19, 'Courage and swiftness, friends,
and desperate fighting are our only
salvation'. 'The 1578 English
translation ... uses Marston's very
words—"Boldnesse and speede"' (K).

77. *his sinew*] probably referring to the
strength of Massinissa's arm rather than,
as Wo. suggests, to Syphax's sinews.

80. *close*] concealed.

82. *thick*] rapid, frequent.

IV.i.

0.1 viols] This first use of these
instruments in the music of the play may,
Ingram suggests, p. 155, 'offer a clue for
the instruments used for the "infernal
music"' at line 101.

3. *vein*] small channel within the earth.

4. *damps*] Bu.'s emendation is supported
by Sophonisba's pleasure in the sweetness
of the air on leaving the vault; see also *AR*,
I.iii.74 and III.ii.93.

9. *nimbly*] K. argues that the Q correction
is unlikely to be authorial since the copy of
the form carrying this emendation also
contains a feeble attempt to deal with a
garbled passage at line 128. It is difficult,
however, to see why anyone other than the
author would make such a distinctive
emendation of a passage which is not
obviously corrupt, unless we are to
imagine a proof-reader offering his own
guess to avoid an awkward repetition of
'just' earlier in the line.

24. *furies*] avenging deities, represented as
winged women who avenged crimes,
especially crimes against the ties of kinship.

25. *stretched*] strained.

31. *pale*] enclosure.

35. *O ... maids*] Wo. compares
Trissimo's *Sophonisba* (1515), 'O, che
felice stato, E'I tuo ... etc.'

46. *I'll ... pearl*] Here, and in the passage
which follows, Syphax demonstrates to an
extreme degree his inability to perceive
Sophonisba in any terms but that of his
own sexual gratification.

52. *use*] make use sexually.

53. *strain*] tendency or disposition.

56. *formed*] perfect.

57. *worth*] merit, deservingness.

63–5. *Corruption ... sin*] sexual perversity
is all you will achieve even if you frame
your lust to the height of sinful
imagination.

68. *or ... hate*] i.e. diminish my hatred for
you.

72. *taste*] 'Cf. Montaigne, III,v, "*It is the
deare price makes viands savour the
better*" (p. 110). There is little similarity,
but Montaigne, like Marston, is dealing
with necrophilia' (K).

77. *We ... suit*] a double negative, i.e. we
urge our suit by 'fair usage', etc.

98–101. *whose ... inhabit*] Cf. Lucan,
Pharsalia, 'Considering it a crime to
occupy an ordinary decent house, she
avoided the town and kept on good terms
with the infernal powers by squatting in
tombs out of which she had driven the
ghostly tenants' (VI, trans. Graves, p. 141).

99. *Contemns*] scornfully refuses.
coverture] roof.

101. Infernal music] see IV.i.o.1n. This
music probably comes from under the
stage; see Introduction, p. 10. Q's placing
of the stage direction indicates that
Syphax's words from 102ff. are
accompanied by music and the appearance
of Erictho whose qualities he invokes. By
delaying the stage direction until line 125,
Bu. robs the episode of this built-in
atmosphere and denies the abruptness of
Erictho's eventual interruption of Syphax's
speech.

102–110. *A loathsome ... sulphur*] Cf.
Pharsalia, 'Her aged face was lean and
loathsome, of Stygian pallor, and matted
hair hung over it. She never appeared in
daylight and quitted the tombs only on wet
or cloudy nights, when she went to catch
and bottle whatever lightning happened to
fall' (VI, p. 141).

108. *From*] K's emendation ignores the implications of lines 100–01.

naked] neglected.

110. *quick sulphur*] lightning.

111. *cerecloths*] waxed sheets for embalming; cf. *AR*, III.i.10.

112–8. *But . . . hand*] Cf. *Pharsalia*, 'If the corpse was not cremated, but placed in a stone sarcophagus—to dry up its moisture, arrest corruption and harden the marrow in its bones—Erichtho always attacked it with greedy passion. She used her fingers to scoop out the glaring eyeballs, and gnawed the pale nails off its withered hands' (VI, p. 142).

119–22. *she bites . . . horror*] Cf. *Pharsalia*, 'If one of her relatives were laid out for burial she would bend over the body, pretending to kiss it, but covertly nip off nose and ears, and then, having prized the mouth open, do the same with the tip of the tongue—mumbling inarticulate words into the dead mouth, which conveyed a wicked secret to the ghosts of the Underworld' (VI, p. 142).

119. *gelid*] frozen, icy cold.

127. *Nice*] 'unwilling,' fastidiously chaste.

128. *Be . . . Jove*] i.e. be jovial. K's support of O's reading is also worthy of consideration here on the grounds that the Q compositor may easily have confused 'Love' and 'Iove' in the holograph.

130. *beasts*] Roberts, 'The "Beasts of Death" in Marston's *Sophonisba*', *N & Q*, June 1975, p. 248, refutes Wo.'s acceptance of Q's reading 'heastes' ('promises or determinations') in preference to the Q variant 'beastes', on the grounds that Marston is here following Lucan's *De Bello Civili*, VI.485–6.

135–8. *The king . . . must*] Cf. *Pharsalia*, 'Instead of invoking the Olympians with the usual hymn offered by suppliants . . . she would pollute their altars with smoking lumps of incense snatched from a burning pyre. No sooner had she stated her demands than the Gods granted them, for fear of being subjected to a second spell' (VI, p. 141).

149. *Flamens*] priests devoted to the service of a particular deity.

153. *vively limned*] drawn in a lively manner, 'drawn to the life' (Bu.).

154–5. *draw . . . lust*] Cf. Montaigne, III.v, 'What harme cause not those huge

draughts or pictures which, wanton youth with chalke or coales draw in each passage, wall or staires of our great houses?' (Ure, p. 85).

161. *charnel-house*] a house for dead bodies, a vault in which the bones of the dead were piled up.

167. *lazy*] sluggish.

175–6. *Nor dare . . . light*] 'For this Erichtho episode Marston has borrowed some of the properties of the Cupid and Psyche legend' (Wo.). Venus, jealous of Psyche's beauty, dispatched Cupid to make her fall in love with some ugly creature. Cupid himself, however, became her lover though urging that, since he visited her in the dark, she should never see him.' See Apuleius, *The Golden Ass*, Bks. IV–VI.

179. *raised*] excited, with bawdy quibble.

182. *heaved*] removed, shifted (to another place). Although there is no change of place indicated here, it would seem appropriate that the transformation of the location be attributable to Erictho's supernatural powers. Such an interpretation would go some way to meet the problems explored by Chambers, *ES*, III, 148–9. This scene provides a good example of the imaginative flexibility of the Elizabethan stage and its audience. See Introduction, pp. 9–11.

187. *My . . . sense*] i.e. my appetite controls my reasons and behaviour. Syphax again declares that he is entirely controlled by his base passions.

188. *Without a man*] 'outside a man's sense' (Bu.). Alternatively the text could be punctuated 'Without, . . .' i.e. a man whose wisdom is not his sense is of no value.

189. *sickless*] free from disease.

194, 198, *Erictho*] O's reading destroys the echo effect which Marston seems to offer as a parallel to 'Io to Hymen!' in I.ii; see Introduction, pp. 9–10.

198.2. *canopy*] Presumably the bed-curtains and not the tester are intended here. See Adams, pp. 282–3. It seems that Erictho is using the music to stimulate and manipulate Syphax's erotic expectations; consequently it is appropriate for the music to identify the area where his passions are to be gratified. The musicians could easily be housed behind the bed-curtains to achieve this effect if Erictho and Syphax were careful when entering Syphax's bed. At line 208 the song comes from *above*; see Introduction, pp. 10–11.

205. *strict gripes*] close embraces.

207. *Raise . . . Venus*] i.e. stimulate sexual strength.

209. *nuptial hymns*] Nuptial hymns are, of course, singularly inappropriate since Syphax's anticipated pleasures are to be enforced by Erictho's evil magic; Marston carefully parodies the musical and vocal effects of I.ii.

210. Cantant] they sing; presumably the chorus used in I.ii.

211.1. in . . . SOPHONISBA] 'It is not quite clear from the text whether she deceives him (Syphax) by showing him a "snowy image" of Sophonisba like the image of Florimell in Spenser . . .' (Ure, p. 84). It is possible that the actor playing Sophonisba also played Erictho here, but, since her face is veiled, it is more likely that Erictho presents the character by a change of costume. The decision will depend on what the audience should understand of the situation. There are advantages in both courses; if Erictho takes the role here the audience may perceive a sharp sense of the irony of Syphax's expectations; if Sophonisba appears at this point the audience is likely to experience a considerable shock at the discovery in V.i. Marston here combines concepts of Renaissance witchcraft with the classical witchcraft of his source; cf. *W.Ed.*, III.i.75–7.

213. *'Bove thunder sit*] i.e. may you be more powerful than Jove.

216. *spite*] be angry or annoyed.

V.i.

0.1 bass lute . . . treble viol] Ingram, p. 155, notes that these instruments have already been associated with love-making by Syphax when they announced Erictho in her disguise as Sophonisba at IV.i.198.

4–6. *Why . . . love?*] cf. *Wi.* I.ii.172.

6. *dotes*] befools, infatuates.

7. *More ignorant*] utterly ignorant.

8. *thirsty womb*] to beget a demon was regarded as 'the most terrible punishment to manhood' (Ingram, p. 156).

16. *philters*] love potions, charms; cf. *Wi.*, I.ii.

17–18. *we . . . Brain-sleights*] i.e. we would have employed damnable brain-tricks. We may take 'brain-sleights' to indicate a

higher order of difficulty than 'philtres', etc., see Introduction, p. 7. Alternatively, if Bu.'s emendation is accepted ('deigned', condescended to), Erictho would be admitting here that her magical powers were ineffective, hence her resort to mere trickery; see Harris, p. 67.

21.1. slips . . . ground] i.e. through a trap-door.

offers . . . her] seeks to attack her with his sword.

23. *we—*] Q's pointing offers a weak repetition of Syphax's previous question. It seems more likely that he is on the verge of imagining greater horrors.

37. *give't*] Q's 'gift' (i.e. endow) is possible though strained.

38.1 altar . . . ariseth] If we assume that the altar is trapped (see III.i.117.1–2n) the stage must have possessed at least two traps.

46. *Made . . . unfortunate*] i.e. whose bad heart justly suffered misery.

49. *next . . . ten*] i.e. (presumably) at the next encounter ten thousand fell.

55. *Where poisoned*] the implication is that Asdrubal took poison.

68. *wings*] figuratively as hastening their advance but also in the military sense of providing the flanking forces to the main body of troops.

75. *shelf*] a sandbank or submerged ledge or rock.

V.ii.

0.2 halberds] weapons combining the properties of spear and battle-axe, consisting of a sharp-edged blade ending in a point and a spear-head, mounted on a handle five to seven feet long.

1. *Part the file*] i.e. divide the ranks.

13. *seize*] occupy.

22.1. up to the mount] i.e. up to the hill (see l. 13), presumably an upper or raised acting level from which Scipio can observe subsequent events.

25. *break up*] break open.

37. *genius*] the attendant spirit allotted to every person at his birth.

40. *My . . . arm*] 'So Mezentius in the *Aenied*, X.772: "Dextra mihi deus"' (Bu.).

47. *only*] uniquely, solely.

49.2 passeth . . . throne] Scipio's throne must be brought on either at the opening of the scene or at this entry.

54. *mean*] moderation.

69–86. *Sophonisba . . . I.*] Marston follows Livy closely in presenting Syphax's version of events; see Livy, XXX.14.635.

79. *hymeneal*] formally 'marital' but here, presumably, 'passionate'.

81. *Threw*] Q's variant reading seems to offer another example of Windet's persistent, but unreliable, proof-reader; see Introduction, p. 28.

85. *try*] test, experience.

90. *new-laughed*] presumably 'newly befriended amidst laughter'; Bu.'s emendation gives easier sense, but Q's reading suggests Marston's penchant for 'new' coinages.

94. *will him*] direct, require him.

96. *now . . . law's*] i.e. now she is under our jurisdiction.

97. *Wise . . . cause*] i.e. Wise men should not anticipate or deal with the events but always forestall the cause.

V.iii.

13–28. *Let . . . bend for.*] 'With this supplication of Sophonisba's compare the parallel passage in Trissimo's tragedy' (Wo.). Some of the detail of Sophonisba's speech may also derive from Livy; see XXX.12, p. 633.

15. *to heart*] to take to heart, fix in the heart.

31. *Leda*] Jupiter visited Leda in the form of a swan. Helen of Troy was born of their union.

32. *Soft music*] 'This is the first meeting since the interrupted wedding night, and they seem to take up from that night's quiet music' (Ingram, p. 157).

34. *nectar. Think—*] Sophonisba appears to collapse in mid-sentence here; but Bu. accepts O's 'nectar-skink' and glosses it as a draught of nectar, although *OED* records no such usage before 1824. Bu.'s reading receives possible support from 'nectar-dew' in *Jack Drum's Entertainment*, III.199. (ed. Wood).

49. *Cneius*] See I.i.40–2n. Massinissa, or Marston, confuses Gnaeus Cornelius Scipio, Scipio's father, with his uncle.

52. *cross*] contrary, in opposition.

82. *maze*] confuse.

104. *of . . . story*] Sophonisba reveals her self-conscious sense of her exemplary behaviour and fame.

111. *Incomprehence*] boundless (only citation in *OED*).

V.iv.

10. *t'affect*] to seek to obtain.

15. *Insensibly*] imperceptibly.

20. *misdoubt*] mistrust.

23. *joy*] enjoy.

26. *grace*] honour, give credit to.
hold . . . sense] i.e. esteem it gentle understanding.

28–9. *bear . . . breast*] i.e. to give limited tolerance to Massinissa's rebellious passion.

36.1 *to a single voice*] either for a single vocalist or the instruments play exactly the same notes. Ingram, p. 157, notes the 'simple and forceful comparison' that this musical effect makes with the 'ostentatiously loud' entry of Scipio at the beginning of the scene.

47. *minion*] idol.

48. *faintings*] declines.

57. *Small . . . flow*] cf. 'Small sorrows (griefs) speak, great ones are silent' (S664, and see also W130 and W123).

58. *Heave*] rise, mount.

Epilogus

3. *Another's voice*] the playwright's voice.

4. *thus formed*] thus instructed; 'in this attire' (Wo.).

5. *sensed*] having wit or sense.

10. *taxings*] accusations, censures.

16. *more . . . wit*] Marston's desire for intelligent appraisal is characteristic; cf. *The Fawne*, 'To my Equal Reader' and Prologus.

THE WITCH

The Persons

7. fantastical] showily dressed, but also perhaps 'capricious, eccentric'; cf. Lucio in

Meas.

10. *FIRESTONE*] Briggs, *PHT*, p. 76, refers to the tradition of witches having loutish

sons, comparing Caliban in *Tp.*, and *The Fairie Queene*, III.vii.12. The name itself may refer to superstitions attaching to fire; see Scot, XI.4.

13. *FRANCISCA*] a name frequently applied to courtesans in the drama of the period; cf. Marston's *The Dutch Courtesan*, II.i.151, for the common pun 'frank', free, loose; see also G. K. Hunter, 'English Folly and Italian Vice', *Jacobean Theatre*, eds. J. R. Brown and B. Harris, 1960, p. 109.

16. *HECATE*] moon-goddess and also divinity of the underworld; and, as a combination of these, goddess of witches. 'Hecate' was also disparagingly applied to a woman meaning 'hag' or 'witch' (see *1H6*, III.ii.64). The qualification 'the chief witch' here would seem to endorse Briggs's view that 'this type of nickname was one assumed by the witches and that the head witch of the coven called herself Hecate' (*PHT*, p. 82). MS's spelling 'Heccat' and the evidence of the song at III.iii.39 (see Appendix) indicates that the name is not trisyllabic in this play.

17–18. *STADLIN, HOPPO*] 'The names of two well-known warlocks' (Briggs, *PHT*, p. 21); for their respective talents in witchcraft see I.ii.134ff. and 144ff.

20. [*Three*] *other Witches*] Hecate makes it clear at V.ii.37 that she is habitually accompanied by 'five sisters'. From Hecate's enquiry at I.ii.8 it seems clear that Hellwain and Puckle are two of the remaining 'sisters'.
HELLWAIN] Perhaps connected with 'Hecla's Hell-wain, the waggon in which the souls of the dead were carried'; see Briggs, *PHT*, p. 21.
PUCKLE] a kind of bugbear; the name of a familiar spirit. (Briggs, *PHT*, p. 21).

25. Ravenna] So little concern is given to the Italian setting by the dramatist that a Scottish accent is used for north Italy at II.i.171, local London references occur, e.g. at I.ii.229 and at V.iii.54 Urbin is substituted, fortuitously, for Ravenna.

Epistle

2. Thomas Holmes] Probably not the musical composer since he is not heard of before his appointment as lay-vicar of Winchester in 1631; for a discussion of the most likely candidates from among the several persons recorded with that name

during the period, including the suggestion that the acquaintance may have arisen out of Middleton's contacts with the city, see Wayne H. Phelps, 'Thomas Holmes, Esquire: The Dedicatee of Middleton's *The Witch*', *N. & Q.*, April 1980, pp. 152–4.

6–7. *ignorantly ill-fated*] Most critics have taken this phrase to indicate that the play was a failure on the stage, but see Anne Lancashire, pp. 161–81, and Introduction, pp. 13–14.

7. *Witches . . . law condemned*] The act of 1563 against 'Conjurations, enchantments and witchcraft' was replaced by a much harsher and more far-reaching act in 1604 which put a new continental emphasis on pacts with evil spirits; see Thomas, pp. 526–7, and Introduction, p. 2.

8–9. *imprisoned obscurity*] Theatre manuscripts were not the possession of the dramatist but of the theatre company, in this case the King's Men; see Bentley, *Profession*, pp. 62–87.

I.i.

0.1 ACT 1 SCENE i] MS's consistent use of Latin phrases to mark act and scene divisions may reflect the habits of the scribe, Ralph Crane, rather than the wishes of the dramatist; see *The Duchess of Malfi*, ed. J. R. Brown (Revels) p. 8n, and cf. *Soph.*

3. *by . . . heaven*] i.e. by the betrothal of the lovers themselves, witnessed by Fernando (see IV.ii.2ff.). Whilst such a contract, with or without witnesses, was held to be binding, it was none the less forbidden by law because of its secret nature. Sebastian's belief that such a betrothal constitutes a legal marriage is an important factor in determining his subsequent behaviour in the play. See Schanzer, pp. 81–9, and Wentersdorf, pp. 129–44.

8. *fastening*] i.e. in marriage.

12. *devil . . . sheep-skin*] proverbial; cf. 'The white devil is worse than the black' (D310).

13. *Clapped it up*] settled it.

24. *That . . . counsel*] proverbial (C702).

27. *sensible*] feeling.

29. *act*] experience.

32. *banquet*] sweetmeats, fruits and wine following a meal, served in a different

room (see l. 67 below).

34. *obeys*] i.e. is obeyed.

35. *marriage*] trisyllabic.

38. *duke's*] MS's 'king's' may indicate that Middleton altered his conception in the course of composition; cf. V.iii.54n.

44. *malego*] malaga, a white wine from the town of that name.

black-jack] leather jug for drinking beer.

45. *small... water-rat*] Small beer was thinned with water.

56. *traded*] prostituted.

60. *comfortable*] comforting, consoling.

61. *miss*] manage without.

62. *perfumers*] employed to prepare and sweeten rooms before use. Possibly the word should be taken with the preceeding 'gentlemen' on the analogy of 'gentleman-usher'.

67. *suckets*] sweetmeats.

68. *take 'em kindly*] bawdy innuendo; *take it*, 'to accept amorous advances'.

69. *complement*] personal accomplishments, qualities.

74. *termers*] dissolutes who frequented London when the law courts were in session; cf. Middleton's *The Family of Love*, 'To the Reader'.

75. *well-booted*] with bawdy innuendo.

84. *Amsterdam*] The resort of persecuted and often extreme Puritans.

85. *Geneva*] During the Marian persecution many English Protestants emigrated to Geneva. Sugden notes that almost all the numerous references to Geneva in the plays of this period are scornful and sarcastic.

85–6. *she... Queenhithe!*] The legend, dramatised in Peele's *Edward I*, was that Queen Eleanor, after denying her murder of the Mayoress of London, prayed that the earth might swallow her if she lied; whereupon she sank into the ground at Charing Cross and rose again at Queenhithe (a quay in Upper Thames Street).

87. *holy*] Amoretta is referring ironically to Almachildes's charge of religious fanaticism. Crane consistently spells 'holy' as 'holly' in the MS (II.i.222, V.i.13, V.iii.61); thus R's emendation is unnecessary.

88. *tail*] bawdy.

89. *headstrong*] drunk.

93. *country-house*] MS's spelling 'cuntry' indicates the bawdy implication; cf. *Ram*

Alley, I.i.65.

94. *fire-drake*] will-o'-the-wisp.

kind] amorous.

95. *conclusions*] experiments, perhaps with bawdy suggestions; cf. *Tit.*, II.iii.68–9.

96. *yet*] still to come.

97. *Bacchus*] God of wine.

110. *period*] stop.

111. *skull*] Middleton makes the duke's action a more calculated one than his source suggests: 'Then mooved by the crueltie of his nature, hee made a cup of her fathers hed, whereof (in memorie of the victorie) he used to drinke... hee celebrated a solemne feast in Verona, whereat, beeing by drinking much, become very merry, and seeing the skull of Comundo full of wine, hee caused the same to be presented to the Queene Rosmunda, who sat over against him at the table (saying unto her, with so loude a voice that everie one might heare him) that she should now at this feast drinke with her father: which speech pearced the Lady to the heart, and she forthwith determined to revenge the same' (Montaigne, *The Florentine History*, trans. Thomas Bedingfield, 1595, ed. W. E. Henley, 1905, Vol. 2, p. 31).

124. *straight*] straightaway, directly.

126. *fate*] R's emendation makes Antonio's remark into a grim joke but the MS reading makes good sense as an intimation of ill-destiny.

128. *fails*] misses the mark.

133. *Sister*] R's emendation is unnecessary since Antonio appears here to be persuading his sister, Francisca, of the need to comply with the Duke's whim.

140. *since*] ever since; or possibly the MS is corrupt here.

144. *round*] (1) a military patrol, (2) a drinking ceremony.

149. *ne'er tossed pike*] Unlike Sebastian, Antonio has not been to the wars referred to at the opening of the play.

I.ii.

0.1. *Enter* HECATE] Despite the suggestions of elaborate effects in the MS's s.d. the cauldron business is kept off-stage during this scene. D's restriction of the entry to Hecate centres attention on her initial invocation and suits the pattern of this scene which, unlike III.iii and V.ii,

works by a series of private interviews, not
spectacular group effects. The MS offers no
exit for the witches during this scene and
Firestone makes it clear at lines 186ff. that
they are to be imagined as tending the
nearby cauldron off-stage.

1–7. *Titty . . . dam*] Nosworthy, p. 34,
thinks it unlikely that MS's italics indicate
singing here; it is more likely to indicate
the formal nature of Hecate's invocation.

7. *devil-dam*] supposed more terrible than
the devil himself; see A. A. Barb, 'The
Mermaid and the Devil's Grandmother',
*Journal of the Warburg and Courtauld
Institute*, XXIX (1966), 1–23.

10. *gallops*] boils (*OED* cites this passage
as the first usage).

blue enough] Blue flames were associated
with witchery and apparitions; cf. *R3*,
V.iii.180, 'The lights burn blue. It is now
dead midnight' and *Caes.*, IV.iii.273ff.

11. *seeton*] not in *OED*; a substance
presumably having the property of turning
the flames more blue. R's 'seeten' suggests
that he has knowledge of such a chemical.
D's 'seething' (i.e. boiling) seems
inappropriate as it refers to the contents of
the cauldron, not the flames as Hecate's
words suggest; but it should be noted that
the verb 'seethe' occurs in the source for
this passage (Scot, X.8) and it may be that
Hecate is contemplating extra boiling to
compensate for the lack of heat in the
flames.

12–13. *nips . . . azure*] It was a common
supersition that elves pinched sluttish
maids; cf. *Wiv.*, V.v.42–3.

16. *second hour*] Hecate is meticulous in
observing the correct conditions for her
witchery. Here she seems to be referring to
the rising of the moon (as opposed to the
sun, the 'first hour'), when the witches are
due to take their flight.

18–45.] closely based on Scot, X.8, who,
having listed the ingredients copied here by
Middleton, comments, 'By this means . . .
in a moone light night they seeme to be
carried in the aire, to feasting, singing,
dansing, kissing, culling, and other acts of
venereie, with such youthes as they love
and desire most'.

18. *unbaptisèd*] thus unprotected; see
Scot, 'Then he teacheth them to make
ointments of the bowels and members of
children, whereby they ride in aire, and
accomplish all their desires. So as, if there

be anie children unbaptised, or not garded
with the sign of the crosse, or orizons; then
the witches may and doo catch them from
their mothers sides in the night, or . . . after
buriall steale them out of their graves, and
seeth them in a caldron, untill their flesh be
made potable' (III.1); cf. also Jonson's
MQ, '6th Witch. I had a dagger, what did I
with that? / Killed an infant, to have his
fat' (ll. 175–6).

23. *pricks or stops*] dots or punctuation
marks.

26. *leek*] like (the obsolete form is used
here for the sake of the rhyme).

29. *coll*] embrace.
use] bawdy.

30. *pleasure us*] please us sexually.

31. *incubus*] Witches were commonly
thought to be enjoyed by the incubus of
particular persons. Scot sceptically
recounts the story of Bishop Sylvanus who
was defamed for having slept with a nun,
until it was explained that an incubus had
assumed his shape (IV.5).

33. *got'st*] copulated with, possessed.
Whelplie's] Perhaps fictional, the name
indicating the youth and nature of
Stadlin's victim.

34. *black . . . yellow*] Black is the usual
dress for such devilish assignations; yellow
seems used here for its association with
love; see Linthicum, pp. 47–50.

35. *spoiled*] violated.

36. *mounting*] riding in the air and riding
sexually.

37. *second hour*] see note to l. 16 above.

38. *magical herbs*] All these ingredients
are mentioned by Scot, X.8.

40. eleoselinum] mountain parsley.

41. Aconitum] wolf's bane, noted by the
Elizabethans as a deadly poison; see *2H4*.,
IV.iv.48, 'though it do work as strong as
aconitum or gun-powder'.
frondes populeus] *frondes populeas*,
poplar leaves. Hecate's grasp of Latin
terminology seems less secure in this
passage than at V.ii.18–25.

43. sium] yellow watercress.
acarum vulgaro] *acarum vulgare*, common
myrtle.

44. Pentaphyllon] cinquefoil.

45. Solanum somnificum] *solanum
somniferum*, deadly nightshade. 'It would
certainly produce hallucinations, with a
considerable amount of vascular
excitement' (Ellis).

45. *et oleum*] and oil, perhaps referring to the olive.

46–7. *Is ... needles*] In Scot's tale from New Romney in Kent the parents of a girl fallen strangely ill are informed by a cunning-woman that a witch 'wrought the maidens destruction, by making a hart of wax, and pricking the same with pins and needels' (XII.16).

48–9. *farmer's picture ... yet*] cf. 'pictures made in wax will cause the party for whom it is made to continue sick two whole years, because it will be two whole years ere the wax will be consumed' (*The Examination of John Walsh ... touching Witchcraft*, 1566, ed. Rosen, p. 70). The time lag for such destruction becomes an important issue to the Duchess later in the play; see V.ii.4–8.

53–56. *They ... breedings*] A most commonly cited motive to provoke the witch's *maleficium*; see Thomas, p. 663.

53. *barm*] yeast, leaven.

54. *charmings*] a variant form of 'churnings'; it was a common complaint that witches disrupted the preparation of butter.

55. *brew-locks*] perhaps a variant of 'brew-lead', a leaden vessel used in brewing.

batches] bakings of bread.

forspoke] bewitched.

56. *breedings*] hatchings.

meet] even.

59. *after evensong*] i.e. after their attendance at evensong which may be assumed to have given them some protection from the effects of witchcraft.

60. *sop*] sup, draught; Roberts, pp. 217–18, suggests that the 'sop' here may relate to instances of cows giving blood instead of milk.

63. *dewed-skirted*] Crane's transcription 'dew-d-skirted' is a good example of his use in the MS of the hyphen 'in place of, or by mistake for, an apostrophe' (Greg, 'Some Notes', p. 214).

70. *twelve ... night*] The expiry time of contracts with the devil; see *Faustus*, Sc. XIX.

74. *bakers*] referring to the baker's dozen.

75. *six ... hundred*] thus Hecate is 117 years old.

76–77. *give ... cast*] give you an extension; or, perhaps, give you another chance.

78. *first apple*] i.e. Eve's in the Garden of Eden.

79. *costermonger*] apple-seller.

80. *pricked*] marked; with obvious bawdy play.

81. *shed*] spill.

82. *hour*] referring back to 'second hour' above, ll. 16 and 32.

87. *posset*] hot milk curdled with ale or wine as a restorative.

91. *How ... straight*] proverbial (K155, T110 and T115).

straight] straightaway.

94. *the Nightmare*] Demon commonly supposed to oppress the sleeper by sitting on his chest and so inducing bad dreams.

96. *The great cat*] The size of the cat, at least as large as a boy actor (see below I.ii.228ff.), might be indicative of its power; see Rosen, p. 31 and cf. *W.Ed.*, V.i.43–4n.

105–8. *Urchins ... Puckle*] Middleton has converted Scot's fine denunciation of the catalogue of 'bugs' that make us 'afraid of our owne shadowes' (VII.15) into a formal invocation by Hecate of kindred spirits.

105. *Urchins*] small mischievous fairies sometimes thought to take the form of a hedgehog.

Hags] an evil spirit in female form.

106. *Silens*] wood-gods (from the 'sileni' of Greek mythology), a species of satyr. Crane seems to have mis-read his text as a command on Hecate's part. Scot's 'sylens' from which Middleton derives his term, is possibly a misprint for 'sylvens'.

Kit-with-the-candlestick] Jack-o'-lantern, will-o'-the-wisp.

Tritons] Briggs, *Anatomy*, p. 20, suggests mermen and merrows as native equivalents.

107. *the Spoorn*] a special kind of spectre whose particular name has not survived in folk-lore.

the Mare] see note to I.ii.94.

the Man-i'-th'-oak] a spirit supposed to inhabit an oak; Briggs points to the rhyme 'Fairy folks / Are in the oaks' (*Anatomy*, p. 21).

108. *the Hellwain ... the Puckle*] Middleton's inclusion of two of Hecate's sisters in the play in this list derived from Scot is perhaps a sign of hasty composition (Harris, p. 81).

the Fire-drake] see note to I.i.94.

A ab hur hus!] In Scot, XII.14., these words, followed by an etcetera, are mentioned as a charm against the toothache but it is difficult to see how this effect could be conveyed to an audience without a ludicrous break in the mood of Hecate's conjurations. It is more likely that Middleton borrowed the formula from Scot to add an occult element of *gravitas* to Hecate's invocations; where he intends comic deflation of witchcraft he employs the loutish son Firestone or the drunken client Almachildes.

120. *all ... suppers*] proverbial.

125. *firk*] drive, shoot.

126. *ointments*] see note to l. 18.

129. *takes me bravely*] pleases me exceedingly.

sworn] i.e. in the compact with the devil.

133–48. *Is't ... ground*] Middleton follows Scot closely, 'Stafus ... had a disciple called *Hoppo*, who made *Stadlin* a maister witch, and could all when they list invisiblie transferre the third part of their neighbours doong, hay, corne, etc., into theire owne ground, make haile, tempests and flouds, with thunder and lightning; and kill children, cattell, etc.' (XII.5).

137. Anno Domini] i.e. the date of erection, commonly inscribed in the moulding of the fire-place or on the fire irons at the back of the grate; cf. the havoc which accompanies the murder of Duncan in *Mac.*, 'Our chimneys were blown down' (II.iii.53).

138. *sweet place*] ironic; cf. *1H4*, 'Why, they will allow us ne'er a jordan, and then we leak in your chimney and your chamber-lye breeds fleas like a loach' (II.i.18–20).

140. *They ... picture*] The age of the sitter as well as the date was commonly included in portraits at this time. Five pounds was a substantial sum of money.

141. *curtain*] Pictures were commonly protected by curtains; see *Tw. N*, I.v.218–19.

152. *starve up generation*] destroy the capacity to procreate. James I, in the notorious case of the Essex divorce, supported the commonly held notion of the power of witchcraft to induce sexual impotence; see Introduction, p. 14.

162–4. Chiroconita ... ends] Scot suggests that these poisons were outdated: 'marrie in their steed we have hogs turd and chervill, as the onlie thing whereby our witches worke miracles' (VI.3).

163. Archimadon] 'which would make one bewraie in his sleepe, all the secrets in his heart' (Scot, VI.3).

marmaritin] 'whereby spirits may be raised' (Scot, VI.3).

164. *sort*] fit.

166–7. *As ... sheets*] listed by Scot among experiments supposed to engender love or hate (VI.7).

167. *socks up*] sews up a corpse into a shroud.

168–9. *A privy ... sunset*] Abuse of the dead body of a murderer (other criminals would be cut down before evening) is also claimed by one of the hags in Jonson's *MQ*, ll. 179–82.

172. *We ... wedlock*] Witches were commonly shown as having only limited power over the human spirit. Specifically here the powerlessness to disrupt the marriage sacrament is prefigured in Mephistophilis's response to Faustus's request for a wife (*Faustus*, V, 141ff.); cf. also *Mac.*, I.iii.24–5. and see *Soph.*, V.i.3ff.

173. *jars*] discords.

175. *our master*] i.e. the devil.

176. *patient miracle*] a Biblical reference to Job's patient endurance of sufferings, including boils on his skin. Middleton probably derives this reference from the discussion of Job's case in Scot, V.8, but the image 'a thick scurf o'er life' has a wider application than this, relating to the malevolence of witchcraft in the play.

the work itself] i.e. the marriage sacrament.

183. *first oath*] a reference to the diabolic compact.

185. *bravest*] most handsome, finely dressed.

187. *pipkin*] small earthenware pot or pan used in cookery.

188. *tumbling-cast*] somersault.

191. *honesty*] chastity.

192. '*I ... covered!*'] a phrase normally applied to head-gear.

195. *flat*] dull, incompetent.

198. *in incubus*] see note to l. 31 above.

203. *thou'rt a witch*] i.e. for guessing my errand; proverbial (W585).

204. *dry ones*] The joke, extended at l. 210, relates to Almachildes' heavy drinking.

206–10. *remora ... pismires*] taken from Scot, IV.7.

206. *remora*] a sucking fish, which was

supposed to have the power of stopping a
ship's course by adhering to the rudder.

207. *suck-stone*] sucking fish.

208. *sea-lamprey*] often used with bawdy
innuendo; cf. *The Duchess of Malfi*,
I.i.336–7, 'And women like that part
which, like the lamprey, / Hath ne'er a
bone in't' (Revels ed.).

210. *pismires*] ants.

215. *haberdasher's wife*] presumably by
trade well-equipped with good-sized
pockets for the purpose; cf. Mother in
Middleton's *Women Beware Women*,
III.ii.186–7 (Revels ed.).

216. *marchpane*] marzipan, a typical
banqueting sweetmeat; its capacity for
being moulded into elaborate effigies of
birds and beasts would make it an
attractive gift to witches.

217. *fitted*] suited, served; also bawdy.

218. *paddock-brood*] frog-brood; frequent
among witch familiars. Cf. *Mac.*, 'Paddock
calls', I.i.9.

220. *berayed*] befouled.

wet sucket] wet suckets (preserved fruits)
were served before dry ones; see
Markham, *English Housewife* (1615), II,
78.

229. *The Cat ... ordinary*] the London
ordinary or eating house in Cheapside near
the Cross.

234. *fatter ... laughing*] proverbial (L91).

II.i.

13. *pearl ... cullis*] in the making of the
cullis (a rich broth) pearls and gold were
dissolved.

14. *consumption*] wasting disease, with
allusion to gonorrhoea; see *Lr.*,
IV.vi.128–9.
and] but.

16. *goldsmith*] i.e. as part of the cure for
venereal disease.

21. *nobles*] gold coins worth
approximately 33 pence; slightly more than
the 'going-rate' for strumpets suggested in
Barry's *Ram Alley*, IV.ii.1647ff.

22. *ponado*] panada, boiled and flavoured
bread pudding.

36. *make merry*] have sex.
friend] euphemism for lover.

38. *rocking*] i.e. in the cradle.

43. *venturing*] sexually bold; *OED* 8 gives
'venture' as 'prostitute'. For similar
laments at a too ready fertility, see

Touchwood Senior in Middleton's *A
Chaste Maid in Cheapside*, II.i.

49. *chewets*] minced meat or fish pies.

51. *help forward*] eggs were thought to
have aphrodisiac qualities.

60. *powder-up*] to salt or preserve meat,
applied figuratively here in relation to a
projected long sea-voyage.

64. *More ... should*] Sebastian's charms
from Hecate have rendered Antonio
sexually incapable.

74. *gamester*] lecher, debauched fellow.

77. *leave tobacco*] The plight of the wife
of a smoker is elaborated by James I in his
Counter-blast to Tobacco, 'either she must
also corrupt her sweet breath therewith, or
else resolve to live in a perpetual stinking
torment' (Miniature Books, 1954, p. 36).

79. *toy*] trifle.

80. *knights' wives in town*] The jibe here
lies in the devaluation of knighthood in the
early years of James I's reign, a frequent
joke in the city comedies of the period; see
Eastward Ho!, IV.i.167–8.

86–7. *statute ... fiddlers*] Minstrels
'wandringe abroad' were included in the
statutes against vagabonds of 1572, 1598
and 1604; see Chambers, *ES*, IV, 269, 324,
336.

104. *Quicker*] quibble on the senses
'faster' and 'more pregnant'.

113. *a good bit*] referring to her
pregnancy.

114. *broke ... sinner*] referring to the
injunction of fasting until after morning
church service.

117. *yard of lawn!*] i.e. by way of a bet.
lawn] fine linen.

119. *old shirts*] for use during the actual
child-birth.

124. *cold ... means*] because of last
night's failed activity in bed.

125. *fault*] bawdy quibble on the meaning
'crack, flaw' (*OED* 4).

125.1. *Song*] This song survives in a MS
folio copied by John Wilson *c.* 1650
(Bodleian MS. Mus, b.1.f.21) and in John
Gamble's *Commonplace Book* (New York,
Drexel MS. 4257, No. 32); see Nosworthy,
pp. 230–1 and Appendix below.

137. *spoils*] corrupts.

172. *heal verray*] health very; parodies of
Scottish dialect were prevalent, and
punishable, at this time; cf. *Eastward Ho!*,
IV.i.197–8 and note (Revels ed.).

181. *down*] i.e. for the child-birth.

182. *speed*] deliverance.

192. *conceit*] personal opinion.

205. *he's no content*] i.e. Antonio has no sexual gratification.

207. *the cold disease*] i.e. sexual deprivation.

210. *throughly*] thoroughly; the two-syllable form was common.

214–16. *What ... joys*] an orthodox sentiment; cf. *Faustus*, III, 78ff.

219. *red*] used here as an intensive, as well as being the colour traditionally associated with love.

228. *I've ... venture.*] Sebastian reminds himself that the courage he needs to sustain his present role is less than he has shown formerly in military action ('upon a breach').

II.ii.

1. *toy*] whim.

7. *foot-post*] messenger who travels on foot.

8. *charm*] Roberts, pp. 218–19, traces this practice and the way in which it is handled by Middleton to Le Loyer's *A Treatise of Spectres*, where a young man tried to win the love of a girl by magical means obtaining scrolls of virgin parchment from a sorcerous priest and 'finding his mistresse in a place fitte for the purpose, he conveyed the paper into her bosome, whilst himselfe made semblance that he was but playing and jesting with her' (fol. 138).

11–14. *Necte ... necte.*] Taken from Virgil's eighth eclogue, except that Amaryllis is changed to Amoretta, 'I take three colours, Amaryllis, in three knots. Come, twine them, Amaryllis, and say "These are the chains of Venus that I twine"' (trans. E. V. Rieu, Penguin, 1949). Le Loyer glosses this passage 'Which woordes ioyned and used with a ceremonie of certaine knottes made in a ribande or lace of three severall colours, were held to have such power that they in whose name they were pronounced, should presently feele themselves stricken in love' (fol. 143v).

13. *boughts*] knots, twists.

14. *Nodo*] *modo* in Virgil, the mistake being copied from Le Loyer but also suiting Middleton's fun with Latin translation.

necte] *necto* in Virgil.

18. *construction*] (1) expounding (the Latin charm); (2) interpreting behaviour.

20–24. *Let ... boy*] Middleton again made comic use of misconstrued Latin in *A Chaste Maid in Cheapside*, I.i.66ff. (Revels ed.).

22. *turned colours*] perhaps a play on the figurative sense 'surrender' as well as a literal reference to the twisted colours of the charm.

27. *hellcat*] either evil woman or witch; *OED* cites this as the first usage.

brain of a cat] cf. *MQ*, l. 194, where Jonson glosses his text, 'another special Ingredient and of so much more efficacy, by how much blacker the Cat is'.

31. *cleanly*] neat, elegant.

33. *ordinarily*] in the normal way.

40. *rudest*] least sophisticated, roughest.

42. *thing*] bawdy.

43. *make all split*] wreck havoc, create hell.

47. *when ... time*] while there's still time.

62. *confusion*] overthrow, ruin.

74. *tricks*] sexual strategems.

103. *Thy ... is*] The Duchess is called Rosmunda in the source, the change being necessary so that the charm works equally on both women.

123. *case altered*] proverbial (C111).

125. *venturous*] amorous.

126. *flesh and blood*] proverbial (F367).

129–32. *You ... list*] Bromham, 'The Date', p. 152, suggests that Amoretta's reference to 'best folks' may well be a reference to the Essex annulment, and to the way in which Frances Howard was able to use the influence of the King himself to obtain it so that she could marry her lover. See Introduction, p. 14.

135. *clipped name*] i.e. injured reputation, 'the metaphor is from the clipped wing of a bird in a snare' (Deighton); Bu. derives 'clipped' from 'cleped' (called, proclaimed) but this offers a more strained reading whereby the snare is imagined to operate by means of a decoy bird-call.

II.iii.

6. *Well ... sides*] i.e. heavily pregnant.

7. *drab*] slut, strumpet.

9. *scape*] breach of chastity.

12. *to a hair*] exactly.

14. *purse*] perhaps in the sense 'scrotum' and, by extension, maintaining a man's sexual freedom; cf. *W.T.*, IV.iii.614–16.

22. *quick ... cleanly*] i.e. tailoring will make a good training for stealing.

30. *safe-guard*] outer skirt or petticoat worn by women to protect their dress while riding, often made of expensive materials; see Linthicum, p. 188.

31. *probably*] plausibly.

dabbled] bespattered.

32. *marked*] noticed it.

34. *woodcock*] generally 'fool', but also meaning 'prostitute'.

36. *box*] cuff.

41. *At*] after.

46. *I'll ... least*] at a conservative estimate.

47. *caudles*] warm drink with wine or ale, sweetened and spiced, given especially to women when lying-in and also to their visitors.

48. *of ... departure*] used up a week ago.

54. *whips*] rather laboured play on the idea of the use of whips to punish lechery.

III.i.

3. *handled*] cheated.

5. *tries*] play on 'tests' and 'tries sexually'.

11. *gotten*] sexually possessed.

11–13. *'Tis ... bird-lime.*] cf. the proverb, 'A woman either loves or hates to extremes' (W651).

31. *act of force*] rape.

proud] sexually potent; cf. *Sonn.* 151.

36–7. *'Tis ... too*] Almachildes complains that this sexual pleasure not only makes him breathless but subsequently denies him breath, i.e. his life.

40. *Of*] in respect of.

47–8. *For ... somewhat*] probably proverbial; cf. 'Let everyman have his own' (M209).

53. *That time*] i.e. the opportunity for the deed.

III.ii.

2. *quean*] whore.

7. *prick-song*] written vocal music, with a joke at Antonio's impotence with Isabella in the following line.

close] fixedly or privately.

15. *envious*] malicious.

17. *fail*] misinterpret.

condition] disposition.

22. *city-tuck*] If the MS reading is correct the phrase probably has the force of 'city-fashion' (see *OED* 7 'ducks and tucks'); Bu.'s conjecture is attractive, though, and

would have a more dismissive edge, 'city trash' (*OED* truck n. 4b; see also 'truck' v. 5b. 'to have sexual intercourse with').

27. *at a strange stand*] perplexed.

36. *one ... family*] i.e. a prostitute.

37. *Rutneys*] not mentioned in Sugden; perhaps a resort notorious to the audience, but the bawdy innuendo in the name suggests that it may be fictional.

43. *sirrah*] Gaspero uses the form of address implying his own superiority to the disguised Sebastian who has only recently been taken into the service of Isabella.

44. *Thinkst ... Gasper*] Gaspero is unaware of the witchcraft that Sebastian is practising against Antonio.

52. *fled to shifts*] resorted to expedients, evasions.

65. *confusion*] ruin.

70. *wished her to*] recommended her to (in marriage).

75. *speed*] applicable to the issue of Francisca's journey as well as its rapidity.

83. *rod*] a measure of five and a half yards.

85. *bleak*] pale.

86. *sharp*] peaked.

88. *travelled*] a play on the meaning 'laboured' (with child) as MS's spelling 'travaild' suggests.

91. *hand*] handwriting.

100. *strangeness*] 'shyness as a stranger' (Ellis).

103. *shake hands with*] say goodbye to.

107. *his*] i.e. Aberzanes'.

112. *churching*] the public appearance of a woman at church one month after bearing a child to return thanks and to be 're-sanctified'; see Thomas, pp. 42–3 and 68–9.

113. *'Give you joy'*] Presumably the congratulations of neighbours attending the ceremony. This phrase is not to be found in the service of *Thanksgiving of Women after Childbirth* although the emphasis in the ceremony was shifted, after 1552, from 'purification' to 'thanksgiving'.

117. *Misdeeds ... enough*] proverbial (cf. M1315 and T117).

119–20. *She ... too!*] proverbial (W649).

123. *cast*] considered, but also a play on the meaning 'vomit' which is picked up in the next line.

134. *conceit*] understanding or imagination.

139. *fit*] punish.

143. *conceit*] idea.

152. *lightness*] wantonness.

155. *apparent*] evident, plain.

191. *fortnight's journey*] There has been no opportunity for Sebastian to learn of Antonio's forthcoming absence.

192. *country*] bawdy.

207. *stand*] persist.

217. *prefer*] recommend.

III.iii.

0.1 [three other] *Witches*] Hellwain, Puckle and one unnamed witch; see note to 'The Persons', 20.

1. *brisk*] finely dressed, spruce.

2. *rich*] magnificent.

3. *take ... mile*] see I.ii.18–45n.

5. *Heard...owl*] welcomed here as a signal for the witches' activities; cf. *Mac.*, II.ii.3–4, 'It was the owl that shrieked, the fatal bellman / Which gives the stern'st goodnight'.

7–8. *bat ... fill*] The notion of vampirish familiars was a peculiarly English one; see Thomas, pp. 530–1 and cf. *W.Ed.*, II.i.147 and IV.i.153ff. and *1H6*, V.iii.2–23.

12. *ointments*] a necessary preliminary to flight; see I.ii.18–45n.

14. *betimes*] speedily.

14.1 [Exeunt ... HECATE]] The suggestion in the 1810 edition that the witches ascended here, besides raising the question of feasibility in terms of available stage-machinery, produces a serious risk of up-staging Hecate's later elevation with her familiar at l. 62.

15. *a-birding*] usually applied to bird-catching (cf. *Wiv.*, III.iii.206) but here humorously to describe the witches' night flight.

17. *mortality*] Suggesting that death will ensue as a direct result of the witches' flight; later Hecate refers to 'the red-haired girl / I killed last night' (V.ii.55).

22. *brave plump ones*] probably eggs, as the next line would seem to suggest.

25. *marmartin*] Gareth Roberts suggests that the joke in Firestone's version of the herb may lie in an allusion to the tract entitled *Mar Martine* (1589), attributed to Lyly, written as part of the Marprelate pamphlet war.

26. Marmaritin] See I.ii.163n.

mandragora] a soporific from the plant mandrake; cf. *Oth.*, III.iii.334, 'not poppy, nor mandragora' and *Ant.*, I.v.4–5, 'Give me to drink mandragora ... / That I may sleep out this great gap of time'.

27. panax] panace, all-heal.

pan] head; or, perhaps, socket of the thigh-bone; the actor must choose which to signal to the audience.

28. selago] the club-moss, *Lycopodisum Selago*; according to Holland's *Pliny*, XXIV.xi.II.193, like the herb 'savine', from the tops of which a strong poisonous drug can be made.

29. *Hedge-hyssop*] *gratiola officinalis*, noted for medicinal qualities.

how ... cuttings] Hecate seems to fear for the secrecy of her own special herbs.

30. *by moonlight*] the propitious time; cf. Jonson's *MQ*, where all the items are collected 'since the Evening Starre did rise' (l. 162). By contrast the slips of yew in *Mac.* (IV.i.27–8) are taken in total darkness.

31. *moon-calf*] monstrosity, congenital idiot.

36. *noise*] company (of musicians).

37.1 Song] A divided song as the MS's stage directions indicate, with responses to Hecate coming from above.

38–76. Come away...] See Appendix for the music to this elaborate song. It seems from the stage-direction in the folio of *Mac.*, 'Sing within. Come away, come away, etc.' (III.v.33), that this song was interpolated into revivals of that play and may itself have been suggested by Jonson's *MQ*, 'Sisters, stay; we want o[ur] Dame. / Call upon her, by your name, / And the charme we use to say, / That she quickly anoynt, and come away' (ll. 48–51).

60–1. *own language*] Firestone describes this as French at V.ii.31, but this may be a joke at that language's resemblance to a cat-like spitting to Jacobean ears.

62. Going ... *MALKIN*] A feat which would be possible with Jacobean stage-machinery 'particularly if the cat was played by a boy' (Harris, p. 170).

63. Malkin] a diminutive of Matilda, Maud; here Hecate's affectionate name for the cat; the name was often applied to animal familiars and female spectres; cf. *Mac.*, I.i.8.

64. dainty] choice, precious.

67. *toy*] flirt.

69. our mistress'] Several readings have some claim to authority here: 'crystal'

attractively picks up moonlit suggestions in 'shines fair' (l. 66) and elsewhere; 'over misty', a plausible mis-reading by Crane, might indicate the height of the witches' venture which is drawn attention to several times in the text. However, Nosworthy's explanation is perhaps the best: 'The seas are fountains drawn up by ['our mistress'] the moon' (p. 229). This reading is further supported by the close associations, especially in this scene, of Hecate with the moon.

70. steeples] MS's 'Steepe' is possible, but metrically less desirable than Davenant's reading which is supported by 'In moonlight nights o'er steeple-tops' at I.ii.22.

IV.i.

3. *rub out*] manage without.

7–8. *I ... brimstone*] an echo of *Ham.*, 'I know a hawk from a handsaw' (II.ii.385).

7. *bawd ... shop*] The two were regarded as inseparable; see Marston's *The Malcontent*, 'as a bawd with aqua-vitae' (V.i.20) and cf. *R.&J.*, III.ii.88.

8. *wildfire*] a name for erysipelas and various inflammatory eruptive diseases; associated here with venereal disease and hence strumpets; cf. *1H4*, III.iii.39.

beadle from brimstone] beadles were noted for their severity in punishing offenders; see *Lr.*, IV.vi.160.

13–14. *A ... hair-bracelets*] parodying moralistic plays and pamphlet titles of the day, e.g. Heywood's *A Warning for Fair Women* (1599); a hair-bracelet was a fashionable love-token, associated with death in Donne's 'The Relique' and 'The Funerall'.

19. *rudeness*] ignorance.

23. *crosses*] thwartings, vexations.

38. *take ... upon*] feign.

43. *spoon-meat*] 'broth in which poison could be easily administered' (Ellis).

48. *countenance*] set off, grace.

52. *popular*] plebian, low, vulgar.

60. *Dearer*] more intense.

64. *rankness*] corruption.

74. *up*] risen in rebellion.

78–9. *two passions ... sorrow*] A crude echo, perhaps, of Cordelia's divided mood, *Lr.*, IV.iii.17ff.

82. *her*] herself.

94. *Mischief ... friend*] proverbial (M996).

IV.ii.

7. *This ... offer*] a view that Sebastian retracts at ll. 95ff.

23. *make use of*] see Introduction, pp. 17–18 for discussion of Sebastian's muddled plot here.

25. *she*] Isabella.

26. *him*] Antonio.

27. *he*] How Sebastian could involve Antonio in this way is obscure; see Introduction, pp. 17–18.

compound] collude, conspire with, but perhaps also 'coit'.

35. *Closely*] secretly.

take] get into.

37. *a-work*] bawdy.

45. *When ... mainly*] cf. 'Of a little spark a great fire' (S714).

46. *business*] bawdy.

53. *allusion*] comparison.

59. *feed*] either of G's conjectures make more convincing sense than MS's 'feel'; 'feed' is preferable as a more likely copyist's error.

81. *stuff*] bawdy.

82. *bold strumpet*] Are we to assume that she met Florida at the door?

90. *disease*] disturb.

95. *I ... sinful*] Besides the offence of deception, contemporary church opinion would have regarded Sebastian's consummation of his 'marriage' to Isabella before it had been publicly solemnised, as fornication and a deadly sin; see I.i.3n.

109. *affect*] love.

117. *Man ... disposing*] proverbial (M298).

123. *else ... go*] Sebastian now wants to abort Florida's mission.

125. *Sin ... does.*] proverbial; cf. 'Sins are not known till they be acted' (S477).

IV.iii.

9. *resolved*] convinced.

16. *cries*] snores.

disease] disturb.

18. *spiced*] dosed with a spiced drug.

posset] restorative night-drink.

22. *gasp*] Obvious name puns were not uncommon; cf. Heywood's *A Woman Killed with Kindness*, VI, 167 (Revels ed.), 'Ay, Nick, didst come in the nick?'.

28. *stir enough*] bawdy.

36. *his own lodging*] his own bedroom. Drees, misunderstanding the use of the term 'lodging', prefers the corrected MS

reading, but Francisca's instructions are to ensure that Gaspero is discovered at the very least to be suspiciously absent from his own bed.

37–46.] A largely off-stage sequence held together by Francisca's alert listening; MS's attribution of words to Francisca at l. 40 makes little sense since she wishes Antonio to use his sword.

37. *Here's*] i.e. in Gaspero's chamber.

43. *spoiled*] destroyed.

53–5. O . . . *merry*] cf. *Oth.*, III.iii.342ff., and also the proverb 'Better be a cuckold and know it than be none and everybody say so' (C876).

101. *new man*] Sebastian disguised as Celio.

V.i.

0.1. *ANTONIO*] MS's substitution of Sebastian here and in the first two speech prefixes is odd and presumably indicates Middleton's change of plan in composition; cf. I.i.38 and V.iii.54.

2. *untrussed*] with the breeches' tags untied.

3–4. *The . . . it*] Antonio questions Aberzanes's sense of his own worthiness by contrasting slaves who may escape death when 'honester men' perish ('go to't').

9. *long weapon*] bawdy.

27. *starting-holes*] loopholes.

light] get to the point.

28. *play*] dealing (with bawdy innuendo).

41. *friend*] lover.

50. *it*] the wine.

51. *strong bill of divorcement*] The difficulty of obtaining divorce during the early seventeenth century may be gauged by the notorious case of the Earl of Essex, which Bromham suggests ('The Date', p. 152) may be alluded to here; see Introduction, p. 14.

55. *poison*] Antonio has instructed Hermio at IV.iii.108 (in a whisper) to poison the wine which the three have now drunk.

59ff.] This information has been witheld from the audience until this point; see Introduction, pp. 18–19.

60. *falsely . . . falsely*] (1) deceitfully and (2) mistakenly.

75. *sound*] free from venereal disease.

78. *light horse*] courtesan.

87. *conceit*] apprehension.

abuse] deceive.

88. *For*] in respect of.

93. *wears*] possesses.

95. *loud*] vehement.

110. *sureness*] as a witness to confirm events.

111. *mistaken*] i.e. stabbed in mistake for Isabella.

114. *she*] Isabella.

134. *Flatters*] promises.

V.ii.

0.1 [ACT V] SCENE ii] This scene and the final one are incorrectly numbered by Crane but there is no sign that a scene has been omitted.

2. *fitted*] supplied.

3. *gifts . . . subtle*] ingredients conferring both sudden and subtle deaths.

4. *picture . . . wax*] see I.ii.48–9n.

5. *blue fire*] see I.ii.10n.

14. *closely*] possibly means 'swiftly' as well as 'privily' (or even perhaps 'completely'); see *OED* 'close' adj. and adv.

17. *scrupulous*] distrustful.

greatness] D's emendation is attractive but unnecessary here since Hecate is referring to the social rank of the Duchess.

18–25. Cum . . . traho] D suggests that Middleton's source for this quotation from Ovid's *Metamorphoses*, VII.199, is Bodinus's *De Magnum Daemonomania* rather than Scot, since Hecate's speech here omits the line '*Vivaque saxa, sua convulsaque robora terra*' after l. 22 in the same manner as Bodinus. Scot's translation of the complete passage is as follows:

> The rivers I can make retire,
> Into the fountains whence they flo,
> (Whereat the banks themselves admire)
> I can make standing waters go,
> With charmes I drive both sea and clowd,
> I make it calme and blowe alowd.
> The vipers jawes, the rockie stone,
> With words and charmes I breake in twaine
> The force of earth congeald in one,
> I moove and shake both woods and plaine;
> I make the soules of men arise.
> I pull the moone out of the skies.
> (XII.7).

26. *woods walk*] cf. Birnam Wood in

Mac., IV.i.97–8.

27–8. *spirits ... marbles*] among Faustus's and Prospero's capabilities; see *Faustus*, VI, 26ff., etc., and *Tp.*, V.i.48–50.

28. *marbles*] marble tombs.

29. *involved*] underhand.

31–2. *for ... Latin*] Ghosts and devils were commonly thought to converse in Latin; cf. Beaumont and Fletcher's *Night Walker*, II.i, 'Let's call the butler up, for he speaks Latin, / And that would daunt the devil'. For the cat's French see III.iii.60–1n.

38. *howlet-time*] see III.iii.5n.

43. semina cum sanguine] seed with blood.

47–8. *conscionable*] reasonable.

49. *lizard's brain*] mentioned by Scot as an ingredient in a love cup, IV.7.

51. three other *Witches*]] Hecate refers to 'five sisters' (l. 37 above).

52. *marmaritin*] see I.i.163n.

53. *bear-breech*] popular name for the herbaceous plant of the genus *Acanthus*, brank-ursine.

55. *red-haired girl*] Red-heads were thought to be especially noxious and powerful in poisoning; here clearly the intention is to crown the potency of the poisonous brew. In Massinger's *A Very Woman*, a red-haired slave is priced above others because

> He will poyson Rats,
> Make him but angry, and his eyes
>   kill Spiders;
> Let him but fasting, spit upon a
>   Tode,
> And presently it bursts, and dies;
>   his dreams kill
>   (II.i.31–4, *Plays and Poems of Philip Massinger*, ed. Philip Edwards and Colin Gibson).

57. *acopus*] soothing salve, anodyne.

59.1. A charm-song] A song which seems also to be used in *Mac.*, at IV.i.43. Briggs, *PHT*, p. 51, suggests that the first line is a quotation from a ballad on the witches of St Osyth's from which Scot also quotes. Long is unable to trace any music for this song but suggests that, like the first witches' song in III.iii, it was 'accompanied by a broken consort located, probably, above the stage' (p. 197).

66. Liard, Robin] see above I.ii.3–8.

71. libbard's bane] leopard's bane, a plant of the genus *Doronicum*; 'libbard' is an archaic form of 'leopard'. Nosworthy's

suggested emendation is based on the mistaken assumption that the ingredient referred to here is 'lizard's brain' mentioned at ll. 49 and 53. The MS reading is further supported, as T. H. Howard-Hill observes ('"Lizard's Braine" in Middleton's *The Witch*', *N. & Q.*, Dec. 1973, pp. 458–9), by a similar reading in Jonson's *MQ*, l. 189.

72–6. Nosworthy suggests that the variants (see textual collation) were 'evidently made to render the song more suitable for use in *Macbeth*. Whether they possess Shakespearian authority is an open question' (p. 230).

73. younker] youngster.

82. burden] accompaniment.

83. *Let ... strike*] cf. *Mac.*, 'I'll charm the air to give a sound' (IV.i.129); and also Glendower's musicians who 'Hang in the air a thousand leagues from hence,' in *1H4*, III.i.225–6.

strike] play.

84.1. *The Witches' Dance*] From a similar stage-direction it would seem that this dance was also used in *Mac.* at IV.i.131 and may have been taken from or inspired by Jonson's *MQ*, where the description of movements in the dance suggests effects that might be suitable here: 'with a strange sodayne Musique, they fell into a magicall Daunce, full of preposterous change, and gesticulation, but most applying to their property: who at their meetings, do all things contrary to the custome of Men, dauncing back to back, hip to hip, their handes ioyn'd and making circles backward, to the left hand, with strange phantastique motions of their hands, and bodyes' (l. 344–50). See Appendix for the probable music to this dance.

V.iii.

0.2 *FRANCISCA, ABERZANES*] As these characters have no lines to speak in the final scene they are omitted by many editors. MS's inclusion of Hermio in this general entry is clearly a mistake (see l. 21 below).

3. *this woman*] Florida.

17. *her ... her*] Florida and Isabella respectively.

41. *passion*] passionate sorrow.

47. *Your ... knowledge*] having acted as your servant cannot have made me unrecognisable.

50–1. *One . . . here*] Gaspero refers to his gaping wounds.

54. *Ravenna*] Presumably MS's 'Urbin' survives from an earlier draft; cf. I.i.38 and see note to 'The Persons', 25. Urbino, an Italian city, was frequently used as a setting in dramas of the period and may have served as a convenient provisional location for Middleton during composition. Unfortunately the necessary revision leaves a clumsy metrical line.

65. *Ends . . . now*] Either some words have dropped out of the text here or MS's 'ever' is a misreading. Clearly a verb referring to Almachildes's death is required to make

sense of the passage.

74. *As . . . desertful*] It is possible that there was a topical allusion here which would have been understood by the contemporary audience.

88. *worthy and unequalled*] ironic. *piece*] masterpiece of villainy.

92. *injury*] that of drinking healths out of the skull-cap of her killed father as we have seen in I.i.105ff.

105. *time . . . about*] cf. the proverb 'Time reveals all things' (T333).

108. *known her better*] i.e. sexually.

116. *blinded*] blindfolded; see III.i.1ff.

126. *practice*] conspiracy.

THE WITCH OF EDMONTON

Actors' Names

4. *OLD BANKS*] Sugden suggests that since Banks appears both here, and in the earlier play, *The Merry Devil of Edmonton*, as Banks, the Miller of Waltham, it 'seems to indicate that he was a study from the life'.

5. *W. MAGO*] William Mago was perhaps a hired minor actor in the Prince's Company. He is twice named as a 'Carthaginian Officer' and an 'attendant on King Prusias' in the cast list of the King's Men's production of Massinger's *Believe As You List* (1631). See Bentley, II, 506. Mago is not referred to elsewhere in the play.

6. *W. HAMLUC*] 'Hamluc is generally said to be an actor's name slipped into the text of *The Witch of Edmonton*, though it is quite possible that the dramatists selected the name and that no actor is indicated at all' (Bentley, II, 459–60). Bentley conjectures that Mago and Hamluc performed in the original production rather than in the revival. Hamluc enters at IV.i.14 '*with a thatch and link*' and is given two brief speeches.

11. *YOUNG CUDDY BANKS*] Cuddy from 'cudden', ass, a born fool

15. *POLDAVIS*] Although Young Banks refers to Poldavis at III.i.60 he makes no appearance in the play.

Argument

1. *distich*] a couplet containing a complete idea.

Prologue

PROLOGUE] It is evident from ll. 5–10 that the prologue was written for the play's revival. Theophilus Bird and Ezekiel Fenn, who played Winnifride, were both members of Queen Henrietta's Company in the mid-1630's, thus dating the revival c. 1635. Bentley suggests that Fenn was born in the parish of St Martin-in-the-Fields in 1620. He also played Sophonisba in Nabbes's *Hannibal and Scipio* for Queen Henrietta's Company in 1635. See Bentley, II, 433.

1. *Edmonton*] village in Middlesex, seven miles north of London.

2. *A Devil*] a reference to *The Merry Devil of Edmonton*. See Introduction, p. 21.

13. *Master Bird*] Probably the son of the actor William Bird, he had a long theatrical career which extended into the Restoration period. He first appeared in female roles for Queen Henrietta's Men in the mid-1620s and had graduated to male roles by 1635. Bentley suggests a friendship between Bird and Ford since the former's name is affixed to the prologues of two

plays and to the dedication of one which were written in whole or in part by the dramatist. See Bentley, II, 378.

I.i.

3. *gossips*] newsmongers or tattlers, but the more strict meaning may also apply here—'godparents'.

15. *thrift*] prosperity, success.

38. *Waltham Abbey*] Waltham, or Waltham Cross, a village in Hertfordshire, 12 miles north of London; just across the border of the county is Waltham Abbey or Waltham Holy Cross.

58. *double*] presumably 'doubly strong'; but a second, ironic, meaning is also possible—'deceitful'.

63–7. Frank's oath is here ironic in that in breaking it by his subsequent bigamous marriage to Susan he indeed brings about his ruin.

70. *behoveful*] advantageous; necessary.

82. *stews*] brothel.

95. *gentleman*] It was common practice for the children of the gentry and aristocracy to be educated by serving in the households of their social superiors.

120. *present*] immediate.

121. *occasions*] needs, requirements.

143. *there*] Bo., following *Q*'s 'that', suggests that the possible sense is, 'But what is that which can be brought forward to acquit me of prior knowledge?' On. speculates that 'that' refers to Frank's preceding explanation.

153. *cuckoo*] cuckold.

156–7. Gi. reads *Q*'s speech prefix as an appellation. Strict adherence to the metre would support this and On. argues that Winnifride who, a few lines later, repents of her past 'deeds of lust', would not speak in this way to her former lover. However, it is possible to argue that Winnifride is referring to the financial arrangements between Frank and Sir Arthur and, perhaps naively, has concluded that her past indiscretions have been buried.

159. *Suddenly*] very soon.

160–2. *Then . . . virginity*] Bo. conjectures that '*Then . . . happiness*' may be corrupt and that an emendation ''twere' is desirable. He suggests that the lines may be interpreted 'If this has been cleanly carried, it should be my happiness that I repent rather than any happiness that I have deceived Frank'. More simply one may

suggest that Winnifride finds happiness in repenting that she did not bring Frank the dower of her virginity.

169. *practise*] to scheme or intrigue.

183. *resolve you*] put you out of doubt.

201. *Unfile*] withdraw, delete; the reverse of *file*, OED, 3, 1b.

210. *fine*] cunning, artful (*OED* 11).

222. *fools have fortune*] proverbial (F536).

I.ii.

12. *Men . . . mortal*] proverbial (M502).

15. *tarriers*] hindrances, obstructions.

25. *There . . . bags*] The meaning here is obscure, but bags are often associated with money-bags, e.g. Middleton's *Women Beware Women*, I.i.100 (Revels ed.). Thus On's conjecture that Carter is suggesting that Frank 'might very well have gotten someone uglier than Susan along with such a large dowry' has some substance.

29. *bread . . . fare*] Old Carter's emphasis on the homely fare offered to his guests shows his pride in his yeoman status and accentuates the range and richness of the play's social texture.

30. *kickshaws*] a fancy dish in cookery, chiefly contemptuous: a something French, not one of the known 'substantial English' dishes.

31–2. *Barber-Surgeons' Hall*] Built in the reign of Edward IV in Monkswell Street near Cripplegate. Corpses, especially those of criminals, were brought there for dissection and their skeletons were occasionally preserved.

32. *anatomy*] a skeleton; a skeleton with the skin left, a mummy.

34. *Valentine's day*] 14 February. Traditionally the day upon which the birds chose their mates and lovers chose their sweethearts.

38. *a loose . . . shoe*] Old Carter's meaning is unclear but probably refers to the idea that such apparel is appropriate for pregnancy. Certainly loose gowns were frequently associated with moral 'looseness'. However Linthicum, p. 183, seems sceptical of such innuendo. A straight shoe was presumably a tight-fitting one, here suggesting the constraints of the marriage bond. 'Shoe' often has a bawdy innuendo; see *The Shoemaker's Holiday*, I, 148 (Revels ed.).

38–9. *Win 'em and wear 'em*] proverbial

(W408), a version of the form 'Win her and wear her' (sc. as a bride).

49. *yea and nay*] Matthew's injunction, 'Let your communication be, Yea, yea; Nay, nay' (Matt. V.37) came to be regarded as a particularly earnest oath.

52. *Flatter ... it*] probably proverbial.

55–6. *The fly ... done*] proverbial, 'the fly (moth) that plays too long in the candle singes its wings at last' (F394, citing this example).

64. *resolvèd*] certain of it.

76. *roaring-lads*] young men who behaved in a noisy, riotous manner; see Middleton's *A Fair Quarrel* and *The Roaring Girl*.

77. *rake-hells*] scoundrels, vile debauchees.

78. *prizes*] contests.

81–2. *five ... weight*] Old Carter reveals a very sceptical opinion of Warbeck.

83. *West Ham*] a village four and a half miles from London; now part of Greater London.

84. *Enfield*] Enfield in Middlesex, about eleven miles north of London.

88–9. *Honest ... then*] proverbial; a variation of 'Honest men and knaves may possibly wear the same cloth' (M528).

98. *stale*] decoy, bait, stalking horse. *fond*] foolish.

99. *Wilt ... wasp*] allusion to the proverb 'As angry as a wasp' (W76).

100. *firk*] trounce.

106.] Previous editors' interpretation of Warbeck's remark as an aside is not necessary. Susan's subsequent response suggests that he addresses her.

113. *He ... her*] probably proverbial.

114. *Mew!*] a derisive exclamation.

117. *huswives*] hussies.

126. *clew*] a ball of thread or yarn which guides or threads a way through a maze. *wind ... out*] extricate, disentangle.

132. *instate*] confer.

175. *Which ... night*] Gi. suspects textual corruption here but the line, though short, makes sense.

181. *quick*] alive.

186. *mainly*] strongly.

204. *I ... Dunstable*] honest and straightforward; a reference to the proverb: 'As plain as Dunstable Highway' (D646).

211. *at a burden*] at one birth.

211–12 *The nursing ... milk*] i.e. the cost of the nursing and employing a wet-nurse

will not fall upon you.

217. *motion*] proposal.

218–9. *Let ... together*] a double meaning with an allusion to the dance tune 'The Shaking of the Sheets' often used as the basis of a sexual joke; see Dekker's *The Shoemaker's Holiday*, XVI, 83 (Revels ed.).

226–7. *No ... him*] probably proverbial.

II.i.

3–4. *'Cause ... together*] Goodcole records 'Her body was crooked and deformed, even bending together' (sig. A4v), and later notes 'she was a very ignorant woman' (sig. C1). Elizabeth Sawyer is consistently presented by the dramatists in a sympathetic light which may reflect the influence of Scot, who writes of witches who, 'being poore and needie, go from doore to doore for releefe, have they never so manie todes or cats at home, or never so much hogs doong or charvill about them, or never so manie charmes in store' (XV.31). On. also quotes Heywood's *Gynaekaeon* (1624, p. 399) 'all such are for the most part stigmaticall and ouglie, in so much, that it is growne into a common Adage ... As deformed as a Witch'.

8–13. *Some ... nurse*] Goodcole records Elizabeth Sawyer's confession, 'I have bene by the helpe of the Divell, the meanes of many Christians and beasts death; the cause that moved mee to do it, was malice and envy, for if any body had angred me in any manner, I would be so revenged of them and of their cattell. And do now further confesse, that I was the cause of those two nurse-childrens death ...' (sig. C2).

12. *Forspeaks*] bewitches, charms. *bewitch ... corn*] either blasting it as it is growing, spoiling it once harvested, or transporting it; cf. *Wi.*, I.ii.145–8.

25. *maw*] stomach.

26. *Hag*] (1) an evil spirit, daemon, or infernal being in female form; (2) a witch; (3) an ugly repulsive old woman often with implications of viciousness or maliciousness. Old Banks's comments would seem to suggest the second and third meanings here. Cf. *Wi.*, I.ii.105.

27. *curmudgeon*] avaricious churlish fellow; miser.

36. *Familiar*] 'The familiar spirit, or imp

is an almost exclusively English (and Scottish) contribution to the theory of witchcraft... The Devil, so it was held, having made a compact with the witch, gave her a low ranking demon in the shape of a small domestic animal to advise her and perform small malicious errands, including murder' (Rossell Hope Robbins, *The Encyclopedia of Witchcraft and Demonology*, 1959, p. 190); cf. *Wi.*, III.iii.7–8n.

36.1 Morris Dancers] Cuddy Banks and his companions are preparing for their morris dance, a form which was remarkably popular in the sixteenth and seventeenth centuries; see Chambers, *MS*, I, 195, and Philip Stubbs, *Anatomy of Abuses* (1583), sigs. N6v–7.

37–8. *A... pipe*] The instruments most generally favoured to accompany the morris dance in earlier times were the pipe and tabor, and the fiddle; see Arthur Peck, *The Morris and Sword Dances of England* (n.d.), p. 7.

38. *leash*] set of three; thus five sets of three bells which would be attached to the dancers' legs; see the title-page of *Kemps nine daies wonder* (1600) which illustrates Kemp dancing from London to Norwich.

39. *Double*] 'in names of musical instruments... sounding an octave lower in pitch' (*OED* A.4.b).
Crooked Lane] a lane which ran from New Fish Street to St Michael's Lane, London. Sugden records that on Fish Street Hill there was an old inn called the Black Bell and suggests that the reference to double bells is an allusion to the inn.

41. *Trebles*] instruments of the highest pitch.

42. *altitudes*] high notes.

43. *mean*] a middle or intermediate part in any harmonized composition. Young Banks puns on 'mean' at l. 45 in the sense of inferior in rank or quality.

45. *fellow Rowland*] although Young Banks refers to the second morris-dancer as Rowland, Q does not identify him in the speech prefixes. Rowland has been taken to be the actor Rowland Dowle, one of the King's Men, although Bentley (II. 425) does not think this likely.

46. *counter*] counter-tenor. Young Banks puns on hunting-counter, i.e. to follow the scent of the game in the reverse direction. Hoy conjectures on a further quibble on

'Counter' as 'a name for the two London debtors' prisons'.

48. *Enville Chase*] Enfield Chase. Q's spelling probably records the contemporary pronunciation. The chase was a hunting preserve, a dozen miles north of London, stocked both by Elizabeth and James; see also l. 68.

51. *fore-horse*] leader, lead horse in the team.

52. *fore-gallant*] the chief performer or leader in a morris.

55. *hobby-horse*] 'A character common in folk festivals throughout Europe, and probably a survival of the primitive worshipper clad in the skin of a sacrificial animal. He rode a wooden or wicker framework shaped like a horse... In England the hobby-horse became a necessary accompaniment of the Morris dancers and sometimes the Mummers' (Hartnoll).

57. *Midsummer-moon... ye*] allusion to the proverb 'It is midsummer moon with you' (M1117), a time of lunacy and strange occurrences; cf. *MND.*

57–8. *When... wane*] proverbial (W555).

64. *forget the hobby-horse*] an allusion to a popular catchphrase (cf. *Ham.*, III.ii.130). It is likely that the hobby-horse was omitted from May-games and festivals in the face of Puritan disapproval.

68–9. *cast thy stuff*] quit or throw away your worthless ideas (*OED* '*stuff*' 8b).

76. *caparisons*] trappings.

78. *bosses*] metal knobs on each side of the bit of a bridle.
new saffroned o'er] newly coloured with saffron, i.e. an orange-yellow.

86. *'uds me*] God save me.

89. *her tother eye*] Elizabeth Sawyer had only one eye as Goodcole records: '*Quest[ion]. How came your eye to be put out? Answ[er].* With a sticke which one of my children had in the hand, that night my mother did dye it was done; for I was stooping by the bed side, and I by chance did hit my eye on the sharpe end of the sticke' (sig. D1). Such deformities were commonly held to be characteristic of witches; see Harrison, p. 55.

91. *Ungirt... proverb*] proverbial (U10).

92. *a riding knot*] a hanging (running) knot; 'Cuddy will take the chance of being unblessed (and hence prey for the devil), and use his girdle as a noose' (On.).

94. *abide ... crossed*] a reference to the popular belief that to cross the devil's path or to confront him exposed one to his malign influence; see *Ham.*, I.i.127. There may also be a second meaning, i.e. to make the sign of the cross.

98.1 SD] It is difficult to interpret this SD. On.'s conjecture that 'Cuddy and his companions may have assumed positions which they thought would keep them from directly crossing the path of the devil supposedly with Mother Sawyer but invisible to them' is not entirely convincing. It may be that the postures they adopt are intended as some means of protection from her influence or, perhaps, a way of showing their dislike of her or a means of tormenting her.

100. *ground*] basis, foundation.

102–5. *I ... blood*] It was a popular belief that witches fed their familiars with their own blood either by scratching themselves or allowing the familiar to suck blood from the witch's mark, an 'unnatural' mark on the body which was insensible to pain and which was sometimes thought of as a teat. 'And they all three said, that they a little above the Fundiment of *Elizabeth Sawyer* the prisoner, there indited before the Bench for a Witch, found a thing like a Teate the bignesse of the little finger, and the length of halfe a finger, which was branched at the top like a teate, and seemed as though one had suckt it, and that the bottome thereof was blew, and the top of it was redde' (Goodcole, sig. B3v). The act of 1604 (see *Wi.*, Epistle, 7n.) makes reference to the entertaining and feeding of familiars. See Thomas, p. 530, Kittredge, Ch. 10 and *Wi.*, III.iii.7–8. Elizabeth Sawyer testified, 'The place where the Divell suckt my bloud was a little above my fundiment, and that place chosen by himselfe, and in that place by continuall drawing, there is a thing in the forme of a Teate, at which the divell would sucke mee. And I asked the Divell why hee would sucke my bloud, and hee sayd it was to nourish him' (Goodcole, sigs. C3–3v). Cf. Harrison, pp. 21–2.

109–11. *I'd ... age*] Russell suggests that Elizabeth Sawyer is here referring to her body.

121. *Ho ... own*] 'The first time that the Divell came unto me was, when I was cursing, swearing and blaspheming ... the first words that hee spake unto me were these: *Oh! have I now found you cursing, swearing and blaspheming? now you are mine*' (Goodcole, sigs. C1–C1v).

121ff.] In the episode in which Elizabeth Sawyer makes her contract with the devil-dog Dekker draws heavily on the source. See Introduction, pp. 22–4.

133–6. *make ... blood*] On., citing Perkins, *Discourse of the Damned Art of Witchcraft*, ed. 1610, pp. 41ff., comments that 'without such "a deed of gift" the pact would be one-sided'. It would appear from the text that Elizabeth Sawyer has given both body and soul to the devil and is therefore damned. However, some writers on witchcraft argued that such compacts were invalid since one could not renounce the benefits of baptism. Faustus is consigned to Hell because of his own fear and despair in refusing to seek Christ's mercy, *Faustus*, XIX.

147. SD] Gi.'s expanded SD offers actors and audience a more graphic piece of stage-business than Q. In the 1981 RSC production Elizabeth Sawyer scratched her chest to let blood in order to complete the contract.

153–65. *Go ... touch.*] The devil's power to injure the faithful was held to be very limited. See note to *Wi.*, I.ii.172 and cf. Mephistophilis in *Faustus*, 'His faith is great; I cannot touch his soul; / But what I may afflict his body with / I will attempt, which is but little worth' (XVIII, 87–9).

155. *I wonnot*] I will not.

158. *curst*] malignant, perversely disagreeable (*OED* 4). Gi.'s emendation is perhaps only marginally preferable in that Q's 'curs'd' i.e. deserving a curse, damnable, makes equal sense.

169. *orisons*] prayers. When asked if the devil asked her to pray to him Elizabeth Sawyer replied, 'he found me once praying, and he asked of me to whom I prayed, and I answered him, to Jesus Christ; and he charged me then to pray no more to Jesus Christ, but to him the Divell, and he the Divell, taught me this prayer, *Santibicetur nomen tuum*. Amen.' In response to a further question she replied, 'I was not taught it by any body else, but by the Divell alone; neither doe I understand the meaning of these words, nor can speake any more Latine words' (Goodcole, sig. C4v).

176–90. Sanctibicetur nomen tuum] a parody of the Lord's Prayer, 'Hallowed be thy name'. '*Sanctibicetur*' replaces '*sanctificetur*'. Although some editors have partially or completely regularised the spelling of *sanctibicetur*, Q's varied spelling is retained here since it might be argued that the dramatists wish to suggest Elizabeth Sawyer's ignorance and weak hold on the charm which the Dog has taught her.

181. Contaminetur] polluted or defiled.

186. *The . . . noster*] the devil's 'Our Father', the lord's prayer.

191. *Gammer*] a rustic title for an old woman, corresponding to 'gaffer' for a man.

195. *by this*] by this time. She anticipates that the devil will, by now, have completed his work against Banks.

199–200. *a . . . God-bless-us*] obscure, though probably a euphemism. Russell conjectures a person addicted to praying.

201. *ka me . . . kob you*] a variation of the proverb 'Ka me, ka thee' (K1), i.e. scratch my back and I'll scratch yours.

215. *As a pike-staff*] proverbial (P322).

219. hisce auribus] by these ears.

220. *burbolt*] a kind of blunt-headed arrow used for shooting birds.

223. *for three lives*] an allusion to legal terminology for land or property held for the lives of three persons.

226. *hilts*] the handle of a sword or dagger.

238. *back-friend*] a backer or supporter but also, ironically here, a pretended or false friend.

239. *An*] if.

240. *catchpole*] sheriff's officer or sergeant.

241. *woundy*] extremely, excessively.

dudder] shudder or shiver.

shake . . . aspen-leaf] proverbial (L.140).

247. *goblin*] a mischievous and ugly demon.

Latin] see Wi., V.ii.31–2.

260. *codlings*] green or young peas with a bawdy quibble on 'cod'.

268. *at eaglet*] The meaning is obscure and editors have suggested various emendations. We.'s 'an eaglet' has been accepted by Hoy who suggests that 'Cuddy is employing the familiar image of the eaglet who throughout its youth . . .

ventures forth on expeditions of prey under guidance and protection of a parent bird'. Gi.'s emendation, 'a taglet' or tendril, suggests that Young Banks would cling to Kate. More satisfactory, perhaps, are Ba. and Bo. who suggest that 'eaglet' refers to a game or gaming; thus Bo., '*to make* is a common contemporary term for winning or taking a trick, or series of tricks, at cards'; and *OED* lists 'eagle' as an early eighteenth-century term for a gamester. Support for this interpretation is provided by A. V. Judges's gloss on *eagle* as a member of a group of confederates cheating at cards or dice. He it is who ultimately wins (see *The Elizabethan Underworld* (1930), p. 525). It may be, therefore, that Young Banks has hopes of assuaging his sorrows by winning at cards or dice.

II.ii.

4–5. *Wedding . . . knot*] proverbial (W232). Old Carter's remarks turn out to be ironically appropriate.

8–9. *promise . . . debt*] proverbial, 'Promise is debt' (P603).

14–15. *won . . . her*] see I.ii.38–9.

19–21. *Were . . . a-wool-gathering*] probably proverbial.

22. *You . . . string*] proverbial, 'To have the world (fortune) in a string' (W886).

29. *compass*] measure, proper proportion, regularity. 'Arrows shot compass-wise, that is, with a certain elevation, were generally considered as going more steadily to the mark' (Gi.).

32. *Cuckold's Haven*] A point on the Surrey side of the Thames about a mile below Rotherhithe Church. It was traditional on St Luke's Day, 18 October, for a butcher of Eastcheap to commemorate King John's cuckolding of a miller by erecting a pair of horns on a pole there. See *Eastward Ho!*, IV.i.

38.1. SD] Q's placing of the SD is dramatically satisfactory whilst D.'s relocation delays the entrance too long. In the RSC 1981 production Frank and Susan entered at 'come,' in l. 40.

40. *Sheffield knives*] 'a pair of knives was a common wedding gift, being a symbol of the two-fold union' (Hoy). Sheffield was already famous for cutlery. *OED* and Sugden cite this passage.

44–5. *No . . . done*] 'I have given this short

speech to Somerton. Warbeck's reply sufficiently shows that it could not be spoken by Carter' (D.). Bo. adds that Warbeck's use of the familiar address, *thou*, at l. 46. would be inappropriate for Old Carter.

46. *things ... standing*] in the circumstances, with a bawdy quibble on 'standing'.

58. *censure*] judgement, opinion; but also adverse judgement or unfavourable opinion.

59. *Till ... deride*] Warbeck's meaning is unclear. Gi. believed that the line is addressed to Frank 'and conveys some obscure hint of a knowledge of his former connection with Winnifride' and that it is evident from what follows that it awakens his conscience. It seems more likely that the line is addressed to Susan since she has treated Warbeck scornfully in I.ii.40–54. The general sense may be that since Susan is now a bride she should give up her scornful attitude to Warbeck. We.'s emendation 'new elected' does not resolve the problem.

61. *barrels ... a-tilt*] a reference to running at the quintain, a popular imitation of jousting or running at the ring, in which a barrel was used as the target. See Wickham, I, 38–9.

69. *accents*] words.

88. *nice*] shy, coy.

92. *passionate*] susceptible to swift changes of mood.

96. *conceit*] fanciful notion or opinion.

97. *Diana*] the moon-goddess, patroness of virginity.

99. *Cupid*] the God of love. He was said to carry arrows of gold to cause love and arrows of lead to repel it.

101.] Q's break here perhaps suggests that the compositor was unable to decipher the first word of the line in the MS.

102. *Adonis*] a youth beloved by the goddess Venus.

112. *Hydra*] the fabulous many-headed snake whose heads grew as they were cut off.

124. *pretend*] Frank's meaning is ambiguous, for 'to pretend' can mean both 'to use as a pretext' and 'to lay claim to'.

128–9.] Q's reading suggests that Frank's lines refer entirely to Winnifride and are interpreted by Susan that she has died. It is plain however that Frank is preoccupied

with the guilt of his bigamy and it is more likely that 'The poor girl!' refers to Susan's naive generosity. Thus Susan's response at ll. 129–31, more appropriately, refers to the palmist's prediction. Bo. objects to giving Frank's lines as an aside as 'an un-Elizabethan staging whereby Frank's aside is taken by Susan as an unspoken hesitation to answer her and she is therefore forced to repeat her question'. This does not seem insuperable (cf. *R3*, IV.ii.99–106, where Richard's lines are sometimes delivered as aside), and by making Frank's lines an aside there is a gain in the dramatic emphasis on his torn conscience, although there is some loss of dramatic ambiguity.

128. *She ... thee*] i.e. she has my marriage vow before you.

152–3. *Like ... me*] an allusion to the behaviour of the lapwing which distracts enemies by feigning distress at a distance from her nest. Also proverbial, 'The lapwing cries most when furthest from her nest' (L. 68).

163. *flam*] to deceive by a sham story or trick. *OED* cites this example.

166–7. There is no need to make this an aside since at one level the lines are complimentary if we take 'fond' as 'loving', and so can be accepted by Susan. The ironic second sense of 'fond', i.e. foolish, should be appreciated by the audience.

III.i.

4. *If ... serve*] an allusion to the proverb 'A word to a wise man is enough' (W781).

9. *Maid Marian*] Robin Hood's companion and a figure in both May-games and Morris dances.

19. *cherry-pit*] a children's game which consists in throwing cherry stones into a small pit or hole. On. suggests that the reference may be less than innocent since, as *OED* records, the term was originally used for the hole itself. *OED* cites this example.

34. *Chessum*] Cheshunt in Hertfordshire, some four miles north of Edmonton.

39. *stila ... traveller*] a reference to the Gregorian calendar adopted on the continent in 1582 but not accepted in England until 1752.

41–3. *Ask ... there*] a reference to the unpunctuality of soldiers' pay.

43. *hard by*] very nearly.

50. *cut*] misfortune (*OED* 4).

53. *caroche*] coach.

59. *The ... remembered*] see II.i.64n.

60. *Poldavis*] see Actors' Names. Hoy, citing Nashe's *Have With You*, III, 13, comments that poldavy was a coarse canvas used for sailcloth and that the name was often applied to 'clowns or rustics, or the lowlier order of tradesmen'.

67. *water-dog*] a dog trained to retrieve waterfowl for huntsmen. The term provides Young Banks with an opportunity for extended punning.

69. *Katherine's Dock*] Young Banks quibbles on his love's name and the landing place near St Katherine's Hospital east of the Tower of London.

74.1–2. SD] It is possible that the actor playing Katherine also played the Spirit entering in a mask which he then removed.

76. *take ... maid*] The means by which spirits achieved physical manifestation was a matter of some debate. On. cites Jonson's *The Devil is an Ass* I.i.134–41, alluding to the various views on this although the parallel is not exact since the Devil in that play orders Pug to reanimate the body of a hanged cut-purse.

77–8. *We ... runaways*] see II.i.153–65n.

82. *Barking Church*] Allhallows, Barking, on the north side of Great Tower Street at the east end.

89–93. *Stay ... highway*] Young Banks adapts the popular ballad, 'When Daphne Did from Phoebus Fly', to his own purposes:

When Daphne from fair Phoebus
    did flie,
The west winde most sweetly did
    blow in her face:
Her silken scarfe scarce
    shadowed her eyes;
The god cried 'O pitie,' and held
    her in chace.
'Stay, nimph, stay nimph,' cryes
    Apollo,
Tarry and turn thee; sweet
    nymph, stay!'

See W. Chappell, *Popular Music of the Olden Time* (1855–9), I, 338.

98. *Pond's almanac*] a popular almanac annually published in London from 1604 by Edward Pond. He died in 1629. Young Banks's speech contains a number of such puns.

99. *Gravesend*] a port on the south bank of the Thames, thirty miles below London.

dog-days] The hottest and most unwholesome period of the year variously calculated as beginning between 3 July and 15 August and lasting for up to fifty-four days.

101. *mangie*] mange.

102. *Limehouse*] a district, noted for its tanneries, on the north of the Thames opposite Cuckold's Haven.

104. *Hist*] listen.

109. *reading tongue*] We. conjectures a pun on 'Reading' but On.'s suggestion of a connection between the phrase and Banks's subsequent remark about Aesop's Fables seems more likely.

111–13. *Aesop's ... water*] Aesop tells of a dog who, carrying a stolen piece of meat in his mouth, lost it whilst crossing a bridge when he saw his shadow and that of the meat in water below. Believing he had seen another dog carrying meat, he dropped his own prize in attempting to rob his supposed rival and so lost all.

115. *My ... Tom*] 'Quest[ion]. *By what name did you call the Divill, and what promises did he make to you?* Answ[er]. I did call the Divell by the name of *Tom*, and he promised to doe for me whatsoever I should require of him' (Goodcole, sig. C4).

119. *ingle*] strictly a boy-favourite; a catamite. *OED* also records familiar friend or chum as a misused meaning. Although the latter is more appropriate here, *OED* does|not record|such a usage|before 1821.

123. *jowls*] jaw-bones.

131. *Ningle*] i.e. ingle; see above l. 119.

132. *maids*] Young skate or thornback. Banks puns here ironically and unconsciously.

133. *fishmonger*] a cant term for a procurer or a pimp.

140–1. *I ... too!*] Both characters allude to Biblical sayings, Luke, XVI.13, 'No servant can serve two masters' and Matt., VI.24, 'Ye cannot serve God and Mammon'. Such precepts became proverbial (M322).

146. *neuf*] fist.

149. *Devil of Edmonton*] an allusion to Peter Fabell in *The Merry Devil of Edmonton*; see Introduction, p. 21.

150. *dog*] follow.

III.ii.

5. *cheek*] i.e. tearful cheek.

6. *singled*] alone.

7. *It calls*] i.e. my tearful cheek recalls.

11. *eclipse*] an eclipse was often regarded as a portent of future misfortune.

17. *dowry... sin*] the dowry which Susan brought with her.

29. *hire*] payment, wages.

44. *rudiments*] basic instructions.

56. *dor*] beetle.

66. *label*] From the context it is apparent that Susan gives Winnifride a jewel or pendant ear-ring, although OED does not record such a usage. Hoy cites Rowley's *All's Lost By Lust*, I.ii.69–72, as a similar usage of 'label'.

75. *shift*] change place or role with a further and ironic meaning perhaps, i.e. to employ shifts or evasions or practise fraud.

97. *lubric*] lascivious, wanton (OED citing this example).

scapes] transgressions.

103. *it*] i.e. the label.

106.1. SD] Gi.'s relocation of Winnifride's exit allows Susan to address her whilst she is still on stage.

107. *happily*] perhaps.

123. *behind*] hidden, OED 3b.

132–4. *The... long*] Hoy cites Pliny, *Naturall Historie*, VIII.16 (trans. P. Holland, 1601, p. 201) and Topsell, *The Historie of Foure-Footed Beastes* (1607) p. 466, as examples of this observation.

III.iii.

0.1. SD] The Dog is invisible in this scene to all but the audience.

14.1 DOG *rubs him*.] The degree to which the Dog's action provokes Susan's death is left unclear. On. goes so far as to argue that by means of the Dog's touch here Frank is possessed by the devil; more likely, in view of the Dog's remarks at II.i.163–5 and ll. 2–3 above, the action serves to confirm Frank's hidden impulses. See IV.i.189n.

15. *Thank... that*] Frank here appears to be sub-consciously responding to the Dog's action rather than speaking directly to Susan as Gi. suggests (on the assumption that Frank refers to the 'incidental mention of their parents being stirring'). It seems preferable to take the whole of Frank's speech as an aside articulating the inner stirrings of his murderous intent.

21. *fine*] skilful.

37. *The... minute*] Gi. conjectures that Q's punctuation could scarcely be correct since the devil did prompt Frank's action, and his emendation of the punctuation suggests Frank's conscious knowledge of the devil's part in the murder. This seems inappropriate since the Dog is invisible to Frank who shows no knowledge of his assistance at ll. 72–4. Q's punctuation allows his remark to generate a dark irony so characteristic of much of the play.

39. *dogged*] followed like a dog, pursued or tracked, but with obvious irony.

40. *intelligent*] sensible, sagacious.

41. *'Twas... motion*] Susan's remark is sharply ironic since the audience recognises that the devil has had a hand in crystallising Frank's murderous intention. Although Roman Catholics held that there were personal good spirits or guardian angels, such beliefs were held to be superstitious by most Protestant theologians and writers. See Thomas, pp. 562 and 589.

67. *heal*] i.e. to conceal the source of.

dressing] directing, guiding; also with an ironic play on the sense 'tending a wound'.

75. Exit DOG.] Q. makes no provision for the Dog's exit but it seems sensible that he should exit before the entrance of the parents since the focus of the scene's final movement is on their grief and the identification of the alleged murderers. Gi., followed by a number of later editors, places the exit after l. 71. A more pointed dramatic irony may be gained if the Dog exits after l. 75, as in the 1981 RSC production, having overhead Frank's remarks, ll. 72–4.

85. *Think... do*] i.e. consider what men subjected to violence may be forced to do.

93. *Here's... heard*] Old Carter refers to Susan.

94. *branched*] embroidered with gold or needlework representing flowers or foliage.

96. *Binal*] double, twofold. (OED cites this passage).

101. *Bob me off*] fool me, mock me.

III.iv.

14. *morris-ray*] morris-array.

14–16. *The... bell*] Gi. notes that 'the end of this tale frequently forgets the beginning. Cuddy had more than once declared that he would have all *trebles*, no *means*, or *bases*; yet we have Father Sawgut arranging his counters, tenors, and bases as usual.' The criticism is untheatrical since it is likely that the dramatists were chiefly interested in the dramatic effects of Cuddy's punning in II.i.

23.1 and *DOG*] The dog is, of course, invisible to all but Cuddy and the audience.

31–3. *we . . . no*] proverbial (M262).

43–4. *my . . . bewitched*] cf. Heywood and Brome's *The Late Lancashire Witches* (1634), III.i, where the fiddlers are bewitched.

44. *'The Flowers in May'*] a dance tune, now lost.

45. *against the hair*] against the grain.

50.1. *DOG . . . morris*] Despite the worries of previous editors, audiences have little difficulty in accepting the dramatic convention of invisibility. The 1981 RSC production made no attempt to signal or hint at the Dog's invisible status, which audiences easily accepted, even to the point of the Dog playing the fiddle handed to him by Banks; cf. *Faustus* and *MND*.

55. *Flat*] undeniable, downright.

70. *fit*] a sudden and transitory state of inaction (OED 4a) or paroxysm of lunacy.

80. *middle zone*] a reference to the tropical zone where the sun is always overhead.

81. *goes alone*] i.e. walks without a shadow.

IV.i.

1–2. *glanders*] a contagious disease in horses, the chief symptoms of which are swellings beneath the jaw and discharge of mucous matter from the nostrils. (OED cites this example).

4. *long of*] on account of, because of.

5. *took*] caught, found.

6. *thrashing*] the term may also carry sexual implications.

7. *polecat*] courtesan, prostitute.

12–14. *Our . . . us*] The third Countryman's comments also carry sexual connotations.

14.1. *W. HAMLUC*] see note on Actors' Names, l.6.

link] torch.

17–18. *A . . . in*] 'And to finde out who should bee the author of this mischiefe, an old ridiculous custome was used, which was to plucke the Thatch of her house, and to burne it, and it being so burnd, the author of such mischiefe should presently then come: and it was observed, and affirmed to the Court, that *Elizabeth Sawyer* would presently frequent the house of them that burnt the thatch which they pluckt of her house, and come without any sending for' (Goodcole, sigs. A4–A4v). Goodcole's scepticism as to the value of such practice is transferred to the Justice, see l. 41.

23. *trot*] beldame, hag.

53–66. *So . . . please*] cf. Gifford, 'A third man came in, and he sayd she [a witch] was once angry with him, he had a dun cow which was tyed up in a house, for it was winter, he feared that some euill would follow, and for his life he could not come in where she was, but he must needes take up her tayle and kisse under it' (*A Dialogue Concerning Witches and Witchcraftes*, 1593, sig. l. 4v). It is likely that Gifford is the source of Banks's anecdote. Certainly Sir Arthur's response and the Justice's admonishment reflect something of Gifford's sceptical attitude to witch belief.

53–4. *back-side*] backyard.

64. *she . . . burning*] In England the punishment for witchcraft was hanging not burning. In most witch-trials the accused were indicted for murder or attempted murder by witchcraft; see Harrison.

91–2. *she's . . . her*] see II.i.102–5 and note.

91. *bruited for*] openly reported to be.

103–34.] Elizabeth Sawyer's remarks articulate a range of social criticism which is common in the drama of the period. The dramatists generate some sympathy for her plight by providing such comment. See Introduction, p. 25.

113. *Flanders mares*] a breed of heavy and powerful horses used to draw carriages.

114. *French butterfly*] a vain or gaudily attired person, often a courtier, having affected French manners or clothes.

117. *gardens*] Gardens were often used as resorts for immoral purposes; see *Ram Alley*, I.i.11–12.

119–20. *Are . . . these*] cf. Gifford (sig. A4v) where the rustic, Samuell, complains that they are living in the worst part of England, inhabited by 'naughty people' and Daniell replies 'Naughty people: where shall a man dwell, and not find them? swearers, liars, raylers, slaunderers drunckards, adulterers, rioutours, unthriftes, dicers, and proude high minded persons'. (Cited by On. who suggests that one might almost call the play a dramatised version of Gifford's point of view.)

122–24. *Now . . . witch*] cf. Scot: 'One sort of such as are said to bee witches, are women which be commonly old, lame, bleare-eied, pale, fowle, and full of wrinkles; poore, sullen, superstitious, and papists' (I.3). The presentation of Elizabeth Sawyer parallels Scot's sympathy and scepticism.

132–3. *As . . . his*] It was a popular belief that swarms of bees could be hived or reclaimed by beating on pans and basins, but Hillman suggests such action was merely a way of claiming ownership of the swarm (note to Thomas Tusser's *Five Hundred Points of Good Husbandry*, repr. Oxford, 1984, p. 287).

143. *denier*] a small copper coin used as a type of a very small sum.

146–8. *By . . . fury*] Sir Arthur takes it that Elizabeth Sawyer has divined his relationship with Winnifride. It was sometimes believed that witches had such powers but it seems more likely that her comment is general rather than directed towards him.

152. *Clapped*] set vigorously.

160. *fine tricks*] The 'tricks' which the Dog has performed recall many of the complaints made against witches; see Harrison, pp. 23–4 and 39–44 and also Scot I.4.

Let's tickle] 'Tickle' can mean to touch pleasurably. In the 1981 RSC production the characters rolled on the floor together, whilst in the Bristol production (1984) Elizabeth Sawyer tickled the Dog's stomach.

162. *nipped . . . child*] See II.i.8–13n.

163. *Pearl*] a common name for a dog (Hoy).

170–73. *That . . . heart?*] 'She was also indited, for that shee the said *Elizabeth Sawyer*, by Diabolicall helpe, and out of her malice afore-thought, did witch unto death *Agnes Ratcleife*, a neighbour of hers, dwelling in the towne of *Edmonton* where shee did likewise dwell, and the cause that urged her thereunto was, because that

Elizabeth Ratcleife did strike a Sowe of hers in her sight, for licking up a little Soape where shee had laide it, and for that *Elizabeth Sawyer* would be revenged of her' (Goodcole, sigs. Blv–B2).

173. *quean*] hussy, loose woman.

177. *the art of grinding*] 'The erotic metaphor is at least as old as the Old Testament (see, for example, *Job* 31:10) "Then let my wife grind unto another, and let others bow down upon her"' (Hoy).

179. *Hoyda!*] exclamation of surprise.

184. *I . . . face*] It was widely believed that a witch's *malificium* could be removed by drawing her blood and particularly by scratching her face. See Roberts, *N. & Q.* vol. 30, No. 2, pp. 111–14.

189. *Touch her*] cf. Harrison, p. 69, 'the said Spirit *Dandy* appeared vnto this Examinate, and said, Thou didst touch the said *Duckworth*; whereunto this Examinate answered, he did not touch him: yes (said the spirit againe) thou didst touch him, and therefore I haue power of him: whereupon this Examinate ioyned with the said Spirit, and then wished the said Spirit to kill, the said *Duckworth*: and within one weeke, then next after, *Duckworth* died'. See also II.i.153–65.

190. *paned hose*] breeches made in panes or strips, or in pleats which parted slightly, showing a rich lining and which were liable to break at the seams.

191. *Lancashire hornpipe*] an obsolete wind instrument, said to have been so called from having the bell and mouthpiece made of horn (*OED*). Lancashire had a reputation for witchcraft due to the witch epidemic of 1612.

199.1. SD] Bo. indicates that the Dog follows Old Ratcliffe and the Country-fellows off-stage and returns at l. 247. There seems to be no good reason for this; indeed, the presence of the Dog during the intervening action serves to increase the ironic tension. In the 1981 RSC production the Dog observed the subsequent events from the top of a notch post.

200. *Mother Bumby*] The heroine of Lyly's comedy (1594) who was a wise woman rather than a witch.

203–4. *she . . . old*] an allusion to the proverb 'There's no more harm in him, than in a devil of two years old' (On.).

212. *brains . . . wool-gathering*] proverbial (W582).

217. *Newgate*] Elizabeth Sawyer was imprisoned in Newgate prison where Goodcole was, according to the title-page of his pamphlet, her continual visitor.

218. *burn ... witch*] see note to l. 64 above.

230. *Puppison*] Probably equivalent to 'his puppyship' (Ba.).

234. *court-foisting*] foisting, cheating or breaking wind silently; generally a term of abuse or contempt.

235. *water-spaniel*] a retriever in the hunting of water-fowl.

237. *wife ... home*] to behave improvidently, proverbial (D632), with implications of immoral behaviour.

238. *Paris-garden bandog*] mastiff or bloodhound used in bear-baiting at the Bear Garden at Paris Garden on Bankside, Southwark.

240–1. *Black Dog of Newgate*] legendary spectral dog who haunted the prison at execution time. See Thomas Dekker, *Selected Prose Writings*, ed. E. D. Pendry (1967), pp. 20 and 337.

245. *The devil in St Dunstan's*] a reference to the Devil Tavern near Temple Bar and St Dunstan's Church in Fleet Street. Its sign represented St Dunstan pulling the Devil's nose with his pincers.

246–7. *Temple-bar laundress*] Laundresses had a reputation for easy virtue; see *Ram Alley*, I.i.85.

255. *Gammer Gurton*] reference to the heroine of the comedy *Gammer Gurton's Needle*, printed in 1557 and attributed to William Stevenson.

261. *spit in thy mouth*] a gesture of affection which was believed to please dogs; cf. Marston's *The Malcontent*, III.i.147 (Revels ed.).

267. *biting's conscience*] On. argues for and accepts the nineteenth-century editors' punctuation which places 'conscience' in apposition to 'Dog'. Q's punctuation, however, makes sense and also implies a possible extension of the devil-dog's influence to Sir Arthur.

IV.ii.

3–4. *all ... flea*] proverbial, 'It is but a flea-biting' (F355).

17. *idle*] delirious.

65.] The Dog's entrance and his joyful behaviour and dance emphasise the devil's influence in Frank Thorney's fate. The Dog exits as soon as the crime is discovered.

68. [*Discovers ... pocket*] Although Q provides no SD it is clear from ll. 115–18 below that Katherine discovers the knife but immediately dissimulates.

69.2. *Spirit* of *SUSAN*] The nature of the Spirit is ambiguous. Since Susan died forgiving Frank Thorney it is unlikely that it is her ghost returning to torment him. On., citing Robert H. West, *The Invisible World* (1939), suggests that the Spirit might be interpreted as an impersonating devil managed by the Dog. Frank subsequently suggests that it was a figment of his imagination (ll. 84–5). In any event the Spirit's entrance heightens the dramatic pathos of the scene.

79–80. *A ... winding-sheet*] ghosts commonly announce impending deaths in plays of the period; see *The White Devil*, IV.iv.123–5 (Revels ed.).

85. *Some ... sleep*] proverbial (W455).

100. *freebooter*] one who goes in search of plunder.

109.2.] Once again the Dog enters to witness the revelation of Frank Thorney's guilt. The Dog's pawing of Frank suggests that he claims him for his own.

115. *else*] if it is not believed.

126. *urinals*] glass vessels employed to receive urine for medical examination or inspection.

128. *bag*] sack in the body containing poison (OED 11).
imposthumes] swellings or cysts on any part of the body; but here, figuratively, moral corruption.

132. *there's ... one*] i.e. death; see Tilley W148.

162. *posies*] short mottoes, originally a line or verse of poetry and usually in patterned language inscribed on a knife, within a ring, as an heraldic motto.

178. *fire ... bedstraw*] 'A proverbial expression for *more concealed mischief!*' (Gi.). An allusion to the proverb 'It is a dangerous fire begins in the bedstraw' (F272).

187. *arraign*] accuse, charge. Winnifride's remarks seem confused. She appears to refer to Old Carter here and, certainly, he interprets it thus. Yet this makes little sense. She may be attempting to retrieve her admission that Frank Thorney has

confessed or it is possible that 'this father' refers to Frank. The problem would be resolved if 'arraign' could be glossed as 'sue to', but *OED* records no such usage.

192. *tacklings*] gear, used figuratively here for clothes.

193. *trull*] concubine, strumpet.

194. *Newgate birds*] prisoners in Newgate Gaol.

196. *served thee*] served thee [Old Carter] badly.

197. *worst punishment*] damnation, as well as execution.

V.i.

7. *Revenge ... life*] cf. 'Revenge is sweet' (R90).

8ff.] The language given to Elizabeth Sawyer may seem incongruous for a village witch. However, its intensity is dramatically effective in articulating her state of mind and generating sympathy for her situation.

18. *bulch*] a rare form of *bulchin*, a bull-calf, here, 'a term of endearment' according to *OED* which cites this example.

19. *swart*] black.

34. *Why ... white*] 'Question. In what shape would the Divell come unto you? Answer. Always in the shape of a dogge, and of two collars, sometimes of blacke and sometimes of white' (Goodcole, sig. C2v).

36. *dogged*] cruel, sullenly obstinate. *list*] choose.

39–40. *devil ... lamb*] see *Wi.*, I.i.12n.

43. *Why ... me?*] 'Quest[ion]. Would the Divell come unto you, all in one bignesse? Answ[er]. No; when hee came unto mee in the blacke shape, he then was biggest, and in white the least; and when that I was praying, hee then would come unto me in the white colour' (Goodcole, sigs. D1–D1v). Cf. *Wi.*, I.ii.96n.

47. *rivelled*] wrinkled.

53. *puritan*] hypocritical.

68. *Choose ... burned*] i.e. Whether you choose to confess or not you will be executed; see IV.i.64n.

79. *mittimus*] a warrant committing a person to prison.

86–8. *He ... innocent*] 'Significantly, Cuddy, the natural, ... recognises the devil's claw in the foul work which has been going on' (On.).

88. *innocent*] idiot, simpleton, with a secondary sense of an innocent person.

100–01. *She ... goose*] Young Banks's comment reflects the rational scepticism found in Gifford's *A Dialogue* in which Daniell vigorously argues that witches are servants of the devil and thus have no power or influence of their own. 'I know that witches and coniurers are seduced and become the vassals of Satan: they be his servants, and not he theirs' (sig. B3r).

101. *goose*] also having the sense of 'female simpleton' and sometimes 'prostitute'.

116–18.] see II.i.36n.

124. *broker's*] a dealer in second hand furniture and apparel; a pawnbroker.

128–37. See II.i.122n.

138. *rook*] a cheat, swindler or sharper in gaming (*OED* 2b).

144–7. *An ... place*] cf. *Faustus*, V, 147–50. and *Soph.*, IV, 212ff.

144. *twines*] embraces.

145. *clip*] embrace.

155. *stroy*] destroy. See II.i.12n.

156. *etc.*] 'Here, it would seem, the actor supplied additional *maleficia* from popular superstitution' (On.). Whether the Master of the Revels would have allowed the possibility of such improvisation is, however, doubtful.

158–60. *if you ... in you*] The use of water-spaniels for duck-hunting was a popular pastime for London citizens.

162. *Moll Cutpurse*] Mary Frith (c. 1589–1662) adopted male clothes and a masculine way of life. She was noted for her skill with the sword and in later life was notorious as a whore, bawd, cutpurse and receiver. She was the heroine of Middleton and Dekker's *The Roaring Girl*.

166. *staved off*] driven off or beaten with a staff or stave. (*OED* cites this example.)

168. *the wheel*] a tread-wheel connected to a spit.

171. *arming*] to be carried in a lady's arms. (*OED* cites this as its only example.)

183. *shug in*] *OED* cites this one example and conjectures a forced use of 'shug' as a variant of 'shog', thus perhaps meaning to force one's way in, shove in. *countenance*] patronage.

184. *Briarean*] an allusion to Briareos, one of the hundred-handed giants of Greek mythology. *footcloth-strider*] rider of a horse covered

with a richly worked horse cloth.

187. *dragon's tail*] an allusion to
Revelation, XII.3–4, '. . . and behold a great
red dragon having seven heads and ten
horns, and seven crowns upon his heads.
And his tail drew the third part of the stars
of heaven, and did cast them to the earth'.

194. *we . . . procession*] presumably
Young Banks refers to the ceremony of
beating the bounds.

196. *Tyburn*] the site of the gallows close
to the junction of Oxford Street and
Edgware Road in London.

197. *Thieving Lane*] A short street in
Westminster. It was the way by which
thieves were taken to the Gatehouse
prison: hence the name Thieven Lane,
corrupted into Thieving Lane.

198. *Westminster Hall*] the great hall of
Westminster Palace which housed law-
courts and was often used for state trials.

199. *stairs*] presumably a reference to the
landing stage at the Bankside where the
bear-baiting houses were situated.

V.ii.

13. *going . . . way*] to the gallows;
proverbial expression for something going
amiss (W168).

V.iii.

0.1–2.] As On. points out, there is some
confusion in the stage directions here since
Old Thorney speaks of Frank as though he
were not on the stage although Q's stage
directions suggest that he is present. It
seems better that Frank Thorney with his
guards should pass across the stage to be
followed by the entrance of the other
characters. Note that Q signals Frank's re-
entrance to execution at l. 52.2 .

13. *but*] than.

15–16. *grieve . . . forceth*] cf. 'Never grieve
for what you cannot help' (G453).

28. *Who . . . mine?*] Elizabeth Sawyer can

have no knowledge of the Dog's
involvement in Susan's murder although
she has an indirect connection with its
results via her willingness to help Young
Banks to court Katherine.

39. *Westminster dog-pigs*] male or boar
pigs. Pigs sold at Bartholomew Fair were
called Bartholomew-boar-pigs but the
reference to Westminster here is obscure.

39–40. *Bartholomew Fair . . . for*] The
longing of pregnant women for
Bartholomew Fair roast pig is illustrated in
Jonson's *Bartholomew Fair*, I.v.148–56 and
I.vi.19–41 (Revels ed.).

42–5. *Though . . . be*] 'Quest[ion]. *What
moves you now to make this confession?
did any urge you to it, or bid you doe it, is
it for any hope of life you doe it?* Answ[er].
No; I doe it to cleere my conscience, and
now having done it, I am the more quiet,
and the better prepared, and willing
thereby to suffer death; for I have no hope
at all of my life, although I must confesse, I
would live longer if I might' (Goodcole,
sig. D1v).

52.1.] Bo.'s stage direction has Elizabeth
Sawyer's exit followed by the country-
people. Although this may seem
appropriate in that they have followed her
on stage there would seem to be an
advantage in their remaining to witness
Frank Thorney's confession so that his
didactic sentiments reach a wider stage
audience.

84. *fact*] crime.

151. *but . . . passed*] except that my true
love is pledged.

158. *thousand marks*] a considerable sum;
a mark was worth thirteen shillings and
fourpence, i.e. two thirds of a pound
sterling.

162. *tottered*] swing to and fro, especially
at the end of a rope.

Epilogue

1. *sort*] choose, select.

7. PHEN.] see Prologue note.

TEXTUAL COLLATION

THE TRAGEDY OF SOPHONISBA

To the General Reader
4. blank] *O;* black *Q.*

Argument
0.1. Argument] *Argumentum Q.*
1. height] *O;* haight *Q.*

Interlocutors
INTERLOCUTORS] INTERLOCUTORES *Q.*
7. CARTHALO] Carthalon *Q, but* Carthalo *throughout text.*

PROLOGUS
23. sit] *Q;* see't *conj. Bu.*
25. hear] heare *Q;* beare *conj. Wo.*
29. *quaesiverit*] *O;* quisiverit *Q.*

I.i
ACT I SCENE i] ACTUS PRIMUS SCENA PRIMA *Q.*
37. prows] *Q;* powers *O.*
38. ooze] *Bu;* ouse *Q;* house *O.*
42. three hundred hundred] *conj. Wo;* 30000 *Q.*
68. we. To] *H;* we, to *Q;* we to *conj. this ed.*

I.ii.
[ACT I] SCENE ii] SCENA SECUNDA *Q.*
4–5. *You . . . undóne. /* Humblest service.] *Bu;* one line in *Q.*
14. find.] find; *O;* find us *Q.*
35.1 *antiquely*] *Q;* anticly *Bu.*
41–2. She . . . chaste / *Io . . . Hymen!*] one line in *Q.*
48. rusheth;] rusheth, *O;* rusheth. *Bu;* rusheth *Q.*
55. t'lame] *Q;* claime *O.*
56–7. Load . . . shame / *Io . . . Hymen!*] *Bu;* one line in *Q.*
60–1. Prosper . . . divining. / *Io . . . Hymen.*] *Bu;* one line in *Q.*
65. fear. Resolve,] *K;* feare, resolve, *Q.*
76. anchor] *Q;* Ancor *O;* rancour *Bu.*
slight] *Q;* flight *K.*
78. now taught] *O;* taught now *Q.*
101. rapes] *Q, O;* rape *Q. var.*

111. opposed] *O;* apposed *Q.*
115, you] *Q;* we *O.*
118. fill] *O;* full *Q.*
121. we] *O;* yee *Q.*
125. joins] joynes *O;* ions *Q.*
we] *Q;* yee *Q. var.*
126. fall] *Q;* fell *O.*
clusters] *O;* glusters *Q.*
132–3. You . . . fortune!] *Q; given to Hanno in O and to Bytheas by Wo.*
132. sad] *conj. Wo;* said *Q.*
133. [*Tearing his hair*]] *Bu.*
142. dishonoured. Asdrubal] *Q;* dishonoured Asdrubal *O.*
144. th' god] *O;* God *Q.*
147. loved] lou'd *O;* loud *Q.*
149. unlaced] unlacd *O;* unlac'd *O;* unlacked *Bu.*
161. well-strung] *O;* well-strong *Q.*
163. am I] *O;* I am *Q.*
167. Arms' fate] Armes fate *Q;* Arm'd hate *conj. Bu.*
169. my] *O;* me *Q.*
177. grateful] *Q;* graceful *O.*
182. too] to *Q;* so *O.*
188. kings—ingratitude—] Kings Ingratitude *Q;* kings ingratitude *O;* kings' ingratitude *Bu.*
192. ample] *Q;* simple *H.*
193. have] *O;* hath *Q.*
195. this] *Q;* these *O.*
210. By] *Q;* My *O.*
211. his] *Q;* thy *O.*
214. fields] *K;* field *Q.*
230. lifeful] lifefull *Q;* lightfull *O.*
233. *Fame . . . gain!*] *K; not italicised in Q.*
233. Act.] Act. / *Actus primi finis Q.*

II.i.
ACT II SCENE i] ACTUS SECUNDI SCENA PRIMA *Q.*
2. wood] *Q;* wooed *conj. K.*
3. stand] *Q;* stands *O.*
14. are one] *Q;* are not one *O.*
31. adultery, murder,] *Q;* murder, adultery, *O.*
32. Nay, . . . Pish!] *this ed.;* Nay . . . left /

246

Pish . . . *Q*; Nay, . . . left / Pish / *Bu*.
　37. of it] *Q*; it O.
　39. Carthage, well advised] *Bu*; Carthage
well advised, *Q*.
　39. come] *Bu*; comes *Q*.
　43. *courts*] *Courtes Q*; *Court* O.
　51. hundred hundred marble] *conj. Wo*;
hundred marble marble *Q*.
　60. soldered] *Bu*; sodderd *Q uncorr.*;
soderd *Q corr.*; soulderd O; souldred H.
　82. my honour] *Q*; mine honour O.
　83. vow] *Q*; vowes O.
oath] *Q*; oaths O.
　88. slake] *Q*; slacke O.
　89. feel] feele *Q*; cell *Q var*; feele O; sell
O *var*.
　91. Charge . . . great /] *Q*; Charge home, /
Wounds . . . great K.
　96. ever] O; over *Q*.
　98. with] *Q*; by O.
　99. doubtful] doubtfull *Q*; double O.
　104. [*Sophonisba*.]] *H*; *speech prefix two
lines later in Q*.
　106. Is . . . is.] Wo; *this question and
answer appear twice at the bottom of one
page and the top of the next in Q and O
follows although there is no change of
page.*
　109. me] *Q*; us O.
　113. head's] O; heads *Q*.
　123. wrong. As] K; wrong as *Q*.
　125. torture] O; orture *Q*.
　127. you] *Q*; yee O.
　134. *not*] O; and *Q*.
　135. *See . . . see.*] *Bu*; See as things are
things, are not, as we see O; *See as thinges
are things are not, for we see Q.*
　155. her] *this ed.*; thy *Q*; his O.
　160. thee, contemning] *Q*; thee-
contemning *Bu*.
　164. not one] K; no one *Q*.
　166. know] *Q*; now *Bu*.
　170. *vows'*] *Bu*; vows *Q*.

II.ii.
[ACT II] SCENE ii] *Scena Secunda Q*.
　0.3 *cuirass*] *Bu*; *curaes Q*; *cures* O.
　11. my] *Q*; my [*own*] *Bu*.
　15. and I am] *Q*; and am *Bu*.
　20. may let a] *Q*, O; melt at a *Q var*.
　21-2. Too . . . revenged] Too forward
bleeds abroad, and bleed bemond, / But
not revengd *Q*; Even bleed to death,
abroad, and not bemoan'd / Neither
reveng'd O.
　32. Carthage. Cease] K; Carthage cease *Q*.

　40. Apollo Pythian] *set well apart in
italics in Q and O.*
　43. (*To Gelosso*) Most . . .] *Bu*; most only
man, *to Gelosso Q*.
　44.1. draw] drawe *Q*; drane *Q var.*, O.
　52. fleshless] O; fleshlesh *Q*.
　54. [GISCO . . . *poison*.]] K.
Gisco, live:] Gisco (　　) live *Q*, O; Gisco
yet live *conj. Thorssen.*
　76. Not, Jugurth] Not Jugurth *Q*; No
Jugurth K.
　77. Off] *Bu*; of *Q*.
[*Discovers himself.*]] *this ed.*
　81. abode] K; abods *Q*; abodes O.
　83. fate] *Q*; fare H.
　87. in most] *Q*; into O.

II.iii.
[ACT II] SCENE iii] SCENA TERTIA *Q*.
　4. piece. Were] peece: were *Q*; peece were
K.
　5. sung] O; song *Q*; said K.
　9. clear] cleare *Q*; free O.
　11. clasped] clasp'd O; claps'd *Q*.
　27. assured] *this ed*; Afeared *Q*.
　42-3. hate / Shall] K; hate. / Shall *Q*;
hate. / I O.
　63. Dull rest our men] *Q*; they all obey O.
　75. rage-strong] O; rage strong *Q*.
　79. Of ten, six thousand fell] *Q*; Six
thousand fell at once: O.
　83. struck] O; strooke *Q*.
　89. Massinissa] O; Massinissas *Q*.
　99. Not.] K; Not? *Q*.
　108. Brook . . . powers!] Brooke open
scorne, faint powers O; Brode skorne
oppen faind powers *Q*.
　113. *Exeunt*] Exeunt. / *Actus Secundi
Finis Q*.

III.i.
ACT III SCENE i] *Actus Tertii Scena Prima*
Q.
　0.1 *Organ . . . act*] *placed before act
heading in Q*.
　0.1 *his*] *Q*; *with his* O.
　0.2 *twined*] *twon Q*; *twound* O.
　0.2-3 *nightgown-petticoat*] *this ed*;
nightgown petticoate *Q*; *nightgown* [*and*]
petticoat Bu.
　23. of good men, shame!] of goodmen
shame *Q*; and good mens shame? O.
　25. O . . . fame] O; O save / thine own
(yet) fame *Q*; O save thine own sweet fame
K.
　27. bear out] beare out *Q*; bar out *Bu*.

28. me, Syphax. Know] me. Syphax know O; my Syphax know; Q.

38. noble] Q; feeble conj. Bu.

46. love's fight is] Q; loves fight and O; loves flight and O var.; love's sight and H.

51. No,] K; Not Q.

59. good speed, speed,] O; good speed speed Q; good speed, adew K.

64. their maids. Hold] Deighton; their vails, hold Q; their—Vails: hold Bu.; their Vails. Hold K.

67. Be, get,] Bee, get, Q; Be yet; Bu.

70. height] O; haight Q.

100. Against] O; Againe Q.

111. do] Bu; to Q, O.

112. place] Q; space Bu.

117. lick] Q; like H.

118. All . . . depart] printed as part of the dialogue in O.

133. pangs] O; pangus Q.

143.1–2. [and . . . drink.]] K; & & &. Q.

145. Which . . . king] Bu; which don / The King Q.

163. They . . . curtains] Q corr., O; printed as part of the dialogue in Q uncorr.

163–4. There . . . bride/A naked . . . undressed] K; one line in Q.

165–6. There . . . comes.] this ed.; as prose in Q.

172.1. She descends] Q corr., O; printed as part of the dialogue in Q uncorr.

177–8. When . . . Hence / Stay . . . steps.] H; one line in Q.

190. not—] not – – – – Q; not. K.

194. Think, or] Q; think I, or O.

204. then fly] then flie K; the Flie Q; that fly Bu.

208. bear] Q; bar Bu.

III.ii.

[ACT III SCENE ii] Scena Secunda Q.

8. breathes] K.; breath Q.

9. fees] O; sees Q.

thee] this ed; these Q.

14. may] Q; can O.

15. most grateful] Q; gratefull O.

17. thee] Bu; the Q.

24. Gelosso!] O; Gel. Q.

37. Rome's] this ed.; Romes, Q; Rome, Bu.

38. me with] Bu; me worth Q.

45. Libya] Libea Q; Libian O.

46. No] K; not Q.

60. And beggars treasure heaped;] Q; A beggar's treasure-heap, Bu.

72. amaze] Q; a maze Deighton.

77. sinew] Q; sinne O; sin Bu.

83.1. depart.] depart. / ACTUS TERTII / FINIS Q.

IV.i.

ACT IV SCENE i] ACTUS QUARTI SCENA PRIMA Q.

0.1 Organs . . . act.] placed before act heading in Q.

4. damps] Bu.; dumps Q.

6. leagues] Q; leages Q var.

9. nimbly] Q; justly Q var., O.

25. stretched] O; streachd Q.

73. Think, Syphax] Bu. gives this as an aside.

83. [Re-enter ZANTHIA]] this ed.

86–9. Let . . . speed / When . . . bleed / Syphax. When . . . rot. / Sophonisba. Syphax . . . not.] O; Let . . . not / Thus . . . friends / Partakers . . . flourish / Their . . . recompensed. / I . . . not. Q.

88. When . . . rot] Q; Where plots most flourish, there manure must rot. conj. Grierson.

89.1. Ex[eunt] . . . Guard]] Bu; Sopho: Exit Q.

101.1–2 Infernal . . . ceaseth] Q; after line 125 in Bu.

111. From] Q; For K.

113. New . . . turn] Q; But newly grav'd, whose entrailes are not turn'd O.

119. gelid] gelled Q; gellid O.

128. Be all full of Jove] Bu; be al full of Iove Q; be all full of love O; By awful Jove conj. K.

130. beasts] O; beastes Q; heastes Q var.

133. uncurls] uncurl's O; uncurlde Q.

138. breath's] O; breathes Q.

152. sound] Q; sounds O.

153. limned] Bu; lim'd Q; limb'd O; limbs H.

164. choke] choake Q; choakes O.

165. drought] O; drough Q.

181.1 [Exit ERICTHO]] K.

182. Whither] Bullen; Whether Q.

184. unformed] unform'd Q; uniform'd O.

189. sickless] sicklesse Q; sickness' Bu.

194. Erictho. (Within.)] Q; s.p. omitted in O.

198. Erictho. (Within.)] Q; s.p. omitted in O.

198.1. softly] O; softlyd Q.

199. Syphax.] Sy. O; not in Q.

209. Now] Q; Two O.

211. spite] O; spigh Q.
213. sit] Q; sits O.
216.1 bed.] bed / ACTUS QUARTI / FINIS. Q.

V.i.

ACT V SCENE i] ACTUS QUINTI SCENA PRIMA
Q.
0.1. A base ... act] placed before act
heading in Q.
1. Syphax.] O; Sc. Q.
7. More] Q; mere Bu.
13. height] O; haight Q.
15. well-strung] Bu; well strong Q.
16. hell's charms] this ed.; Hels charmes
Q; Hell-charms Bu.
17. damned] dam'd Q; deigned Bu.
22. breathe] Bu; breath Q.
23. we—] this ed.; we? Q.
26. being] Q; beings O.
37. give't] giv't O; gift Q.
52. fury] Q; Furies Bu.
55. Where] Q; When O.
70-3. Direct ... hear] this ed.; Direct ...
Cirta / Hark ... cittye. / Sy. Helpe ...
march, / Beate ... thou / Q.
72. leaders march] Q; leaders O.

V.ii.

[ACT V] SCENE ii] SCENA SECUNDA Q.
1. Scipio. Stand!] Q; So. Stand, Q var.
Scipio. Part] H; So. Part Q.
8. our] Q; out H.
22. Sound ... cask,] K; Sound on, /
Iugurth ... caske. Q.
26. nor sued] O; nor's adue Q.
41. not] O; and Q.
73. made] Q; wade Q var.
76. once] O; one Q.
81. Threw] Q; There Q var, O.

clasps] Bu; claspt Q, O.
89. crown] crowne Q; crownes O;
crown's Bu.
90. new-laughed] this ed; new laughd Q;
new-leagued Bu.
94. him give up] Q; give him up O.
96. now our law's] Bu; now our lawes Q;
'neath our laws conj. Bu.

V.iii.

[ACT V] SCENE iii] Scena Tertia Q.
4. or] Q, O; of Q var.
6. of] Q; for O.
26. not much] Q; not now O.
now we crave] Q; we doe crave O.
34. nectar. Think –] this ed; Nectar,
thinke Q; Nectar, skinke O; nectar-skink
Bu; Nectar, think – K.
35. bear] beare Q; bar Bu.
50. struck] O; strooke Q.
67. Salute] Q; Laelius. Salute Bu.
108. Fame-greedy] Bu; Fame greedy Q;
Fame, greedy H.

[ACT V SCENE iv]] no scene division in Q.
2. tongue] tong Q uncorr.; tongs Q corr.;
tongues O.
5. from] Q; for O.
she] Q, O; he Q var.
32. soul] soule Q; soul['s] Bu.
34. th'whole] Q, O; th'ole Q var.
46. breathe] Bu; breath Q.
50. like] Q; like to O.
51. more bright] Q; the more O.
59.2 Exeunt ... remains.] Exeuntque,
manet Ma. Q.

EPILOGUS] text in italic in Q.

THE WITCH

The Persons
THE PERSONS] separate columns in MS for
male and female characters.
16. HECATE] D; Heccat MS.

EPISTLE] italic script in MS.

I.i.

ACT I SCENE i] Actus Primus: / Sce[n]a
Prima MS.
38. duke's] D; King's MS.

52-3.] This ed.; Why ... though / my ...
Reputation, MS.
61. know] D; knew MS.
73. they] MS; then conj. G.
81-2.] This ed.; I'll ... more / 'Tis ...
little MS.
87. holy] this ed.; holly MS; silly R.
94-5.] D; like ... kind / Girles ... try /
conclusions MS.
126. fate] ffate MS; face R.
133. Sister] MS; since R.

137. act] *MS;* art *R.*
140. since] *MS;* set *or* sure *conjs. this ed.*

I.ii.

[ACT I] SCENE ii] *Sce[n]a 2a. MS.*
0.1. *Enter* HECATE.] *D; Enter Heccat: &*
other witches: (with Properties and
Habbits fitting.) MS.
1–7.] *This ed.; Titty . . . Suckin / and . . .*
Robin / white . . . red Speritts: / Deuill-
Toad . . . Dam. MS.
8. Hellwain] *D;* Hellwin *MS.*
Puckle] *D;* Prickle *MS.*
11. seeton] Seeton *MS;* seeten *R;* seething
D.
22. o'er] *conj. G;* or *MS;* on *R.*
33. Whelplie's] *R;* wlelplies *MS.*
42. black] *R;* back *MS.*
44. *Pentaphyllon] D;* Dentaphillon *MS.*
50. [*Exit* STADLIN]] *D.*
54. charmings] Charmings *MS;* churnings
R.
58–9.] *This ed.;* Of . . . Hog: / fell . . . too.
MS.
60. sop] *This ed.;* Soape *MS.;* soupe *R;*
sup *D.*
61–4.] *This ed.;* each . . . Snakes / shall . . .
Dayrie-wenches / shall . . . Curssing: *MS.*
63. dewed-skirted] *This ed.;* dew-d-
skirted *MS;* dew-skirted *D.*
65. frothy] froathie *MS;* swathie *R., D.,*
Bu.
82. portion] Portion *MS;* potion *conj. this*
ed.
91. villain] Villaine *MS;* '*Villanie is a*
possible reading' (G).
96–8.] *D; prose in MS.*
106. Silens] *G;* Silence. *MS;* Sylvans *D.*
108.1 *Enter* SEBASTIAN] *D; after line 106 in*
MS.
111. religious] *MS, G;* religion's *R. (G's*
reading of MS is probably correct, but R's
is possible since MS's raised stroke may
not be part of the 's' as G. assumes.)
115. wretched] *MS;* th'wretchedst *conj.*
G.
127. as] *D;* and *MS.*
168. gristle] *D;* Grizzell *MS.*
179. grant, you greater . . .] *D;* graunt you
(greater . . . *MS.*
183. to—the] *This ed.;* to; the *MS;* to the
D.
203–4.] *This ed.;* why . . . think / thou . . .
drie / nay . . . drie-ones. *MS.*
208. sea-lamprey] *D;* Stalamprey *MS.*
must't] *This ed.;* must' *MS.*

210. pismires] *D;* Pize mires *MS.*
229. Fiddle?] *Fidle? MS;* Fidle's *R.*
234. *Exit.*] *Exit Finis Actus pri[m]i. MS.*

II.i.

ACT II SCENE i] *Actus Secundus. / Sce[n]a*
pri[m]a. MS.
46. once] *MS;* 'oure' *is a possible reading*
(G); our *R.*
50. currant-custards] *D;* Curran-Custards
MS.
128. *married]* Married *MS;* Marrid'g *Bod.*
131. *women]* woemen *MS;* woman *Bod.*
138–9.] *D;* that . . . comes / with . . . borne
MS.
197. into] *MS;* unto *D.*
198. *Exeunt . . .Gentleman]] after line 199*
in MS.

II.ii.

[ACT II] SCENE ii] *Sce[n]a 2a. MS.*
5. Ate] Eat *MS.*
9. wound about] woond-about *MS;*
rоund about *R.*
13. boughts] *D;* Bouts *MS.*
29. nethermost] *This ed.;* hethermost *MS;*
hithermost *D.*
81. [*Picks up ribbon*]] *this ed.*
104. It's] 't has *MS.*
108–9. About . . . perform.] *one line in*
MS.
114. competent] *D;* Computent *MS.*
116. *Enter* ALMACHILDES.] *D; entry at line*
112 in MS.
123. ruled] *1810;* rude *MS.*

II.iii.

[ACT II] SCENE iii] *Sce[n]a 3a. MS.*
8. fashion] *conj. G;* fashion: *MS.*
17. on] *R;* one *MS.*
31. [*Looks in mirror*]] *this ed.*
55. *Exeunt*] *Ex[eun]t / Finis Actus 2i. MS.*

III.i.

ACT III SCENE i] *Actus Tercius / Sce[n]a*
pri[m]a MS.
10. [*Attempts . . . himself*]] *This ed.*
51. [*Kisses him*]] *This ed.*

III.ii.

[ACT III] SCENE ii] *Sce[n]a 2a. MS.*
22. city-tuck] Citty-tuck *MS;* city-truck
conj. Bu.
58. her] here *MS.*
61. *Enter* GASPERO] *after line 59 in MS.*
113. fine] *R;* five *MS.*

163. secrecy] secrecie *MS*; service *R*.
166. *Enter* ISABELLA] *alongside line 164 in MS*.
184-5. What's . . . toward?] *D*; *one line in MS*.

III.iii.

[ACT III] SCENE iii] *Sce[n]a 3a. MS*.
4-5. O . . . yet?] *one line in MS*.
14.1 [*Exeunt . . .* HECATE.]] *D*; They ascend. *1810*.
27. Here's . . .] *This ed.*; *in MS 'Fire-' is written half a line too high as if the scribe were uncertain to which line it belonged (G)*; Firestone. Here's . . . *R*.
37. They are there] *this ed.*; They are they *MS*.
38. *Come*] *MS*; O come *Dr*; Oh come *1673, Dav*.
43. *Stadlin*] *MS*; Stadling *1673, Dav*.
45. *Hoppo*] *MS*; Hopper *1673, Dav*.
Hellwain] *MS*; heelway *Drexel, 1673, Dav*.
46. *lack*] *MS*; want *1673, Dav*.
49. *There's . . . down*] *MS*; heare comes one downe *Dr*; Here comes one, it . . . *1673*.
50. *coll*] *MS*; cull *Dr, 1673, Dav*.
53. *sweet*]*MS*; fresh *Dr*.
56. *still*] *MS*; well *Dr*; fair *1673, Dav*.
62. *go, now*] *MS*; goe, o now *Dr*; go; now *1673*; go and now *Dav*.
64. *pleasure 'tis*] *MS*; pleasure in this *Dr*; Pleasure's this *1673, Dav*.
65. *ride*] *MS*; sail *1673, Dav*.
67. *And sing and dance*] *MS*; and (   ) and singe *Dr*; To sing, to toy *1673, Dav*.
69. *Over seas, our mistress' fountains*] *D*; Ouer seas, our Mistris Fountaines, *MS*; Over misty hills and Fountaines, *1673*; Over hills and misty fountains *Dav.*; Over hills our crystal / mistress fountains *Dr*.
70. *steeples*] *1673, Dav.*, *Dr*; Steepe *MS*.
73. no yelps] *MS*; nor yelps *Dr, 1673, Dav*.
74. not] *MS*; nor *Dr, 1673, Dav*.
75. Or] *MS*; nor *Dr, 1673, Dav*.
79. *Exit*] Exit. / *Finis Actus Tercius MS*.

IV.i.

ACT IV SCENE i] *Actus Quartus. / Sce[n]a pri[m]a. MS*.
23. crosses] Crosses *MS*; curses *D*.
53. Governor.] *MS*; Governor. [*Speaking within*] *1810*.

IV.ii.

[ACT IV] SCENE ii] *Sce[n]a 2a. MS*.

10. man] Man *MS*; men *D*.
22. *Enter* FLORIDA] *alongside lines 19 and 20 in MS*.
40. fortnight's] *D*; forthnights *MS*; forth nightes *conj. G*.
59. feed] *conj. G*; feele *MS*; fill *conj. G*.
123. [*Aside*]] *This ed*.

IV.iii.

[ACT IV] SCENE iii] *Sce[n]a 3a. MS*.
15. [*Snoring within*]] *This ed*.
36. his] *Reed*; *MS has 'er' apparently written over 'is' (G)*.
37. Here's] heeres *MS*; there's *R*.
40. [*Florida.*] [*Within*]] *D*; Fra. *MS*.
56-7. Come . . . too] *one line in MS*.
68. ruinous] *D*; Ruynes *MS*; ruines *R*.
77. knowledge] *MS*; conscience *R*.
111. *Exeunt*] Ex[eun]t / Finis Actus Quarti *MS*.

V.i.

ACT V SCENE i] *Actus Quintus. / Sce[n]a pri[m]a MS*.
0.1 ANTONIO.] *R*; Sebastian. *MS*.
1. *Antonio.*] *R*; Seb. *MS*.
3. *Antonio.*] *R*; Seb. *MS*.
63. her] *MS*; 'er' *altered from 'is' G*; his *R*.
80. doe] *D*; -Doa *MS*.
89. off] *D*; of *MS*.
114-15. [*Governor.*] If . . . lust.] *R*; *given to Florida in MS*.
127-8.] *This ed.*; Did . . . my *Master?* / Is. how . . . to night? / *Her*. then . . . Madam *MS*.

V.ii.

[ACT V] SCENE ii] *Sce[n]a 3a. MS*.
11. may] *MS*; be *conj. G*.
12. Here's] *1813 Var.*; her's *MS*.
17. greatness] Greatnes *MS*; creatures *R*.
49.1-2. [FIRESTONE . . . *them*.]] *D*.
62-7.] *D*; *arranged as three lines in MS*.
62. *Titty, Tiffin*] *MS*; Tiffin, Tiffin *Dav*.
66. *Liard*] *R*; Liand *MS*; Lyer *Dav*.
70. *Put*] *MS*; O put *Dav*.
O *put*] *MS*; put *Dav*.
71. *libbard's bane*] *MS*; Lizard's braine *Dav*.
a grain] a graine *Dav.*; againe *MS*.
72. *The . . . the*] *MS*; Here's . . . here's *Dav*.
73. *younker*] *MS*; Charm grow *Dav*.
74. *there's all*] *MS*; all these *Dav*.
and rid] *MS*; 'twill raise *Dav*.

75. *of the red*] MS; *of a red Dav.*
76. *All [Witches.] Round . . .*] R; *all Round MS.*

V.iii.
[ACT V] SCENE iii] *Sce[n] a. 4a. MS.*
0.1–2. *Enter . . . Servants.*]] *This ed.; MS includes* HERMIO *and erases an entry for Antonio; D. omits* FRANCISCA *and* \ ABERZANES. |
24. *How!*] How? MS; Who? *conj. D.*
54. *Ravenna*] *This ed.; Urbin MS.*
64. *Enter* DUCHESS] *alongside lines 62 and 63 in MS; Enter* DUCHESS *and* AMORETTA *D.*

65. Ends] *This ed.; ever MS; conj. D. lacuna.*
Ends . . . now. / Better . . . ours.] *one line in 65–6. MS.*
74. *done't*] D; *done MS.*
80. *[A . . . dead.]]* D.
83. *thee*] MS; *there 1810.*
93. *Perform*] Performe R; *performes MS.*
95. *an*] MS; *as conj. this ed.*
101. *accuser*] Accuser MS; *accusers R.*
110–111.] *This ed.; Nay . . . then / In . . . bold MS.*
123. *[Rising . . . her.]]* D.
135. *Exeunt*] Exeunt. / *Finis Actus Quinti. MS.*

THE WITCH OF EDMONTON

Prologue
PROLOGUE] *italics in Q with the exception of* Edmonton *(line 1),* Once . . . ever *(line 10) and* Bird *(line 13).*

I.i.
5–7. *You . . . satisfaction*] We.; *You . . . man; / I . . . satisfaction Q.*
55. *how—*] We.; *how Q.*
70–1. *Thus . . . house*] We.; *one line in Q.*
76–7.] *as verse We.; as prose Q.*
80. *duty, you*] We.; *duty. You Q.*
110–12. *Thou . . . Already?*] We.; *Thou . . . promise. / We . . . Already? Q.*
121–3.] *as prose Q.*
129. *thy*] Gi.; *not in Q.*
143. *there*] Gi.; *that Q, Bo., On.*
146. *thoroughly*] Gi.; *throughly Q.*
147. *passed*] *this ed.; past Q; past? We.*
151. *witty, witty Frank*] Q; *witty, witty, Frank We.*
153. *the*] Q; *thee, conj. On.*
156–7. *Winnifride. . . . past*] Q; *given to Sir Arthur by G., D., Rh.*
163. *lewdness*] *conj. D.; laundress Q.*
188. *thoroughly*] We.; *throughly Q.*
210. *cold*] *conj. Gi.; old Q.*

I.ii.
5–6. *Hertfordshire*] We.; *Hertforshire Q.*
9–13.] *as verse Bo.; as prose Q.*
26–7.] Q; *as verse Bo.*
29. *yeoman's*] Yoeman's Q.
33.1. *Enter . . .* KATHERINE] We.; *after line 34 in Q.*
40–8.] *as verse We.; as prose Q.*

52–3.] *as verse We.; as prose Q.*
64–5. *Master . . . deceive*] *one line in Q.*
106. *Frank . . . ha!*] Q; *as an aside We.*
108. *Salutes them.*] Q; *Kisses them Gi.*
113–14. *Marry / A servingman?*] Q; Marry, / A servingman? *We.*
175. *Which . . . night,*] Q; *Which x x x x travellers, day and night, Gi.*
190–201.] *as verse We.; as prose Q.*
210. *Marry, and*] We.; *Marry and Q.*

II.i.
13.1 *Enter . . . Banks*] *after line 14 in Q; after line 16 in We.*
28. *ache*] We.; *aches Q.*
cramp] We.; *cramps Q.*
39. *First Dancer.*] *this ed.; 1 Q; also 2, 3, 4 below Q.*
51–2. *fore-horse in a*] Bo.; *fore-horse i'the Gi.; fore-horse i'th' Rh.; Fore-horse, Q.*
52. *fore-gallant*] We.; *for gallant Q.*
92. *knot*] Gi.; *knit Q.*
98. *All.*] We.; *Omnes Q.*
121–3.] On.; *as prose in Q.*
144. *Then*] We.; *When Q.*
147. *Sucks . . . lightning*] Q; *She pricks her arm, which he sucks. Thunder and Lightning Gi.*
Seal't . . . mine.] We.; *Seal't . . . blood. / See . . . mine. Q.*
150–1. *And . . . Banks*] *one line in Q.*
158. *curst*] Gi.; *curs'd Q.*
216. *daughter*] Q; *daughter? We.*
239. *An*] We.; *And Q.*
240. *talons*] We.; *Talents Q.*
267. *an*] We.; *and Q.*

268. at eaglet] *Q; an eaglet We.; a taglet Gi.*

II.ii.

38.1 SD] *Q; after 'care' in line 39 in We., Gi.; after line 47 in D., Rh.*

44. Somerton.] *Gi.; Cart. Q.*

48–51.] *as prose in Q.*

59. now] *Q; new We.*

62. Exit] *Q; Exit [with* SOMERTON] *We.*

63–96.] *We.; as prose in Q.*

82. more,] *Gi.; more Q.*

101. In thy] *We.;—In thy Q; * * * in thy Gi.*

119–21. Two ... me?] *We.; prose in Q.*

126–34. I hope ... goodness] *as verse We.; as prose Q.*

128. poor] *poot Q.*

128–9. [Aside] ... me] *Ba.; she ... me as aside in Gi.*

134–5. Sir ... fate] *We.; Sir ... you / Yet ... fate Q.*

139. Prithee, prithee] *Prithee, prithe Q.*

139–59.] *as verse in We.; as prose in Q.*

166.] *Q; [Aside] D., Rh., Ba.*

III.i.

1. First Dancer.] *this ed., 1 Q; also 2., 3., 4., below in Q.*

4. Young Banks.] *Q's speech prefix throughout the scene is 'Clow'.*

58. All] *this ed.; Omn. Q.*

66.1 SD] *Bo.; ... is come. / Enter the Spirit in the shape of a Dog. We., Gi., Rh., Ba.*

89–93.] *as prose in Q.*

94.1 SD] *We.; Ex. Spir. and banks Q (at line 95).*

104.1 barks] *braks Q.*

III.ii.

34. her] *conj. D., Bo.; here Q.*

37–8. Go ... thee] *Gi.; one line in Q.*

46–7.] *We.; Tush ... necessary. / On, ... brief. Q.*

62. from] *Rh.; for Q.*

74. them] *We.; then Q.*

104–5.] *Gi.; Prithee ... thee, / And ... instantly Q.*

106.1 SD] *Gi.; at line 105 in Q.*

107–09.] *Rh.; Pray ... last / Service ... sight. Q.*

109–10.] *Gi.; Why ... other / Business ... part. Q.*

III.iii.

4–5. What ... ever] *Bo.; one line in Q.*

22–6.] *We.; as prose in Q.*

25. earnest] *We.; earst Q.*

37. The ... minute] *Q; The Devil did not prompt me till this minute: conj. Gi.*

64.1. She dies] *this ed.; Moritur Q.*

71.1. DOG ... him.] *Q;* DOG *ties him and exit. Gi., Rh., Bo., On.*

76–82.] *We.; as prose in Q.*

87. To] *We.; to Q.*

104–5.] *Ba.; When ... Slut? / Alas ... now? Q.*

114. full] *sull Q.*

III.iv.

2–4.] *We.; The ... kinde / To ... Morrice. Q.*

7–8.] *one line in Q.*

14. Sawgut.] *Gi.; Fidl. Q (and throughout the scene).*

17. First Dancer.] *this ed.; 1 Q; also 2 below.*

40. All.] *We.; Omn. Q (and below).*

50.1–2. SD] *following line 49 in Q.*

59–60.] *Gi.; Sir ... hope / You'll ... power; Q.*

62. Somerton and Warbeck.] *this ed.; Ambo. Q.*

68. an] *We.; and Q.*

IV.i.

5. First Countryman.] *We.; 1 Q; also 2., 3., below.*

14.1. HAMLUC] *We.; Hamlac Q.*

16. All.] *We.; Omn. Q, and below.*

86. to?] *this ed.; to. Q.*

165. churning] *We.; churming Q.*

199.1 SD] *We.; line 198 in Q; [*DOG *goes after.] Bo.*

267. there's] *We.; there Q.*

biting's conscience] *Q; biting, his conscience We.; biting—his conscience Gi.*

IV.ii.

12–14.] *We.; each speech one line in Q.*

16–17. Why ... asleep] *We.; one line in Q.*

24–5. Why ... calling?] *Bo.; one line in Q.*

25–7.] *We.; Yes ... place / To ... this Q.*

49–50.] *We.; Slaves! ... Slaves! / Speak ... them Q.*

61–2.] *We.; How ... ear. / Stay ... higher. Q.*

61. Lute plays] *Gi.; at end of line 60 in Q.*

62–85.] *We.; as prose in Q.*

93–4.] *this ed.; one line in Q.*

105–14.] *We.; as prose in Q.*
118–22.] *We.; as prose in Q.*
137. sin's] *We.*; sins *Q.*
138–43.] *Bo.; as prose in Q.*
143.] *SD placed after line 143 in Q.*
149–50.] *We.; as prose in Q.*
156–9.] *We.; as prose in Q.*
160.1. Katherine] Katharaine *Q.*
168–9.] *Gi.; as prose in Q.*
172–3.] *We.; as prose in Q.*
179. upon] *We.*; on *Q.*
179–82.] *We.; as prose in Q.*
184–8.] *We.; as prose in Q.*

V.i.

34–5.] *We.; as prose in Q.*
37. sheet] *We.*; Sweet *Q.*
44–5.] *We.; as prose in Q.*
55–6.] *We.; one line in Q.*
58–9.] *We.; as prose in Q.*
81–3.] *We.; as prose in Q.*
86. *Young Banks.*] *Clown. Q (throughout the scene).*
87. amongst 'em] *We.*; amongst 'um *Q.*
89.1. [DOG] *barks. No!*] *We.*; no. [Barks] *Q.*
99. *Young Banks.*] Dog. *Q.*
110–13.] *as prose Bo.*; True …
devilishly. / I … at. / The … with, /
But … ha! *Q.*
125. that, fool? It] *Gi.*; that? fool, it *Q.*
138. rook?] *We.*; Rook. *Q.*
162. Moll Cutpurse] *We.*; Mal-Cutpurse *Q.*
170. your] *Gi.*; you *Q.*

V.ii.

0.2 KATHERINE] *We.*; Kate *Q.*

V.iii.

6–7. But … thither] *We.; one line in Q.*
7–9. Poor … too] *On.*; Poor … see /
Thee … too. *Q.*
14–15.] *We.; one line in Q.*
15–19. Daughter … them] *Bo.; as prose in Q.*
20.1. *execution*] *Fexecution Q.*
29–30.] *Ba.; as prose in Q.*
33–5.] *Rh.; as prose in Q.*
35–6.] *We.; one line in·Q.*
52.1. [*Exeunt … Officers.*]] *this ed;*
[*Exeunt* SAWYER *with Officers, Country people follow.*] *Bo.*
61–2. To … execution] *We.; one line in Q.*
113. I] *We.; dropped out in Q.*
115–18.] *We.*; I, … see / Thee … her: I …
thou / Had'st … have / Done … them./ *Q.*
122–3. *Warbeck. And … you*] *We.; one line in Q.*
123–31.] *We.; as prose in Q.*
131–3.] *We.*; Take … last / Tears …
Frank! *Q.*
133–4.] *We.*; Gentlemen, to / Comfort …
Q.
151–4. And … troubled] *Bo.; as prose in Q.*
155. *Justice.*] *We.*; Cart. *Q.*
159–60.] *We.; one line in Q.*
165. had] *We.*; has *Q.*

EPILOGUE] *in italic throughout in Q.*

APPENDIX

Music for *The Witch*

Music is used on the following occasions:

(*a*) II.i.125–32: 'In a maiden time professed', a song by John Wilson, transcribed here from the Bodleian Library MS. Mus. b.1.f.21 (also extant in Dx. MS. 4357, No. 32):

In a Maiden time pro-fest yᵉⁿ wee say that life is best, tast-ing once yᵗ mar-rid'y life, then wee on – ly praise yᵗ wife, there's but one state more to try, wᶜʰ makes woman laugh, or cry Widdow Widdow, of theise three, the mid-dle's best, and yᵗ give me.

Two further verses are given in the MS:

Cupid is an Idle toy
never was there such a boy
yf there were, let any show
or his quiver or his Bow
or a wound by him and they gott
or a broaken Arrow shott
    Money money makes us bough,
    there is no other Cupid now

Whilst ye wold [world?] continued good,
people loud [loved] for flesh, and bloud
Men about them bore the dart
that would catch a womans hart
wemen likewise great, and small
with a pretty thinge they call
    Cunny Cunny wun the Men
    And this was all the Cupid then

(*b*) III.iii.38–76: 'Come away, come away, Hecate', probably by Robert Johnson,[1] is given here in the version from the Drexel MS. 4175. Liiii. (a setting is also extant in Fitzwilliam MS. 52. D. ff. 107v–08):

and then I mounte, I will but noynte and then I mounte heare comes one downe to

fetch his dues a kisse, a cull a sip of blood and why thou

stayest soe longe I muse, I muse, since y^e ayre soe freshe and good:

ô art thou come what newes, what newes all goes well to our de -

-light, ei - ther come or els re - fuse, re - fuse now I am fournisht

for the flyght, now I goe, ô now I flye Mal-kin my sweete

spiritt and I ô what a dayn - tie pleas - ure is this to

ride in the aire whē y^e moone shines faire, and ⟨feast⟩ ∝ singe, ∝ toy, ∝ kisse,

o - uer woods, highe rockes, ∝ mountaines o - uer seaes our {cris - tall}{mis - tris} fountaynes

o - uer steeples, towers, ∝ tur-retts, wee fly by night mongst troopes of spiritts:

no ringe of bells to o^r eares sounde, no howles of

woolves, nor yelps of hounds, no nor the noise of____

wa - ter breach, nor can-nons throate o^r height can reach.

(c) V.ii.59–76: 'A charm-song about a vessel'. No music has been traced for this song.[2]

(d) V.ii.85.1: '*The Witches' Dance*'. The following dance, probably by Robert Johnson, may well be the dance used here and also in *Macbeth*.[3] It is taken from B.M. Add. MS. 10444:

NOTES

1 See John P. Cutts, 'The Original Music to Middleton's *The Witch*', *Sh. Q.* 7 (1956), pp. 203–9. The song reproduced here is taken from Cutts's article.

2 See John H. Long, *Shakespeare's Use of Music: The Histories and Tragedies*, Univ. of Florida P., 1971, p. 197.

3 For a discussion of the relationship of the two witches' dances in this MS to Jonson's *MQ*, Middleton's *The Witch* and Shakespeare's *Macbeth*, see John P. Cutts, 'Jacobean Masque and Stage Music', *Music and Letters*, 35 (1954), pp. 185–200. The version printed here is taken from Mary Chan, *Music in the Theatre of Ben Jonson*, 1980, pp. 201–2.